COAL AND MEN

MINING CAMP IN WEST VIRGINIA

COAL AND MEN

An Economic and Social Study
of the
British & American Coalfields

BY

Harold M. Watkins

B.Sc.(Econ.) Lond.

Travelling Lecturer in Economics
Glamorgan County Council
Social Science Research Fellow of
the Rockefeller Foundation

WITH A FOREWORD BY

PROFESSOR

John R. Commons

University of Wisconsin, U.S.A.

LONDON
George Allen & Unwin Ltd
MUSEUM STREET

FIRST PUBLISHED IN 1934

TO
THE COAL-MINERS OF GREAT BRITAIN
AND
THE UNITED STATES

PREFACE

ONE may reflect on a problem for many years and yet be too busy or too lazy to collect the relevant facts. Brought up in a small market town in North Wales, I came into the South Wales coalfield when the coal-mining industry was flourishing. I had previously worked in a Government Department in London, in Broadmoor Criminal Lunatic Asylum (not as a patient!), taught at a seaside boarding school and at a Grammar School in Lancashire, and studied at a university college. Two years spent in the South Lancashire coalfield had to some extent familiarised me with life in a British coal-mining community, but it was not till I took up a teaching post in the Rhondda Valley, lived in miners' homes and began to concentrate on the study of Economics that I became interested in the economic and social phases of the coal problem. For there was a coal problem even in those days of comparative prosperity. There were industrial conflicts about wages and unionisation, there were commercial difficulties, the housing conditions were shocking (the kitchen bath was almost universal), facilities for the education of adults and for recreation were meagre in the extreme, the social habits of the miners and the owners were unrefined if not definitely coarse (drunkenness was rampant) and there was an enormous waste of valuable human material. It was this wastage that impressed me most as a young man, and it has been the pith of the coal problem for me ever since. It is now thirty years since I came into the South Wales coalfield, and it is still this aspect of the problem that concerns me most: indeed, the worsened economic conditions have intensified its seriousness.

When therefore in 1928 I was fortunate enough to be awarded a Research Fellowship by the Rockefeller Foundation (now styled the Social Science Research Council), I was delighted to be disturbed out of my business of lecturing or my laziness of pondering into the pleasurable activity of researching and field work in the American coalfields. I had submitted as my thesis "A comparison between the economic conditions of the South Wales coalfield and those of one or more American coalfields, with special reference to the effect of such conditions on the educational and civic development of a mining community."

But after a year spent in the American coalfields I enlarged the scope of my study. In order to investigate the working conditions I had been down several mines in the pivotal fields—the Pennsylvania Anthracite, the Pennsylvania Bituminous, Illinois, West Virginia, Alabama and Colorado. I had surveyed the social conditions everywhere and had had fruitful discussions on the technical, economic and sociological aspects with a large number of experts in each field. I was already familiar with all the British coalfields except the most recently developed, Kent. So I spent the second year at the Harvard University Library and the Congressional Library at Washington in researching and planning a comparative study of the British and American coalfields generally, from the angle in which I was specially interested.

This book is the outcome of that planning. It is now nearly four years since the first paragraphs were written. Preoccupation with my normal work prevented the completion of the task on my return from America, and more than once in despair of finishing it I almost gave up the idea of publication, but it seemed worth while to persevere because no study on the same lines had ever been published either in Great Britain or in America. The literature of coal hitherto has been preponderantly technical. The social aspects of the industry have been neglected in both countries. Certain English economists, it is true, have devoted some attention to the British industry from the economic and social angle. The late Professor W. Stanley Jevons concentrated on the problem of the conservation of coal resources, and although this is no longer a pressing problem his book was worth writing if only for one thing he said on the coal question:

"This is a question of that almost religious importance which needs the separate study and determination of every intelligent person."

His son, Professor H. Stanley Jevons, also interested himself in the coal question, and in his *British Coal Trade* he deals at some length with the housing conditions, the social life of the mining communities and the various types of British miners. Lord Passfield, still best known as Sidney Webb, has made a notable contribution with his valuable *Story of the Durham Miners*. Professor R. H. Tawney, who was a member of the Royal Commission on the Coal Industry, 1919, has written an able pamphlet on the Nationalisation of the Mines and may almost be regarded as the miners' economist. Mr. G. D. H. Cole has interested himself specially in the Labour aspects of the industry. Mr. J. F. W. Rowe has done a scholarly study of Wages in the Coal Industry.

On the American side Professor J. R. Commons, well known everywhere as an authority on Labour and Trade Union questions, has given considerable attention to the economics of the coal industry. Professor Walton H. Hamilton and Miss Helen R. Wright, with their two books *The Case of Bituminous Coal* and *A Way of Order for Bituminous Coal* have made valuable contributions to the solution of American coal problems. Mr. Isador Lubin, as the title of his book *Miners' Wages and the Cost of Coal* indicates, is interested in the human side of the industry and, in collaboration with Miss Helen Everett, wrote an extraordinarily good book on the economic and psychological aspects of the British mining situation under the title of *The British Coal Dilemma*. Mr. Arthur Suffern's *The Coal Miners' Struggle for Industrial Status* is the standard work on that subject in America. Professor Carter Goodrich has specialised in an interesting phase of the question in his study entitled *The Miners' Freedom*. Miss Elsie Glück has directed attention to the problem of leadership in the unionisation of American miners by taking the life of John Mitchell as her text. Quite recently Miss Anna Rochester wrote a book called *Labor and Coal* in which are given graphic pictures of living and working conditions and an interpretation of the economic struggle in the American coal industry, while some attention is paid to the contrast between the American coal problem and the problem in Great Britain and Germany.

But no British or American economist has made anything like an exhaustive comparative study of the economic and social conditions in the two sets of coalfields. The author does not claim that his is a complete study. But at least it is far the most exhaustive attempt yet made. Research work takes weird and wonderful forms whose serviceableness it is sometimes not easy to appreciate. It is hoped that readers of this work will not be left in doubt that it was worth while doing. Industry should be organised to serve the best human ends, and waste of good human material is at least as deplorable as the failure to secure the fullest use of machinery in a plant. The miners of Great Britain and America, as a result of the conditions prevailing in the coal-mining industry, have fallen far short of the glory of possible development. Achievement socially and politically has been greater among the British miners, for reasons which will presently appear, but mining communities in both countries have had a "raw deal" and the world is the poorer for their denial of opportunities to live a spacious and dignified life.

When the thirteenth International Physiological Congress met in Boston in August, 1929, I attended the opening meeting at Harvard and heard Professor August Krogh deliver his address on "The Progress of Physiology." Among other wise things he said:

"In a recent small book of instructions for medical writers I find the statement that what is needed in scientific papers is facts and again facts and still more facts. I venture to disagree emphatically with this statement. Facts are necessary of course, but unless fertilized by ideas, correlated with other facts, illuminated by thought, I consider them as material only for science. I am prepared to submit the thesis, revolting though it may seem, that too many experiments and observations are being made and published and too little thought is bestowed upon them."

I have naturally assured myself of the reliability of the data used in this book and, almost as naturally, wasted a great deal of time in searching out material, but I have deliberately avoided the use of copious statistics and meaningless facts. I too have long felt the need of fertilising thought, particularly in social investigations. Hard, straight thinking and concentrated reflection sometimes generate ideas that may contribute far more to a higher civilisation than tomes of barren facts however impressive and however patiently accumulated. I hope it may be found that I have succeeded in making the happy combination of facts and ideas which has been my aim throughout.

Words fail me in any attempt to express my gratitude to the hundreds of very delightful people in all parts of the United States who in countless ways helped and befriended a wandering scholar from Wales. My investigation was made passible by the Rockefeller Foundation, and my being a Rockefeller Fellow enabled me to enter all gates at which I knocked except those which guarded the entrance to the men's unions: to these I was admitted by other credentials. But it should be made clear that I have received no assistance whatever from the Foundation or from any other source in connection with the publication of this book, and I have felt free to criticise the Rockefeller policies in the conduct of the coal industry in the Colorado field.

Everywhere professors and instructors in economics, history, sociology, industrial psychology, geography and education; engineers and specialists in mining; housing and recreation experts; government department officials; librarians; officials of operators' associations and of the miners' unions, particularly those of the United Mine Workers of America; operators themselves and a large number of mine-workers—all gave most generously of their time and knowledge. Indeed, the extraordinarily kind hospitality of Americans is a thing to be experienced to be believed. Among those to whom I feel a special debt of gratitude are Professor J. R. Commons, Professor Carter Goodrich, Professor Walton Hamilton, Professor J. H. Willitts, Mr. Isador Lubin, Miss Helen Everett and her husband, Dr. Meiklejohn, Miss Helen Wright, Miss Margaret Hodgen, Miss Hilda Smith, Dr. Joseph K. Hart, Miss Josephine Roche and Mrs. Esther Henshaw. But perhaps no one gave me more valuable direct assistance than Mr. F. G. Tryon, Head of the Statistics Division of the Bureau of Mines, Washington. A finer official I cannot conceive that any government department in Great Britain or America could have.

This is not the place to acknowledge private hospitality, but there is a kind of kindness which is of great value indirectly in the pursuit of an investigation, and I should be ungrateful if I did not refer especially to the rest and refreshment which I always found at the home of Mr. and Mrs. Irving O. Hunt, of Wyoming, Pennsylvania, in the intervals between visits to the coal-mines, some of which they themselves arranged. Mrs. Victor Berger, of Milwaukee, with her daughter Doris Berger Welles and her husband, also befriended me in this way. And one of my most fruitful and enjoyable sojourns in the States was the period spent in the home of Mr. and Mrs. Ed. Wieck at Belleville, Illinois. Himself a miner, Mr. Wieck gave me the privilege of an insight into the home life of an American coal-digger, and he and his wife, who had written articles in the American *Nation* on coal problems, were of invaluable help in many ways.

In the course of writing these pages I have become a debtor to many other people. I wish to acknowledge the unfailing courtesy and valuable assistance of the Librarians of the Harvard and

Congressional Libraries and their staffs, of Mr. Harry Farr, Librarian of the Cardiff Free Library, and his staff, and of Mr. S. O. Moffett, Librarian of the University Library, Cardiff. The officials of the South Wales Miners' Federation have at all times been ready to furnish me with information. I am indebted also to the South Wales Coal Owners' Association and to Councillor Edgar Chappell, an expert on housing in South Wales, for the loan of manuscript material relating to the social conditions of the South Wales coalfield. Mr. G. D. H. Cole helped me to decide on the title of the book, Professor R. H. Tawney has made one or two friendly suggestions as to its organisation and Mr. Stanley Unwin has shown more than a professional interest in its publication. But I owe most to the encouragement and sympathetic prodding of my wife, who, either in America or at home, has never failed me with her unerring judgment.

HAROLD M. WATKINS

CARDIFF

May 1934

FOREWORD

A COMPARATIVE study of economic conditions in England and America is, for me, the most illuminating of economic investigations.

When Mr. Watkins visited Madison at various times and told me and my students of his comparisons and contrasts in the greatest of basic industries for both countries, I recognized, for us, the importance of what he was doing. I had made, some twenty-five years before, along with others, a comparative study in England and America of private and public ownership and operation of what we name in America, municipal "public utilities." At another time I supervised a comparative study of "restriction of output" by capitalistic and labour organisations in the two countries. When I returned to Wisconsin, after the former investigation, and was called upon to assist the State Legislature in drafting a Bill for the regulation of private and public operation and capitalisation of these "utilities" in this State, it was what I learned in England, compared with what we knew in our own State, that became the most convincing argument before the legislative committees and the basis of the legislation adopted.

Here are two countries with the same common-law history, the same reverence for private property, the similar customs and traditions, but with us the judicial sovereignty of fifty supreme courts interpreting as many written constitutions.

Coal and iron are the two basic industries for both countries, in war and peace. Substitutes may be found in part, but these remain supreme. The biggest labour organisations in both countries are those of the coal-miners, the membership in the United States at one time reaching more than three hundred thousand and in Great Britain about a million. But in England they speak one language. In America I have counted as high as thirty nationalities, races or languages in the coal-miners' union. In America one branch, anthracite coal, has been monopolised for forty years by evading the anti-trust laws. In the other, bituminous coal, the competition has been, at times, terribly destructive for both the owners and the labourers. In England the first labour member of parliament was a union coal-miner—Alexander

Macdonald. In America the first labour member of the President's Cabinet was a union coal-miner. In America I attended, in 1901, the then recently organised interstate conference of employers and employees of the bituminous industry. I named it "constitutional government in industry," because it reminded me of the origins of the British House of Lords on one side in their own right as owners, and the House of Commons on the other side, a representative body elected by several hundred local unions. They jointly made the legislative rules governing the industry, irrespective of the several State legislatures. And now after thirty-five years of watching and writing about our American coal industry I read eagerly this first comparative study of the industry in two English empires.

JOHN R. COMMONS

MADISON, WISCONSIN

CONTENTS

LIST OF ILLUSTRATIONS

CHAPTER I

HISTORICAL AND ECONOMIC IMPORTANCE
OF COAL

CHAPTER I

HISTORICAL AND ECONOMIC IMPORTANCE OF COAL

COAL, with the metallurgical arts based on its use, is the basis of modern industrial civilisation. Twenty million years ago the coal of the world had been put to bed kissed by the sun, lullabied by the shifting seas and tucked in by the paternal mountains. Rarely, intermittently man disturbed the profound sleep of the ages as he stumbled, here and there, on the discovery that the black, soft rock would burn and give off heat. But it was not till less than two centuries ago that he began to realise the value of coal, nor even yet does he fully appreciate its multifarious potential uses.

There are evidences that prehistoric man worked and smelted certain metals, and the making of arms seems to have been an industry of great antiquity, but the fuel was obtained direct from the forests. Wherever it was found necessary to generate heat by burning, there were ample supplies of wood to hand. This condition lasted for several centuries, and, broadly, it was only when the supplies of "charcole" gave out as population and civilisation advanced that the need for a compact fuel of high calorific power was felt. The word coal itself is not very old and was originally a suffix, as in "charcole," but a knowledge of its use undoubtedly existed before the Christian era. Charles Wilkins, in his interesting, if somewhat unscientific, treatise on Coal, published in 1888, gives several quotations from the Bible containing obvious references to the substance we call coal. But perhaps the earliest reliable reference to the supposed use of coal occurs in a work on *Stones*, written by Theophrastus, said to be the favourite pupil of Aristotle. There is some doubt as to the date, Tonge[1] giving it as 238 B.C. and Arber[2] as about 315 B.C. but there is no doubt of what he wrote. He says: "They call those fossil substances Anthracite (or Coal) and when broken up for use they are of an earthy character; nevertheless, they inflame and burn even like charcoal. These are found in Liguria and Elis in the way to Olympias, over the mountains, and are used by the Smiths." There are other historical references which

[1] *Coal*, p. 2. [2] *The Natural History of Coal*, p. 1.

show that the Greeks and Romans were acquainted with the use of coal.

It seems clear also, from the discoveries of geologists and missionaries, that the Chinese in a period of remote antiquity had some knowledge of the nature and properties of coal and that they turned it to account in the manufacture of porcelain, gunpowder and paper.

There seems to be no doubt that coal was worked by the Britons long before the Roman occupation, and that the Romans engaged in the mining of coal in Britain. Tonge[1] writes: "Many of their stations were situated in close proximity to the outcrops of valuable seams; tools of a peculiarly Roman type have been found in old colliery workings; the plan or system of working has been discovered to be of a design associated with art as practised by the Romans; finally, coal and coal cinders have at several places been found in excavating Roman stations in various parts of England." But the earliest historical reference to the existence of coal in Britain is that found in the Saxon Chronicle of the Abbey of Peterborough: "About this time (A.D. 852) the Abbot Ceolred let the land of Sempringham to Wulfred, who was to send each year to the Monastery '60 loads of wool, 12 loads of coal, 6 loads of peat, 2 tuns full of fine ale, 2 neats carcasses, 600 loaves and 10 kilderkins of Welsh ale, 1 horse also each year and 308 starlings and 1 night's entertainment.' " Till the thirteenth century coal did not enter into general commerce, but in the ninth, tenth and eleventh centuries it had often been given to the Monks as an offering or, as in the case of the Abbey of Peterborough, in compensation for the letting of land.

Coal, in the modern sense, was originally referred to as "pitcole," "earthcole" or "seacole," and towards the middle of the thirteenth century "seacole" conveyed by ship from Newcastle (a port on the north-east coast of England) was being used by the manufacturers in London.

In 1239 Henry III, confirming the Charter of Newcastle-on-Tyne, granted a licence to the citizens to "dig coals and stones in the common soil outside the walls and convert them to their own profit." From this licence may be dated the foundation of the coal trade.

In the year 1281 the Newcastle coal trade had become so

[1] *Coal*, p. 3.

extensive that laws were enacted for its regulation. The smoke from the burning of coal caused considerable annoyance to the prelates, nobles and gentry of London, who complained they were unable to stay in the town because of "the noisome smell and thick air caused by burning cole." Nothing is heard of the complaints of those sections of the population who were not prelates, nobles or gentry. This probably was because they were obliged to remain in the town; in any event they were politically impotent. The complaints of those who were able to leave the town resulted in a proclamation forbidding the use of coal. It is not recorded whether there was any "bootlegging" in coal at that time, but its use increased steadily with the development of trade, and Queen Elizabeth narrowed the prohibition to the point of forbidding the burning of coal in London during the sitting of Parliament, as it was feared that "the health of the Knights of the Shires might suffer during their abode in the Metropolis." In 1634 a duty of four shillings per chaldron was imposed on imported sea coal, an interesting indication of the national policy of attempting to keep the expanding trade a close national preserve. The gay and needy Charles I exploited the industry to the extent of a shilling for every ton of coal sold by a syndicate which he allowed to be incorporated in 1638 with the monopoly of selling all the coal of Newcastle, Sunderland and Berwick in London at exorbitant prices. In 1662 Charles II raised funds to the tune of £200,000 by imposing a tax on every hearth or fireplace in England. As Englishmen have never adopted the central heating system there was little chance of evasion! They still cling to their fireplaces, to the great discomfort of American visitors!

In the seventeenth century two English ships were carrying cargoes of coal to foreign ports, and though there was the prejudice against smoke and smell in the chief towns of France, the Netherlands and Germany, many coal-mines were being worked in those countries before the close of the century.

Apparently the first reference to the existence of coal in what is now the United States of America occurs in the Journal of Father Hennepin, who observed a seam of coal on the banks of the Illinois River as he travelled through that region in 1669.[1] It was not till a hundred years later, however, that either bituminous

[1] *History of the Coal Miners of the United States*, Andrew Roy.

or anthracite coal was mined in America. Anthracite coal was first used for blacksmithing purposes in the Wyoming Valley in Eastern Pennsylvania in 1768, but it was not till 1812 that it was used in firing furnaces when the Fairmount (Pa.) Nail and Wire Works made the discovery that the black rock would get red hot if it was undisturbed instead of being constantly stirred. The Monongahela River mines in the Pittsburg district were the first bituminous mines to be worked; the coal was apparently used for domestic purposes from the earliest settlement of the country. It is difficult to assign a reliable date for the first working of this soft coal, but it seems to have been in general use among the inhabitants of Pittsburg by the beginning of the nineteenth century, and there are records of shipments to distant markets in 1803 and 1817. The early methods of hauling coal in these first shipping mines are interesting as being indicative of the pioneer stage of coal-mining. In one of them the coal was tied up in raw hides and rolled down the hill to the river bank, where it was emptied into wagons; the hides were carried back to the pit mouth to be reloaded. An improvement on this primitive raw hide haulage was made by framing two saplings together to form shafts for a horse, a box being fastened at the rear end of the saplings. Underground the miner first used a wheelbarrow in hauling the coal from his room or "place" to the mouth of the mine. Later he was assisted by dogs; the dog was harnessed up to the front of the car and the miner pushed behind. Stories of the affectionate care of the miner for his dog remind one of the more modern instances of the wonderful ways in which "pit ponies" in Great Britain respond to humane treatment. A remarkably fine type of miner working in the South Wales coalfield once said to the author, "Why, my little pony will do anything for me in reason. Of course, you mustn't try her too hard, and I treat her kindly, you know. Intelligent? She's a damned sight more intelligent than some of my butties!" Just as ponies and mules have supplanted the dog, so they in time will be superseded by the locomotive. Already in America to a great extent and in Europe to some extent "live stock" in a mine is a thing of the past. It was interesting in exploring one of the mines in Pennsylvania to find that the mules' stalls were no longer used as stables. Everything points to the inevitable trend towards the mechanisation of the coal-mining industry.

We have seen that coal-mining grew steadily more extensive in England from the thirteenth to the seventeenth century. But the means of pumping water out of the mines were still primitive and inadequate. An improvement was made by Thomas Savery in 1698 with his invention of a pump worked by the condensation of steam. By means of a practical prime mover he used steam to create a vacuum. By 1705 Newcomen had got a great beam clanking back and forth by means of an atmospheric engine, which if its boiler did not burst and its valves melt out could coax a little water out of the bottom of a coal mine.

There was a growing demand for iron at the time and this stimulated the production of coal. Indeed, the growth of the coal trade is bound up with the development of the iron industry. The forests of the southern and western counties of England had been largely consumed for smelting iron, and Dudley's use of sea and pit coal for this purpose spurred inventors to improve methods of mining coal. The steam engine of James Watt filled the need. The gifted young maker of mathematical instruments discovered a better way of condensing the steam and creating the vacuum than to disgage the cylinder every few seconds by dousing cold water over it as Newcomen had done. He contrived a second metal box to which the steam could regularly escape and be condensed and so prompt the cylinder, now steadily hot, to transform ever more of the heated coal into energy. The new engine was used to clear the mines of water, in the sinking of shafts and in bringing up the coal from the pit. This application of steam power soon resulted in a rapid development of all the English coalfields. The consequent increased production of coal gave a great impetus to the iron, copper and tin industries; with the assistance of the steam engine, the forge and the rolling-mill increased the output of their products; the enormous growth of the metallurgical industries meant a demand for more and more coal and the coke derived from it, notwithstanding the effect of Neilson's invention of the hot blast which was to reduce from seven to two tons the amount of coal necessary to transform iron ore into a ton of the finished product.

The extraordinarily rapid increase in the industries, commerce and population of Great Britain from the middle of the eighteenth century to the beginning of the twentieth is a tale that has been told a thousand times. It is, indeed, a fascinating story and invests the study of history with a dramatic content unique in the economic life of man. For many centuries industry had been carried on with little change of process. The weaving of cloth and the ploughing of the fields were much the same in the seventeenth as they had been in the eleventh century. It is a mistake to think of the Industrial Revolution as something that was so sudden that it had no relation to what had gone before, just as it is to suppose that the invention of Watt or anyone else is entirely the product of his own brain or experience, but taking a broad sweep of industrial history one cannot but be impressed by the astonishingly accelerated pace of economic development in England as the result of the radical changes in the technique of manufacturing industry which were made during the period so generally described as the Industrial Revolution.

This comparatively sudden burst of industrial activity opened a new era which has been variously described as the Age of Steam, the Coal Age, the Machine Age. Perhaps the most appropriate appellation is the Power Age, or more recently and perhaps more accurately as the Age of Energy. But as Mr. Stuart Chase says in his most informative and challenging *Men and Machines*: "If the power engine was the hero of the industrial revolution, iron and coal were its parents. The three together formed the new holy family of materialism. Acting and reacting upon one another in countless combinations, they made possible the billion horses which are either serving us or running away with us to-day.

"The coal mine fed the engine and the engine in return pumped water out of the mine; hoisted coal out of the pits; helped to carry it by rail and water to its destination. Coal smelted the iron, and its coke helped to make the steel out of which the engine could be formed."

Another quotation from the same source will serve to bring this brief historical survey up to date:

"Now changes come thick and fast. Dynamite succeeds black powder. Cars pushed by hand give way to mules, and finally to dwarf locomotives. The iron hoisting bucket disappears before a cage-like freight elevator for handling cars direct from the working levels to the surface. The skip hoisting equipment is introduced. The hand shovel is supplanted by mechanical loading machines. The individual steam plant is replaced by a central power station, furnishing current for lights, electric hoists, air compressors: pumps and motors for underground haulage. Finally come multiple car tipples, automatic hoists, coal-cutting machines (in coal mines), elaborate ventilating systems and a steam turbine for the central power plant. Nor is the end in sight."

Mr. Chase might have included that marvellous machine known as an "entry driver" which the author has seen at work in that wonderfully equipped No. 2 Orient Mine at West Frankfort, Illinois. The machine drives an entry or bores its circular way into the coal seam, thus cutting the coal from the face; picks it down and loads it into the cars in one continuous, automatic operation. It is of interest to note that this mine holds the world's record for one day's output, i.e. 15,000 tons, and in December, 1928, was producing 12,000 tons as a daily average.

As in Great Britain so it was the trinity of coal, steam and iron that opened up the Power Age in the United States and enabled the settlers of that vast country, like an immense prairie fire, to sweep from east to west.

But the industrial revolution in the United States did not get well under way till the 'sixties; electricity and oil have added their contribution to the building up of what is surely one of the most marvellous material civilisations in the history of the world.

ECONOMIC IMPORTANCE

The evolution of coal through all its stages is so gradual that it is difficult to define its various grades. The customary geological classification, ignoring peat which is not yet coal, and graphite which has ceased to be coal, is into six grades, namely, lignite, sub-bituminous, bituminous, semi-bituminous, semi-anthracite and anthracite. For all economic purposes this classification is simplified into three grades: anthracite, bituminous and lignite.

Anthracite or hard coal is of uniformly high heating value and burns without causing any smoke nuisance. The freedom from smoke is a blessing to the housewife, a boon to the real estate dealer, an inducement to the health of the city dweller, and it artistically improves the view from the Woolworth Tower or the Empire State Building. One cannot but be impressed by the difference in clarity between elevated views of London and New

York. Broadly speaking, London uses bituminous coal (the smoking chimneys are far more typically characteristic than winter fogs): New York uses anthracite. In recent years oil has been much used instead of anthracite and the operators in the anthracite industry are greatly concerned about the growing competition from this source. The operators have always presumed on the possession of a monopoly of smokeless fuel for domestic purposes but the strike of 1922 shook their commercial complacency. One result of that strike, which lasted for five months, was that a great many people had resort to oil and made the discovery that it was an extremely convenient fuel, installed with the minimum of physical effort and regulated automatically. Part of the market that was lost to oil has been regained, but the anthracite operators are now very alert to every measure for promoting the use of their own product and have an elaborate organisation for advertising its merits, and, incidentally, for discouraging the use of oil. They are faced by a difficult commercial problem—how to place anthracite on the market at a price sufficiently low to induce the consumer to forgo the convenience of oil. We shall have more to say of oil later.

But there is the householder who cannot afford the luxury of anthracite or oil: economic necessity forces him to use bituminous or soft coal which, though it gives off a thick, dense smoke and on the average is of slightly lower heating value in the raw state than anthracite, yet is relatively cheaper. It is estimated that the cost of production of anthracite is approximately twice that of bituminous coal which is found in flat, close-to-the-surface beds, whereas anthracite mining is made more expensive by a complicated geological occurrence, involving folded strata, depth, water and association with thin seams of slate: the cost of preparing anthracite for commercial use (the building of breakers, with their elaborate machinery for cleaning, sorting, etc.) is also greater. A visitor to a bituminous mine feels that the "show" is over on reaching "air" again, but on stepping out of the cage of an anthracite mine he begins on a tour of a coal *works*. In America anthracite is mined almost exclusively in North-East Pennsylvania, which is a district of heavy freights and where the industry has been developed by the railroad companies, from the beginning. A considerable proportion of the available supply is already exhausted, and it has no capacity for yielding by-products to reduce its cost: at any rate the capacity has not yet been commercially exploited. Its domestic use may be continued by those who can afford it but the task of supplying the home must fall for the most part on bituminous coal.

Bituminous coal has several advantages. It is relatively cheap, it is widely distributed, being mined commercially in no fewer than thirty-two States, and there are still enormous reserves in the various coal-producing areas. It has been estimated that in the case of the United States only one per cent of the reserve has been used. But the smoke nuisance created by its use is certainly a serious objection. Apart from the health and civic objections which in a well-ordered social community would be a justification for preventing its use altogether, there are strong commercial inducements for robbing the coal of its smoke, for the smoke represents the most concentrated value in soft coal. If this value can be extracted and used towards reducing the cost, while at the same time a smokeless fuel for heating use can be produced, the objections will be converted into real benefits. Several processes for the manufacture of an artificial anthracite which would have these desirable results have been experimented upon. If any specific industry were in need of artificial anthracite it would soon develop a process to the point where it could be economically applied. But since it is only the public interest that demands it the public must wait till the need is felt by industry. If natural resources were exploited with a single eye to the public weal such an invention would soon be successfully applied and the inventor, instead of having to beg an individual company to adopt the new process, would be engaged by an appropriate public authority and be regarded as a public benefactor. The manufacture of a synthetic anthracite is, however, no longer a technological problem. It was of great interest to the author to break anthracite with Mr. Hugh Archbald, consultant mining engineer, mine superintendent and author of *The Four Hour Day*, an excellent little book which shows the social and economic possibilities of applying engineering to the problem of hours. Picture two men sprawling on the floor of a room in Scranton, Pa., the one an interested economist from South Wales, the other an American engineer in love with his invention in the form of a stick of synthetic anthracite which he fondly handled as he told how for four years he had experimented on various processes

c

and minutely described the one he finally adopted, occasionally breaking off a piece to show how clean and convenient it was. For six hours they talked of coal, economics and engineering, the only break being a discussion of fish over lunch, occasioned by the delicious trout caught and cooked by Mr. Archbald himself. The engineer has produced anthracite artificially: the problem is no longer one of technical processes but of the economic and social application of inventive skill.

Lignite is often described as "brown" coal—the Germans call it *braunkohl*—though all deposits are not of this colour, those which have been subjected to the greatest pressure for the longest periods being the darkest. It contains a high percentage of water, varying from 30 to 40 per cent and is therefore of low heating value. Its chief economic use is in the production of electricity. At a place called Rucksack, a few miles out of Cologne, there is an extensive lignite mine, worked on the "stripping" principle, i.e. the coal is scraped off the surface by huge mechanical "shovels" and tipped on to wagons. The brown coal feeds an adjoining electricity plant which supplies a considerable zone in the Rhineland with electric light and power. The Germans, partly stimulated by the economic stress of the World War, have constructed special machinery adapted to the use of lignite for certain manufacturing purposes. But in America, which has more than 90 per cent of the world's reserves of lignite, it is little used for fuel requirements. Lignite is mined in many countries and its use is likely to increase as the higher grade coals become dearer but in the current industrial type of world the anthracite and bituminous coals alone have any great importance.

The future utilisation of lignite as a source of heat and power lies in its burning in powdered form, with the effect of gaseous fuel in compression into briquettes through complete gasification in gas producers or by carbonisation with by-product recovery. The American Bureau of Mines has shown that one ton of air-dried lignite may be made to yield 8,000 to 10,000 cubic feet of gas, 17 pounds of ammonium sulphate, one gallon of oil, 50 pounds of tar, and one-half to two thirds of carbon residue convertible into briquettes approaching the value of anthracite. It is also used in the nitrate and glass industries.

The chief use of anthracite is for domestic and office heating purposes. The Pennsylvania field supplies the New England market and the South Wales anthracite field, the only important deposit of anthracite in Great Britain, exports the bulk of its product to European countries, where it is used in central heating stoves. Canada and the United States also import Welsh anthracite. The small sizes are used for steam coal in small factories like laundries, power plants, and for heating greenhouses. A small amount—about 7 per cent—is consumed by railroads in the United States and at one time anthracite was used as an industrial coal, the greater part of the iron and steel manufactured in the United States less than sixty years ago coming from anthracite blast furnaces. It is probable that the use of natural anthracite in industry and transportation will gradually diminish: the reserves are small and they will be husbanded for domestic purposes.

The largest uses of bituminous coal in most coal-producing countries are for power in manufacturing plants, for heating houses and other buildings and for locomotive service. Next to these in importance come its utilisation for steamer fuel, as blast furnace fuel (in the form of coke) and as a raw material itself in the manufacture of illuminating gas and by-products. In the case of some countries (notably Great Britain), the export of coal to another country is an important way of marketing the output.

A large proportion of the coal used in the world is utilised for the purpose of developing power for running manufacturing plants. At the time of the Industrial Revolution in England, this use of coal was regarded as its main future utilisation. England's position as the foremost commercial power of the nineteenth century was based largely on her coalfields which provided the power for her manufactures. This is still the most important utilisation of coal. In addition to its direct use as a manufacturing fuel, coal has important effects on manufactures through its stimulus to the development of transport within the producing country itself. Cheap coal for transportation was a factor in England's industrial development, but the classic example is the United States where the distances are so great that the transport use of coal has a tremendous bearing on the general industrial situation. Despite the rapidly increasing use of petroleum and electric power for transportation purpose in the United States, a very considerable proportion of its coal production will probably continue to be used in this way for a long time to come.

The use of coal as a raw material is also important. When

bituminous coal is heated strongly out of contact with air, it is not burnt but distilled and in the process of this distillation several groups of products are used. The fixed carbon and ash which were in the original coal remain in the form of coke and in addition the more volatile constituents of the coal separate out in the forms of gas, ammoniacal liquor and coal tar. We have already seen that coke for blast furnace use was adopted in England in the middle of the eighteenth century. Illuminating gas was not made for use till 1798 when the first private gasworks was constructed for an English factory. Public gasworks followed in London in 1813, in Paris 1815 and in Berlin in 1826; since then they have spread all over the industrialised world. But alike in the ovens which produced coke for the blast furnaces and in the gasworks which manufactured illuminating gas, the coal-tar was practically wasted. It was not till 1856 when Perkin discovered the aniline colours which could be produced from the tar that any serious attempt was made to utilise this product, though small quantities had been treated previously in order to make benzene and illuminating oils. The manufacture of aniline dyes and other coal-tar products spread rapidly, Germany soon taking the lead. Before the last war no other country had developed this manufacture to any great extent, but since the war, during which foreign supplies were cut off from England and the United States, there has been a marked development of the by-product side of the coal industry, especially in those two countries; indeed there are experts who believe that the only hope for the industry in England lies in the utilisation of by-products.

Mr. Edwin C. Eckel, an American civil engineer, in his valuable book *Coal, Iron and War* gives a table indicating the uses to which the world puts its coal, excluding the portion used at the mines for pumping, etc., which the United States Geological Survey for anthracite and bituminous utilisations during 1915, estimated as 3·9 per cent of the total. Mr. Eckel, basing his table on the world output of coal in 1913 and certain outstanding features of American production of hard and soft coal at that time, says that the results are not precise but apparently no previous estimate of the sort had been made so that they may be accepted tentatively. The table, which is given opposite, is sufficiently indicative of the use-distribution of coal, despite subsequent changes.

In some countries the shipping of coal to other countries plays an important part in the national economy. This is particularly true in the case of Great Britain which for several decades has exported a considerable proportion, on an average about 30–40 per cent of its coal supplies as a means of paying for imports of foreign food supplies and raw materials. In 1931 the British export of coal was just 30 per cent. Here is a country possessing abundant supplies of coal of excellent quality, relatively cheaply mined, and where the collieries are so near the seaboard that transportation to ports is not a heavy item. The late Professor W. S. Jevons two generations ago in his able treatise, *The Coal Question*, discussed in masterly style the wisdom of England's policy of exporting coal, of "draining itself of its life-blood," and many

	Metric Tons	Per cent.
Manufacturing purposes	562,000,000	43
Heating buildings	250,000,000	20
Locomotive fuel	230,000,000	18
Coke	150,000,000	12
Steamer fuel	75,000,000	6
Illuminating gas	12,000,000	1
	1,279,000,000	100

other writers who have devoted their attention to estimates of the duration of the supplies have expressed grave fears of the consequences of exhaustion.

It is ironical to realise that to-day England's problem is not the danger of producing too much coal but the difficulty of finding markets for the coal produced. Few experts are concerned now about the problem of exhaustion; they believe that long before reserves are exhausted at the present rate of consumption other forms of fuel will have been invented and brought into use. The immediate problem is to increase consumption, and with the growing competition of oil and hydro-electricity, improved methods of combustion and the increasing indirect use of coal for the generation of gas and electricity, all resulting in a substantial reduction in coal consumption, it is assuming far greater urgency than the question of conservation of supplies ever had.

The United States at present exports only about 4½ per cent of its coal production, but as the exports of the north-western European nations decline, and as the United States changes from being a producer and exporter of raw materials to a producer and exporter of manufactured goods, thus having a freight differential similar to that now enjoyed by coal exports from Great Britain, it may be expected that it will gradually become the successor to the present exporting nations of Europe. This change, however, will not only be gradual but will be a long time in developing. The United States is too far distant from the great coal-consuming markets, and while probably its exports to Europe will continue on a level above the pre-war figure, they can hardly form more than a small proportion of Europe's requirements in the immediate future.

No other country possesses such huge reserves and in no other country with large unexploited reserves has there been the same development of mines and transportation systems as in the United States.[1]

Less important uses of coal are the use for power and heat at the mines and for bunker purposes. A greater percentage of the coal is used at the mines in Great Britain than in the United States and at the anthracite mines in both countries than at the bituminous mines. The percentages vary from year to year but 10 per cent and 3 per cent may be taken as roughly indicative of the difference. This relatively greater use at the mines in Great Britain is due to the fact that its mines are much deeper and consequently more power is required for raising the coal and for pumping water out of the mines. The average depth of English mines is 1,000 feet whereas in the United States anthracite mines average 460 feet and bituminous mines 250 feet. Further, the more limited reserves prevent England from discarding the lower grade coal as is done in the United States and more power is needed to operate the sorting and washing machinery.

In view of the small export trade of the United States it is natural that very little coal should be used for bunker purposes, not much more than 1 per cent of the total production: this compares with more than 5 per cent for British coal.

There is one other form of coal utilisation which while perhaps not strictly economic exercises an extremely important influence

[1] *The World's Coal Resources*, J. E. Orchard, Harvard University.

on economic developments through its use in the manufacture of explosives for military purposes. A lack of toluol is said to have come near to causing the defeat of Great Britain in the early days of the European war. Indeed, the last war showed more clearly than any previous war the advantage of possession of supplies of coal for the making of munitions and gave a new political importance to the distribution of coal throughout the world. This is probably one reason why the Economic Committee of the League of Nations is devoting some attention to the world supplies of coal. Its summary report entitled *The Coal Problem* is an excellent statement of the problem approached from the standpoint of the desirability of organising and distributing the mineral wealth of the world on a more co-operative basis than the existing unorganised chaotic competitive system which harbours such dangerous potentialities of war. Political parties in all industrialised countries are now paying close attention to questions relating to the ownership or control of mineral wealth, such as the policy of nationalisation or of international regulation.

It seems remarkable that a single, partly developed unit of industry can have such a vital and far-reaching bearing on human welfare but this is undoubtedly true of the products of coal. Attempts have been made by certain writers, notably Jeffrey,[1] to establish a close correlation between coal and civilisation. France and Spain both suffer economically from a lack of coal resources. The decline in the birth-rates of France and Spain is attributed not to natural sterility, for French Canadians and the Spanish peoples of South and Central America are exceptionally fecund, but to the lack of adequate resources in coal. The population of Great Britain and Germany steadily and rapidly increased with the development of industries based on coal and these countries are assumed to have advanced in civilisation. More recently the United States made tremendous strides in growth of population and industrial development after its vast coal resources were applied to the iron and manufacturing industries. Sweden and Denmark in the eighteenth century were important European powers but to-day, owing to their poverty in coal and despite their able and energetic population, they rank lower than all the coal-producing countries. The emigration of the Irish, the people of the Highlands of Scotland

[1] *Coal and Civilisation.*

and of the Southern Italians to other countries is traced to lack of coal resources.

So runs the argument, which seems to imply that a growth of population and industrial development based on coal necessarily indicates an advance in civilisation. The French people, however, might claim that they are more civilised than the people of the United States and one assumes that the Greeks and Romans who used charcoal as fuel, not coal, reached a high level of civilisation. The correlation where it can be established with any degree of closeness applies only in the modern industrial world and presupposes an accepted definition of civilisation anyway.

But it is clear that coal is a commodity of enormous economic importance in the economy of the modern world. It is the original source of the greater part of our artificial heat and light and power. The home industry and commerce are largely dependent upon its adequate supply. It adds to the comfort of man; it furnishes him with the energy of a billion horses and with a thousand products of utility and beauty, while it contains within itself the potentialities of blowing him and his civilisation to smithereens.

CHAPTER II

ANALYSIS OF PRESENT WORLD COAL SITUATION

WITH PARTICULAR REFERENCE TO
THE TRADE OF GREAT BRITAIN
AND THE UNITED STATES OF AMERICA
AND
OF POSSIBILITIES OF DEVELOPMENT

CHAPTER II

ANALYSIS OF PRESENT WORLD COAL SITUATION

WITH PARTICULAR REFERENCE TO THE TRADE OF
GREAT BRITAIN AND THE UNITED STATES OF AMERICA
AND OF POSSIBILITIES OF DEVELOPMENT

THE ascertained coal resources of the world aggregate about
7,260 billion gross tons. It is difficult to grasp the significance
of this colossal figure, and without wearying the reader with a
table showing how it is made up it will suffice to indicate the
proportionate shares of the various continents; 69 per cent of
this total is in North America, 17 per cent in Asia, 11 per cent
in Europe and 2 per cent in Oceania. Africa and South America
have relatively unimportant deposits. Additional deposits have
been discovered in Western Canada, Russia and China but
reliable estimates as to their extent are not available.

The late war resulted in some important changes in the political
distribution of coal resources. From Germany, France obtained
the coal in Alsace-Lorraine and the Saar Basin—the latter for
a period of fifteen years with the possibility (subject to a plebiscite)
of repurchase by Germany at the end of that period. The field
lying at the junction of the former German, Austrian and Russian
Empires has also been redistributed. Poland obtained the parts
lying within German and Russian Poland and Austrian Galicia,
while the remainder of the Austrian portion now belongs to
Czechoslovakia. The ownership of the richest part of the field,
lying in Upper Silesia, is divided between Germany and Poland,
the bulk of the reserves belonging to Poland. The Austrian
Empire has also lost the deposits in Dalmatia, Bosnia and
Herzegovina to Yugoslavia. But all these changes were made
within Europe itself and do not affect the continental distribution.

More than one half of the total coal reserves of the world are
located in the United States. The most workable portions of
these huge reserves are situated in the Eastern section of the
country, where practically all the anthracite deposits and most
of the best steaming coals are to be found. Canada ranks next
to the United States in aggregate coal resources but 70 per cent

of them is lignite and she only produces about one half of her needs. The industrial regions of Ontario and Lower Quebec import considerable quantities of both anthracite and bituminous from the United States. On the other hand the seaboard area of New England receives shipments of New Brunswick and Cape Breton coal while the American North West depends to a considerable extent for its supplies upon Alberta and British Columbia.

South America and Africa are unimportant factors in the world's coal trade. Australia has reserves of high quality coal ample to supply its needs for generations. The deposit of New South Wales is all good bituminous and is the principal bunker fuel of Australasia. It is shipped in considerable quantities to the Dutch East Indies, Singapore, Colombo and even to the West Coast of the United States and of South America. Asia's coal reserves are not definitely known but they are believed to rank second only to those of North America. China possesses unsurpassed stores of anthracite while its bituminous reserves rank next to those of the United States. Exploitation of Chinese resources however has scarcely begun; they constitute the reserves of the more distant future. China's output is little more than sufficient to meet her own requirements. Japan normally has a considerable surplus which is exported to Shanghai, Hong Kong, the Philippines and Singapore. Asiatic Russia also has extensive but almost unknown deposits, mainly lignitic. India and Bengal possess considerable reserves of bituminous coal, used chiefly for coking and locomotive purposes; they are too soft for effective use as steam coal. Considerable anthracite fields exist in Indo-China.

The major coal resources of Europe are comprised in four main regions. These regions are: first, the British fields which lie for the most part near the sea, and produce coal of high quality and great variety; second, the Rhine Valley fields including the Ruhr Basin in Germany, the Saar Basin, formerly German and now under French control, the Namur fields in Belgium and the mines in North Eastern France; third, the fields at the juncture of Poland, Germany and Czechoslovakia; fourth, the Donetz Basin in Southern Russia, bordering the Black Sea. The coal in this region is mainly of high-grade bituminous and anthracite: the development of an export trade in coal has been hampered by the lack of bulky imports to balance an outward movement of coal.

Extent of resources is one thing; extent of production is quite another.

We have seen that the world's coal resources aggregate about 7,260 billion gross tons. For many years past, the world production has averaged less than 1,200 million metric tons. Europe, though ranking third in point of resources, produces more than one-half of the world output and is the leading coal-exporting continent. Of the European share, the United Kingdom produced about half before the war and accounts for between 40 and 50 per cent to-day. Germany's share is about one-fourth. Far below these rank France (with a steadily increasing output), Czechoslovakia, Poland, Belgium and Russia.

The following countries shewed an increase in production for the world trade from 1913, a typical year prior to the war, to 1926:

Poland	from no production to 2·6 per cent	
Japan	from 1·6 to 2·3	per cent
China	from 1·0 to 1·4	per cent
Belgium	from 1·7 to 1·8	per cent
India	from 1·2 to 1·5	per cent
Canada	from 1·0 to 1·2	per cent
S. Africa	from 0·6 to 1·0	per cent
Chile	from 0·09 to 1·0	per cent
Spain	from 0·3 to 0·46	per cent

In 1931 the world output of coal, as estimated by the United States Bureau of Mines, was 1,256,000 metric tons, a drop of 157,000 tons from the 1930 total. Russia, the Netherlands, Poland, Spain and India were the only major producing countries to record gains in 1931. The United States continued to be by far the largest producer, with 343,014,000 tons of soft coal and lignite, and 54,005,000 tons of anthracite.

There is no correlation between the amount produced and the amount exported. The United States produces about 20 per cent more of the world's coal than Great Britain, but exports only about 4½ per cent of its production, four-fifths of which is consigned to Canada, whereas Great Britain exports about 30 per cent of its production. In October, 1932, her exports were 4,835,800 tons, rather more than 29 per cent of the total production, which was 16,371,500 tons. These two countries and

Germany are the only ones in a position to export coal in large quantities. In 1913 Great Britain handled about 50 per cent of the export coal trade of the world; Germany about 30 per cent and the United States about 15 per cent. The British percentage is now about the same as before the war; the German trade has shrunk somewhat and the American has increased slightly. Poland, Japan, Australia and South Africa export small quantities, but are unimportant factors in the world coal trade, though Poland is developing in importance as a coal-exporting country.

We have seen that although the United States is one of the three leading exporting countries, it is relatively to Great Britain and Germany unimportant as an exporter of coal. It is a striking fact, for instance, that whereas the total production of coal in the United States in 1925 was 531,890,000 gross tons, its exports amounted to only about 16 million gross tons—about 3 per cent. There are several reasons for this condition.

In the first place, the domestic requirements are so large as to absorb the great bulk of the entire production. The tremendous development of railroads and the rapid growth of great coal-consuming industries, such as iron and steel production, have stimulated the domestic demand in a very remarkable degree.

In the second place, the position of the mines, situated mainly in the Appalachian Mountains, necessitates an expensive railroad haul of 200 miles or more to the seaboard and this expense effectually offsets any advantage which American operators may have over British and German employers in the matter of cost of production. British export coals are within 10–15 miles of the sea.

In the third place, ocean traffic in American coal is handicapped by the comparative absence of bulky return freight. Coal is bulky and the other commodities in the production of which the United States possesses a greater advantage than she does in the mining of coal, are also bulky, wheat, cotton and heavy iron and steel products. Most American imports are of small bulk and high value. From the standpoint of the ocean carriers, it has not been found profitable to add coal to bulky commodities already transported in outgoing traffic. Great Britain, on the other hand, imports bulky commodities and utilises coal as outward ballast. Reasons of minor importance sometimes advanced are the relative inexperience of American shippers in dealing with foreign buyers and their alleged unwillingness to adapt themselves to the methods and practices of these buyers. To-day these reasons appear to be lacking in any force they may ever have had.

The bulk of the exports goes to Canada, Italy, France and the Spanish American nations. Canada takes practically all the surplus of anthracite though in recent years she has begun to import anthracite from South Wales, which has to that extent displaced supplies from Pennsylvania. The trade with France has steadily declined since the war because of the payment of German reparations in coal and of reviving British competition. For the same reasons the trade to Italy has shrunk somewhat. A similar shrinking tendency is observable to other European countries and to all South American countries except Brazil. Shipments to Mexico, Central America and Cuba are increasing, but have not yet reached pre-war levels.

The United States is not regarded seriously as a rival for European business. The British Coal Commission Report, 1925, made some interesting comments on this feature: "In normal times, America is not a serious competitor in markets in which Great Britain is interested, except in South America, although some American coal always finds its way to Europe and the Mediterranean." "The Americans come into the market spasmodically when there is a chance. It is not the regular trade that ours is." This chance is usually provided by long strikes like those of 1921 and 1926 in England with the consequent high prices. Several witnesses before the Commission pointed out that a very slight difference one way or the other in the British price would bring in or exclude considerable American competition.

The coal industry of the United States then is largely self-contained, the overwhelming bulk of its production being consumed at home, and only in exceptional circumstances has it any important direct contact with foreign countries.

The international problem, therefore, is mainly confined to Europe. Before any attempt is made to describe that problem some attention must be given to certain normal features of the industry.

Considerable progress has been made in recent years in the introduction of mechanical power into coal-mines, especially in the United States, but this should not obscure the fact that wages constitute an exceptionally high proportion of total costs as compared with most other industries. This proportion has been authoritatively estimated as two-thirds. Owing to the expense and time involved in opening new mines to take advantage of an increase in demand, any increase in demand has in normal times led to a rapid rise in profits and any decrease to an equally rapid reduction. In some cases, as in West Virginia, mines can be opened without heavy capital outlay but it is generally true that profits tend to fluctuate to an exceptional degree; and as the margin for immediate economies except out of wages is a small one, any depression in the industry is likely to affect wages or employment with exceptional rapidity.

The statistics of consumption in recent years, however, show that demand for coal is remarkably steady and is normally but little affected by changes in price over short periods of time. Mr. Alfred Morgan, a South Wales working miner (one of the author's students) who became a technician, shows this very clearly in an article published in the *Economic Journal*, December, 1926—"The Coal Problem as seen by a Colliery Official"—and gives the following interesting export figures for the United Kingdom for the March quarter, 1924 and 1926.

COAL EXPORTS

March Quarter	Quantity, Tons	Average Value s. d.	Total Value £
1924	15,705,950	24 4	19,270,422
1926	13,190,584	21 7	12,031,042
Reduction .. 2,515,366		Loss .. 7,239,380	

More recent English experience illustrates the characteristic inelasticity of the demand for coal. Between April, 1927, and March, 1928, the average export price of coal showed a reduction from 18s. 6d. to 15s. 9d. but consumption remained almost unaffected. Coal exports amounted in tonnage to 5·7 millions in the first month and 5·8 millions in the last month of the period. The total quantity of coal produced in four weeks at the beginning of the period was 19·1 million tons, and at the end of it was 19·9 million tons. A similar illustration may be given from American experience. In 1920, when the price was the highest on record, the American people bought more bituminous coal than in any year before with one exception. In 1921, when millions of tons were sold at the bare operating cost of production no cut in price could induce the American people to buy more than they needed.

This characteristic of inelasticity of demand of coal is one that should never be lost sight of in any discussion of prices and the consumption of coal: one has only to think of automobiles to appreciate it, for by contrast the demand for automobiles has increased steadily with a reduction in price. This characteristic of the trade in coal was concealed to a large extent before the war by the constant and rapid increase in the total amount required. Consumption then increased roughly in proportion to the growth of industrial production. Between 1886 and 1913 world consumption advanced at a rate of rather more than 4 per cent per annum. Production in that period was quintupled in the United States, trebled in Germany and increased in the United Kingdom by 80 per cent. Towards the end of this period these three countries supplied the needs of those which were lacking in coal deposits, and of their total net exports the United Kingdom accounted for nearly two-thirds: her exports in 1913 amounted to approximately 100 million metric tons—more than one-third of her output and almost one-sixth of the total value of the total volume hewn in Europe during that year; by 1928 her exports had dropped to 68 million tons and by 1932 to 57·15 million tons, a decrease of 7½ per cent as compared with 1931. These figures are significant of the change that has occurred since the war in the British coal trade particularly, and in the European situation generally.

In 1913, 605 million metric tons of coal were mined in Europe and of this total probably more than one-sixth entered into international trade. The war largely stopped this trade. Countries which had been dependent on external supplies had to develop their own resources or seek other forms of fuel and power. During the course of the war many mines were gutted and in 1919 and 1920 the price of coal soared to unprecedented heights. Those who had surplus coal to sell reaped the full measure of the advantage offered. A powerful incentive was given to consumers to search for every means of economising its use and for every available alternative source of energy. During the last decade, therefore, very rapid progress has been made in the scientific conservation of heat, in the extraction of the maximum of energy from coal burnt, in the exploitation of water-power and in the generation

of electricity from inferior qualities of coal—lignite, peat, etc.
This incentive towards economy and towards the discovery of
alternative sources of energy occurred at a moment when a
revolution was being created in the means of transport by the
more extended use of the internal combustion engine deriving
its motive power from oil products.

In 1928 only 594 million metric tons of coal were mined in
Europe, 11 million less than in 1913. It is difficult if not impossible
to attribute the respective weights for the reduction in demand
to the special forces generated by the war and to the normal
progress of scientific discovery. What concerns us here is the
highly important cumulative effect of all the influences at work.
Thus about one-third of the mercantile marine of the world is
now adapted for burning or otherwise using oil as compared with
3·4 per cent in 1914. The change in naval consumption is even
more striking: at least 90 per cent of the British Navy now runs
on oil. The increase of hydro-electric power generated in Italy
is equal to a coal consumption of some 9 million tons per annum.
In 1913 more than 84 per cent of the total energy employed in
the United States was derived from bituminous coal and anthracite; in 1927 the proportion had fallen to below 64 per cent.
It is estimated that in Germany an economy of 10 per cent has
been effected in the use of coal in industry by means of improved
boilers, furnaces, etc. Moreover, with modern processes it is
possible to employ inferior grades of coal which used to be considered as waste products.

As a result of these new industrial requirements, the world
consumption of coal and lignite in 1928 was only 4 per cent
greater than in 1913. During the same period the production
of raw materials and foodstuffs and the trade of the world had
grown by well over 20 per cent and in view of the economies
in manufacturing processes there is little doubt that the output
of industrial goods increased by considerably more than that
percentage. This failure of coal to keep pace with industrial
development is strikingly shown in the case of the United States.
There the consumption of coal was only 3·3 per cent higher
in 1928 than in 1913, whereas industrial production in 1925 was
about 70 per cent greater and rose still higher till 1930 when
a decline set in.

Thus though the economic activity of the world is beyond

question substantially greater than it was fifteen years ago, its consumption of coal has only increased during the whole of that period by an amount approximately equal to the normal increase in a single year before the war. Statistics also show clearly that in the same period the growth in the world consumption of coal has been very much slower than the increase in general agricultural production.

A more important characteristic of the present problem than the unresilient nature of the demand for coal is the large margin of surplus or excess capacity of the industry. By capacity is meant the immediate power of existing mines to produce coal without the investment of any additional fixed capital. And the excess capacity is equal to the difference between the amount which existing mines, without any additional investment of fixed capital, could produce and the amount of actual output. *The present margin of surplus capacity is the main cause of the trouble in the coal industry in all the highly industrialised coal-producing countries of the world.* Demand, as we have seen, is almost stationary, yet the capacity of production has generally increased. It has increased partly because States cut off from their normal sources of supply during the war were driven to open up their own deposits, partly as a result of the normal progress of the industry, and partly owing to the special incentive which the depression of recent years has given to more scientific and economical methods of production.

The most striking example of the first of these influences is the Netherlands, whose production increased from 1·9 million tons in 1913 to 10·7 million tons in 1928. Spain whose production increased by 50 per cent, Japan 46 per cent, and India 30 per cent were also affected by the inadequacy of the supplies from their habitual sources during the war and early post-war years. The fields which have been opened in Campine have raised the Belgian output by some 2½ million tons per annum. Germany, to make good her territorial losses, has doubled her production of lignite and to-day raises 8 million tons more coal in German Upper Silesia than she did fifteen years ago.

With demand increasing but slightly, all this war-created development has resulted in the closing of many mines, the partial working of others and widespread unemployment among mine-workers. Moreover it is believed by some experts that

the channels of trade have been affected by deliveries of coal
under the reparation clauses of the treaties of peace. The immediate reactions of these conditions have been most severely felt
in the United Kingdom whose markets in France, Italy and other
countries were diminished by German reparations coal deliveries.
In 1913 British mines raised 292 million tons; in 1928 they raised
244 million. Unemployment has been acute in the British coalfields since 1921 and to-day, January, 1934, there are 370,000
British miners wholly unemployed, for whom there is no immediate
prospect of absorption in any other industry. Meanwhile the
output derived from the present territory of France is about
7½ million tons and that from the present territory of Germany
about 10 million tons greater than in 1913.

But the change in the sources of supply fails by itself to bring
out fully the disproportion between productive capacity and
demand. In Europe generally the efficiency of the industry has
been very materially improved. Thus the French mines in the
Pas de Calais and in the Nord have been completely reorganised.
In the latter district 70 per cent of the coal is hewn to-day with
the aid of mechanical power. The proportion so hewn in the
Ruhr is stated to have risen from 2 per cent in 1913 to 83 per
cent in 1927.

These changes have led to the creation of a margin of surplus
capacity which has been reliably estimated at about one-quarter
in Germany, from one-quarter to one-third in the United
Kingdom and about one-half in Poland. When, therefore, during
the coal dispute of 1926 British production dropped by 119
million tons and her net exports by 64 million, the other countries
in Europe were able to increase their output by 41 million tons.
The remaining deficit was practically made good by the United
States. In normal years, as we have seen, the United States
does not sell in Europe. But the ability of her industry to respond
to any sudden demand is such that, whenever prices rise above
a certain point, whenever one of the great European producers
is temporarily disabled, she can throw upon the markets all the
coal required. In 1926, though British production owing to the
so-called "general strike" was less by 119 million tons, world
production fell off by only 2,300,000 tons. Everything goes to
show that the present capacity of the United States is extremely
elastic, and that Europe can produce all the coal she and her

external markets require while working far below her full capacity. The two great producing continents of the World have developed their power to supply, while demand lies quiescent.

It is this pronounced lack of equilibrium between demand and immediately available productive capacity that is at the root of the problem. Actual production is never likely to exceed demand by a very large margin. A slight proportionate excess is enough, under the conditions that have been indicated, to depress prices below a remunerative level, to bring about an accumulation of stocks, which will force this tendency further and to cause crisis and stoppages. But if behind any given excess of production there were not a much larger excess of productive capacity the "slack" might be taken up by the growth of demand even at the slow rate of the post-war period. It is the interest of each individual producer to exploit the present surplus capacity though it is to the detriment of producers as a whole to have it exploited; the industry does not act as a unit in any sense of the word and consequently there is no effective pressure on the companies new or old to prevent further unnecessary expansion. This conflict between the interest of the individual operator and that of the industry as a whole is clearly seen in the United States where almost twice as much coal as the country needs can be produced. There is no State or Federal regulation of production and apparently there is nothing to prevent an individual operator or company from adding to the already superfluous aggregate production. To open a small new mine in West Virginia, for example, needs but little capital and as capital for investment purposes has been plentiful in recent years, there is no difficulty about the initial outlay. When, because of a war or a strike the prospect of profits has seemed good there has been a rush to exploit the nation's vast coal resources; capital has been raised and it has been an easy matter to secure miners, drive shafts, lay tracks, and obtain the coal. The capacity of the old mines has been increased by new or improved machinery. During the extent of the boom the individual operator has reaped a harvest but when the slump has followed the aim of all the operators has been to keep their mines going until the next boom. During the slump the small man or the weaker companies have been eliminated, but with every new expansion more adventurers have been attracted to the industry.

In Europe it is not so easy to open up new mines—the capital outlay is heavier and the physical conditions of working the mines are more difficult—but a similar situation exists there.

It has been estimated that if only the United Kingdom, Germany and Poland produced up to their existing capacity the total European output would be increased by one-fifth.

Everywhere is this disequilibrium between capacity and consumption. It is the chief cause of the sickness of the industry. In Europe it has led to a struggle among the exporting countries to secure new markets or to maintain old ones. In the United States it means an increasingly keen and an increasingly chaotic competition for a share of the domestic market. The industry is a victim of the vagaries of a competitive economy without any group control. Coal resources are privately owned and coal-mining has in the main been carried on by business men who have owned lands or who have leased them from private owners on a royalty basis. Unrestricted competition might be expected to act as a brake to slow down the process of over-expansion which it has engendered. Over-expansion and its consequent operation of many of the mines on a part-time basis might be expected to result in bankruptcy for the more inefficient mines, and in accordance with orthodox classical economics we should expect such mines by reason of their extra-marginal nature to close down. Economic forces should in the long run ensure the production of coal by the more efficient mines. Mine capacity under the free play of competition should adjust itself automatically to the coal consumption requirements of industry at large. Producers unable to produce at a profit should be literally forced out of the industry. But competition in the coal industry has failed to meet the reasonable expectations of the theorists in this respect. Of bankruptcies there is no end but bankruptcy does not force the more inefficient mines out of existence. The capital investment in coal-mining represents a permanent investment of a highly specialised sort. The equipment for coal-mining cannot be utilised for any other industrial undertaking. A coal operator may be driven out of business, but this does not mean the permanent closing down of a mine. The investment is fixed, capital losses are written off, and the mine with the lower investment charges remains to plague the industry.

Coal operators overshadowed by the fear of financial loss

have sought refuge in lower costs, and as wages comprise the major cost of coal production the way out for the operator seemed to lie in the introduction of the machine. For a century the mine refused to admit the machine. The physical conditions under which the processes of coal-mining have been carried on were not hospitable ground, but in response to the spur of combining increase of output with diminished costs of production machines have been devised for the winning of coal in spite of physical obstacles and there has been a remarkable development in the application of machinery to coal-mining.

Professor Carter Goodrich in *The Miner's Freedom* has made a most interesting study of the effect of the growing mechanisation of the coal industry on that freedom from close factory supervision which has until recently characterised the work of the miner. It is clear that even the coal industry is at last succumbing to the onslaught of machinery and that the miner is destined to lose his peculiar freedom.

The following particulars relating to this development in the United States are of striking interest. In 1890, 6 per cent of the total coal mined was undercut by machinery. By 1900 the percentage had increased to 25, by 1913 to 51, and to-day about two-thirds of the total is produced by this method.[1] Recently there have been considerable developments in the use of machinery for loading and of conveyors for transportation, and it is believed that the number of completely mechanised mines will increase rapidly in the next few years. At present it is only the largest mines that have mechanical loaders and conveyors, though the author has seen loaders in use in a very small mine in Illinois and there is little doubt that they will become more and more the general practice.

Uncontrolled resort to machinery and operation on a large scale, however, have further complicated the position by adding to the capacity of the industry. Mechanisation helps the individual company but does not solve the problems of the operators as a whole. It is in line with the development of industrial technique generally, but unregulated, it only makes confusion worse confounded. It also aggravates the problem of unemployment. Free enterprise has not placed production in the hands of the economi-

[1] I am indebted for these figures to Mr. F. G. Tryon, Director of the Statistical Division of the Bureau of Mines, Washington, D.C.

cally fit. Both the fit and the unfit have continued to survive and more miners have remained in the industry than the industry, as at present conducted, can support. As a result, under-employment has been chronic, and the life of the labourer is increasingly beset by harassing anxieties.

The policy of cutting down the wage bill has been tried and proved a failure. Since the slump set in towards the close of 1920, European employers have acted on the assumption that by reducing wages they would enlarge their markets. Those countries engaged in export trade reaped some advantage of a temporary character, but the competition in reducing wages, as for example between Great Britain and Germany, apart from its injurious effects on the purchasing power of the mining community as consumers of other goods, is a fertile source of stoppages resulting in heavy financial losses as well as of serious psychological damage resulting from hostile discontent among the wage-earners. The same thing is true of wage-reducing competition among the bituminous operators of the United States; the competition among the operators in the anthracite field is more nominal than real, because there the rival interests have merged in a unified organisation which attempts to regulate prices and wages by agreement among the various companies. Even in the anthracite industry, however, the futility of the policy of cuts in wages is being realised and the best brains in the industry are concentrating on technical improvements, advertising, etc., designed to stimulate a bigger demand for anthracite and particularly to combat the growing rivalry, based mainly on convenience, of oil. In the American bituminous fields there is perpetual chaos—periodical wage reductions, rivalry between union and non-union operators, bankruptcies, disregard of agreements, bitter strikes, eviction of miners from their homes, importation of "scab" labour and occasionally armed conflicts. One feature of industrial relations in the United States that impresses an English investigator is that industrial disputes are literally in the nature of civil war. Ludlow; the armed march of West Virginia; Herrin; Lattimer—these are black spots bespattered with the red blood of fighters in the lawless struggle for industrial rights. You may see wild shootings and killings in the streets of Chicago in this year of grace 1933, but these are part of the course of crime run by gangsters and racketeers. During the author's stay in that city, seven men were placed against a wall and shot with cool calculation. But to appreciate the bellicose character of the fight between American coal operators and the miners, turning mainly on the issue of unionisation, you should see the spot in a peaceful field at Herrin, in the Illinois coalfield, where "scabs" were mercilessly slaughtered—of the manner of the killings no man dare tell—or the scene of the "Ludlow Massacre" of brave miners in the remote, romantic coalfield of Colorado; or the two little graveyards overlooking the village of Lattimer, Pennsylvania, which are the final resting place of fourteen Polish miners shot for attempting to persuade some of the men working in the mine down the road to join the union; or the wild mountain ridge near Logan—the scene of the "Armed March of West Virginia."

During the author's sojourn in the Pittsburg district, a Polish miner named Barkoski was foully murdered by the "Coal and Iron" Police for his suspected activities. In the year following his return to Wales a serious situation arose in the coalfields of South-eastern Kentucky.

Numerous writers have investigated the situation in Kentucky, particularly in Harlan and Bell Counties. Some of these individual investigators and certain parties of experts accompanying well-known men seem to have met with anything but a friendly reception. There appears to be reliable evidence, for instance, that the Waldo Frank party from New York were actually "beaten up." A group of ministers of religion who spent some time in the disturbed districts issued a report on their visit. This report shows that the plight of the miners was brought on by the arrogant attitude of the non-union coal operators who used their control of public officials to further their wage-cutting practices and to dominate the coal areas. While the operators claimed that no miner was dismissed for belonging to a union and that they merely insisted on the open shop, there was practically universal testimony from the miners that knowledge of union connections resulted in immediate dismissal. Union officials informed the group that nearly four thousand miners were on a black list in the County of Harlan for activities in connection with various unions. It was found that company ownership of houses prevailed with the usual power of eviction being used by the company to discipline recalcitrant and striking miners. Wages were generally

paid in scrip which the operators' group declared to be acceptable
in all stores. This the miners denied. The miners claimed that
the practice of charging higher prices in company stores prevailed.

The report states that two sections of the County, one centred
in Pineville and the other in Middlesboro, had raised $17,500
for relief, which was dispensed through the Welfare Leagues.
This relief was augmented by Government flour dispensed through
the Red Cross, the American Friends' Service Committee,
which supplied food for the children and milk for pre-school
children and expectant mothers; carload lots of food from other
sources and packages of seeds for vegetable gardens; 2,419
families had applied for relief, which was described as being
obviously inadequate. Incidentally it may be said here that the
American Friends' Service Committee, which has an elaborate
organisation for the relief of distress in necessitous districts
throughout the States, is still active in dispensing relief in the
Kentucky and the neighbouring West Virginia coalfields. The
author had the pleasure of meeting the Chairman, Henry J.
Cadbury, at Harvard, and has been kept informed of relief work
in these areas by Mary Kelsey, one of the most devoted and
sacrificial voluntary relief workers imaginable, whom he first
met in Philadelphia and with whom he has discussed relief
plans in America on her annual visits to South Wales since.

Officials of the United Mine Workers of America allege that
by the use of gunmen and other similar means in the 1931
disturbances, the operators have made it extremely difficult
for the union to organise the miners in South-eastern Kentucky,
though they believe that the non-union operators will eventually
fail and that the union will prevail. The fight has not been a
bloodless one. In May, 1931, four men were slain arising out
of the Ewarts clash.

In May, 1932, the Senate appointed a Sub-Committee to
investigate conditions in the coalfields of Bell and Harlan Counties
of Kentucky.

American coal history is studded with pages of bloody encounters, massacres and murders. It is a common thing to find
a gun in a miner's home in America, especially in the newer
coalfields and those which are unorganised. The men feel they
must be prepared for emergencies and they would rather run
the risk of breaking the law, which forbids the keeping of arms,

than feel utterly defenceless "if anything should happen." The author himself was advised in all friendliness to carry a revolver in certain coalfields! But wage-cuts have carried us to battle-grounds! We shall have occasion to return to this distressing feature of the industry.

The policy of lengthening the working day has also failed to solve the troubles of the coal industry. There is no lack of material on the effects of hours of labour on output. Economists and psychologists have devoted a great deal of attention to such studies. It is not intended to discuss them further here.

It is always difficult to assign responsibility for a decline in output consequent on the shortening of working hours because other factors have to be taken into account. In Great Britain the growing age of the industry is a most important factor. The increasingly difficult physical conditions, the increasing length of haulage distances from the face to the pit head or tipple, the increase in the proportion of men employed on work other than coal-getting, e.g. maintenance work like roofing, track-repairing, etc., the extent to which machinery can be economically used— these are factors that have to be considered in comparing the *per capita* output of Great Britain and that of the United States. By 1913 the annual production per man in Great Britain had fallen to 59 tons less than the average for the decade ending 1888. The American miner had actually increased his yearly output by 100 tons.[1] In explaining this remarkable contrast far more weight is to be given to the differences in physical conditions than to the relative number of hours worked. Within Great Britain itself there are striking differences of output as between the older and newer fields. In the Durham field, where coal has been mined for nearly five hundred years, the *per capita* annual production between 1889 and 1907 fell approximately 89 tons. In the newer South Wales field the decline between the same years, the men working the same number of hours, was 20 tons per man.

It does not follow that the length of the working day is an immaterial factor, but there has been a tendency in some quarters to give it undue weight and to underestimate the importance of the other relevant factors.

It would be easy to give examples of an increased output

[1] Royal Commission on the Coal Industry (1925), *Report*, Vol. I, p. 127.

following upon a reduction in hours, and psychologists have done a valuable service in showing that as a general rule and within limits a worker does more efficient work the shorter the working day. On social grounds the shortening of hours is to be encouraged. It was therefore greatly regretted by all who realise the social importance of a reduced working day that the British Government in 1926 changed the seven-hour law of 1919 to what was virtually an eight-hour law, thus setting back social progress to 1908 when for the first time an eight-hour law had been enacted. The British Coal Commission of 1925 found that some part of the decline in output was to be explained by the shortening of working hours, that is, from eight to seven. And the employers believed that the reversion to the eight-hour day, by increasing output, would reduce price and consequently stimulate consumption. Without giving statistical tables shewing the output and consumption since 1926 it is therefore sufficient to emphasise the all too evident fact that an increase in the miner's working day in Great Britain as a remedy for the economic troubles of the industry has not proved successful. Complaints of inability to find a market for the coal produced are as loud to-day as in 1925 and the lengthening of hours has not reduced unemployment in the coalfields.

The whole policy of price-cutting by reductions in wages and by lengthening the working day has failed to justify the expectations of its sponsors. All it can do is to give a temporary competitive advantage to a particular country. But it is no solution of the world problem. The same forces are at work throughout the world. The demand for coal, bituminous and anthracite, tends to shrink. Greater economy in the utilisation of coal, the use of oil, hydro-electric power, the increased output of lignite and the discovery of new uses for it, the development of native resources by countries that formerly imported coal, all have contributed to a reduced demand even during a period of falling prices.

The only ways in which the demand can be materially increased are by the discovery of new methods of coal utilisation, particularly of by-products, and by a development of other industries such as iron and steel. Technical improvements in the organisation and management of mines, stimuli in the form of prohibitions, duties, preferential railway freight rates, subsidies on export, lower wages and longer working hours—these local and national measures, while affording some competitive advantage to a particular country for a time, merely accentuate the nationalistic competitive scramble for markets and do little to stimulate aggregate consumption. International agreements concerning output, markets, prices, wages, hours and the abolition of existing artificial restrictions and stimuli would do much to improve the condition of the industry as a whole by minimising cut-throat competition, by reducing the gap between world capacity and demand and by improving the social conditions of the workers, but even these most desirable improvements cannot give coal a new lease of life. The positive problem of coal as a commodity is how to increase the demand for it and we have indicated the main ways—new uses for coal and a growth in the volume of industrial operations.

Perhaps the most hopeful development lies in the possibility of making the extraction of oil from coal by the process of hydrogenation a commercial success. The intensification of unemployment and the decline of prosperity of colliery companies have stimulated research along the lines of this process and of low temperature carbonisation and pulverisation of coal. It is now pretty generally realised that the use of raw, untreated coal is doomed and that the throwing of raw coal into the furnace is doomed to become a thing of the past.

Engineers appear to be divided as to the relative merits of the various methods of coal treatment. Some put their faith in pulverisation. By this process the coal is powdered to a fine mash which is capable of flowing like oil. It is burned through a carburetter similar to the device on motor cars. In America pulverised coal has been used for heating homes. The coal is delivered in tank wagons and piped into basement tanks connected to heating plants. Thermostatic control provides the last word in convenience to the user. The utilisation of powdered fuel is growing and, according to the experts, including Sir Richard Redmayne, will doubtless eventually have a wide application both on land and sea for steam-raising, but in its use at sea it has to compete with oil, which at present is prime favourite although in point of saving of fuel and labour and flexibility of operation coal dust closely approximates to oil. The use of pulverised fuel allows of the employment of inferior and, consequently, cheaper qualities of fuel than those usually burnt under boilers.

Others are concentrating their efforts on the method of low temperature carbonisation by which coal is "baked" at a temperature of about 600 degrees centigrade, producing oils and other chemicals as by-products. The advent of the crude oil motor engine makes the utilisation of low temperature oils much more attractive from a commercial standpoint, but the method produces a smokeless fuel for the open grate and this raises the difficulty of demand for the open grate fuel.

Hydrogenation has the advantage that, with the exception of a small quantity of gas, there are no by-products, though there is the difficulty of disposal of the residue of coke. But the liquid fuel is the main product. This is obtained by treating coal with hydrogen at a high pressure; in the Scientific Research Department of the British Government at Greenwich, the pressure is 3,000 lb. per square inch. The report of the British Fuel Research Department for 1930, states that with suitable plant, from 120 to 130 gallons of petrol could be taken from each ton of coal so treated. The large consumption of oil and spirit in Great Britain gives special interest to any scheme which would enable them to be produced in that country. In 1930, the imports of oil and spirit into Great Britain amounted to 2,403,377,670 gallons.

On the lowest estimate of 120 gallons per ton hydrogenated, the production of that quantity of oil and spirit would require the treatment of 20 million tons of coal. Since one ton of coal is required to treat one ton of coal by hydrogenation, that makes a total of 40 million tons. As the coal has to be crushed for this treatment, a further claim is made for the use of the small coal, which has for so long been a drug on the market. To have such a large, steady home demand would mean new life to the industry.

Whether it would be an economic proposition depends on several factors. It is always difficult to fix costs of production in this class of work until large-scale plant has been fully tested out. Then there is the question of the relation between the import price and the home price. Dr. C. H. Lander, Director of the British Fuel Research Department, told a conference in 1930:

"It would appear, from careful analysis of such data as are available, that the petrol could be produced at a price which is beginning to bear close relationship to the import price of petrol, if the effect of a preferential duty is taken into account."

Since then the price of petrol has risen in consequence of the revenue tax (standing in November, 1932, at 8d. a gallon) and this rise in price should have the effect of stimulating the home production of the liquid fuel. It has to be borne in mind, however, that to drop this tax on home-produced petrol would obviously mean a loss of revenue.

A further difficulty is to obtain official estimates of the capital cost or plant, and of royalties for patent rights about which there is a great deal of secrecy.

In spite of the existing adverse factors hydrogenation seems to be the most promising success. The scientific problem has been solved. It is now a matter of financial enterprise in which the State will probably be the dominant interest.

The following statement derives a certain importance from the fact that it was made by Sir Harry McGowan, Chairman of the Imperial Chemical Industries Company:

"I am quite satisfied that it is now practicable to build in this country a plant for the production of petrol from bituminous coal. A plant to hydrogenate 1,000 tons of clean dry coal a day could produce No. 1 motor spirit and sell it at present retail standard prices with a small profit, after allowing for all costs of raw material, manufacture, repairs, obsolescence and distribution.

"It is not contended, however, that such a profit as the above would attract capital. It is mentioned as an indication of the fact that the hydrogenation process has already reached a stage at which only a very slight rise in the price of petrol is required to render it a self-supporting commercial proposition."

One other process demands attention—the colloidal process. It has excited considerable public interest recently, particularly since the Cunard Shipping Company's experience of colloidal fuel. The success of this company's experiment with its s.s. *Scythia* in burning 150 tons of a mixture of 60 per cent oil and 40 per cent coal seems to have established a definite future for this type of fuel.

The chief difficulty in the past has been the grinding of the coal to the necessary fineness. Mills for this purpose are forthcoming, grinding in two stages and without classifying. The first mill will bring the coal down from duff size to 75 per cent through 200 mesh. At this stage the coal is mixed with the oil. It then passes through the second mill, where it is reduced to the fineness of 600 mesh which makes it possible to prepare a mixture of 60 per cent coal with 40 per cent fuel oil, having the same viscosity as natural fuel oil.

The burning point can be fixed at will, within a radius of 80° F. to 300° F., so that it may be used as a fuel in automatic furnaces, pre-heating not being necessary.

It is claimed that colloidal fuel has certain definite advantages over fuel oil. Owing to its high specific gravity it requires much less space than fuel oil. The sixty-forty mixture, with a specific gravity of 1·17, would require only a little over 30 cubic feet: fuel oil would require 38 cubic feet and coal 42 to 45 cubic feet per ton. A fuel tank having a capacity of 20,000 cubic feet would hold slightly over 500 tons of fuel oil. The same tank would hold 650 tons of colloidal fuel.

The total heat value in the fuel oil would be 21,365,120,000 B.Th.U.In the colloidal the total heat value would be 23,827,731,200 B.Th.U.—a difference of approximately 10 per cent in favour of colloidal.

It is also claimed that the cost of manufacturing colloidal fuel would be very small in comparison with other known methods for the utilisation of coal, except, of course, hand firing.

There are possibilities for colloidal fuel for central heating purposes. At the present moment in London alone some 500,000 tons of fuel oil are used for central heating. It is estimated that colloidal fuel could take its place at half the cost. Smelting furnaces and tinworks are now going over to fuel oil. Colloidal is quite suitable for both these industries.

The only disadvantage in colloidal fuel is the tendency to coke at a temperature around 470° F. It is believed that with suitable burners this difficulty can be overcome.

A small experimental plant is now being erected to deal with the coal in all the operations necessary for the finished colloidal fuel.

Many mining engineers believe that the colloidal process is the most promising of all—the cheapest and the one most likely to result in a largely increased consumption of coal.

The negative aspect is to regulate output with an eye on demand—the old problem of adjusting production to consumption. In the solution of this problem international arrangements are essential and the Economic Committee of the League of Nations has done a signal service in emphasising this need.

The coal industry is a declining industry. Whether it will ever again be as prosperous as it has been is a moot point. Present world economic forces would seem to be against a complete recovery. Coal no longer holds an unrivalled position as a source of energy or heat. The old monarch may again "call for his pipe and call for his bowl," but will he ever again feel cheerful enough to "call for his fiddlers three"?

E

CHAPTER III
SOME ASPECTS OF
AMERICAN INDUSTRY AND POLITICS

SOME ASPECTS OF
AMERICAN INDUSTRY AND POLITICS

AMERICAN industry is so immense that the mind boggles at the attempt to view it as a whole. One is fortified by such a work as *Recent Economic Changes* which surveys the most important industries and presents a mass of valuable material. But it is almost impossible to generalise about the economic condition of American industry *in toto*. It is more fruitful to analyse each of the basic industries, separately. It may be worth while however to attempt to indicate the characteristic features of the *conduct* of industry in general.

The United States, in its application of machinery and technological improvements to industry, has much to teach Great Britain and indeed the rest of the world. In no other country is there such a marvellous combination of a high degree of technical skill and extremely rich economic resources. This *conjunctur* has produced a volume of wealth unsurpassed in the history of the world and has been responsible for a new human species— the multi-millionaire. In many cases huge fortunes have been made as the result of exploitation of human labour and natural resources such as cotton, coal, cattle, oil, but the distinctive feature of American industry is the application of science, more especially in the form of machinery, to raw materials and in the building up of a marvellous system of transportation. One may be acutely sensible of some of the defects of a machine civilisation but from the standpoint of sheer mechanical achievement one cannot but be tremendously impressed by what one sees in the United States. Machinery has been harnessed to industry in other countries, notably England and Germany, and, more recently, Russia, but in America it has been developed and applied to such an extent as to mean something almost new in the way of industrial civilisation.

The readiness to discard obsolete machinery is also a notable feature. This is due partly to the fact that American industrialists, unlike British, are not traditionally set in conservative habits of running a business and partly because they expect the new machinery to yield increased profits. As with machines so with men. The human machine is also scrapped as soon as it becomes obsolete, as soon, that is, as the iron machine offers higher returns. American industrialists do not go into business for the benefit of their health; in this they are not peculiar but in their single-minded devotion to the pursuit of making profits quickly and making them big they are uncommonly ready to experiment, and if necessary to scrap machinery—metal and human. They dispose of the less productive instruments as advantageously as possible though it is not a rare thing to see a huge obsolete machine which no one will spend the money even to remove.[1] About the human machines they are not conspicuously more concerned; if a new machine will result in a net profit it is nobody's concern what happens to the men who are displaced—they will find other jobs, of course. And until recently there was a remarkable degree of occupational mobility so that men need not for long remain unemployed. But to-day it is not so easy even in the United States for unemployed men, especially in the textile and coal-mining industries or even in the automobile industry, to get other jobs. In the absence of a national scheme of unemployment insurance it is impossible to obtain any reliable estimate of the unemployed from year to year, from month to month. In Great Britain and Germany any investigator can readily ascertain the official figures of unemployment through the machinery of the national insurance scheme. In the United States to-day the estimates range from 750,000 to 4,000,000. Such estimates are lacking in value because there is no accepted understanding as to what constitutes unemployment. It is good to know that plans are being made in the 1930 Census to get something in the nature of a reliable record of the number of unemployed people based on an agreed definition of unemployment. The results of the Census may well indicate the desirability of a national scheme of unemployment insurance. It is safe to predict that sooner or later some such scheme will prove desirable

[1] Perhaps the most remarkable instance in recent years was the scrapping by Mr. Henry Ford in 1927 of valuable plant as the result of his adoption of a new model for his car—the scrapping of model T and the adoption of model A. I am assured by one who is in Mr. Ford's confidence that it is impossible to state the value in dollars, even in approximate terms, of the scrapped plant, but everybody knows the change was made at an immense cost.

if not a necessity.[1] Meantime there is no social provision for men and women thrown out of employment as the result of changing economic and technological conditions. Some large private corporations have systems of old age pensions, eight States have State Schemes of old age pensions and it may be that unemployment insurance will proceed on similar lines. There are a few corporations which have schemes of unemployment benefit, but they are very exceptional. There is only one State that has established a system of unemployment insurance, namely, Wisconsin. The underlying principle of the Wisconsin law is that industry should bear the cost of unemployment, with a view to preventing it, as workmen's compensation laws have tended to prevent accidents. The employers are to have an opportunity until July 1, 1933, to fulfil the purposes of the Act without legal compulsion. If by July 1, 1933, the employers, who employ altogether 175,000 employees, have voluntarily established plans which comply with the provisions of the Act, the compulsory system provided by the Act shall not take effect. Otherwise it shall take effect on July 1, 1933.

Broadly, benevolent paternalism at its best takes care of the workers only when they are employed. In the United States to-day the unemployed are expected unaided by an Employment Exchange to fit in wherever they can find a temporary niche in industry and if they fail to do so they may be looked after by a charitable organisation and receive turkey and plum pudding at Christmas or they may drift into the army of "down-and-outs."

American industry seems to be in the stage of benevolent paternalism, not always too benevolent. Even where the personal relationship is remote owing to the size of the undertaking the sense of responsibility for the welfare of the employees is reflected in the attitude and policy of the corporation. The welfare schemes of some of the biggest business concerns, e.g. Filene's of Boston and Dennison's of Framingham near Boston, are extraordinarily good, expert economists or psychologists being commissioned in some instances to prepare the schemes. In the remarkable works

---

[1] This was written in 1929. Most authorities now (1932) give the number of unemployed as being somewhere in the region of 11,000,000. Mr. William Green estimates that there will be 13,000,000 by January, 1933. National unemployment insurance has not yet arrived but it is appreciably nearer.

of the Columbia Conserve Co. of Indianapolis the workers have a considerable share in the conduct of the business. It is said that even the owner, Mr. Norman Hapgood, has to ask the permission of the employees' council if he wants to take a day off. The fact that the joke has been made—it is not literally true—shows how exceptional the conditions at these works are.

Where there is still a fairly close personal relationship as in certain parts of the coalfields like Southern West Virginia, the operator thinks and speaks of his employees as "my people." And in many cases he treats his people well enough—gives them houses at fairly low rents, provides medical and nursing service at reasonable rates, builds a cinema or amusement hall where there may be a few books and newspapers, and perhaps classes in mining instruction for men and in some communities cookery classes for the women who, after cooking the Sunday dinner, are expected to attend a Bible Class conducted by the operator's wife. "His people"—yes, but they must be good children—all one large happy family. In other words, all belonging to one large happy company, company houses, company stores, and all. In still other words, no Union! Any sign of a desire to have the Union come into the close community and soon some of the houses are empty; undesirable elements are quickly expelled. There can be no toleration of the Union "which only upsets things, and the men would be worse off." No, it must be a purely personal, private affair. "My men must do a fair day's work and I'll give 'em a good day's pay! As a matter of fact they are quite happy—it's those damned agitators who try to make them discontented! But they won't get into this section while I'm around! I pay them good wages, what more do they want?"

There is a good deal of loose talk about the American belief in the policy of high wages. The impression has been created that there is something peculiarly American in the belief in the wisdom of paying high wages. It is difficult to prove that the American standard of living is higher than the English partly because the population is three times greater, far more varied in ethnic composition and spread over a very much bigger area, and partly because of the different values attached to the component factors in the standard of living. It is so largely a geographical and subjective comparison. A friend of the author's in Vienna, who had spent two years continuously in America, told him he would rather live in Vienna on £250 a year than in New York on $10,000 a year. The difference in the cost of living as measured by the prices of commodities in so far as Index Numbers can help is not eight times greater in New York than in Vienna, yet the Viennese lecturer preferred Vienna because he could live a more leisurely and artistic life there. The miners of West Virginia are paid higher wages than the miners of South Wales but the miners of South Wales would not change places with the miners of West Virginia because the South Wales miners have won a measure of freedom from industrial autocracy and of political independence which would be denied them in West Virginia, and they value freedom and independence far more than an extra dollar a day even now when earnings in South Wales are so low (a man is lucky if he makes $15 or £3 a week) and unemployment is so high (93,254 in October, 1932, in the South Wales field alone). It has been suggested that the measure of economic political and social freedom should be included in any conception of the standard of living. It would be exceedingly difficult to gauge and assess this freedom absolutely or even relatively but so it is to compare elements in national standards of living that can supposedly be reduced to money terms, e.g. public services like education, music, drama, libraries, parks, police protection and health services. At any rate there is much to be said for the adoption of the principle of the recognition of economic freedom as a factor in the standard of living.

In spite however of difficulties in comparing standards of living it is probably true that the American standard in point of material real wages is the highest in the world. There are black spots like agriculture, coal-mining and the textiles. But with the help of statistics a trained observer can fairly safely conclude that the average wage-earner in the United States is better off economically than the average wage-earner in Great Britain. Automobiles may not be an entirely satisfactory index of wages and allowance must be made for mortgage ownership or instalment buying in a considerable proportion of cases, but the sight of hundreds of cars outside a coal-mine in Southern Illinois was certainly an impressive one. If one sees a car at the pit-head in Wales one may be sure it belongs to the owner or the manager or the engineer, but here were hundreds of cars owned by miners who drove to and from their work, some two or three miles, some ten to twenty miles, many returning to homes of which they were the owners. It is ridiculous of course to assert, as the author has often heard it asserted, that "the working men have all got cars." It would be interesting to know exactly what proportion do own a machine. Statistics indicate that one in five of the general population owns a car but there are no statistics to show the proportion of the industrial working population and in many coal-mining sections the proportion would be more like one in twenty; moreover it should not be forgotten that a car is a necessity to a large number of miners to enable them to get to work, almost as much so as the tools or machines they work with underground. It is too optimistic to conclude from seeing the enormous numbers of cars on the roads on summer Sundays that this is a land of unspotted prosperity. The fact that 16 million workers earn less than $25 a week should serve to preserve a sense of perspective. And yet when all is said, the working class in America is probably more prosperous than that of any other country, judged by ownership of automobiles, houses, radios, electric domestic appliances, quality, quantity and variety of food, clothing, shoes, visits to "shows" and money spent on weekly and monthly magazines of the lighter, more exciting sort. It is not easy to assess the results of this standard of living. Some observers assert that it makes the people happier; a shrewd French professor has said that the automobile has contributed greatly to the happiness of the American workers, if only by providing opportunities for "necking parties"! There may be some point in the observation since it might mean they would be less disposed to interest themselves in industrial disputes, political questions, and problems of freedom as they became more able to afford to "enjoy" themselves. But this is not the place to discuss whether "necking parties" promote happiness! What is important here to emphasise is that the "American philosophy of high wages" is due not so much to a belief in the wisdom of the policy as to the fact that economic conditions have hitherto made high wages and big profits simultaneously possible. It is true that the effect of high wages in one industry in increasing the consumption of goods produced in another has been so marked that to preach the philosophy of high wages was to preach to the converted. Mr. Henry Ford paid his employees high wages because he could afford to and because it paid him to do so.

The success of his policy in catering to the demand of an army of consumers for a low-priced car enabled him to pay high wages.[1] If his business had not prospered he could not have paid high wages however firm his belief in the principle. There are operators in the Coal industry who believe in paying high wages, who would like to pay good wages, but owing to the competition of operators who do not, their business is damaged and they are unable to pay high wages. American business men believe in the policy of good wages but whether they pay them or not depends on the prosperity of their own industry and the power of the union where it functions. There are many enlightened employers in England who believe it is economically sound to pay high wages but to-day most industries there are in such bad case that one does not hear so much about the efficiency of high wages as about the necessity for reducing wages.

American industries have paid relatively higher wages because they have been relatively more prosperous than industries in Europe; if they should be reduced to the present economic plight of British industries no amount of fine talk about the philosophy of high wages will keep them high.[2]

An interesting feature of American industry and business is the way in which the owners encourage their employees to make suggestions for the improvement of the business. It is a common practice for the workers in machine shops, factories, mills, etc., to be invited to send in suggestions to the management, which sometimes offers a financial reward, or to compete for prizes advertised in the company's own magazine. There are now several thousands of these company magazines. On the day which the author spent in making a tour of the Armor Swift Meat Packing Works in Chicago a meeting was held in a large well-equipped hall of the firm's salesmen from all over the country. The chief business of the meeting was the discussion of possible ways of making the selling side of the concern more successful.

---

[1] Since I wrote the above lines I came across the following statement in the *Boston Evening Transcript* of November 23, 1929:—

"Wages are not in the discretion of the employer, but in the productivity of the business."

HENRY FORD

[2] Since these words were written many American industries have seriously declined and wage levels have been appreciably lowered.

Such meetings, not confined to salesmen, are held periodically and by most of the large-scale enterprises so that employees are continually thinking of ways of improvement. A coal-miner in the Western Pennsylvania field suggested to the manager a different method of cleaning and lighting the lamps and he is now the colliery lampman; he had had experience of the job in Wales and the manager availed himself of it. This practice of encouraging suggestions from employees appears to be decidedly more prevalent in America than in England.

The gap between the management and the men in the coal industry is perhaps not so big as in other industries and it is true of course that there is not the same kind of industrial and business aristocracy in America as in England, but, except in times of strikes, the relations between master and man in the United States are generally more intimate, open and friendly than in Great Britain. The employer was perhaps but recently an employee himself, and he feels that many of his workmen may one day be employers themselves. There is always the type of employer which was so common in England during the industrial revolution, the "boss" who, unable to adapt himself to his new status, abuses his power by abusing his men. This type is not infrequently met with in the coalfields but it is an exceptional type; most of the employers, where there is any personal relationship at all, show a more friendly attitude than do their English counterparts. The managers and engineers too seem to be less aloof from the men; many of them have studied a little psychology and realise the wisdom of trying to understand the other fellow's point of view even if the other fellow has to obey his orders.

There are also more men and women trained for personnel administration and welfare work employed in industry in America than in Great Britain. In times of dispute between the owners and the workers these officers are expected to line up with the management and it becomes the duty of the personnel specialist to write articles in the company's magazine shewing the men where they are wrong and the employer's case in the best possible light. In normal times, however, these officers are remarkably successful in promoting happy relations and comfortable conditions of work and recreation. All these agencies and methods of encouragement are quite frankly designed to get the best out of the workers—"they give you better service"—and the sentimental

ASPECTS OF AMERICAN INDUSTRY AND POLITICS 77

talk of a fatherly interest in them is not to be taken too seriously.

Closely allied with the spirit of getting service is the boast of giving service; the motive of getting service is disguised by paternal sentimentalism, the motive of giving service is thinly veiled as the desire for dollars. The parting exhortation—"Thank you, come again" is peculiar to America; it is flattering to the unsuspecting foreign visitor, but as he becomes more sophisticated in American ways it serves as a constant reminder of the psychology of salesmanship.

Into the service of the great god Service is pressed also the whole chain of clubs that stretch across the vast country, the Rotary, Kiwanis, Lions, etc., and a great variety of women's clubs. Mr. Charles Merz, in *The great American band wagon*, writes of these clubs in a realistic, not to say a sarcastic vein. The reader who is interested is referred to that entertaining book. This kind of service seems to be a remarkable blend of the commercial and the social; it is good business and it is "doing good." Some of these clubs contribute large sums to various organisations engaged in philanthropic, charitable work and many individual members will give generously in response to an eloquent appeal. A characteristic method of raising funds for any object, e.g. the development of a district with a view to increasing business possibilities, or to give the kiddies a treat (Americans have a tender spot for kiddies), is to appeal for contributions just as an auctioneer asks for bids. "Who will give a thousand dollars?" Loud clapping follows the announcement of the name. "Five hundred dollars?" and so on down to smaller amounts, the flagging enthusiasm of the gathering being gingered up occasionally by an exhortation from the conductor of the "drive," sometimes a hired professional, to "give him a hand."

There is a club in Pittsburg, Pa., called the Hungry Club, which in some respects is unique in America, if not in the world. Its conception of service seems to be based on toleration arising from understanding. The members, for the most part business and professional men and women, meet weekly at lunch to hear an address by an expert on his special topic. The author heard talks on Old Age Pensions, Mass Education in China and the Coal and Iron Police. Dr. Yen, an expert on education in China, made an eloquent, powerful speech which obviously impressed the five or six hundred members present. The prospectus of addresses, and talks with the enterprising, enthusiastic secretary, Mr. Cooper, Warden of the Kingsley House Settlement, revealed the wide range of subjects covered by the various speakers. It seems that the members are glad to hear speakers on any topic, even of a political character, e.g. Communism or Conservatism, provided the speaker is an authority on his subject. Time is allowed for questions. The gatherings are quite an interesting experiment in the field of adult education of a popular kind, and appear to serve a useful purpose in promoting breadth of view and tolerant understanding in matters of politics, religion, international relations and even in the industrial world, where attitudes of mind are apt to be sharply opposed and fixed by economic interest, especially in Pittsburg, the centre of one of the most important industrial regions of the world and the battleground of some of the bitterest struggles between employers and employees in the steel and coal trades.

A further development of the conception of service is to be found in the way in which men who have amassed fortunes in business or industry apply a proportion of their wealth to social services of various kinds. The names of Andrew Carnegie and John D. Rockefeller, Sr., readily occur to the mind. The whole world knows something of Carnegie's endowment of libraries; the Peace Foundation is perhaps not so widely known, but it has done and continues to do work of significant value, especially in the way of research in the promotion of international peace. The name of Rockefeller is associated in the public mind with the endowment of Universities and other educational institutions, though few people realise the immense amount of valuable research work that is done, especially in the field of medicine and the social sciences, under the auspices of the Rockefeller Foundation. Some idea of the importance of this Foundation may be had from the fact that in 1928 alone it spent $24,000,000 in support of medical research, educational work generally and peace projects in all parts of the world. Incidentally this expenditure means a very considerable interchange of experience of thousands of students, ranging from the young graduate with his honours thick upon him to the mature professor who has passed from honours to interest in his special study; as these students are of a wide range of nationality also and visit many countries it is reasonable to suppose that such expenditure is calculated to promote friendly international relations. A further evidence of the Rockefeller family's international spirit is that remarkable institution on Riverside Drive, New York, known as International House, which is a kind of residential club for students, particularly post-graduate students from other lands. It was established to relieve the loneliness of the foreign student on his coming to America and to serve as a clearing-house of ideas and opinions. When the author stayed there he talked with men and women of something like thirty of the sixty-two different nationalities represented among the seven hundred residents, each one in the United States to pursue a special course of study or to undertake an investigation of some sort. A considerable proportion of the residents are native Americans, always ready to help the visitors to a preliminary understanding of the new country, they in turn finding something to learn from the visitor about the institutions and life of his country.

There are several other funds established for the award of Fellowships and Scholarships to enable students from abroad to visit America and American students to go abroad, e.g. the Commonwealth (Harkness), Davidson and Rigg Funds. Also there are many important Foundations on the lines of the Carnegie and Rockefeller Foundations such as the Russell Sage, Guggenheim, J. C. Penny and Judge Baker Foundations and the Twentieth Century Fund (Filene's). The Russell Sage Foundation, named after Mr. Russell Sage, a wealthy business man, devotes considerable attention to problems of industry and from time to time publishes the results of its investigations to the great benefit of students of industry and the social fabric.

Gradually a tradition is being built up that the successful rich business man is not a good citizen unless he liberally supports social work, charitable enterprises, institutions of higher learning, research foundations, hospitals, schools of music, museums of art, libraries, or what not. The motives impelling the accumulation of large fortunes are not always easily traceable; the desire for power, sometimes economic, sometimes political, often a combination of both; the desire for social distinction, often dictated by the wife or daughter; the desire for security and early retirement from a life of close confinement to work, regular hours of business, etc.; the desire to "provide handsomely" for one's children—that these are potent avowed motives there is not much doubt.

It is more difficult to ascertain whether a man's desire to become
rich in order to "do good with his money" has been a conscious
motive in many cases or whether the "doing good" has followed
after the accumulation of a fortune in response to other motives;
or in the course of "playing the game" with its chances of luck,
exploitation, gambling. Someone has cynically observed that the
money is made first and then some way of spending it has to be
found. And the tradition of patronage is sufficiently strong to
ensure that ways and means of disposing of any surplus can be
found very easily. But whatever weight is to be attached to the
desire to "do good" as an incentive, the attitude of regarding
one's wealth as a trust seems to be somewhat characteristic of
the successful business type in America.

To a certain extent this is true also of Great Britain. Rich men
in that country to-day are not so numerous nor so rich as in
America though hospitals and universities are still largely dependent
on private benefactions. But gradually the tradition of patronage
is giving way to a critical attitude towards the wealthy. The
feeling is growing in England that no man has the right to be
very rich and that no amount of private expenditure on hospitals
or universities justifies the possession of great wealth. The whole
tendency of taxation is towards a redistribution of income. Even
among wealthy people themselves there is not the comfortable
complacency that characterised the "lady bountiful" attitude.
They shew an increasing tendency to attempt to justify their rôle
in society. There is not the same enviable distinction in England
to-day in being rich that there seems to be in the United States.
It has been suggested that this is because it is easier to become
rich in the United States, but if this were the true explanation
one might reasonably expect that the difficulty in becoming
rich in England would add to the distinction. A more reliable
explanation probably is that England is gradually becoming
more socialistic, while the United States is still highly individualistic. Any suggestion of public ownership and control of
a basic industry like coal-mining, the railroads, land or banking
is regarded as revolutionary in America and outside the realm
of practical politics, whereas in Great Britain it is discussed
with as much reality as the tariff or prohibition is in America.
The author followed the presidential election of 1928 with close
interest and was impressed by the contrast in content of the

issues before the public in America and those discussed by the candidates, electors, and in the press at recent general elections in Great Britain. In the presidential election interest appeared to be centred mainly round prohibition, questions of religious freedom, farmers' relief and the control of water-power schemes. The last question was an issue of considerable political and economic importance, but it was over the other three issues that the great majority of the electorate got most excited. The author found it difficult to share the general excitement as to whether a man might drink a glass of beer or not, be a Catholic or a Protestant or whether the farmer should get the benefit of special legislation. He could not help thinking of corresponding issues in the history of English politics, e.g., local option, Catholic Emancipation, the Disestablishment of the Established Church in Wales and the Corn Laws—issues belonging to the last century with the exception of local option which may possibly assume a minor importance in future elections, but about which the electorate will never get excited. Voters in England to-day are becoming more and more interested and well versed in economic problems of industry like the nationalisation of the mines or the land; of finance like the public ownership and control of the Bank of England and the Joint Stock Banks; of transportation, like the nationalisation of the railways; of trade like the exports credit schemes, and Trade Facilities Acts; of taxation like heavy inheritance taxes; of redistribution of income in the form of increased public provision of services like schools, clinics, milk for infants, houses at low rents, pensions for widows and retiral pensions at sixty years of age, family allowances; problems relating to unemployment, trade unions, minimum wage Acts, hours of labour, conditions of work; problems of international trade, e.g. resumption of trade with Russia, of imperialism, and war. English voters are not yet proof against stunts but they are growing more critical of unimportant issues and more insistent that politicians shall be serious students of the industrial and social organisation, of international affairs and of the art of government.

All this is not to say that English electors are more intelligent than American. It is probably true however that their intelligence has been directed far more closely and over a longer period along channels of interest in political and economic issues. For

F

a generation now the industrial workers of Great Britain have been "attending college" during the winter months after their day's work in the mine, mill or factory, the cream of them also spending a full-time month or so at a summer school. In this way they have developed a remarkably well-informed and highly critical interest in problems of philosophy, politics, economics, civics; in art, literature, music, etc. A considerable number of these students have become members of the House of Commons; a large number, including more than seventy of the author's own students, have become members of the various bodies of local government—the county council, the town council, the urban and rural district councils and the parish council—while many others have attained to responsible positions in their trade unions. The many thousands of the rank and file students, though perhaps not prominent in public affairs nor distinguished in the fields of literature or music, are all men and women of some influence in their own circles, and thus indirectly raise the general level of interest.

In addition to those who attend classes and pursue systematic courses of study there is a huge scattered audience of people running into hundreds of thousands every week throughout the winter, who attend political meetings all over Great Britain to hear a member of Parliament, a candidate or one of the local party leaders speak on a topic of current political interest. These meetings are attended by many women who in this way become interested in politics and learn a great deal from the speeches, many of which are highly educative even though delivered from a party platform. Such meetings are not confined to any one political party though they are to a far greater extent a part of the regular machinery of propaganda of the Labour Party than of the other parties, but taken altogether they constitute quite an important form of adult education in the field of politics. It is the common experience of speakers that they have to be sure of their facts and armed at all points to meet the criticism and answer the questions that invariably follow the speeches.

Political meetings are not a feature of the normal life of American people; the topics of the speakers are generally but remotely concerned with the problems of industry and there is a grievous lack of Classes in the social sciences designed especially for industrial workers; the provision of facilities for education in elementary and high schools and in institutions of higher learning such as Universities, Institutes of Technology, etc., is probably greater than in any other country in the world but facilities for the education of adult industrial workers in the social sciences are probably more inadequate than in any other industrialised country in the world, certainly than in England or Germany. The United States is the classic home of democracy but it can hardly be called the home of an educated democracy. One cannot help but be impressed for instance by the contrast between the typical American miner and his counterpart in Great Britain— both splendid fellows in their own way; the working conditions and particularly the hazards of their occupation seem to breed certain fine qualities. The American miner is clever at tinkering with an automobile or a radio and can talk knowledgeably about house property, insurance and even investments; if he belongs to the union he may occasionally discuss it but his criticism will probably be in terms of personalities rather than of principles. The British, more particularly the Welsh miner, is not interested personally in investments or house property. He would like to possess a motor car and a wireless set but he cannot afford such luxuries and the fact is that he is more interested in helping to get bread and butter, with perhaps a piece of cake, for all his "butties" and their wives and kiddies than in getting a car for himself. And that bread and butter must have no taste of charity! So you will find him eagerly interested in economic and political theories and problems and able to sustain an argument with remarkable knowledge, courtesy and sincerity. If he finds you are interested he will take you to his home or lodgings where you will probably be amazed at his collection of books, bought with hard-earned shillings and ranging over a wide field of litera- ture other than economic or political, including probably his favourite poets. The personal library is perhaps less common now in these days of unemployment and underemployment but the librarian of the local municipal library or of the workmen's institute will tell you that the demand for "serious" books is far greater than he can meet. The Universities and public authorities are rendering valuable assistance in the effort to improve the supply, largely by a system of distributing boxes of books to classes of students all over the country. It goes without saying that he is a member of his union and it is probably no exaggeration to say that no union in the world has a better instructed and more critical rank and file membership than the South Wales Miners' Federation.

It is frequently said that the lack of political and intellectual interests characteristic of the American working man is explained by his relatively high standard of living. People engaged in political propaganda and pioneers in the field of adult education complain that it is extremely difficult to arouse and maintain the interest of the industrial workers who, they say, are too comfortable to respond to appeals for mental exertion. Individual prosperity in the form of ownership of an automobile, radio, a home, to say nothing of investments, is apt to make a working man indifferent to the kind of industrial and political problems that exercise the minds of European working men. This explains much, but it is not the whole of the explanation, and a high standard of living is not the only cause of apathy; indeed in England in recent years it has been a not uncommon experience that apathy has been greatest in districts where unemployment and distress have been most acute. One has often heard some such comment as "the poor devils are too much worried about their bread and butter to take any interest in politics." Below a certain standard of living people cannot be expected to show much interest in public questions—they are "too poor to care"—but above a standard that ensures adequate food, clothing, housing and a reasonable margin for the little luxuries of life there seems to be no reason why people should not cultivate other than their own private interests. If this were not so, the great majority of teachers and university students, who at least have an adequate physical subsistence, would be incapable of public spiritedness or social mindedness whatever training they might undergo, and all efforts to raise the standard of living of the workers as a basis for the wider diffusion of culture and "thinking straight" would be doomed to failure. It may be that the relatively high standard of living of American workmen, combined with the lack of educational facilities of the kind provided in Great Britain and also with some defects of their educational training before they became workmen, is an adequate explanation of the low level of political interest in the United States. And if such facilities were provided and the grades school training improved it is reasonable to suppose that the results would be seen in a working population more keenly interested and better instructed in matters of public importance, notwithstanding the high standard of living. It might be argued that the existing relatively low physical standard of living in England and particularly the extraordinarily severe unemployment of the last few years explain the demonstrations of disaffection which have disturbed the authorities in many parts of the country, especially the coalfields. There is little doubt that the continued unemployment acts as a spur to people's political thinking—when men lose their jobs they begin to ask questions—but as a generalisation it would probably be true to say that the adult and workers' education movements and the regular political meetings have been an important factor in the development of a high standard of intelligent interest in social, political and industrial matters. One might even hazard the prediction that if unemployment were cured and the standard of living of the workers of Great Britain were appreciably raised and if the processes of adult education were continued, the level of informed, critical interest would continue to rise.

As there is no immediate prospect of the absorption of the unemployed, the prediction can hardly be put to the test for some years. But what an opportunity exists in America! The prospect however of the capitalisation of this opportunity seems as remote as the chances of the abolition of unemployment in Great Britain.

So the industrial workers of the United States, apart from struggles over wages or hours which are waged on their behalf by trade unions, are rarely if ever stirred about problems of economic control. Indeed the trade unions themselves have advanced little beyond collective bargaining and there are great stretches of industry still ununionised. The fact is that America is still essentially a land of *laisser-faire* and the prevailing atmosphere is an atmosphere of prosperity. It may be that *laisser-faire* will continue to flourish indefinitely, that employees will assume an increasingly greater share of ownership of corporation stock, that the United States will present something new in the way of ownership and control of industry—something radically different from the line of European industrial evolution, and that the workers will have no need to concern themselves seriously about politics. Or it may be that, like England, it will develop along the lines of imperialistic expansion in seeking an outlet for its increasing production, that the law of diminishing returns may operate on a large scale, with the consequent probability of a lowering of the standard of living—in a word, that the new capitalism in America may fail to "deliver the goods." Time alone will show, but the author's confident prediction is that it will fail to do so within the next decade or two.

The results of the 1932 Presidential election have just been published. The following headline, which appeared in an English newspaper two days after the election, is significant—"Mr. Hoover defeated by Trade Depression."

NOTE—Since this chapter was written economic events have moved with an almost startling rapidity which has seriously disturbed the complacency of the advocates of the New Capitalism. Mr. Roosevelt's Administration has introduced changes in the conduct and control of industry of a remarkable if not revolutionary character, especially in the regulation of hours and wages. There has been a considerable reduction in unemployment but the net result of all the changes will probably be a decline in the standard of life of the American people.

CHAPTER IV

GENERAL COMPARISON OF THE COAL INDUSTRY IN THE UNITED STATES AND IN GREAT BRITAIN

PANORAMA OF MINING CAMP, PENNSYLVANIA

GENERAL COMPARISON OF THE COAL INDUSTRY IN THE UNITED STATES AND IN GREAT BRITAIN

SECTION A

HISTORICAL AND GEOGRAPHICAL

As we have shewn in the first chapter the development of the coal industry had much earlier beginnings in Great Britain than in the United States. By the end of the thirteenth century coal was being got or mined in most of the existing British fields, though at that time the coal was not used for household purposes but almost exclusively by smiths and lime-burners. It was not until about 1570 that it came into common use for household purposes, and its employment for smelting did not become general till the early part of the eighteenth century. Reference was made in the first chapter to the French Jesuit missionary, Father Hennepin, by whom the earliest mention of coal in America was recorded. He saw traces of coal on the banks of the Illinois River in 1679, more than four hundred years after the first shipment of coal from Newcastle to London. In his journal he marks the site of a "cole mine" above Fort Crecolur, near the present town of Ottawa. In 1750 the Virginia bituminous mines were opened and worked on the James River, near Richmond. About eighty years ago Sir Charles Lyell, the English geologist, visited these mines and wrote an interesting account of his geological explorations in the Richmond coalfields. These Virginia mines were the first coal-mines opened for the market in the United States. Owned by an English company and competing only with English coals they enjoyed for some time the exclusive coast-wise trade of the Union. The cost was so great, however, that few individuals used the Richmond coals in the large coast cities but burned wood for many years after the mines were opened. This region has declined very considerably in economic importance owing apparently to the many troubles and faults in the coal seam; to the increased expense of mining in the deep shafts necessary to reach the coal; to backward methods of mining and to the abundance of cheaper and better fuel from other fields. Five years after the Virginia mines began operation coal was discovered in Ohio by one Lewis Evans, probably a Welshman.

Anthracite was first discovered in Rhode Island in 1760. But the beds were thin and irregular, full of faults, saddles and troubles. Many attempts have been made to work these coals by operators of experience but the attempt to compete with the great Pennsylvania beds was found to be useless and their works have been abandoned. It was unfortunate for the United States that both the earliest bituminous and anthracite deposits to be worked had such serious geological defects. Had Nature provided a more bountiful formation which would have given a boundless bed of bituminous coal in Virginia and another of anthracite in Rhode Island—both at or near tide water—the long haul from the inland fields to the seaboard, which has proved such a heavy handicap, would have been avoided. But if Nature was niggardly near the sea she has been extraordinarily generous inland. If England has had the advantage of proximity to the coast, the United States has a tremendous advantage in point of quantity, the American fields exceeding the British as 37 to 1.

Just as the Richmond fields in Virginia soon lost their importance when better, cheaper and larger quantities of coal were discovered in Pennsylvania, so the anthracite industry quickly passed from Rhode Island to the richly endowed though limited area in the extreme north-eastern corner of Pennsylvania. This compact field is of great importance in the existing economy of the United States. The production of anthracite in the other fields combined amounts to less than 1 per cent of the output of the Pennsylvania field and the exhaustion of this field will mark the virtual end of hard coal supplies in the United States. Anthracite coal was first discovered by a company of Connecticut pioneers in the Pennsylvania field in the Wyoming Valley at the mouth of Mill Creek, near Wilkes-Barre, in 1762. It is said that two brothers named Gore, blacksmiths who were members of the Connecticut Colony that settled in the Wyoming Valley, were the first to use anthracite in America; they used it in their forge fires in 1768. There is some doubt as to this date, and Mr. Edward W. Parker, Director of the Anthracite Bureau of Information, gives 1770 or maybe 1771. In 1770 coal was discovered in the middle region of this field near Shamokin. During the Revolutionary War in 1776, anthracite was taken to Carlisle for the United States Army. It was taken to Harrisburg in boats or arks, and from there hauled in wagons to Carlisle. This was the first shipment of anthracite coal ever made in America.[1] In 1784 Thomas and William Penn granted the privilege of mining coal in the "Great Seam" opposite the town of Pittsburg "at the rate of £30 for each mining lot extending back to the centre of the hill." Anthracite was first discovered in the Lehigh region of the field in 1791, by a poor hunter named Philip Ginter, near the present town of Mauch Chunk. Reading Howell's map of Pennsylvania, published in 1793, indicates coal near Tamaqua. Seven years later William Morris took a wagon load of this coal to Philadelphia, a distance of nearly 100 miles, but was unable to sell it. The first authentic record of anthracite being successfully burned in a stove is in 1803, and it was not until 1804 that the method of successful use was applied in Philadelphia. At that time an operator who attempted to sell black stones to the public as coal was regarded as an impostor. The story is told that Colonel George Shoemaker, of Pottsville, loaded nine wagons of anthracite at Pottsville and hauled it to Philadelphia: he managed to sell two and gave the other seven loads away. One of the loads was bought by White and Hazard, operating wire-works at the Falls of Schuylkill. "A whole night was spent in the effort to make the coal burn, when the hands in despair quit their work, but left the door of the furnace shut. Fortunately, one of the workmen forgot his jacket, and returning found everything red-hot!" Thus was learned the important lesson in making an anthracite fire—to let it alone!

There is a well-defined interval between the early discoveries of coal and the beginning of commercial and industrial operations. It is a transitional period of pioneer effort and great interest, but we cannot pursue it here. It is sufficient for our present purpose to stress the fact that the coal industry is much older in England than in America. As we have seen the beginnings date back more than four centuries earlier, but discoveries are not so important as uses. There is about a century, however, separating the general employment of coal in the two countries. By the early part of the eighteenth century the industry was an important

[1] W. J. Nicolls: *The Story of American Coals*, p. 60.

element in the national economic structure of England. It was
not until the beginning of the nineteenth century that coal came
into general industrial and commercial use in America. Yet
to-day the United States produces considerably more than twice
as much as Great Britain and almost as much as the whole of
Europe. The American coal industry is like a lusty, full-blooded
youth, prodigal and reckless of his easily-produced energy—
that of Great Britain has passed through this stage and finds it
increasingly difficult to produce half as much energy as its youthful successor. "The British conditions of to-day show what we
must face in the Appalachian fields before many decades, when
our thick and easily accessible beds are gone!"[1] Closely linked
up with the relative youth and prodigal output of American
mines are the more favourable physical conditions of mining in the
newer country. But before comparing these it would seem
desirable to have a general idea of the geographical setting of
the two sets of coalfields.

I. COALFIELDS OF THE UNITED STATES

Thirty years ago an American writer said "In fact, the geography
of American coals is to-day, practically, a description of the
United States."[2] This statement probably would not be quite
so closely applicable to-day, and yet there would still be a large
measure of truth in it. Thirty-two of the forty-eight States of the
Union make regular returns of coal shipments (let it be explained
to the English reader that a "shipment" does not necessarily mean
transfer by ship but a transfer of goods from one place to another
overland or by water) in their annual reports, from more than
eleven thousand mines, interspersed at irregular distances over
a vast territory, extending from the Atlantic Ocean on the east
to the Pacific on the west—a distance of 3,000 miles—and
from the Canadian boundary on the north to the Gulf of
Mexico in the south—a distance varying from 900 to 1,500 miles
approximately. This immense region embraces the States of

[1] *Comparison of Physical Conditions in British and American Coal
Mines*, p. 2. By F. G. Tryon and Margaret H. Schoenfeld. An excellent
study, on which I have drawn largely for part of this chapter.
[2] W. J. Nicolls: *The Story of American Coals*, p. 72.

Alabama, Arizona, Arkansas, California, Idaho, Nevada, Oregon, Colorado, Georgia, Illinois, Indiana, Iowa, Kansas, Kentucky, Maryland, Michigan, Missouri, Montana, New Mexico, North Carolina, North Dakota, Ohio, Oklahoma, Pennsylvania, South Dakota, Tennessee, Texas, Utah, Virginia, Washington, West Virginia and Wyoming. Two other States, Rhode Island and Nebraska, have deposits of coal within their borders, but are not now producing any tonnage and therefore are not counted among the coal-producing States. To establish geographical lines, circumscribing the coalfields of the United States, would therefore be to include the boundaries of all these (thirty-two) States—a truly enormous territory. Alaska lies outside this territory but should be included in the list.

The coalfields of the United States are commonly divided into seven major regions, distinguished by their geographical location, and in some cases with no distinct line of demarcation between continuous regions. These major divisions, in the general order of their location from east to west, are:

> Anthracite Region
> Eastern or Appalachian Region
> Middle Western Region
> Western Region
> South-western Region
> Rocky Mountain Region
> Pacific Coast Region.

Each of these larger regions has been subdivided into many supplementary districts and these latter not infrequently have been still further subdivided. These smaller subdivisions are usually due to variations in the quality of the coal, thickness of the seams, etc. The Pittsburg district, for example, which is itself a subdivision of the Eastern or Appalachian region is broken up into various sections. The western section is known as the Panhandle district; east of this is the Gas Coal field with the Westmoreland Gas Coal field to the north and the Klondyke Coke field to the east with the Connelsville Coke region, which was an important factor in the development of the great iron and steel industries of the Pittsburg district, on the eastern border.

The Anthracite Region

Nearly all of the anthracite coal mined in the United States comes from Pennsylvania but from a comparatively small part of it in the north-eastern corner of the State, the easterly extension of the field being close to the New York State line. This field falls into four natural subdivisions, the Northern, Middle Eastern, Middle Western and Southern. For trade purposes these geographical regions are grouped into three as follows:

The Wyoming Region, embracing the entire Northern field.
The Lehigh Region, embracing all of the Eastern field and part of the Southern field.
The Schuylkill Region, embracing the Western and part of the Southern field.

Of these three regions the Wyoming is far the most important, producing as it does over 50 per cent of the whole output. The next in importance is the Schuylkill region with 35 per cent of the production, the Lehigh region producing the remaining 15 per cent.

Before describing the bituminous regions it is appropriate to record the fact that the output of bituminous coal in the United States is more than three times as large as that of anthracite and that the territory in which the soft coal is found is more than a hundred times as extensive as the anthracite area.

The Eastern or Appalachian Field

This field has been described as "The greatest storehouse of high-rank coal in the United States, if not in the world." The most northerly extension of this huge coal reserve lies in Pennsylvania, just south of the New York State line, which it roughly parallels in its westerly extension over into Ohio, where it nearly touches Lake Erie at Cleveland. From this northerly line it extends in a south-westerly direction, parallel to the Atlantic coast line, down into Alabama, a distance of 800 miles.

The field attains its maximum width of 190 miles at Pittsburg, covering the eastern third of Ohio and nearly the whole of West Virginia. At Huntingdon, West Virginia, it begins to narrow in gradually and at Chattanooga, Tennessee, it is less than 40 miles wide; but farther on in Alabama it terminates in a roughly circular deposit 100 miles in diameter.

This field is estimated to contain nine-tenths of the high-grade bituminous coal in the United States, the excellent quality of which has caused it to be an important if not the dominant factor in the wonderful industrial achievements of the last half-century. Located in the high mountain regions of the Alleghanies, the coal is transported down to the Atlantic seaboard for local use or for reshipment by water in the coastwise, bunker or export trade.

Middle Western Field

This field spreads over three-quarters of lower Illinois, the western or south-western district of Indiana and across the Ohio River, where it forms the Western Kentucky field. The coals here, though of a good grade of bituminous, are of a generally leaner quality than those of the Appalachian field but their proximity to the great consuming centres of the Middle West has given them a substantial advantage in these markets and the field as a whole ranks as second in importance among the coalfields of the country.

In Illinois the two most important subdivisions in point of production are the Central Illinois and the Williamson and Franklin County fields, both in the extreme southern part of the State. The Du Quoin field forms the connecting link between these two fields. North of the Central Illinois field are the Pana, Virden, Springfield and the Peoria and Fulton fields in the order named, and on the extreme northern boundary are the Rock Island, Northern and Wilmington fields, the Wilmington field being less than 50 miles from Chicago. The extension of the Middle Western field into the Western Kentucky field finds the coal there of somewhat better quality than elsewhere in the district. To the north of the middle Western field, in the State of Michigan, there is a comparatively large area of coal about equidistant from the Eastern and Middle Western fields, which takes its name from the State in which it is found. The coal of this area is of indifferent quality and the production of the entire field is no more than that of a single moderately large company in the Eastern field, and if it were not for the advantageous

geographical location of the field it would not have attained to
any importance.

Western Field

The northern extremity of this field terminates 80 miles north
of Des Moines, Iowa, from which it extends due south, across
the north-western corner of Missouri, through Eastern Kansas,
and nearly across the State of Oklahoma. While the field is
continuous throughout, custom has decreed that the southern
extension in Oklahoma be classified as part of the south-western
field. At Lincoln, Nebraska, the field is 275 miles wide and
gradually narrows to a width of 60 to 70 miles in Oklahoma:
the known workable coals are confined to the eastern two-thirds
of this area. The most important field is the Southern Kansas
district. The discovery of oil in Oklahoma has displaced the
coal in many industries but the mines have in the past been an
important factor in the industrial advancement of this section.

The South-western Field

As already indicated this field is merely an extension of the
Western field into Oklahoma. In this State, however, the coal
measures turn abruptly eastward, crossing the Arkansas line
and terminating in a sharp point in the centre of that State.
The coal-bearing measures of this area, extending 50 miles
into Oklahoma and 100 miles into Arkansas, with a maximum
width of 75 miles, contain some very high-grade fuels that are
considered quite comparable with those of Pennsylvania and
West Virginia.

Between the South-western field and the Gulf of Mexico
there is an extensive area of low-grade lignite coal, extending
in a belt of varying width from the Mexican border at Laredo,
through Texas, Louisiana, Arkansas, Mississippi, Tennessee,
South-eastern Missouri, and terminating at the juncture of the
Ohio and Mississippi rivers less than 25 miles from the southern
extremity of the Middle Western field. Attempts have been
made to mine these lignites, but with indifferent results due to
competition with the high-grade coals of the Warrior fields on
the east and the South-western fields to the north-west, but they
will remain to form a supply of fuel for future generations if

they should be required when the existing supplies of high-grade coals have become exhausted.

The Rocky Mountains Fields

Under this general heading are grouped all the numerous fields between the Canadian and Mexican borders. They lie for the most part on the eastern slope of the Rocky Mountains, from which they extend in varying distances into the great plains to the east. The most westerly extension of this field is a series of small isolated areas of sub-bituminous coals which occur in the Glacial National Park, in the vicinity of Missoula and Anaconda, Montana, and at other points. The Great Falls and Judith Basin fields, extending from the vicinity of Great Falls, Montana, about 150 miles east, contain a very good grade of bituminous coal, though with an unusually high ash content. North of these is the Assiniboine field, covering a broad territory but not mined to any extent. To the south-west is the Bull Mountain or Round-up field which has been developed quite extensively in the past decade or more.

East of the fields just described is an enormous area of coal-bearing measures covering the western half of North Dakota, the eastern quarter of Montana, and extending in a broad belt 100 miles wide down into the east central part of Wyoming. Almost the whole of the south-western quarter of Wyoming is covered by another enormous area known as the Green River region. Some of the coals in this district are among the best in the Rocky Mountains and they have been extensively developed on a large scale and over a long period. South of this region is another coal area called the Uinta region which is almost as extensive as the Green River region.

Denver, Colorado, is surrounded by a field which takes its name after that city. Farther south, on the border between Colorado and New Mexico are the Trinidad and Raton fields which form the most extensive deposits of coking coal to be found in the West. These fields have been the most important source of supply for the Western smelting interests. West of the Trinidad and Raton fields and south of the Uinta field is another fairly large coal area known as the San Juan River region. This field has been developed on a considerable scale, the principal operations being at Durango where a very good grade of coke is also produced.

The Rocky Mountains region generally is a region of widely scattered fields, containing the greatest range in qualities of coal of any region in the country. It includes the coal areas contained in the States of Colorado, Idaho, Montana, New Mexico, North Dakota, Utah and Wyoming: some of these lie east of the great Continental divide and some lie west. There is still much to be learnt about this region: apparently the need has not yet arisen for reliable estimates of all the coal measures throughout the enormous field but so long as coal continues to be a necessary industrial and household fuel it may be safely predicted that this region is destined to play an increasingly important part in the economic development of Western America.

Pacific Coast Fields

The important coalfields of the Pacific Coast region are confined to the State of Washington. Coal has been discovered in both California and Oregon and some attempts have been made to develop the fields in the latter State but with only indifferent success. The quality of the coal in both these States is very inferior and it is doubtful if it will prove a factor in the Pacific Coast fuel industry for a very long time to come.

Of the Washington coals, the Roslyn field is the only one east of the Cascade Mountains. It contains a very fair grade of bituminous coal which has been mined quite extensively by the Northern Pacific Railroad. The Kings County field in the immediate vicinity of Seattle contains good grades of bituminous coal and has many large operations. The Pierce County field, close to Tacoma, is credited with the best grade of fuel in the State and has been the scene of active mining. West and south-west of the Pierce County field are the Centralia and Cowlitzs, the coals of which are almost lignitic in character, but there has never been any extensive mining in these districts. The Whatcom and Skagit fields in the northern parts of the State, near the coast, contain a wide range of coals varying from low-grade bituminous to a very fair grade of anthracite but even here mining operations are not on an extensive scale.

II. BRITISH COALFIELDS

There are several points of outstanding contrast between the United States and British coalfields. One is the proportion of

37 to 1 in point of area in favour of the United States: the immensity of the coal reserves and the enormous distances separating the various fields are very striking. In the majority of cases also the coalfields are many hundreds of miles from the seaboard and in some cases considerable distances from their inland markets. In Great Britain most of the coalfields lie close to the coast, some not more than 10 miles and none of them more than 100 miles from the sea. There are many differences in the physical conditions of mining in the two countries, which we shall deal with later, but the mere contrast in size between the two sets of coalfields is tremendously impressive. People in England have a vague idea that the United States is a huge country and that the coalfields are correspondingly bigger than the British, but one has to visit America and tour through at least some of the major regions to realise the vastness of the industry.

In classifying the British coalfields it is not customary to deal with the anthracite region separately as is done in the case of the American coalfields: it is usually included in the South Wales field. The total production is not very great (only 4½ million tons or as 1 to 18 in the United States) and its relative importance to the whole industry in Great Britain is much smaller than that of its American counterpart. Nevertheless it may be well to adopt the American procedure and describe it briefly first, distinctly from all the rest of the coalfields, which are bituminous. In Great Britain, although small quantities are mined in other parts of the country—in Derbyshire and Scotland—anthracite is practically a monopoly of South Wales, where the anthracite district forms the north-western and western border of the coalfield; it covers an area of about 137,000 acres in the western part of the county of Glamorgan, in Breconshire, Carmarthenshire and Pembrokeshire. There is no sharp line of demarcation between the anthracite region and the steam coal area, for the composition of each seam changes gradually towards the west and north-west from the Standard Steam coal in the centre of the fields, to a drier and harder steam coal and finally to anthracite at the border. In the easterly direction the extension of the anthracite seams is cut off by a great fault running from north-east to south-west in the Vale of Neath. From this line of demarcation at Glyn Neath, anthracite coal seams extend westwards for a distance of about 30 miles to Kidwelly in Carmarthenshire.

The mean width of the field is reckoned as being from 8 to 10 miles.

The principal fields in the British Isles are:

The Northumberland and Durham field;
The Yorkshire–Derbyshire–Nottingham field;
The South Wales field; and
The Scottish fields (Ayr–Lanark–Lothian and Fife).

The less important fields are:

The Lancashire field;
The Cumberland field;
The North Wales field (Flint–Denbigh);
The Midland field, embracing North Staffordshire, South Staffordshire, Shropshire (Coalbrookdale), Leicestershire and Warwickshire;
The Forest of Dean field;
The Bristol and Somerset field; and
The Kent field, the most recently developed—within 50 miles of London, to which the nearest field formerly was 90 miles.

In Ireland the coal industry is not a factor of great importance in the national economy but there are two fields which have been developed, that of Leinster (Queen's and Kilkenny counties) being the more important, and the Tyrone field in the North.

Northumberland and Durham Field

The larger part of this field, situated in the extreme north-east of England, lies in the county of Durham. On the western margin the coal measures rise steeply against the Pennine Chain. To the east in Durham they dip under newer strata but in Northumberland they extend to the sea coast and several miles beyond. From pits sunk near the coast the coal is worked for a distance of more than 2 miles out to sea. The field is nearly 60 miles in length from north to south, and its width varies from about 5 to 30 miles. It is roughly speaking of triangular form, the apex being on the sea coast near the mouth of the river Coquet. The area of the visible coalfield is about 590 square miles, that of the part overspread by Permian rocks 125 square miles while the area beneath the sea is roughly estimated at 136 square miles. The under-sea coal is worked by old collieries at Seaham, Ryhope, Monk Wearmouth and by newer mines at Horden and Easington.

This coalfield is the oldest in the British Isles, having been worked since the fifteenth century, therefore a greater proportion of its resources has been exploited than in the case of the other fields, and the production is greater than that of any other field except the Yorkshire coalfield, which covers a much larger area.

The Yorkshire and North Midland Coalfield

This is the largest field in the British Isles. It extends from Leeds to Nottingham, a distance of about 60 miles, and includes considerable portions of the Counties of Nottingham, Derby and York. The area of the proved coalfields is about 1,376 square miles, while a further area of 760 square miles in the Valley of the Trent contains reserves which have been only partly proved. The seams of this field are the thickest in Great Britain, some parts of the Barnsley Bed, so called from the adjacent town of that name, being from 7 to 10 feet in thickness.

Coal has been worked in the country round Leeds, Halifax, Huddersfield and Sheffield for at least two hundred years but only to a small extent. It is only in comparatively recent times that the coalfield has become one of great importance. Its rise is synchronous with the Industrial Revolution, the development of the steam engine and of the iron and steel manufactures. The woollen and worsted industry, which is the staple trade of the West Riding of Yorkshire, has also stimulated the development of this coalfield.

The greater part of the production is for consumption in manufacturing and for household purposes in the immediate neighbourhood or the central part of England, but in recent years strenuous efforts have been made to increase the export trade from Goole, on the Humber, and from Hull, with the result that Yorkshire coals are now strong competitors of the North-eastern and South Wales steam coals in most of the European and distant markets. Within the last thirty years the new fields of South Yorkshire and Nottinghamshire have assumed an increasingly important position in the industry: the mines are newer and are equipped with up-to-date machinery.

The South Wales Coalfield

In many respects this is the principal coalfield of the British Isles, for besides the exceptional quality of the mineral found in it, bituminous and anthracite, it is the largest continuous field, though the superficial area of the basin, estimated at about 1,000 square miles, is exceeded by that of the Clyde Basin. It contains almost as great a vertical thickness of strata as any coalfield in the world, amounting to about 10,000 feet.

It is separated by Carmarthen Bay into two unequal portions. That to the east of the bay stretches to Pontypool, in Monmouth-shire, a distance of 56 miles, and is the larger portion. This is the section popularly known as the South Wales coalfield: it covers almost the whole of the counties of Glamorgan and Monmouth and part of the counties of Brecon and Carmarthen. The greatest transverse diameter is 16 miles, in the meridian of Neath, in Glamorganshire. The smaller portion extends westward to St. Bride's Bay, on the west coast of Pembrokeshire, a distance of 17 miles. The coal resources of this outlying part of the field are small and unimportant.

The general form of the main part of the coalfield is that of an oval basin or trough, lying nearly east and west. It is deeply indented by the bays of Swansea and Carmarthen which spread over the upturned edges of the strata as they cross from shore to shore. The beds also rise and crop out towards the north, beyond which the Millstone Grit and Carboniferous Limestone mark the limits of the coal-producing area.

The Coal Measures come to the surface over the greater part of the region. The land, which has a plateau-like formation, and slopes from north to south, is intersected by a number of deep transverse valleys, including those of the rivers Nedd, Afan, Ogwr, Taff, Rhymney and Ebbw, and their subordinates— the Ely, Rhondda, Cynon, Sirhowy and the Afon Llwyd. These valleys, by exposing many of the coal seams, facilitated in the past the economical working of the coal, which could be obtained by driving adits and galleries from the outcrops along the hill-sides. Up to a comparatively recent period, therefore, the coal-pits were generally shallow as compared with those of the north of England, but during the past thirty or forty years, mining by adits and shallow pits has given place to collieries with pits of considerable depth and capable of a large output of coal. Several collieries exceed a depth of 1,500 feet and some of 2,000 feet. The eastern part of the field is traversed for many miles by an important anticlinal fold, which converts it into two troughs and in this way brings within reach of the miner much coal that would otherwise have lain at too great a depth to be worked.

The character of the coal varies from bituminous in the east to pure anthracite in the west, the famous steam coal—"Admiralty coal"—occurring chiefly in the central part of the field between Llanelly and Neath. Nearly half of the coal of the whole field is steam coal, one-seventh being classed as first-class and about one-third second class steam, while about 30 per cent is bituminous and rather more than one-fifth is anthracite.

In normal times about one-half of the output, consisting mainly of steam coal, is exported. The export of coal from South Wales, like the mining of it, is greatly aided by the transverse valleys which open up easy railway routes and have at their mouths the chief exporting towns—Cardiff, Swansea, Llanelly and Newport. Barry Dock, situated a few miles west of Cardiff, though not at a river mouth, is also engaged in the coal export trade.

The Scottish Coalfield

Several coalfields of considerable importance occur in Scotland in a wide zone extending from the Firth of Forth to the Firth of Clyde. This zone is about 95 miles long and varies in width up to 30 miles. There are about a dozen fields, not, however, geologically distinct, the most important of which are the Lanark, Fife, Ayr and Lothian fields.

The LANARK coalfield embraces the counties of Lanark, Dumbarton, Renfrew, Linlithgow, Stirling and Clackmannan, though in the restricted sense the part lying in County Lanark is the centre of a great industrial district extending from Glasgow up the Valley of the Clyde almost to the town of Lanark. This coalfield has been the industrial centre of Scotland for very many years and practically the whole district is occupied by collieries, many of them in an advanced stage of development.

The FIFE coalfield contains the whole carboniferous series of strata within its area and the seams are of considerable thickness over large areas. The upper series occur in the north end of a basin, along the Fife coast from Dysart to Largo. This basin is continuous under the Firth of Forth with the Lothian coalfield. The coal is now worked to a distance of 2 or 3 miles under the Firth of Forth. The carboniferous limestone series occupy a far larger area, stretching from Elie westwards north of Largo, through Markinch and Lochgelly past Dunfermline to Cidross. It occupies a wide-stretching area of which Dunfermline is nearly the centre. This coalfield of the limestone series is from 15 to 18 miles long, from east to west, and 4 or 5 miles broad.

The AYRSHIRE coalfield lies on the east shore of the Firth of Clyde: it is 330 square miles in area.

The LOTHIAN coalfield is geologically the southern end of the Fife and Forth basin, and covers parts of the counties of Edinburgh, Haddington and Peebles. It is probably the oldest worked field in Scotland.

The coals of Scotland include good and medium quality steam coals, gas and house coals and coking coals: thus they are used for a variety of manufacturing, railway and domestic purposes. A small quantity of anthracite and dry steam coal is mined in the neighbourhood of some of the great dykes and sills of Fifeshire and Ayr, and anthracite coal is also found in a tiny coalfield in the north of the island of Arran, which may perhaps be regarded as a detached portion of the Ayrshire field.

There has been a steady growth of the coal industry in Scotland during the past half century with the exception of the last few years when it has suffered from the general depression.

THE LESS IMPORTANT COALFIELDS

Lancashire and Cheshire Coalfield

This field is separated from the Yorkshire coalfield by the Pennine Chain anticlinal. It has an area of 217 square miles of exposed coal measures, the greater part of which lies in the southern part of Lancashire, with the town of Wigan as the centre of the field. Some of the deepest workings of the British Isles are found in this region at the Pendleton Colliery near Manchester, which has a total depth from the surface of 3,483 feet. The portion of the coalfield lying in Cheshire is small and the output is not more than 2 per cent of the total production of the field. The immense growth of the cotton spinning and weaving industry and ot the machinery manufacture of Lancashire has been greatly facilitated by the abundant supply of cheap coal on the spot.

Cumberland Coalfield

This is a small coalfield lying on the west of the northern extremity of the Pennine Chain, on the opposite side from the Durham and Northumberland field. It is about 25 miles long from north-east to south-west, and about 6 miles wide at its widest point. A feature of this coalfield is the extent of the workings under the sea, which occur all along the coast. At Whitehaven, the coal is being worked under the sea at a distance of 4 miles from the coast. There is some coastwise shipment to Barrow, Liverpool, Manchester, the Lancashire seaside towns and the Isle of Man.

Coalfields of North Wales

The North Wales coalfields cover part of the counties of Denbigh and Flint. North of the Valley of the Alyn they become separated into two portions by the upheaval along the line of a great fault of the Lower Carboniferous Rocks. This is one of the largest faults in Great Britain and has been traced from the sea on the coast of Merionethshire, through Bala Lake, into Cheshire. The tract south of this fault is called the Denbighshire Coalfield, that to the north the Flintshire Coalfield.

The Denbighshire field begins about 3 miles south of Oswestry and extends northward by Oswestry, Ruabon and Wrexham. The length of the field is about 18 miles and it is about 4 miles in breadth at Wrexham.

The Flintshire field is disconnected from that of Denbighshire by the uprise of the Carboniferous Limestone and Millstone Grit over a small tract between Gresford and Hope. From this it extends along the western side of the estuary of the Dee to Point of Aire, a distance of 15 miles, but throughout a considerable part of its range the productive portion is very narrow and greatly broken by faults.

The coal obtained in the North Wales coalfields is used mainly for household purposes and for manufacturing gas, and hardly any is exported.

Bristol and Somerset Coalfield

This Coalfield occupies a basin elongated in a north and south direction, extending from Wickwar in Gloucestershire at the north end, for 25 miles southwards to near Frome in Somerset. The principal parts of the field lie between Bristol and Bath, and in the neighbourhood of Radstock to the south. The coals of this field are of varying quality. The best steam coals have given satisfactory results in ocean-going steamers and there are excellent house coals, good gas coal and ordinary bituminous coking and manufacturing coals. There has been no dramatic increase in the rate of development of this field in the last fifty years, nor are there prospects of future development.

Forest of Dean Coalfield

This is a small field lying north of the head of the Bristol Channel, with Coleford (Glos.) as the centre. The area covered by coal measures is 34 square miles. The seams at present worked yield a rather soft bituminous coal suitable for household, manufacturing and gas-making purposes. Coal has been worked in the Forest of Dean from very ancient times, and there is an interesting system of mineral rights in force in this coalfield which has come down from feudal times, modified only by recent Acts of Parliament. There is much to interest the historian in this field. Production has increased rather markedly during the past half century and the Forest of Dean is now essentially an industrial district.

The Midland Coalfield

In the Midland Counties of Staffordshire, Warwickshire, Worcestershire, Leicestershire, and Shropshire occur a number of coalfields more or less detached from one another and of varying sizes, the largest being the North Staffordshire and the South Staffordshire coalfields.

The NORTH STAFFORDSHIRE, sometimes called the Potteries coalfield because of the dominant industry there, covers an area of about 110 square miles: if the Cheadle district, which forms a detached basin on the east, be included, the area is 128 square miles.

The SOUTH STAFFORDSHIRE coalfield, between Cannock Chase

and Clent Hills, has a total area of about 150 square miles. The celebrated 30 feet seam, which occurs in the neighbourhood of Dudley, and is known as the "ten yard" or "thick coal" is really a combination of several thinner seams, which a few miles away occur separated by intervening sands and shales. This thick seam has been a source of great wealth to the district but it is now almost entirely worked out.

The WARWICKSHIRE coalfield lies between the towns of Coventry, Nuneaton and Tamworth and is about 60 square miles in area.

The LEICESTERSHIRE coalfield is only about 30 square miles in area in its visible portions, but in addition there is a further area of about 55 square miles which has been proved but has not been developed. The centre of the field is at the town of Ashby-de-la-Zouche.

The SHROPSHIRE AND WORCESTERSHIRE fields include the Coalbrookdale, Shrewsbury, Le Botwood, the Forest of Wyre, Dryton and Clee coalfields. These coalfields extend irregularly from Shrewsbury to the River Teme. The total area is about 98 square miles. Some of these fields, including Le Botwood and Dryton, have been abandoned for some years on account of the fewness and thinness of their seams.

Midland coals are for the most part dry and of a bituminous character, suitable mainly for household purposes, and for smelting and manufacturing; there is also a considerable quantity of good gas and coking coal in North Staffordshire. The Midland Coalfields contain numerous seams of ironstone and it was the existence of this mineral in the district that mainly led to the development of Birmingham, Wolverhampton and other large "iron" towns in the "Black Country" region. In North Staffordshire, the coal seams are interspersed with layers of excellent clay, and this association of coal and clay was responsible principally for the development of the pottery industry in this locality.

The Kent Coalfields

These are the most recently developed fields in the land and as there is still some uncertainty about the measures further exploration is necessary.

The limits of the coalfield cannot yet be given with certainty. It is improbable that coal will be found north of a line from Herne Bay to the mouth of the Stour, and the southern boundary keeps to the north of Brabourne and probably runs from Abbot's Cliff towards Wye. Eastwards, the coal doubtless extends under the sea; but whether for more than 5 miles it is impossible to say. Westwards, the boundary is still uncertain though coal is proved practically to Canterbury.

An interesting feature of the development of this field is that the chief company operating it—Kent Coal Concessions, Ltd.— has built several garden villages for housing the miners, and the villages are models worthy of emulation by all colliery companies or local authorities which build.

As Professor Stanley Jevons, himself a pioneer in the garden village movement, says in his chapter on the Kent Coalfields,[1] "There need be no Black Country in Kent." What would he think of some of the dilapidated miners' camps in West Virginia or West Pennsylvania to-day? Oh for the gardenisation of those abject mining villages!

Such in brief outline is the geographical setting of the two sets of coalfields. A study of maps, informed by the exercise of a lively imagination, will emphasise the enormous disparity in size and the difference in distances separating the various fields from one another and from the nearest ports. These differences are significant and yet not so important as the fact that the natural conditions of mining in Great Britain are much more difficult than in the United States. Let us now address ourselves to this aspect of our comparative study.

[1] *The British Coal Trade,* an excellent study on which the author has drawn freely for his description of the coalfields.

SECTION B

PHYSICAL CONDITIONS OF MINING

As a preliminary step it will be helpful to quote a table (pp. 110, 111) setting forth a comparison of technical and commercial conditions extracted from evidence given before the Royal Commission on the Coal Industry (Great Britain) 1925, and published in 1927 by the Economic and Financial Section of the League of Nations in Volume I of its Memorandum on Coal.

The table on p. 114, taken from the comparative study made by F. G. Tryon and Margaret H. Schoenfeld, shews the main differences in the physical conditions of mining in the two countries. The averages given are weighed by the tonnages produced. For each factor an average is shewn for Great Britain as a whole, a second average for the United States bituminous industry, and a third for the United States anthracite industry. These national averages have the weakness of all averages, that they hide the extremes. In Great Britain, as in the United States, natural conditions vary widely and to bring out something of these variations figures are shewn for five of the largest districts. South Yorkshire is given because it has the deepest workings and the largest mines of any of the big fields; Scotland is included because it has the thinnest beds; Northumberland because its workings are relatively shallow; Durham because it still makes use of the pillar and stall system of mining; and South Wales because it is the largest single district. Six American districts are also shewn, representative of both union and non-union conditions. (It should always be remembered that whereas the whole industry in Great Britain is unionised there are some fields in the United States, e.g. West Virginia, which are almost completely unorganised.) Pennsylvania and West Virginia are included as the two largest producing States. Ohio, Indiana and Illinois are not shewn, because their figures of output per man are hardly comparable on account of the large tonnages which they mine by stripping. One of the most interesting features of mining in the United States to an Englishman is strip mining. The coal is literally stripped from the surface of the earth by a huge machine which, though popularly called a

	United States	Great Britain
Approximate annual output capacity	850,000,000 tons	275,000,000 tons
1. Coal Seams	Large available reserves of coal in seams of suitable section for economic working lying at or near the surface. Large proportion of coal hard	Considerable proportions of coal worked from seams thinner than most economical section and lying at considerable depth below surface. Large proportion of coal hard
2. Roofs and Floors	Generally good	Moderate (good, bad and indifferent).
3. Faults	Relatively free from faults	Fairly numerous in the majority of districts
4. Inclination of Seams	Generally flat except in the anthracite region	As a rule fairly flat
5. Inflammable Gas	Relatively free from gas	Gas prevalent in the majority of districts
6. Quality of Coal	Fairly high	Generally high
7. Drainage	Either free drainage or shallow pumping	Pumping demand heavy in many districts

	Generally easy	Generally difficult
8. Sinking conditions for new developments ..	Generally easy	Generally difficult
9. Transport (a) Water	Fairly well supplied with inland navigable waterway, but long distance from deep water to nearest coalfield	Poorly supplied with large inland water-ways, but ideally placed geographically in respect of proximity of coalfields to deep water
(b) Rail	Railway rates per ton-mile relatively low	Railway rates per ton-mile relatively high
10. Markets (a) Inland ..	Good, due to richness of land and of mineral resources and consequent demand for coal to be developed, transported and converted into semi or finished products	Normally good, due to highly industrialised condition of country and intensity of population per square mile.
(b) Export ..	Handicapped by distance from sea-board and particularly by absence of demand for imports of raw materials on a large scale and consequent difficulty in arranging for convenient return freights from countries to which coal is imported	Normally very good, due to high quality coal, proximity of coal to seaboard, and big demand for imports of raw materials facilitating the arrangement of return freights for ships carrying coal on the outward journey

"shovel," looks like a "tank" and like a "tank" rides roughshod over the field, automatically drawing up the coal and tipping it into wagons. (One cannot help wishing that all mining could be carried on in the open air, on the surface.) Iowa is included because its coal is relatively thin, Wyoming for its thick beds and Washington because its beds pitch steeply.

It is a familiar fact, as shewn by the table, that the American soft coal miner produces in a day about four times as much as the British miner. Many factors may contribute to this difference: among others the price of coal, the attitude of labour and the technical standards of management, and the question of how far the observed differences in natural conditions will account for the discrepancy in output per man is one that only the operating engineers can decide. American usage always separates anthracite from bituminous coal but, in comparisons with other countries, there is a tendency to forget anthracite. When anthracite is considered, the margin between output per worker in the two countries is less flattering to American practice. The output per man employed in the anthracite region is 1·79 long tons per day, as against 1·02 tons, the average for Great Britain on an 8-hour basis. Mining conditions in the Pennsylvania anthracite regions are certainly difficult. The author still retains vivid memories of an arduous exploration of a bed pitching at an angle of 45° and was so exhausted after the pull up that he responded to the invitation to scale a perpendicular bed with nothing more articulate than a sickly smile! Yet in point of thickness and depth of workings, the average British conditions are less favourable. The great difficulty of the American anthracite mines is the faulting, folding and steep pitch of many of the beds. Mr. Tryon generously suggests that it might be fairer to match the industry of Britain against American anthracite, but as the British industry is so preponderantly bituminous it may be well that any comparisons, except where anthracite is specially considered, shall relate to the American bituminous industry.

The figures in the table prove beyond dispute that natural conditions in Great Britain are decidedly more difficult than in the United States, though probably the differences are less sharp than has often been supposed by men who have visited both countries. The American who goes underground in British mines asks particularly to be shewn thin beds and deep workings, and he is apt to give a little too much weight to these extreme conditions. The Briton who visits American mines wants particularly to see the Pittsburg and Pocahontas beds and his picture tends to emphasise these wonderful coals at the expense of the thinner beds of Central Pennsylvania, the Southern Appalachians or the South-western Interstate field. The facts are that in spite of her great natural difficulties Great Britain is still working much thick coal, and that in spite of her great natural advantages America has already in some districts resorted to coals much below the optimum thickness. The great handicaps of British mining are not so much thin seams as depth of workings, and faulting and dipping of the measures.

The American operator has little experience of deep mining—"working under cover." To the British employer that is the normal condition and he is handicapped not only by the increased cost of sinking shafts, hoisting and pumping but also by the necessity of meeting difficulties arising from the heavy pressure developed, which makes the maintenance of all openings more difficult; more timbering is required and more work in keeping roads and air ways in repair. As the depth increases pillars tend to crush, and the room and pillar system as practised in America becomes impossible; the longwall system therefore is nearly universal in Great Britain outside Northumberland and Durham.

In the bituminous mines of the United States the workings are still very shallow. In fact 64 per cent of the coal is won through slopes and drifts, and much of it is taken out from above the ground-water level. Even from slopes and drifts that extend under an adjacent hillside, comparatively little coal is now being taken out from under more than 500 feet of cover.

As will be seen from the table on page 114 the average depth of shaft bituminous mines in the United States is 262 feet. The anthracite mines are deeper, Mr. D. C. Ashmead, an authority on the anthracite industry, giving the weighted average depth as 415 feet. But in Great Britain the average depth of all workings is 1,023 feet. Even Northumberland, the shallowest of the British districts, has an average depth of 498 feet, considerably deeper than the average for the United States anthracite mines.

Nothing surprises an English visitor more than the shallow workings: he finds himself at the bottom of the shaft before he has had time to speculate on the depth of the mine.

COMPARATIVE SUMMARY OF PHYSICAL CONDITIONS IN BRITISH AND AMERICAN COAL MINES

Country or District	Feet Average Depth of Workings	Per cent of Output from Large Mines (producing 200,000 Tons or more in 1924)	Average Net Thickness of Beds Mined	Per cent. of Output Cut by Machine	Explosives Used per Long Ton Mined	Safety Lamps in use per Worker Underground[1]	Per cent. Workers of the Coal Surface	Output per Worker per day[2]
			Inches		Pounds			Long Tons
Great Britain	1,023[3]	67·0	50	18·1	0·12	0·97	42·0	0·89 (1·02 in 8 hours)
United States (bituminous)	262[3]	49·0	63	69·5	0·44	Open lamp dominant	61·4	4·07
United States (anthracite)	415	4[4]	80	1·7	0·68	0·33 +	47·5	1·79
South Yorkshire	1,509	95·0	57	10·5	0·04	1·20	42·4	1·05 (1·20 in 8 hours)
Scotland	699	32·0	35	46·4	0·23	0·40	45·2	0·97 (1·11 in 8 hours)
Northumberland	498	73·0	42	26·7	0·32	0·51	35·4	0·89 (1·02 in 8 hours)
Durham	726	72·0	45	16·0	0·14	0·84	33·6	0·88 (1·01 in 8 hours)
South Wales and Monmouthshire	1,089	63·0	54	5·4	0·07	1·05	46·4	0·79 (0·90 in 8 hours)
Pennsylvania (bituminous)	268[3]	54·1	62	64·8	0·21	0·44	64·3	3·81
West Virginia	291[3]	41·8	64	82·0	0·29	Open lamps general	53·9	4·89
Iowa	182[3]	22·4	46	18·5	1·32	Open lamps general	69·3	2·50
Washington	342[3]	48·0	63	10·4	0·50	Safety lamps general	56·9	3·04
Wyoming	186[3]	38·5	101	55·1	0·37	Safety lamps in South	60·2	4·83

[1] Included to show relative occurrence of gas, electric battery lamps and all other types of safety lamp as well as flame safety lamps are included in the figures.

[2] Figures for Great Britain represent a 7-hour day. To facilitate comparison with the United States, the same rate increased by one-seventh is shown in parenthesis.

[3] Data for United States bituminous represent depth of shaft mines only.

[4] Precise data lacking, but as the anthracite operations are on the whole large, the percentage if available would be

The great depth of the British workings has an unexpected effect in another direction. The desire to utilise the heavy investment in the deep shaft once made induces the practice of working out all the coal that can be reached from a given shaft. The smaller mines of the United States are more quickly worked out and are replaced by new ones, and this, coupled with the more rapid growth of the American industry, means that the typical American mine is very much younger than the typical British mine. From the Royal Commission Report (Vol. 3, p. 175) it appears that there are at least 57 mines in England that were opened more than a hundred years ago, and these mines employ nearly 5 per cent of the total number of men in the industry. In fact 73 per cent of the British miners are employed in mines over thirty years old. This is an astonishing contrast to the United States where between the years 1911 and 1923 a total of 8,975 new mines were opened, an average of 690 per year. The contrast may be summed up in the statement that 50 per cent of the men in the American bituminous industry are working in mines opened in the last twenty years whereas in Britain the figure is less than 10 per cent.

The greater age of the British workings, in addition to imposing the handicaps of greater length of haulage, maintenance of air ways and travelling distance from shaft bottom to face, makes for conservatism in mining practice. A new mine starting with a clean slate may introduce changes in methods without serious resistance and may take advantage of the latest developments in engineering practice much more readily. A considerable part of the contrast in mining practice in the two countries is due to this single factor of age.

To justify the deep shafts, a large tonnage is necessary and the result is that, contrary to what many would suppose, the British mines average distinctly larger than the bituminous mines of the United States, not only in number of employees but in output. In mines producing 200,000 tons or less a year the proportion of British mines is much smaller than that of American bituminous mines. Above the 200,000 tons limit, the proportion of British mines is found to be the greater. Mines producing 500,000 net tons or more contribute only 18·3 per cent of the American output, but furnish 27 per cent of the British output.

The thickness of bed worked in Great Britain ranges about

one foot less than in the bituminous mines of the United States. The spread between the extremes of thickness is rather greater in America. Britain still has a considerable amount of thick coal, for 27 per cent of the output is won from beds over five feet thick. On the other hand, the United States is already working more thin coal than is commonly supposed, and 25 per cent of the American product comes from beds less than 4 feet thick. Some British districts average thicker than some American districts. South Yorkshire is now working an average of 57 inches, but it should be remembered that this fine thick coal lies at an average depth of 1,500 feet. In South Wales the average is 54 inches. In Scotland it is only 35 inches. Of the American districts the thickest average coal is reported from Wyoming, 101 inches. Iowa has an average thickness of only 46 inches or less than the British average and the little Osage field in Kansas is working an average of only 21 inches.

In correlating thickness and output per man, however, it should be noted that the average thickness is sometimes deceptive. In American room and pillar practice the output per man falls rapidly in seams below a certain optimum thickness, and thin vein workings will pull down the average tonnage per man per day more than they do the average thickness. For this reason the difference of approximately 1 foot between the averages for Great Britain and the American bituminous mines repesents much more of a handicap for Britain than would at first appear. Moreover the point should be emphasised that those British mines which are favoured with thick seams are generally the ones which are most handicapped by depth. For beds of less than 2 feet in thickness the average depth is 517 feet; but for beds of 6 feet or more the average depth is 1,350 feet.

The use of cutting machines is not itself a natural factor but may be regarded as a reflection of the physical limitations. The cutting machine has been much less widely introduced into Great Britain than in the United States, except in the anthracite mines of Pennsylvania, where conditions make it unnecessary or unmanageable. In many British seams the roof pressure causes the coal to come down easily and reduces the need for cutting machinery. Indeed, it would often be impossible to work the machine across the face because the pressure would bear down and bind the cutter bar, or the coal would even slump and bury the machine. Still, it is clear that the saturation point has not been reached in Britain because the number of mining machines in use there has been increasing steadily from 1901, when 1·4 per cent of the total output was cut by machine, to 1924, when the percentage was 18·7. It is probable that if the demand had increased in the last few years machines would have been installed in many more mines. In 1929 the tonnage of coal cut by machine in the United States was 75·4 per cent of the total output. In Great Britain it was about 30 per cent. In 1931 it increased to 35 per cent.

Not only does the British miner have fewer machines but he uses less powder. Counting all explosives, the United States bituminous miner employs four times as much explosive per ton mined as the British miner, and the United States anthracite miner employs nearly six times as much. Even discounting this ratio on account of the greater use of black powder in America, which is inferior in shattering power to high explosives, the consumption of the American worker is much higher. The difference is explained in part by the fact that in the deep British mines the coal often comes down easily without shooting; in part by the greater danger of gas explosions; and in part by the demands of the market, which places a higher premium on lump coal than the American market does.

The occurrence of gas is difficult to measure but it is generally known that American mines are relatively free from gas, and that in Great Britain gas is prevalent in a majority of the districts. Some light is thrown on this factor by the number of safety lights in use in relation to the number of men working underground. In Great Britain the ratio of safety lamps to men below ground is ·97; in the gassy districts of South Yorkshire and South Wales the ratio rises above 1. In Scotland, where naked lights are in frequent use, it drops to ·40. From the records of the Pennsylvania Department of mines, it appears that the ratio in the anthracite region of America is ·33 (probably low through lack of complete reports), and that in the bituminous districts of Pennsylvania the average is ·44. For mines working the Pittsburg seam in Pennsylvania the ratio is high. In most other parts of the State it is low. In the American bituminous industry as a whole the prevailing type is the open flame lamp. It is surprising to an Englishman to find that he can smoke a pipe underground without feeling that either he is violating any regulation or endangering the safety of others. Of course the use of safety lamps depends not only on the amount of gas present but to a large extent on the safety regulations of the State and the degree to which they are enforced. The standard of enforcement is probably higher in England, which has had factory legislation generally for something like one hundred and thirty years, but apart from this consideration it is undeniable that the British coal industry is much more handicapped by gas.

All of these physical disadvantages increase the number of men who must be employed simply to maintain the workers at the coal face. In the American bituminous mines 61·4 per cent of the men employed are engaged in productive work at the face. The proportion varies with the duties of the men at the face, who sometimes perform auxiliary work such as timbering, elsewhere done by men especially detailed for the purpose; without taking this into account the comparisons between districts are sometimes misleading. It is worth noting, however, that in Great Britain the average is 42·0 per cent and that in some districts it is as low as 34 per cent. Improved practice may conceivably increase this proportion but admittedly the principal cause of the difference between the two countries is the greater natural difficulties in Britain.

There are many other physical factors that exercise an important influence on productivity but that are not susceptible of measurement. The character of the roof and floor tends to vary independently of the depth, and largely controls the system of mining and the amount of timbering required. Faults are much commoner in British than in American mines, and in some districts such as Lancashire and Cheshire, Staffordshire and North Wales they are very numerous. No small part of the difference in output per worker in the two countries is due to this factor alone. Indeed the presence of many faults would cause the rejection of a bituminous property in the United States as unminable under present conditions. Igneous dykes such as are common in several of the fields of Scotland are extremely rare in American mines. In pumping expense the advantage is clearly with the American bituminous mines. What water there is to be pumped is lifted a much shorter distance on the average. In the Pennsylvania anthracite region however pumping is a source of heavy expense;

one has lively recollections of ploughing through six inches of water in a certain mine in that region.

Another adverse condition which the British employer has to contend with is the relatively steeper and more irregular grades of the beds, though it is not generally realised how steep the pitches in some American fields are, e.g. Oklahoma, Arkansas, Washington and some of the Rocky Mountain districts; in the State of Washington 24·0 per cent of the coal is won from beds dipping more than 20 degrees. Many of the mines in the anthracite region are, of course, working excessively steep beds.

It must be emphasised that these other factors are no less important than some of those for which quantitative comparison is made. All of them tend to increase the natural handicaps of the British mines and help to explain the smaller product per worker.

The higher output per worker in American mines is undoubtedly obtained at some sacrifice of human life, for the American accident record compares very unfavourably with British standards. The death rate through fatal accidents for the United States was 4·08 per thousand employees in 1922, as against 1·13 for Great Britain. The British mining law requires relatively more timbering and the authorities are perhaps slower to approve the use of electrical equipment, but even if it could be shewn that the safety regulations have delayed the introduction of electrical and mechanical improvements it is doubtful if British opinion would approve of any relaxation of the present standards of enforcement of safety regulations: indeed the miners' organisations are so powerful that the tendency is to tighten up the administration of factory legislation as applied to mining. The Bureau of Mines and its officials throughout the American coalfields have devoted a great deal of attention to safety practice and done valuable experimental work, but it has to be remembered that the tradition of governmental supervision is short-lived and that inspectors have to contend with the same kind of opposition that English inspectors met with in the good old days of *laissez-faire* when an employer acted on the belief that he could do what he liked with his own. There is as much humanitarian feeling and as much practical expression of sympathy over a colliery explosion in the United States as in Great Britain, but the regulations for the prevention of explosions and accidents are perhaps hardly so exacting or so strictly enforced.

In reflecting on these differences in physical and political conditions, one naturally has to consider the question as to whether they entirely account for the differences in output per man. As has been suggested earlier this is a point that only operating mining engineers can decide. The question is one that no economist can answer, even one who has endeavoured to equip himself by visiting the mines of both countries. It would appear that after every allowance has been made for the natural conditions there remains a margin which must be ascribed to other causes; among others perhaps to the attitude of labour towards the job (labour in America appears to be more docile than in Great Britain); to methods of management and engineering practice (which are probably superior in the United States); and to the higher wages paid to the American miner, who will increase his output if he knows he will "make good money" and who is less concerned about the dangers arising from the stimulation of the acquisitive instinct than the British miner who much as he desires a higher standard of living finds the philosophy of "each for himself and the devil take the hindmost" a little repugnant.

SECTION C

POLITICAL

In addition to all these factors there is a difference in the general prevailing political atmosphere. In Great Britain although the coal industry is still conducted by private enterprise governmental supervision of mining is pretty close and the question of public ownership of the industry is one of practical politics. This puts the employers on their mettle and they try to run the industry in such a way as to reduce public criticism to the minimum in the hope of staving off nationalisation. In the United States the philosophy of *laissez-faire* is still dominant, probably more so in the coal than in any other industry; the nationalisation of the mines is a question of little more than academic interest; and the operators, while having to accept a certain measure of governmental supervision and in some fields accepting the men's union, are not greatly concerned about public opinion.

It would perhaps be unfair to suggest that the following utterance by Senator William H. King, of Utah, before the National Retail Coal Merchants Association at Chicago, is typical of the attitude of American coal operators generally, but it would be difficult if not impossible to match it in Great Britain in post-war days. "Government ownership or operation of coal mines can end only in failure. The Government should say to big business, 'Here's a fair field and no favours for anyone. Let the best man win.' Business should be allowed to go ahead and develop without being hampered by petty government intervention."

It is extremely difficult to contrast the general attitude in the two countries on the question of government control of the coal industry and it is too big a problem to be treated in any detail here. It would be necessary to attempt to define the respective attitudes of the owners, mine-workers, the general body of consumers and of the governments of the two countries. But broadly speaking one might say that that intangible quantity described as "public opinion" appears to be much more disposed in England than in the United States to favour a substantial measure of government control, and even a policy of nationalisation. The Royal Commission of 1925, popularly known as the Samuel Commission, did not favour nationalisation, but Mr. Justice Sankey, Chairman of the Coal Industry Commission of 1919, reported in favour of government ownership of coal resources and of the mines. In the debate in the House of Lords on the second reading of the Coal Mines Bill (April 29, 1930) this same Mr. Justice Sankey, then Lord Chancellor, said, "I have not changed my mind. I still firmly believe that nationalisation is the only solution of our difficulties." No governmental body in the United States has ever recommended anything that even savoured of public ownership as distinct from control. The general feeling—what is often described vaguely yet accurately enough as the "atmosphere"—of the American people seems to be opposed to anything of the sort. There is still a powerful section in British politics actively hostile to the national ownership of the mines but one does not feel in Great Britain that it is a subject one must not discuss. The war brought it into the realm of practical politics. From February, 1917, till March 31, 1921, the coal industry in Great Britain was controlled by the Government. The entire industry was put into the hands of a Coal Controller. Without going into the reasons for the decontrol in 1921 and allowing for the fact that it was a war measure, one may say that it accustomed the British people to the notion of governmental control and the possibilities of public ownership. In the United States, also, certain war-requiring measures of control were instituted but there governmental control was incidental rather than vital and it did not make much of a "dent" on the national thought. It is a rare thing to find an American economist who favours national control or even State control if that control means the dethronement of the god of *laissez-faire*, but some of the best English economists believe in social control of the entire economic process.

It is not to be assumed that there are no laws governing certain phases of the conduct of industry in the United States. There are federal anti-trust and transportation acts, State laws dealing with corporations, investment and finance, truck acts, labour laws and State transportation laws. There are even laws specially applicable to the mining industry. In every coal State there is a more or less elaborate mining code and there is no lack of regulations relating to accidents, ventilation, gas, qualifications of officials, and in some codes, even of the miners themselves. But such restrictions are not much more than irksome interferences.

It is interesting to find that the United States Coal Commission of 1923 unanimously made many recommendations involving a quite serious curtailment of the freedom of private enterprise.

In spite of the recommendations of the Commission however the coal industry is still conducted in the spirit of private enterprise, fettered only by "safety" compromises, and few, if any, of the more important recommendations have been put into effect. One sometimes wonders whether the most valuable use of a Government Commission is not that it collects a fund of research material on which investigators may draw in future studies! Commissions, Hearings, Inquiries, Conferences, books, articles— and yet nothing seems to be done. It is generally agreed, for instance, among coal experts in the United States that in view of the existing excess capacity of the industry the opening of new mines should be restricted if not prohibited. But as far as can be ascertained the Government, although administrator of 50 million acres of coal lands, has not amended the leasing laws to restrict the opening of new bituminous mines.

Something must be said about the ownership of coal lands. It is well known that the industry in Great Britain has suffered from the incubus of the payment of royalties (estimated at an annual value of £6,000,000) to landowners, some of whom, like the Marquis of Bute and Lord Londonderry, own the land of almost entire coalfields. In America ownership of land generally is a comparatively recent development and in the bituminous industry the ownership of coal lands is widespread. Concentration in ownership of bituminous coal lands is not general, due primarily to the fact that coal is being mined in 92 fields (United States Commission, 1923 grouping) and that large acres of land on which coal is thought to exist are awaiting the development of transportation facilities. There are a few fields, however, which form exceptions to the general rule. For example, in the Pocahontas field in West Virginia concentration in ownership of the coal lands is highly developed. Most of the fifty operators in this field in 1920 paid royalty to one of the principal land-owning companies there—the Pocahontas Coal and Coke Company and the Crozer Land Association. More than 95 per cent of the total output of this field in 1920 was produced from lands owned by one or

other of these two companies. The Pocahontas Coal and Coke
Company is much the larger of the two. It owns or controls
about 300,000 acres of coal land. Most of this land lies in West
Virginia but some of it is in the Pocahontas field across the State
line in Virginia.

There are several operating companies in the United States
which own or control large areas of coal lands, not only in one
but in several fields. While such companies are relatively few
as compared with the total number of coal operators, the aggregate
of their land holdings and of their output forms an important
fraction of the total. Three of the principal companies of this
type are the United States Steel Corporation (and Subsidiaries),
the Consolidation Coal Company (and Subsidiaries), and the
Pittsburg Coal Company (and Subsidiaries). The United States
Steel Corporation, through its subsidiary companies, owned lands
in the States of Pennsylvania, West Virginia, Ohio, Kentucky,
Tennessee, Alabama, Indiana, and Illinois. The Consolidation
Coal Company, in its own name or through subsidiaries, owned
or controlled at the beginning of 1923 about 340,000 acres of
coal lands in the States of Pennsylvania, Maryland, West Virginia,
and Kentucky. The Pittsburg Coal Company and its subsidiaries
owned or controlled at the beginning of 1923 about 165,000 acres
of coal lands in Pennsylvania, Ohio and Kentucky.

Notwithstanding the growth of this process of concentration,
however, ownership of coal seams is still distributed among
about 4,000 different persons alike in the United States and in
Great Britain. It is generally agreed by experts in Great Britain
that diversified ownership, with the inevitable accidental surface
boundaries, militates against efficient underground organisation
and layout. The wastes and inefficiencies arising from the existing
system have been the subject of discussion in mining circles for
many years, and various Government investigating Committees
have pointed out the disadvantages.

These have been clearly summarised by the Committee on
the Acquisition and Valuation of Lands (Great Britain) in its
Third Report, 1919 (Cmd. 156), as follows:

1. Owners unwilling to sell or lease.
2. Owners demanding exorbitant terms.
3. Minerals under copyhold or enfranchised land.

4. Minerals in small separate ownerships.
5. Legal disability of owners.
6. Cases of unknown owners.
7. Difficulties in working arising from surface support.
8. Coal unnecessarily left unworked as barriers.
9. Refusal of owners to grant wayleaves on reasonable terms.
10. Difficulty in obtaining surface powers for working or carrying minerals.
11. Restrictive conditions impeding development of minerals.
12. Onerous conditions of leases.
13. Absence of power to regulate the layout of a mineral field.
14. Loss of minerals in working.

The Mining Industry Commission, 1919, and the Royal Commission on the Coal Industry, 1925, both unanimously recommended the nationalisation of royalties but although legislation has removed some of the wasteful features nothing drastic has yet been done by any British Administration. Apart from the economic benefits of State ownership of coal royalties the psychological effect of the abolition of royalties would be highly salutary. There is no issue connected with the conduct of the industry that rouses a meeting of coal-miners to a higher pitch of indignation than the question of royalties. It has been suggested by Sir Josiah Stamp, who was a member of the Macmillan Board of Enquiry which reported on the Coal Industry in 1925, that the outlay of 100 million or 120 million pounds to "remove this cancer, as it were, from men's minds would be well worth while, because it amounts to far more in the industrial psychology than it is really worth."

The system of royalties is a subject of discussion in the coal-fields of America also. The miners feel strongly about it and many engineers condemn it from the point of view of mining organisation but there is little prospect of its abolition in the United States in the near future. One may venture to predict that State ownership of royalties will be an accomplished fact in Great Britain within the next ten years; in the remote future possibly the United States will follow suit.

ECONOMIC—WAGES, HOURS, UNEMPLOYMENT

Continuing with our comparative study we should with any regard for completeness include a statistical treatment of production, prices, profits, and marketing. But the commercial aspects of the industry have always received adequate attention, at least at the hands of statisticians. There is no lack of material bearing on the commercial branch of the trade—current publications of the Ministry of Mines in Great Britain and of the Bureau of Mines in the United States are especially valuable, in addition to which there is an abundance of statistics published in the trade journals and economic periodicals of the two countries, but this is of immediate interest mainly to business men, and while it is of no less importance to the economist on that account there is little danger of neglect or lack of interest. In any event this study is avowedly more concerned with the social rather than the commercial aspects of the industry. And it is the common experience that reliable data dealing with the social activities of men are more difficult to obtain than, say, the number of tons of coal produced by a certain mine in a certain year. But even confining ourselves to activities susceptible of mathematical computation it is much more difficult to ascertain, say, the average wage of the American miner than the average price of American coal. The system of payment of wages is highly complicated in the coal industry in any event but where some fields are unionised and others are not, the difficulty of getting reliable estimates is increased. The length of the working day also is hedged about with qualifications and modifications. Apart from the difficulties caused by varying additions to and subtractions from the time to be spent underground specified in agreements it is impossible to say that the eight-hour day is universal in the United States because there are fields where a nine-hour and even a ten-hour day prevail. Nor is the problem of unemployment within the industry an easy one to handle statistically. Table 24 of *Coal in 1927* published by the United States Bureau of Mines shews that in 1927 the average number of days worked by the bituminous mines was 191 and by the Pennsylvania anthracite mines was

225, and from Table 21 of the same report the reader may glean that the number of men employed in the bituminous mines in 1927 was 593,918, and in the Pennsylvania anthracite mines 165,259.[1] These figures inform one in a general way about employment and the numbers of miners employed in the industry but when one comes to investigate the amount of unemployment, one is faced with the difficulties that are almost inevitable in the absence of a national system of unemployment insurance.

WAGES

In considering the question of wages it is extremely difficult to compare the average earnings of the British and American miners. There are numerous tables showing the daily rates of pay for contract miners, miners' labourers, the various groups of inside day men and of outside day men working in the industry in America, and in the case of the anthracite field it is possible by multiplying the daily earnings of each grade of worker by the number of days worked in the year to get an idea of the annual earnings. Thus in Table 2 of Horace B. Drury's study of Wages in the Coal Industry[2] the average annual earnings for all employees in the anthracite mines in 1921 are given as $1,605, "as those earnings would figure out if it were possible to add together the earnings of the shifting, as well as the full-year employees; and if the shifting employees worked the entire year, not losing any time between jobs."

The difficulties of shewing the earnings of bituminous miners in the United States are greatly increased by the fact that the mines, unlike the anthracite mines, are scattered over the greater part of the country; and while standards of pay are often uniform for extensive areas there are marked differences in the rates between the North as opposed to the South and the East as opposed to the West. There are also important differences between communities in the average days worked. The most serious difficulties, however, arise from the division between union and

---

[1] In 1929 the numbers were 502,993 and 151,501 respectively and the average numbers of days worked were 219 and 225 respectively.

[2] "Price of Coal," *Annals of the American Academy of Political and Social Science*, January, 1924.

non-union areas. Information about rates in the non-union fields is less complete than about those in the union fields; in any case the rates in the non-union areas are by no means uniform. But the root difficulty lies not so much in the attempt to determine non-union earnings in a given year as in the fact that changes in rates in the non-union and union fields have for several years followed quite different courses; so that it is difficult to say what, over a series of years, have been the respective levels of earnings in the union and non-union areas, and it is perhaps impossible to explain the situation by any one figure.

It is of interest, however, to note some of the figures for 1921 presented by the United States Coal Commission.[1] According to their report 18·4 per cent of the full-time tonnage men in non-union fields and 11·3 per cent in union fields earned less than 900 dollars; 66·6 per cent in the non-union and 54·7 per cent in union fields earned less than 1,500 dollars; 9·7 per cent in non-union fields and 12·7 in union fields earned 2,000 dollars; 3 per cent either in union or non-union districts earned 2,500 dollars or more. The same report shews for full-time day workers in union fields median annual earnings of 1,690 dollars, in non-union fields 1,420 dollars. For the lower quartile of day men, the full-time earnings were 1,320 dollars in the union fields and 1,080 dollars in the non-union fields.

Table 2 on page 135 of the September, 1929, *Labour Review* published by the United States Department of Labour, shews that the average earnings in one half-month (it is not generally known in England that coal miners in America are usually paid not weekly as in England but fortnightly or every half-month) in 1928 for eleven representative States, covering union and non-union fields, were 5·50 dollars ranging from 3·86 dollars in Tennessee to 7·04 dollars in Illinois. If we take this average and multiply it by the average number of days worked in the year, we shall arrive at a rough estimate of the average annual earnings in the bituminous mines. The average number of days worked in 1928 was 203, so the average annual earnings work out at

[1] United States Coal Commission—*Report of Earnings of Bituminous Mine Workers in 1921 with Supplementary Comparison with 1920.* Prepared under the direction of Miss Anne Bezanson of the University of Pennsylvania, assisted by Miss Frances Chalufour and Miss Marian Hussey. (Issued October 3, 1923.)

1,116·5 dollars. This is roughly equivalent in English money to £223 6s. od. a year or £4 6s. od. a week.

The British Ministry of Mines is not beset by so many difficulties arising from wide variations of wages, union and non-union fields and marked differences in the average days worked, but like the Bureau of Mines it shrinks from the attempt to form an estimate of the average wage of the worker in the coal-mining industry for the whole country. It does, however, in its valuable quarterly Statistical Summary, estimate the earnings per man-shift worked, and for the quarter ended December 31, 1928, it gives for the first time the value of allowances in kind per man-shift worked. The earnings per shift, 9s. 2·84d. *plus* the value of allowances in kind 4·82d. make up the remuneration of 9s. 7d. per man-shift worked. The total number of shifts worked was 54,226,527; the number of workpeople employed was 850,770. Multiplying the 9s. 7d. by the number of shifts worked per man (roughly 63) we get as the annual wage £120 14s. od. and as the weekly wage £2 6s. 5d.

The American estimate, based on a half-month period and the British estimate, based on a quarterly period, are obviously lacking in exactness and cannot be accepted even in their rough form as representative over a long period, but it has seemed desirable to attempt a broad, general comparison between the wages of American and British miners. So far as the author knows, this has not been attempted before and he is aware of the objections to any attempt to institute a comparison by reference to any one figure for each country, but despite the difficulties and objections it may be hoped that this attempt is not altogether without value. Many people have asked the question, "How do the wages in the coal industry in the two countries compare?" To answer the question at all adequately, one would need to go into the inquiry over a considerable period and compare, say, the pre-war wages with those of last year, taking note of fluctuations during and since the war, and also compare the wages of each specific occupation within the industry or even within each field in the two countries. But without attempting that almost impossible task and in accordance with his plan of dispensing with tables as far as possible, the author ventures to offer these two estimates as being fairly reliable for all practical purposes for the year 1928.

I

Let us say then that the average money wages of the American coal-digger are eighty-six shillings (£4 6s. od.) a week and those of the English coal-miner about forty-six shillings (£2 6s. od.) a week. This is in the ratio of 43 to 23.

But it would be misleading to say on the basis of this ratio that the American miner is almost twice as well off as the British miner. Account must be taken first of the difference in consumers' satisfaction from social services. In the Pennsylvania anthracite region and in certain parts of the unionised fields, e.g. Central and Southern Illinois, the miner as citizen enjoys the benefit of municipalised services like schools, libraries museums, recreation parks, etc., because these districts have for some time been unionised and settled, and in towns like Scranton or Wilkes-Barre in Pennsylvania and Belleville, Illinois, miners are to be found holding office on the local government bodies just as one finds in every coalfield in Great Britain. But in the bituminous non-union fields of the United States the miners are dependent almost entirely on the local operator for anything in the way of social services other than the provision of roads, water supply and schools, and even these in many cases are supplied or controlled by the coal company. The British miner, generally speaking, lives in a house over which the company for which he works has no control, enjoys the usual health and transportation municipal services everywhere, whether he lives in a small mining village or in a large urban district, sends his children to the elementary school, never far away and invariably built and entirely supported by the appropriate local authority; in many cases he himself attends evening classes in technical subjects that will improve him as a miner or in non-vocational studies like economics, economic history, psychology, music or literature —all conducted by public authorities or the local university or some labour organisation; makes use of public libraries, museums, art galleries, parks and other services provided by the municipality. Then there are State services, such as health and unemployment insurance benefits, old age pensions, maternity benefits, clinics, etc. It is impossible to assess the value of these benefits in money terms but there is no question that the British miner is much better off so far as this kind of satisfaction is concerned. Americans find it difficult to realise the value attached by the British coal-miner to municipal services, especially those of an educational and cultural character. A few years ago, one of the author's students, a bright, well-educated miner of about thirty years of age, who was keenly interested in economic problems, politics and trade union organisation as well as Rugby football, left South Wales after being unemployed for about a year and went to the United States where he worked in the mines for several months, earning much higher wages than he had earned in Wales when in employment. He wrote home glowing accounts of the "big money" he was making, but in his letters to the author he spoke somewhat wistfully of the lack of classes in social science "like ours" and remarked that the miners "out here" were not much interested in politics or economics and spent most of their spare time in "riding round" and "going to the movies." It came as a surprise however when he returned to South Wales where he now keeps a small shop (stores) in his native mining village. He confessed to a feeling of home-sickness but said that he would not have returned on that account alone. The reason he returned, he declared, was that he "could enjoy life much better at home and get more out of it—money isn't everything you know"— and it was interesting to hear that what he missed most in America were "the classes in Economics" and political meetings.

This is an exceptional case, and there are many excellent coal-diggers in America of a similar type, but the type is much more common in Great Britain, especially in South Wales, the North of England, and Scotland, than in the United States, and it is important to realise that the "imponderables" are the essence of life to a large proportion of British miners. Higher wages alone will not tempt them to emigrate. Where they do, the results are often disillusioning. In the course of his investigation in West Virginia, the author was told of a young Scotsman who had comparatively recently come over from Glasgow. It seems he started working underground but through a relative he was given a job as clerk in the colliery office at a salary of 1,750 dollars (£350) a year. Unexpectedly our paths crossed a second time and on being pressed—he had to be very careful of what he said— he assured the author that he bitterly regretted having left Glasgow, although he was earning only £3 (15 dollars) a week there as a railway clerk, and he was longing to go back. The tears welled up as he spoke of the loneliness of the life of himself, his wife and kiddie. The suggestion that the lonely feeling would gradually wear off and that, after all, he could afford to spend a little on recreation met with scant consideration. He said there was hardly anything worth while spending money on. He had an automobile, but you soon got tired of running round the same old places and the pictures weren't worth seeing. The only real pleasure he got was from books, but the nearest "decent" library was thirty miles away and he couldn't afford to buy many of the kind of books he wanted; he was saving up with the idea of returning to Scotland, but his uncle knew how much he had saved, and was disgusted at the very notion of his wishing to return to Scotland "where everybody was so poor." The young fellow felt under an obligation to his uncle, but was obviously over-awed by him and generally most unhappy. He complained of a lack of freedom and whispered hoarsely as his uncle came to take me off, "It's like being in a prison!"

Much has been said and written on the relative advantage enjoyed by American miners in the way of opportunities for extra-occupational earnings, particularly by farming. It is true that the British miners are almost entirely dependent on their earnings at the mine, but the author strongly suspected that reports of extra earnings by American coal-miners were exaggerated; at any rate he found little proof of it in Pennsylvania, Illinois, West Virginia or Alabama. The conclusion of Dr. Edward T. Devine, who was a member of the United States Coal Commission (1923), is interesting and important. In his book, *Coal*, he writes:

"Nor is it as if there were supplementary earnings on any large scale either by the miners or by other members of the family. There is not, in fact, much opportunity for them to turn to other work in their free time. Here and there a few work at farming or road building when the mines are idle. Generally speaking, however, such sources of supplementary income are not to be relied upon. Miners and their families for the most part live on the earnings at the mine and what they cannot get from those earnings they go without."

Another factor to be taken into account in the general comparison of the economic lot of the two sets of coal-miners, is the difference in the cost of living. Here again no exhaustive comparison has been made. It is doubtful if any absolutely reliable comparison in the cost of living in any two countries can be made, and the difficulties are increased in the case of the British and

American miners by the fact that Great Britain has no company-owned mining towns, and, therefore, no differences between prices in company-owned and those in independent communities as in the United States. Much has been done in the way of comparison of prices in company stores and those in independent stores. The section on "Cost of Living and Prices" by Bertha M. Nienburg in the 1923 Commission Report contains some interesting and valuable data on American conditions. The author himself makes no attempt to institute a comparison between the cost of living in the two national mining populations and has not sufficient data to form an independent comparison of prices in company commissaries and in independent stores. He also realises the danger of unsupported generalisations but as the result of his inquires in the various coalfields he would say that, whereas the rents paid for company houses are lower than those paid in individual communities, and coal and medical attention cost less, the prices of articles of food and clothing are appreciably higher, ranging from 5 to 10 per cent in company-controlled communities. Strictly, we should compare the relative qualities of houses, food and clothing. Without attempting to appraise articles of food and clothing, the view may be expressed that on the whole the standard of housing is higher in Great Britain, not forgetting the purple patches in America and the black patches in some of the British coalfields; the buildings are more solid and sewage disposal methods, general sanitation and water supply are much better, though, on the other hand, the American houses are more generously spaced—there is nothing of the back-to-back and not much in the way of the houses-in-a-row arrangements which still characterise certain British mining districts. Incidentally, the insecurity of tenure of the miners living in company houses is an element to be taken into account and as about half of the bituminous mine-workers' families live in company patches, it is an important element, particularly in view of the fact that when a mine-worker loses or gives up his job "for any cause whatsoever," he loses the right to occupy his house from the day he ceases to work. There are also certain restrictions, according to some leases, which the British miner, accustomed to control over his own premises, would find irksome, if not intolerable, e.g. that the mine-worker must not entertain or harbour upon the premises persons objectionable to the company, and that neither lodgers nor boarders can be taken into the mine-worker's family without the operator's consent, unless such boarders or lodgers work for the company.

The difficulties of comparing the cost of living first of miners living in company-controlled and those in self-controlled communities in America, and then of comparing an average of the two estimates with an estimate for the British miners are sufficiently obvious. But it is generally believed by those most competent to judge that the cost of living in mining communities is at least as high as the average for a country as a whole. This is almost certainly true of the two countries under consideration; indeed one might safely conclude that the cost of living in the mining districts of both countries is higher than the national average.[1] But for our purpose we will take the national average as being applicable to mining communities. We now require an acceptable estimate of the relative cost of living in the two countries. The most recent investigation to come under the author's notice is that of the American National Industrial Conference Board made in 1929. From this it would seem that the cost of living in America is nearly twice as high as the cost of living in England. Accepting this comparative estimate we are forced to the somewhat startling conclusion that even from a strictly financial standpoint the American bituminous mine-worker is no better off than the British miner. Money wages being in the ratio of 43 to 23 and the cost of living being nearly double there is no balance in favour of the American miner. This conclusion is so different from what one would be inclined to expect as the result of stories, published and unpublished, of high wages, automobiles, radios, ownership of houses, etc., that it will probably be subjected to a good deal of criticism; and in view of the serious difficulties in the way of an absolutely reliable comparison it is naturally of a highly tentative character, but it is offered with a full sense of responsibility as being substantially valid and trustworthy.

[1] The United States Coal Commission furnish an interesting illustration, which the author can confirm from his own experience. It found that prices of food were higher in Scranton and Wilkes-Barre (two large anthracite towns in Pennsylvania) than in working-class neighbourhoods in Philadelphia and Pittsburg on the same date: 10 per cent and 11·2 per cent respectively. In the small anthracite towns where they were lowest they were 3·5 per cent higher than in Philadelphia, 4·8 per cent higher than in Pittsburg.

The author has visited some homes of mine-workers in America that are finer than any he knows in Great Britain; on the other hand he has seen some mining shacks in West Virginia and Alabama and even in Pennsylvania which are worse than anything in the way of housing to be seen in British mining communities. He has discovered some men at work in American mines tending machines who earned as much as 9 dollars in a day; he has also talked with many men who were working "short-time" and others who had been unemployed for two months who were far more miserable and dispirited than many British miners of his acquaintance who have been out of work continuously for four or five years. (When a British miner is unemployed he has at least the unemployment insurance benefit to fall back upon; the American unemployed miner has to rely on what he can "pick up" or upon private charity, and when one contrasts the two types one can hardly resist a smile at all the talk of the demoralising effects of the "dole.") The somewhat loose generalisation has been made that the American miner is better off than the British miner when he is working but worse off when he is not. Relying upon hearsay the author was inclined to accept this as being an acceptable judgment, but personal impressions and the relevant data he has been able to use have caused him to distrust it. The American coal-digger is certainly worse off when he is unemployed; he is not better off even when he is working.

If then we conclude that the American miner is no better off financially we can say very definitely that he is much worse off if we extend the comparison to include the value of social services, civic rights, economic freedom and political independence.

HOURS

A comparison of the length of the working day is not so complicated, though the simple statement that now the eight-hour day prevails in both countries requires considerable modification and amplification. And always it is to be remembered that owing to its relatively small size and its complete unionisation the British Coal industry normally has a more uniform working day over the whole country than is the case in the United States.

In England the eight-hour Law was enacted in 1908. This continued on the Statute Book till 1919 when as a result of the recommendation of Mr. Justice Sankey,[1] Chairman of the Coal Industry Commission, the Government enacted a seven-hour Law. The most recent change was made in 1926 when the Government submitted legislation to Parliament extending the permissible hours of employment underground from seven to eight. This is not the place to recount the dramatic story of the miners' resolute fight against the threatened loss of the seven-hour day, about which many of them felt more keenly even than about a reduction in wages. It is common knowledge that they lost the fight and that the eight-hour law made legally possible the formulation of a wage agreement on the basis of an eight-hour day. In fact, the eight-hour shift became general for underground labourers, though the Yorkshire, Nottingham and Derbyshire coalfield by district agreement (the miners having lost on the issue of the national agreement) work a seven-and-a-half hour shift. There are variations in the number of hours worked by surface labourers, according to local agreements, ranging from 45 to 46½ per week in two of the smaller fields to 51½ in two other small fields, but in all the larger important fields, the weekly hours are 48 or 49. The hours for underground workers include meal-times; those for surface workers usually exclude meal-times. The hours for underground workers are reckoned from the time the last man in the shift leaves the surface to the time the first man returns to the surface. It should be added that in many districts, by local agreement, the shift worked on Saturday is less than eight hours. The miners' love of football is probably mainly responsible for such arrangements. If they cannot themselves play, and the facilities in mining areas are severely limited, they take their sport "by proxy" and flock in thousands to the nearest large town to see a first-class "soccer" or "rugger" match; large numbers of them being quite willing when times are good to lose a shift in order to make sure of seeing the game. If anyone is inclined to regard this as a sign of decadence, let him reflect that for thousands of miners this is almost the only bit of recreation they have in the week, at any rate, in the open air. Incidentally, the author saw more drinking at a Harvard–Yale football game than he has ever seen in a football crowd in Great Britain.

To return to the working day, 1926 virtually meant the restoration of the eight-hour day in England. The present Labour

[1] Now Lord Sankey, Lord Chancellor.

Government contemplates a return to the seven-hour day, though a seven-and-a-half-hour day will probably be as much as it can achieve during its present term of office.[1]

In the United States the eight-hour day in bituminous mining has been in effect in a large percentage of the mines for about thirty years. Section 5 of the Chicago (1898) agreement between the miners and operators of the central competitive field states:

"That on and after April 1, 1898, the eight-hour work day, with eight hours' pay, consisting of six days per week, shall be in effect in all the districts represented, and that uniform wages for day labor shall be paid the different prices of labor in the fields named."

The eight-hour day mines employed 56·4 per cent of the total number of wage earners in bituminous coal-mining in 1903. This percentage increased to 64 in 1907, decreased to 58·6 in 1916, increased to 79 in 1917, to 90·6 in 1918, to 95·5 in 1919, to 97·1 in 1920, the highest percentage during the period, and then decreased from year to year to 93·7 per cent in 1924. From figures published by the Bureau of Mines, the percentage works out at 91·2 in 1928.

In 1903, the percentage of employees in nine-hour day mines was 17·1. This decreased by 1920 to 2·0 and increased to 5·1 in 1924 and to 5·9 in 1928.

In ten-hour day mines the percentage decreased from 26·5 in 1903 to 0·9 in 1920 and to 0·5 in 1921, and increased to 1·2 in 1924. The figures for 1928 shew a reduction to 0·76 per cent. In the anthracite field the eight-hour day is the rule.

The tendency, as will be seen, is in the direction of an increase in nine-hour day mines, and a decrease in ten-hour day mines. Of the 4,087 men returned as employed in ten-hour mines, more than half (2,230) work in the Alabama field; 447 in Tennessee; 432 in West Virginia; and 377 in Kentucky—States in which there is little or no unionisation. It is regrettable enough that four thousand men should be working ten hours a day in coal-mines, but more serious still is the fact that 31,323 are returned as working in nine-hour mines, and it is significant that 15,560 of these (about 50 per cent) are also employed in Alabama. It

[1] This was written in 1930. The "National" Government, elected in 1931, has taken no action with regard to hours, which are still governed by the Act of 1926.

seems unfortunate that an eight-hour day cannot be enforced over the whole of the United States, especially in view of the fact that over a period of thirty years bituminous coal miners have on an average lost ninety-five days a year. This average means employment for 70 per cent of the normal working year and unpaid enforced unemployment for 30 per cent.

In discussing the length of the working day in America it is necessary to distinguish between the established working day and the time actually spent at work. As interpreted in the Union Wage Agreements, the eight-hour day means eight hours of labour at the usual working place, exclusive of time for lunch and exclusive of time spent in going from the entrance of the mine to the working place and back again. In general, this provision applies both to piece workers and day-wage workers underground, though certain classes of day-men have duties to be performed outside the eight hours. Motormen and drivers are ordinarily required to take motors and mules in their own time to and from the stables and the parting or station where they begin hauling, and this time is not counted as part of the day's labour. On the other hand, although the wage agreements specify eight hours of labour it does not follow that men are always at work eight hours in the day. Shortage of railroad cars at the tipple, lack of orders, a petty strike, or a breakdown within the mine may cause it to stop work before the eight hours are over. Time-workers may lose fractional days through sickness or accident. In particular, the tonnage men, who constitute 40 to 70 per cent of the working force, may leave before the mine as a whole stops work because the custom of the industry allows them that freedom. Sometimes they may leave because they have finished their allotted work for the day, sometimes because they feel sick or have other interests to attend to, or sometimes simply because they have earned enough for one day. The nominal working day, therefore, measures neither the length of time spent by the men at work, nor the length of time they are underground.

The differences between the two countries in respect of hours may be summed up in the general statement that until 1926 British miners worked seven and American miners eight hours a day. Now the great majority in both countries work eight hours, with a slight tendency in the United States towards a nine-hour day in the non-unionised fields and a prospect in Great Britain of a return to the seven-and-a-half-hour day and later possibly to the seven-hour day. Mr. Justice Sankey in his report in 1919 recommended that a six-hour day be instituted at the end of 1920 if the economic position of the industry justified it, and the British miners have their mind set on the six-hour day, but it is probable that the next important change will be in the direction of an international arrangement on the question of hours and this would mean the postponement of the six-hour day for a considerable time. In the United States there seems to be a distinct prospect of a six-hour day and a five-day week in some industries in the near future, but the coal industry is hardly likely to be one of them, though it is interesting to note that in 1919 the United Mine Workers formulated a demand for it and shewed that it represented the thirty hours per week which the bituminous coal-mines of the country had averaged in the preceding year.

A reduction in hours of work in the coal industry would be a significant step towards raising the standard of leisure in mining communities. Incidentally, it would help to ease the problem of unemployment within the industry. One of the reasons advanced by the Royal Commission of 1925 against the longer working day was "that perhaps 130,000 men would be added to the numbers unemployed."

UNEMPLOYMENT

The difficulty of ascertaining the volume of unemployment in the United States in the absence of a national system of unemployment insurance has already been referred to. In Great Britain coal-mining is included under the Unemployment Insurance Act so that miners in a position to claim benefit leave their unemployment books at the Employment Exchanges and are returned as unemployed. There is no lack of statistics relating to the volume of employment, collateral employment and labour turnover in the United States coal-mining industry, but the extent of unemployment is difficult to estimate. Dr. O. E. Kiessling,[1] of the Bureau of Mines, estimates that between 1923 and 1928 about 183,000 men lost their jobs; that 2,900 mines were closed down and 210 million tons of mine capacity abandoned. He adds that in spite of the fact that a certain amount of slack has been

[1] In a statement prepared for the Harvard Economic Service.

taken up, the number of days worked in the bituminous mines in 1928 was 203 out of a potential working year of 308 days. Unfortunately, these figures do not provide an adequate basis for comparison. The fact that 183,000 men lost their jobs between 1923 and 1928 gives no indication of the number unemployed in any one year of the period. The fact that the average number of days worked in 1928 was 203 is significant as shewing the comparison with the numbers for preceding years, e.g. 191 for 1927; 215 for 1926; 179 for 1923; and 232 for 1913. The fact that the average number of days worked in the Pennsylvania anthracite mines in 1928 was 217 indicates that they were working 14 days more than the bituminous mines in that year but 8 days fewer than the anthracite mines in 1927 (225). The figures shewing the number of employees in the different years are more helpful. For instance, the fact that the total employed in 1927 was 759,177 (bituminous 593,918; anthracite 165,259), compared with 682,831 (bituminous 522,150; anthracite 160,681) in 1928, clearly shews a reduction in men employed in bituminous mines of 71,768 in the year 1927–28 and of 4,578 in the anthracite field —a total reduction of employees in the whole industry for the year of 76,346, about 10 per cent. By comparing the figures for each two-year period, we can follow the fluctuations in the volume of employment. An exhaustive and inclusive estimate, however, would be a difficult and highly complicated undertaking. The union officials can give figures only for the unionised fields; and for the non-union fields there are difficulties in getting complete figures, especially in those districts where there are several very small mines. Then there is the difficulty arising from discrepancies between State and Federal estimates of unemployment. These difficulties are peculiar to the United States. The author has relied almost entirely on figures published by the Bureau of Mines but he realises that they have to be used judiciously and with caution.

The numbers of unemployed in the British Coalfields shewed marked fluctuations between 1920 and 1925 when unemployment in most of the other industries shewed a steady increase. By May, 1922, for instance, the unemployed who in the preceding November had numbered 157,000 fell to 86,800. Owing to a four months' strike in the American coalfields, British coal which previously had hardly been known to American consumers was imported into the ports of Canada and the United States to the extent of 4 million tons. By the end of the year 1922, the number of registered unemployed was down to 56,000.

The occupation of the Ruhr also gave a temporary stimulus to the export trade. The production of German coal was reduced by over 70 million tons. This meant not only that German consumers were deprived of their fuel supply, but also that the 17 million tons of reparation coal received in the preceding year by France, Italy and Belgium had to be in large part replaced from foreign sources. The natural source was Great Britain and throughout 1923 and early 1924 the British coal industry prospered. The number of men employed steadily increased and by May, 1924, 1,193,700 men were employed in the pits. But as the Royal Commission of 1925 pointed out, the depression which had overtaken other British industries in 1920 had been "lying in wait for the coal-mining industry, but had been warded off by a series of accidents." Certain forces calculated to reduce the regular demand for coal were relentlessly at work and when the results of the last of these accidental factors had disappeared, and the British industry was no longer "helped by the temporary cessation of some normal supplies" it found itself confronted with difficulties which could hardly have failed to come upon it three years earlier.

The forces which shattered the hopes of the coal trade continued to exert their influence with cumulative effect throughout the winter of 1924–25, and conditions had reached such a pass by July, 1925, that 315,000 miners were out of work.

The year 1926 was an abnormal year. From May to November Great Britain was in the throes of one of the greatest industrial struggles in its history. First the whole country was caught up for nine days in the excitement and dislocation of the so-called General Strike, when about 1,500,000 workers, other than miners, left their jobs in sympathy with the 850,000 miners who were resisting the demands of the owners for a reduction of wages, a lengthening of hours and the break-up of the national into district agreements. It was actually more in the nature of a sympathetic suspension of work than a general strike, because at no time was the shutting down of all industry contemplated. The industries directly involved were the transport, iron and steel, building, electricity and gas, and printing trades. In the building trade exceptions were made for those employed on housing and hospital work. Sanitary services were to be continued and there was to be no interference with health and food services. It is true other trades were to be called out later as a "second line of attack" if the General Council saw fit to do so but what was intended by the Trade Union leaders was a short suspension of certain essential services.

From the time the "General Strike" was called off till the end of November the coal industry was paralysed by the struggles which the miners continued to wage, and British industry generally was in a chaotic condition. Work in the coal-mines, except for safety men, practically ceased, and the unemployed outside the coal industry were increased by over 250,000.

As the autumn approached and it was obvious that the Miners' Federation was fighting a losing battle, large numbers of men went back to work in accordance with district agreements, especially in Nottinghamshire and Derbyshire. Efforts to stem the tide proved of little avail and by late November some 400,000 men were back at work.

The end of the stoppage brought immediate activity to the coalfields. Both domestic and foreign demand stimulated production after the seven months' suspension and a year later, November 26, 1927, there were 978,535 men on the colliery books. The industry was working far short of full capacity however, and the unemployed numbered 221,702, i.e. 18·5 per cent of insured persons in the industry. Of these 139,188 were wholly unemployed and 82,514 were temporarily stopped. The percentage of unemployed was 3·2 higher than it was two years before.

On November 24, 1928, the number on the colliery books was 896,214, a reduction in the year of more than 80,000 men. The unemployed numbered 282,293 (176,947 wholly unemployed, 105,346 temporary stoppages), an increase of more than 60,000. The percentage unemployed of insured persons was 25·3 as compared with 18·5 a year before. The figures obviously indicate that the industry, after the temporary spurt in making good the cessation of production in 1926, has steadily lost ground.

The position has grown progressively worse since. In Great Britain by 1932 the number of miners unemployed, wholly and temporarily stopped, had amounted to more than 350,000. At the beginning of 1934 the figure stood at 370,000. In the United States bituminous industry the index number of employment, as reported to the Bureau of Labor Statistics, fell from 106·8 in March, 1929, to 75·2 in March, 1932. In the anthracite industry it fell from 100 in 1929 to 73·7 in March, 1932.

One interesting comparison emerges from these figures which will probably surprise many people who seem to be under the impression that conditions in the American Coal industry are a great deal better than they are in the British industry. As we have seen there was a reduction in the number employed in American mines in 1927–28 of 76,346 from the 1927 figure of 759,177. In the corresponding period in Great Britain there was a reduction of 82,321 from the 1927 figure of 978,535. This means that there were nearly 6,000 more miners thrown out of work in Great Britain during the year, but that there were nearly 220,000 more men employed in the industry in 1927 in Great Britain. So that proportionately there were more men laid off in the American coal industry in that year (not an abnormal year in either country) than in the British industry. This was probably due in part to the larger use of machinery but its broad significance is that the industry in America is by no means immune from the influence of the same forces that are at work in Europe—competition of substitutes, e.g. oil, hydro-electricity, greater economy in the use of coal, etc.

ETHNIC COMPOSITION OF MINING POPULATION

At a certain colliery in the Pennsylvania Anthracite coalfield the author found at work men of the following nationalities: Lithuanian, Polish, Russian, Italian, German, Welsh, English, Irish, Scottish, Negro, Serbian, Austrian, Dutch and American (native-born). In some of the western mines there are Japanese and Mexicans. Where else in the world than America would one find such a racial variety in the coal-mining population? There is a wider ethnic range in some American coalfields than others. One encounters more different foreign-born types in Pennsylvania, for instance, than in Illinois, which is predominantly native white, or in Alabama where more than 50 per cent of the labour is coloured. But in every American coalfield, except perhaps in Alabama, where less than 4 per cent of the mine-workers are foreign born, an Englishman is impressed by the foreign accent of so many of the men, even of those who speak English fluently. And a great many speak English, as the Scotsman jokes, "wi' difficulty". One remembers a certain Polish foreman at an iron ore mine who had to give instructions on the telephone underground. His English was halting, broken, and to an Englishman, almost unintelligibly "foreign." But apparently the officials to whom he was speaking understood him easily for they carried out his instructions without mishap. The engineer did not think that mining hazards were increased by speech difficulties—"the other fellows could understand all right"—though he was emphatic that inability to read was fraught with an element of danger. Everywhere one goes one almost involuntarily contrasts the heterogeneity of American mine-workers with the homogeneity of British miners. An American miner once put it this way: "We are a mixture of Polaks, Hunkies, Dagoes and God knows what; you are all British aren't you?"

It is true that the influx of foreign labour to the British coalfields has been very slight. Even the flow of labour from one coalfield to another, owing to variations in geological conditions and in mining technique, has rarely reached appreciable proportions. To fields where wages were relatively high there was a flow of specialised labour, even in the early days of coal-mining. For instance, in 1697 Sir Humphrey Mackworth, being unable to work the Gnoll Colliery (in South Wales) with local men, imported a large number of skilled miners by road and canal from the coalfields of Shropshire and Staffordshire.[1] About the year 1800 Lord Dudley attempted to introduce into Staffordshire some thirty colliers from the Tyne, a riot broke out and his collieries were threatened with destruction.[2] And when in 1832, attracted by the opportunity of earning in two days as much as they could earn in a week in the lead-mines, sixty "groovers" moved from West Durham to Walbridge, the colliers stopped the engine and threw corves and tubs down the shaft when the groovers were below.[3] But such instances of migration were uncommon. Heredity has always been a large factor in the occupation of coal-mining; for the rest the recruitment has been made principally from the ranks of agricultural workers, lead-miners, quarrymen and navvies, though men of all trades are to be met with in British mines. An interesting wave of migration was the movement of large numbers of Irishmen to the coalfields of Scotland and the West of England between 1815 and the middle of the century. Their descendants have worked in these coalfields since and many of them are to be found to-day in Pennsylvania holding executive positions in the coal trade. Political and agrarian persecution and economic depression in Ireland have contributed valuable elements to the human stock of Scottish, Welsh and American coalfields.

Rarely however has there been any organised effort to introduce "foreign" labour into British coalfields. The principal examples are in Scotland where there were colonies of Germans and Poles, working in pits largely apart from the Scottish miners. Such colonisation was attempted to a small extent both in Durham and South Wales many years ago and for some time there were in South Wales in two or three localities a considerable proportion of Italians and Spaniards.[4] Their descendants are now for the most part café keepers, who serve out drinks and sandwiches

[1] Wilkins, *The South Wales Coal Trade*, p. 28.
[2] Edington, *Essay on the Coal Trade* (1803).
[3] *Report on the Trial of Pitmen for the Riot at Walbridge Colliery*, Newcastle local pamphlets.
[4] H. S. Jevons, *The British Coal Trade*, p. 623.

K

to the younger generation of miners in the evenings. With the
growth of trade unionism in Great Britain any organised introduction of foreign labour became impossible. Broadly speaking
the coalfields of Great Britain have always been manned by
people of English, Welsh, Scottish or Irish nationality. There
are differences—physical, temperamental and linguistic—among
these four nationalities, but compared with the tremendous
variations of race and language in the American coalfields they
seem so slight that a foreigner would experience some difficulty
in detecting them. Even an Englishman when investigating
American coalfields thinks of the miners of Great Britain as being
practically of one type. But when he returns home after spending
a year or two in American coalfields he thinks of American mine-
workers as a veritable melting-pot! So it is, relatively. And yet
a study of the facts serves to correct the impression that American
mine-workers are only "a mixture of Polaks, Hunkies and
Dagoes."

The report of the United States Coal Commission by Miss
Marie L. Obenauer, 1925, contains sections on the mine-workers
(bituminous and anthracite) and their environment that are a
mine of interesting and important information. The following
facts are extracted from those sections of the report. It appears
that nearly 60 per cent of the bituminous mine-workers are native-
born white; another 8 per cent are coloured natives, and rather
less than a third are foreign born. Of the foreign-born, Italy,
Austria, Poland and the British Isles, in the order named, furnish
the largest number of recruits to the industry. These are the
figures for the half-million or more bituminous mine-workers
but they do not shew the prevailing racial characteristics in the
various coal regions. In Pennsylvania, for example, over 55 per
cent are foreign born, and an insignificant number are native
coloured. In Alabama less then 4 per cent of the mine-workers
are foreign born and 53 per cent are coloured natives. The native
white mine-workers predominate in West Virginia, Indiana,
Ohio, Illinois and in the other central Western States.

Nearly 70 per cent of the foreign-born bituminous mine-
workers had been in America for ten years or more in 1920,
and more than 90 per cent had been five years or more. While
the proportions of foreign born among the mine-workers in each
section of the country differ conspicuously, the proportion in

each section whose residence in the United States exceeds five years presents few variations. On the other hand, the numbers of foreign born who have been in America fifteen years or more differ sharply in the several coal States.

Twenty-six per cent of the total number of foreign-born mine-workers in 1920 were naturalised, 16·9 had taken out first citizen-ship papers, and 51·7 were alien (the status of 5·2 per cent not being reported). Here again, figures for all the mine-workers taken together fail to represent the civic status of the foreign born engaged in the bituminous mines of Illinois, where 42 per cent were naturalised, 21 per cent had first papers and 31 per cent were alien; and of Pennsylvania, where 22·6 per cent were naturalised, 14·1 per cent had first papers and 59·7 per cent were alien. In West Virginia less then 10 per cent of the 18,500 foreign mine-workers were naturalised, 9·2 per cent had taken out first papers and 74·8 per cent were still alien in 1920, the status of the other 6 per cent being unknown.

Turning to the anthracite field we find that of the 147,500 workers, 78,000 or about 53 per cent are foreign born, 42,000 coming from Russia and Poland. Almost 97 per cent of the foreign born have been in America five years or over. More than 34,000 or 44 per cent of the foreign born were still alien in 1920. Less than a thousand of these were under eighteen years of age, the age at which first papers can be taken. An additional 10,500 of the foreign born had taken out first papers only, so that less than half of all the anthracite mine-workers born overseas were American citizens in 1920.

Poles are the largest single foreign language group, totalling more than 50,000 men in 1920. The great majority live in Penn-sylvania and there are many more in the anthracite than in the bituminous mines. Polish miners work also in the mines of West Virginia, Illinois, Ohio and other States. On one occasion when the author was making a tour of a part of the anthracite field in the company of one of the United Mine Workers' officials we got out of the car to talk with a small group of miners who were basking in the sun. One of the men was introduced as Mr. David Jones. In appearance he was utterly unlike any Welsh miner known to the author and his heavy "foreign" accent betrayed him. He turned out to be a Pole! "Meet Mr. David Jones!" In American coalfields the name is often a misleading label of the man.

Italian miners are almost as numerous as the Poles and have gone further inland in larger numbers than the Poles. In 1920 some 10,000 were in the anthracite field, 17,000 in the bituminous section of Pennsylvania, 8,000 in Illinois and about 5,000 in West Virginia.

Austrians and Slovaks are found chiefly in Pennsylvania bituminous but also in the anthracite; Russians and Lithuanians chiefly in the anthracite; Hungarians chiefly in Pennsylvania bituminous and West Virginia; Yugoslavians chiefly in Pennsylvania (both sections); and Mexicans chiefly in Colorado and the South West.

Foreign-born workers have not only dug most of the American coal produced during the past hundred years; they have also played an important part in the struggles of the mine-workers. British miners, fresh from union membership in their own country, took the lead in organising the miners in America in the 'sixties and 'seventies. Hungarians, Italians, Poles and Slovaks have taken an active part in the bitterly fought strikes of more recent times.

Closely allied with the racial mixture is the element of illiteracy. A large proportion of immigrants from central and eastern European countries to the American coalfields were unable to speak English and a still larger proportion could neither read nor write any language when they first landed in the United States. Bearing this important fact in mind, one is able to realise to some extent the stupendous task it must have been to reduce illiteracy to its present proportions. Much remains to be done but the results already achieved are quite remarkable. Of the total number of bituminous mine-workers 87·9 per cent now both read and write, the percentage ranging from 83·8 in West Virginia to 96·9 in Indiana. In the light of mining hazard, however, the 11 per cent of the total who neither read nor write, ranging from 2·8 in Indiana to 14·9 per cent in West Virginia, assumes significance. Of the total foreign born from other than English-speaking countries, 22·8 per cent neither read nor write and 12·7 per cent do not speak English. The position is rather worse among the anthracite workers, due presumably to the much larger proportion of foreign born in the mining population generally. Over 29 per cent neither read nor write, and 14 per cent of those coming from non-English speaking countries do not speak English.

The elimination of illiteracy is desirable on broad social grounds, and in America particularly so because inability to read, write and speak English is a stumbling-block in the path towards assimilation. Illiteracy increases industrial hazard and adds to the difficulty of safety work; it is an obvious danger to have men underground who cannot read warnings, instructions, regulations, etc. Organisers of mine-workers also complain that their task is made much more difficult by the racial and language problem. Englishmen who have organised mine-workers in England and in America testify that in the States it is "a much tougher proposition" to build up the union, apart from other considerations, because of the illiteracy and racial mixture of the men. This is a problem that hardly exists in Great Britain. Not only has it a homogeneous mining population; it has also an instructed body of miners and it is a rare thing to-day to find a British miner who can neither read nor write.

ORGANISATION OF EMPLOYERS AND EMPLOYED

Reference was made in the preceding section to the difficulties in the way of organising the mine-workers due to illiteracy. Some attention must now be given to the more general aspects of the organisation of miners and mine-owners, or mine-workers and operators, in the two countries.

ORGANISATION OF MINERS IN GREAT BRITAIN

The outstanding protagonist organisations in the coal industry in Great Britain are the Miners' Federation of Great Britain, established in 1888, and the Mining Association of Great Britain, formed by the owners in 1854. But though the Miners' Federation was not created till 1888 there were miners' organisations much earlier. These early organisations were local and geographical in character. The Miners' Federation itself, as its name implies, is no more than a federation of the district associations, each related to a county as in the case of England, to a country as in the case of Scotland, to a region as in the case of South Wales. Each district organisation possesses complete autonomy in administrative and financial matters, and is free to act independently of any other district. It has the power within its rules to engage in local strikes, to make independent representations to Government departments and generally to take any action whatsoever in the interest of their district membership. In practice this local autonomy is rarely exercised. Strikes, for example, tend to become less of a district or local and more of a national character. It is, however, in these district groupings that the origin and development of trade unionism among the miners of Great Britain is to be found.

Like many other English trade unions the Miners' Trade Union came into being in consequence of the terrible conditions of employment which existed at the dawn of the industrial revolution. The earliest traces of miners' organisations are to be found in the counties of Northumberland and Durham. Their grievances as to wages were localised in character; even their revolts against the lack of adequate safeguards of life and limb were confined to small groups of men and to definite localities. In the early stages of the industrial revolution coal-miners were in a state of practical serfdom. In the Scottish coalfields serfdom persisted until the year 1799 when it was finally abolished by Act of Parliament. In those days there were no Factory Acts and there was therefore no legislation to enforce the protection of the miner from the ever-present dangers of his calling. There were no laws as at present for the regulation of the sex and age of those working in the mine. In those days men, women and children earned their living in the bowels of the earth. The conditions under which they worked were little short of slavery. Tiny children, too frail to stand the fatigue of walking to the place of their labour underground, were often carried to it on the backs of their fathers or mothers. Accidents were numerous; explosions occurred with great force, and frequently. Although the collieries were small, compared with modern collieries, it was no rare thing for as many men to be killed in one explosion as in the case of the bigger collieries to-day. Previous to 1814 no inquests on miners killed underground were held; fatalities were considered to be inevitable, and because of the absence of public criticism of the conduct of colliery proprietors, very little was attempted by way of improvement until the early part of the nineteenth century. It was not until 1835 that public attention was concentrated on the position of the miners. It was then that the House of Commons took an interest in the matter and appointed a Select Committee with wide terms of reference to inquire into the lamentable catastrophes which had occurred and to make representations for the prevention of their occurrence. In 1840 Lord Shaftesbury was responsible for the appointment of a Royal Commission to inquire into the conditions of the employment of children and young persons underground. The report of this Commission revealed that children of five years of age and upwards were employed and that they figured prominently in the death and accident toll of that day. Women of all ages were also employed underground. The jobs of the women and girls were to drag full tubs along roadways for the most part railless, the women being tied to the wheelless tub by belts and ropes. In Scotland they were also employed to carry coal up the ladders in the shaft, where mining was so crude that there was no provision for winding gear and cages for the elevation of the coal to the surface. As a result of the report of the Shaftesbury Commission an Act was passed in 1842 which prohibited the employment of women and girls underground, and excluded all boys under ten years of age. This Act provided for the appointment of one Inspector and it is reported that while on a visit to South Wales he discovered that women were still being employed underground as late as 1851. The author has talked with several miners in South Wales whose fathers worked with women underground. The hours of labour were unregulated. In the winter time men, women and children saw daylight only on Sundays. Even in midsummer the mine-workers were unable to enjoy any social leisure because the gases and fatigue of the day left them thoroughly exhausted. Their lives were a round of working, eating and sleeping. The "truck" system was in full operation and the men and their wives were compelled to spend most of their earnings in the company's store. In many cases they were tolerated in the company's houses only so long as they remained the abject and willing creatures of the colliery owner. At the slightest attempt at revolt they and their families were evicted. They were often robbed of their proper weight of coal by a vicious system under which a workman had to forfeit the whole tub of coal he had filled if any quantity of rubbish—the very smallest amount—was discovered in it: if the tub was not properly packed, owing to the varying sizes of the coal filled, he suffered the greatest injustices.

This, then, was the breeding ground for that spirit of local revolt which expanded and exploded into district and national revolt. This first expressed itself in the desire to combine in self-defence and out of the resulting combination sprang the Miners' Trade Unions.

Before 1835 the miners' struggles were carried on in a purely spontaneous way, without organisation or without the forms of organisation; but from 1835 to 1860 regular trade union machinery was established applicable to the needs of the area. About the year 1840 county unions were formed in Lancashire, Yorkshire, Durham, Northumberland; in certain of the Scottish counties and in certain parts of Staffordshire. At this time a movement sprang up for the closer combination of these county associations. The proximity of these counties one to another enabled contact to be maintained to a certain degree, and in the year 1841 there was born in the town of Wakefield (Yorkshire) the Miners' Association of Great Britain and Ireland. This did not represent a disappearance of county unions but rather a new type of Federation of the county unions established for defensive purposes. This early Federation carried on an intense propaganda during its lifetime. It is recorded that the association employed fifty-three paid organisers, whose duty it was to visit every mine in the Kingdom and to stimulate interest among the miners in the trade unionism of the period. In the year 1844 the membership had been gathered from nearly the whole of the mining districts in the country, and the early records shew that the membership amounted to the extraordinary figure of 100,000 in that year. The Miners' Association of Great Britain and Ireland supported the Durham strikers in their great struggle in 1844. This was the period when Lord Londonderry evicted the miners' families, imported strike breakers, threatened tradesmen with reprisals if they gave credit to the men, and generally expressed the attitude of the capitalists and landowners of that day towards the workpeople, whom they regarded as their personal property. The Durham strike was not successful and three years later the coal trade entered on a period of depression. Wages were greatly reduced, membership of the unions was sensibly diminished and in 1848 the Miners' Association of Great Britain and Ireland dropped out of the pages of trade union history.

Attempts to re-establish the Association were made in the following ten years. These attempts were unsuccessful and, owing to the continued depression of trade, miners' trade unionism had virtually vanished from the industrial horizon by the year 1855. In 1858, however, a national conference was held at Ashton-under-Lyne (Lancashire) which though representing only four thousand men was significant as paving the way for a subsequent conference which marks the beginning of a new era in the history of miners' trade unions. The Ashton-under-Lyne conference was largely due to the efforts of Alexander MacDonald, a Scottish miner who worked his way through Glasgow University by hard study in the winter and hard work in the pit in the summer. In 1856 he went to England and conducted intense propaganda not only among the pitmen but among the people generally. A later conference met in 1863 at Leeds (Yorkshire) and a further attempt was made to revive the old miners' national association.

The National Association in 1863 confined itself more particularly to education and propaganda, mainly inspired by MacDonald. It is claimed that he, more than any other man, was responsible for the passing of the Criminal Law Amendment Act and the Employers and Workmen Act in the year 1871. These Acts did a great deal to consolidate trade unionism in England.

In 1869 the miners of Lancashire and Cheshire started a federation of their own under the name of "The Amalgamated Association of Miners." The first President was Mr. T. Halliday. It secured a large number of adherents from South Wales. To a certain degree it may be said that the Amalgamated Association of Miners and the National Association were rival federations.

In the year 1869 also the Durham Miners' Association and the North Staffordshire Association were definitely established as permanent *district* trade unions. In 1872 the Durham Association, as well as abolishing the "yearly bond" and paving the way for district conciliation and arbitration boards, secured an entirely new method for the regulation of wages. This method, known as the "Sliding Scale System," continued in use till 1914 but it met with opposition from its adoption and it was this opposition that led to the formation of the Miners' Federation of Great Britain. The "Sliding Scale" was a system provided for in the district agreements which regulated wages by the ascertained selling price of coal. The principle in its fullest application was soon recognised to be bad by all the districts which adopted it, and in several of the districts movements grew up which established minimum rates of wages below which wages could not fall despite the fact that the price of coal warranted a reduction on the scales then operating. In later years the opposition to this principle became so intense that no district could belong to the Miners' Federation of Great Britain which had an agreement with the employers containing the principle of the Sliding Scale. During the year 1885 there was a strong movement in the Midland Counties in favour of the abolition of this system of wage regulation. In 1888 the Miners' National Union was split as the result of the action of certain districts which formed themselves into a new group, based on their common opposition to the Sliding Scale. Districts like Durham, Northumberland and certain parts of South Wales clung to the old methods and to the National Union. The Midlands, Yorkshire, Lancashire, parts of Scotland and some few men in South Wales sought new methods. This split resulted in the establishment of the organisation since known as the Miners' Federation of Great Britain. The year 1888 therefore is an important one in the annals of the miners' organisations in Great Britain.

The two so-called national organisations existed side by side for some years. Those in the National Miners' Union were still the same districts of Northumberland and Durham and five-sixths of the South Wales miners. A small section of these latter joined the Miners' Federation but their numbers did not reach the figure of 10,000. It is recorded that in the year 1893 there were at least seven independent miners' organisations in South Wales. There was a certain kind of federation of these seven organisations but it was not until the year 1898 that the South Wales Miners' Federation, as it is now known, came into being. Its first task was to link up with the Miners' Federation of Great Britain and it did this in the knowledge that it would have to abandon the principle of the regulation of wages by the sliding scale. The linking up of the South Wales Miners' Federation and later Durham and Northumberland with the Miners' Federation of Great Britain marked the end of the old National Union. In the year 1908, just twenty years after the birth of the Miners' Federation, the last surviving remnants of the Old National Union were transferred to the Miners' Federation of Great Britain. These were the County Associations of Durham and Northumberland. Durham had in fact applied for affiliation on two separate occasions prior to 1908. It was refused admittance on the ground that it still clung to the old sliding scale and was strongly opposed to the new movement for the establishment of the eight-hours day. In the year 1908 the Eight Hours Act was passed, after half a century of struggle. This accomplishment coincided with the admittance into the Miners' Federation of Great Britain of every district and county organisation throughout the length and breadth of the land.

The miners' organisation then entered upon a new phase. It embarked on a project which is still far from complete. It began the work of establishing national agreements with the employers as a whole. During the war the Miners' Federation of Great Britain was the negotiating instrument with the employers and the Government in securing advances of wages, in operating the machinery of recruitment and selection, in the general control of output, etc. In March, 1919, acting on behalf of all the District Associations, it set forth demands for increases of wages, reduction of hours and the nationalisation of the mines. The Coal Industry Commission was established as a consequence. Officers of the national organisation were appointed to act on the Commission. Everywhere emphasis was laid upon the national character of the Miners' Federation. The decisions of the Commission were national in their application. The advances in wages were the same everywhere. The reduction of hours from eight to seven by the passing of the Act of 1919 became universal.

The nearest approach to a national agreement between the employers and the miners however were the agreements of 1921 and 1924, but experience of these only made the District Coalowners' Associations the more determined to revert to district settlements. The setback to the principle of the national agreement and to the seven-hour day following on the struggle of 1926 has already been indicated in Section D in the study of hours and unemployment.

The miners are members of local branches of their union. The Miners' Federation of Great Britain started in 1888 with a membership of 38,000; in 1900 it was over 350,000; in 1913 it was 642,900; and in 1920 the membership had risen to 947,000. It has since declined steadily year by year and in 1932 the membership was only 501,687. The great majority of the miners belong to unions connected with the Miners' Federation but reference must be made to two unions which stand outside it.

The Miners' Industrial Union was formed by Mr. G. A. Spencer, M.P., and two other Nottinghamshire delegates to a national conference during the eventful year, 1926, who favoured a return to work on terms offered by the owners and the Government, which the Federation rejected. It was a protest against "political" unionism and describes itself as a non-political organisation. It made some progress in the Midlands and a little in South Wales but it is not of any great importance. It grew out of the impatience of a section of the miners after months of struggle and deprivation. It flourished for a time but already it has almost faded out of the picture.

The other organisation also sprang from dissatisfaction with the policy of the Miners' Federation but in this case the criticism was that the Federation was not sufficiently radical in its demands or in its methods. This criticism was sponsored mainly by the so-called Minority Movement, a movement which appears to have taken root in some of the coalfields, particularly in the South Wales field. It is avowedly "working for the overthrow of the existing capitalist system" by revolutionary means and has found expression in the organisation of coal-miners in Great Britain as the British Mine Workers' Union. This union is designed to supersede the Miners' Federation. Its aims and objects include the following

The Nationalisation of the mines and ancillary concerns without compensation and with workers' control, as a step towards the supersession of capitalism by a Socialist organisation of society;

National minimum rates and percentages, with a guaranteed weekly minimum;

A six-hours day and a five-days week.

It is not easy to appraise the importance of this union but though the membership is not very large it appears to be growing in influence by the penetration of its ideas. There are those who predict that it will disrupt the Federation, which has certainly suffered a heavy loss of membership in the last ten years of economic depression, but whether this proves true or not it is common knowledge that the officials of the Miners' Federation are more than a little concerned about the undermining influence of the British Mine Workers' Union.

ORGANISATION OF EMPLOYERS IN GREAT BRITAIN

Turning now to the organisation of employers in the British coal industry, one would have to go back several centuries to find the first instance of association of colliery owners. But the early efforts at organisation were in general purely local, were concerned mainly with the regulation of the price of coal and were of short duration. It was not until the middle of the nineteenth century that the national and district coal owners' associations, as we know them to-day, were founded. The national mouth-piece of the coal owners is the Mining Association of Great Britain, formed in 1854.

Although in recent years the most important work which has engaged the attention of the Mining Association has been the settlement of the principles determining the payment of wages, and the consideration of other questions affecting conditions of employment, such as the limitation of hours of work, these were not among the objects for which the Association was originally established. It was not indeed till after the war that such questions came within the purview of the Mining Association, except in so far as they formed the subject of legislative proposals, for the relations between employer and employed in each of the coalfields were dealt with by the *district* organisations concerned.

The principal object for which the Association was formed was to consider and, if necessary, take action in connection with any proposed legislation which might be likely to affect the coal-mining or kindred industries, and from the early reports of proceedings it appears that the chief matters which it dealt with were the Rating of Mines, Railways Acts, the Mines Inspection Act and the Repeal of the London Coal Tax.

The activities of the Association were not exclusively confined to questions that were the subject of legislation, as two other matters which interested it in its earliest days were the establishment of a Mining College and of Mining Schools and the establishment of a trade newspaper. Later, researches into the circumstances giving rise to and the means of prevention of explosions of coal dust were carried out on behalf of the Association.

In the main, however, up to the year 1914 what may be termed the domestic politics of the coal industry were the exclusive concern of the various district associations, and the attention of the Mining Association was principally devoted to matters coming within the scope of governmental action. With the advent of the war the normal activities of the Association gave place to others directed to the organisation of the coal industry for the prosecution of the war. During the war the Mining Association was represented on a number of Government Committees, and after the war, until the decontrol of the mines in 1921, there were prolonged and difficult negotiations between the Association and the Government with regard to the terms of compensation and other matters arising from the Government possession of the mines.

The emergency legislation of the war period is of less importance however than the impetus which the abnormal circumstances of the war period gave to the demand of the Miners' Federation for the treatment of the whole industry as a unit for the purpose of wage regulation. The economic conditions produced by the war destroyed the relation between wages and prices, which lay at the foundation of all wages agreements in the coal industry. Under Government control, with the whole of the revenue from the sale of coal pooled in the hands of the Government, increases of wages on account of increases in the cost of living were given in the form of flat rates equal in amount to all classes of workers at all collieries. The Mining Association had argued for some time that in an industry like the coal industry, in which wages form about 70 per cent of the selling price, it was necessary to take account of costs of production other than wages as well as the selling price when determining the wage-paying capacity of the industry at any time. A scheme was worked out by a committee of the Association according to which in each district the level of wages should be determined by dividing the proceeds of the industry less the costs of production other than wages in agreed proportions between wages and profits. Towards the close of 1920, with the approach of the end of the period of Government control, discussions took place between representatives of the Mining Association of Great Britain and of the Miners' Federation of Great Britain with regard to the future organisation of the industry, and the principle of the division of the net proceeds of the industry between wages and profits in agreed proportions was accepted by both parties. This principle still operates.

In view of the development of the scope of the work which the Mining Association has been called upon to perform in recent years the constitution and organisation of the Association were revised in 1920. Up to 1920 membership of the Association was open both to District Associations of Colliery Owners and to individual colliery owners but the present rules constitute the Association a Federation of District Coalowners' Associations only. All of the District Coalowners' Associations are members. The District Associations include almost all the collieries of any size, and the members of the Associations produce about 94 per cent of the coal output of the country.

The Rules of the Association define the objects for which the Association is established as being generally to watch and take action on behalf of its members in connection with all matters affecting or which may be likely to affect its members or the mining industry. Among the powers which are specially given to the Association (without prejudice to its general powers), in addition to those with which it has hitherto been endowed, is one authorising the Association to undertake the promotion of research and other scientific work in connection with the industry, and the provision of funds for such work. In pursuance of these powers certain work has already been undertaken, and a Research Association for the coal-mining industry has been established to administer the Research Fund which has been constituted by the Mining Association.

NOTE.—For the foregoing descriptions I have drawn freely on articles in the *Historical Review of Coal Mining*, published in 1924 for the Mining Association of Great Britain by The Fleetway Press, Ltd. The article on "Miners' Organisations" was written by Mr. Frank Hodges, a former Secretary of the Miners' Federation of Great Britain, and the one on "Owners' Organisations" by Mr. W. A. Lee, C.B.E., Secretary of the Mining Association of Great Britain.

ORGANISATION OF MINE-WORKERS IN THE UNITED STATES

Mine workers in the United States have been organised in local unions since 1849 though it was not until 1890 that the federation known as the United Mine Workers of America, the counterpart of the Miners' Federation of Great Britain, was formed. These early local unions were first organised in the anthracite region of Pennsylvania and later in the bituminous southern field of Illinois. It is interesting to reflect that these are the sections where the mine-workers are the most closely organised to-day, and the most generally like British coalfields for that reason. During the period 1849–90 repeated attempts were made to bring all the organised miners into one craft union. In 1861 a convention was held at St. Louis, Missouri, composed of representative miners from Illinois and Missouri who organised the first national union of mine-workers in the United States—

the American Miners' Association. This development appears to have been due largely to the leadership and organising ability of Thomas Lloyd, who was made President, and Daniel Weaver, the Secretary. Weaver's address, issued just prior to the Convention, is a somewhat remarkable document, as the following quotation will suggest:

"In laying before you, therefore, the objects of this association, we desire it to be understood that our objects are not merely pecuniary, but to mutually instruct and improve each other in knowledge, which is power, to study the laws of life, the relation of Labor to Capital, politics, municipal affairs, literature, science, or any other subject relating to the general welfare of our class. Has not experience and observation taught us what one of the profoundest thinkers of the present day has said, that 'All human interests, and combined human endeavours, and social growth of this world have, at certain stages of their development, required organising, and Labor—the grandest of human interests—requires it now. There must be an organisation of Labor, to begin with it straightway, to proceed with it, and succeed in it more and more.' One of America's immortals said, 'To me there is no East, no West, no North, no South,' and I would say, let there be no English, no Irish, Germans, Scotch or Welsh. . . . Come then, and rally around the standard of Union—the Union of States and the unity of miners—and with honesty of purpose, zeal and watchfulness—the pledge of success—unite for the emancipation of our labor and the regeneration and elevation, physically, mentally and morally, of our species."[1]

The reference to the English, Irish, Germans, Scots and Welsh is an interesting indication of the character of the mining population at that time. It was much later that the influx of the peoples of Central and Eastern Europe came and complicated the problem of unionisation.

The American Miners' Association began to spread through the northern portion of Illinois and many of the other coal-producing States. In the Blossburg district of Pennsylvania a local union was organised in 1863. In the Tuscarawas, Mahoning and Hocking Valleys of Ohio local and district associations were organised under different names but their forms and usages

[1] Chris Evans, *History of United Mine Workers of America*, Vol. I, p. 7. I have drawn freely on this work.

resembled those used by the branches of the National Union, with headquarters at Belleville, Illinois. The Tuscarawas district union was named Massillon Miners' Association, organised in March, 1863. In the Schuylkill county region of the anthracite field the Workingmen's Benevolent Society of Carbon County was organised in 1864.

In the years that followed internal dissensions were rife, and consequent upon strikes entered into in the years 1867 and 1868 and the policy of certain operators in compelling the men to sign an iron-clad contract that they would give up the union and resume work at a reduced rate the American Miners' Association lost its hold and gradually dwindled away till it finally succumbed to the depression of 1873.

From this time on local unions continued to organise in Illinois, Pennsylvania, Indiana, Maryland, Ohio and other States.

In the year 1868, a miners' union was organised in the anthracite field of St. Clair, Schuylkill County, entitled the Workingmen's Benevolent Association of Schuylkill County, Pennsylvania. Referring to the first organisation of the Workingmen's Benevolent Association, the miners' journal, the *Coal Statistical Register* of Pottsville, Pa., for 1870 says

"The first combined organisation was effected in Luzerne County about five years ago among the men against these companies, and after a suspension of about four months the men were starved out, and the organisation was partially broken up in that county."

After the defeat of this union in 1869 the fight against the operators was carried on by a secret organisation, with all the ritual of initiation rites and oath-taking, known as the Molly Maguires. It was a fiercely picturesque organisation which employed methods of spying, terrorism and even assassination. It was later exposed and many of those connected with it were sentenced and executed. Conan Doyle, the English writer, wrote a thrilling novel about the Molly Maguires called *The Valley of Death* which gives the reader a vivid sense of the bitterness of the industrial struggle in the anthracite field at that time.

In 1870 the name of Workingmen's Benevolent Association was legally changed to Miners' and Laborers' Benevolent Association.

A convention of miners was held at Bloomington, Illinois,

in 1871, and organised the Illinois Miners' Benevolent and Protective Association but this was short-lived.

In 1872 branches of the Miners' and Laborers' Association of the anthracite region were formed in many of the bituminous States, including Pennsylvania, Maryland, Ohio, Kentucky, West Virginia and Michigan. Indiana, Illinois, and Missouri organised a union known as the Miners' Benevolent and Protective Association, with similar objects in view.

It was gradually realised that the Miners' and Laborers' Benevolent Association was unable to cope with changed conditions due to the expansion of railroads and the broadening of the competitive area.

The various benevolent associations disappeared and steps were taken to form another national association. A convention was held at Youngstown, Ohio, in 1873, largely owing to the initiative of John Siney, and organised a national union entitled the Miners' National Association of the United States of America. John Siney, a man destined to play an important part in the organisation of the mine-workers of America, was elected President of the new organisation. In 1874 this association claimed 224 locals and 24,000 members. But economic conditions proved unfavourable. In the early part of 1876 the mining situation was falling off. Local unions which had to some extent recovered from the effects of the strikes and had begun to pay dues to the national union were now placed in a position that made it very difficult for them to continue because they were unable to get any money for work done. In the Mercer county coalfield of Pennsylvania the miners were paid with cheques (checks), payable with interest six months after date, and later on they were notified that the payments for work done would be discontinued altogether for four months, though provisions could be procured from the company store at Sharon, five miles distant from the mines. These circumstances, together with the national trade depression, undermined the union spirit and brought about a condition that proved too much for the national union and it ceased to exist. In 1876 the books were closed and a deficit of about 700 dollars was met by the Secretary, John James.

The next seven years were again a period of local and State organisation. In 1883 the Amalgamated Association of Miners united the miners of Ohio, Pennsylvania, Maryland and Illinois.

But the long strike in the Hocking Valley in 1884, lasting for nine months, was too great a strain on the organisation. The operators, by importing labour, were able to produce all the coal needed by the trade and the men went back to work on reduced wages.

In the summer of 1885 the question of organising a miners' national union was freely discussed by Ohio miners whose leader John McBride and Daniel McLaughlin, the miners' State President of Illinois, took the initiative in calling a national convention to be held at Indianapolis, Indiana, on September 9, 1885. At this convention the National Federation of Miners and Mine Laborers was formed. Eight months after the formation of the National Federation the Knights of Labor organised the National Trades Assembly No. 135 at St. Louis, Missouri. This action gave the mine-workers two national unions and the rivalry for supremacy that followed for four years was a serious impediment to national unification.

The Knights of Labor was a national organisation that included diverse elements who were interested in the labour movement generally. The Order was not an instrument of the industrial workers in their struggle against the employers so much as an association of idealistic co-operators. It was this pure idealism that attracted to it the sympathetic interest and support of doctors, lawyers, university teachers and business men as well as members of crafts in various industries. It began to form local unions throughout the mining regions in 1877 and 1878 but the inclusion of so many interests in the membership was hardly conducive to a single-eyed consideration of the particular needs of the miners. Professional and business men were not so likely as the miners themselves to insist for example on the necessity of a cessation of work as a means of forcing adjustments in bargaining for improvements in wages, hours and working conditions.

A word must be said here about the so-called "joint movement." The Hocking Valley strike was the culmination of a long series of small strikes and the loss to the operators had been considerable. In December, 1885, representatives of both miners and operators met at Pittsburg, and issued a call for a convention at Columbus in February, 1886. Colonel Rend of the Chicago, Pittsburg and Hocking Valley Coal Company said that the difficulties of the industry had been due to "Competition among the operators, who try to undersell each other. The remedy would be to raise the price of mining reasonably in all coalfields and raise the price of coal accordingly. . . . Let these prices be fixed by a Joint Committee of miners and operators." Evans's comment on the last sentence is interesting. He writes "The thirteen words above expressed by Coal Operator W. P. Rend explain fully the foremost cause for the inauguration of the joint movement between operators and miners."

In 1886 the conference met and settled a scale of wages for the year May 1, 1886 to May 1, 1887. Representatives of both miners and operators were present from Pennsylvania, Illinois, Indiana, Ohio and West Virginia. Machinery was devised for the arbitration of disputes. West Virginia fell out in May, 1887, but the system continued for another year. Trouble was experienced with the Illinois operators who refused to fall in with the other three States in granting an advance of wages. In 1888 they stated they could not be bound by the conference and withdrew. In 1889 the Indiana operators for a similar reason also withdrew, and at a later meeting what was left of the conference adjourned *sine die* without agreement. The joint contract that was intended to benefit both parties came to an end.

Meanwhile attempts had been made to heal the breach between the National Federation of Miners and Mine Laborers and the National District Assembly No. 135, Knights of Labor. There had been a loose agreement between the two organisations in 1887 providing that both should work harmoniously and be represented on boards of conciliation. But after the experience of 1888, especially the action of the Indiana operators in refusing to meet the Knights of Labor, a firmer union was sought by merging both organisations into the National Progressive Union.

The following statement, made by President John McBride at the eighth convention of the Ohio Amalgamated Association, held in January, 1889 at Columbus, Ohio, is worth quoting here:

"Statistics for 1887 place the number of miners and mine labourers in the United States and Territories at 280,000, yet out of this large number less than 60,000 were members of National District Assembly 135, Knights of Labor, and the national federation combined. The constant conflict between these two miners' unions not only obstructed progressive efforts, but at times actually caused reverses. A convention of the two organisa-

tions was called and the members of both were asked to cast
aside all personal bias and to send delegates to the convention,
instructed if need be to kill both old organisations and to erect
from their ruins a union that would be acceptable to miners
everywhere, regardless of their former affiliations. The convention
met in this hall and established, on the 7th of December, 1888,
the National Progressive Union of Miners and Mine Laborers.
The wisdom of the convention's work is evidenced by its endorsement by the members of the late federation, and by a large
per cent of the membership of National District Assembly 135.
The miners and mine laborers that belonged to neither of the
old organisations but who have endorsed the National Progressive
Union exceed in number the entire membership of either National
District Assembly 135, or the federation."[1]

The result was however hardly more than a new name for the
National Federation.

In 1889 the fourth annual joint convention of miners and
operators failed, partly because of conflicting authority owing to
the opposition of the contending force that still remained members
of National District Assembly No. 135 of the Knights of Labor.
The operators therefore refused to grant fair prices for mining
or meet jointly as a competitive field to adjust mining affairs
as heretofore. John McBride, President of the National Progressive
Union, speaking at Indianapolis in December, 1889, said,
". . . but the discordant and demoralized state our forces were
in, together with their weakness financially, seemed to court
the destruction of conciliatory methods and invite a conflict
with operators which could not but end in loss and disaster
to us."[2]

Out of this conflict and failure came the United Mine Workers
of America. In January, 1890, the organisations met jointly at
Columbus, Ohio. The plan of amalgamation proposed that there
be one set of officers and one fund for the new organisation, that
in the process of merging neither organisation should surrender
its "essential features," and that in any local or district a majority
vote should determine the practice of open or secret meetings.
The amalgamation was complete. The Master Workman of
National District Assembly 135 was elected President. The interests
of both groups became a common one.

[1] Evans' Vol. I, p. 410.   [2] Evans' Vol. I, p. 480.

The initial programme of the United Mine Workers was to secure anti-screen laws, a uniform wage scale and the eight-hour day. The abolition of screens has been secured, the eight-hour day has become general though not universal, but the uniform wage scale is still far from realisation. If the new national union had been able to organise the mine-workers throughout the entire industry the position would have been different but with less than a third of the workers even to-day within the union ranks and more than half the tonnage produced by non-union mines the power of the union is strictly limited. The competition of the non-union fields sets a limit to what the United Mine Workers can do. As recently as May 24, 1930, the press published an announcement that the Consolidation Coal Company, the largest soft coal producer in the world, had decided to reduce the wages (12 to 14 per cent) of from 2,500 to 3,000 miners employed by the company in the Fairmont, West Virginia, field.

This Company believes in the "High pay" Plan. The author discussed the economic aspects of this policy, the effects of mergers, price-cutting and cut-throat competition at some length with the President of the company, Mr. George J. Anderson, in September, 1928, and he then pointed out the danger of what has since actually occurred. Competitors, said Mr. Anderson (vide *New York Times*, May 24, 1930), have made several wage reductions, and wage scales alleged to be paid in the district have declined 15 to 25 per cent below the scale established by the Consolidation Company and adhered to by that concern since 1928. Two years ago the company announced the closing of the least efficient mines for an indefinite time in order to give as many miners as possible a regular work time under a proper wage basis. It was a plan which had been urged upon the coal industry from time to time but had never been put into practice by a large producer. The hope was that other companies would follow the example of the Consolidation and thereby regularise the earnings of the miners, stabilise conditions and minimise to a great extent cut-throat competition, which, it was charged, held the industry in an iron grip and was driving it further along the path of disintegration.

"The Consolidation Coal Company still believes in a constructive program of wage and market policies," said Mr. Anderson. "In fact, our efforts to promote them have been greater in Fairmont than elsewhere and have involved larger sacrifices of operation to restrict existing evils. To date ten of our Fairmont mines have been shut down as our contribution toward reducing the glut of unwanted coal. On the other hand, we have seen much of our Fairmont-Pittsburg competition sinking to lower standards of living for labor and to lower standards of business for capital, striving to solve excess capacity by more and more output, deficient income by less and less revenue, trying to repair damaged profits by larger patches of loss. Merciless buying may explain, but does not excuse, business methods of this kind."

Mr. Anderson explained that his company was reluctant to take its present step, but that it had been compelled to do so under the pressure of declining price levels and the policies of "irresponsible producers."

"Needless to add, also, in yielding to the inexorable logic of facts, the Consolidation Coal Company does not yield to its convictions. As it has twice been the last to follow into this dreary path, so it will cheerfully be among the first to abandon it."

The *New York Times* comments:

"Mr. Anderson's announcement caused no great surprise in coal circles, which had been discussing for some time how long the company could continue keeping wages up in the face of what was described as an 'epidemic' of wage reductions, both in the Fairmont field and in the Pittsburg district. Coal trade factors said that Mr. Anderson's statement only indicated but did not fully reveal the distress in the Fairmont field 'from over-production and cut-throat competition.' Bituminous coal, it was said, is now selling for one dollar a ton, whereas the Fuel Administration set the price at 2 dollars a ton thirteen years ago. Reports from the Fairmont field have stated that there has been a steady disintegration of standards in that territory, with many companies defaulting from a month to three months in wages, while some companies have been forced into bankruptcy."

It has been thought worth while to devote some attention to the experience of the Consolidation Coal Company because it shews that plans for limiting excess productive capacity, stabilising employment, prices and wages are ineffectual unless the competition of "irresponsible producers" is removed, and also because it goes to the root of the problem of unionisation.

The United Mine Workers has a branch office at Fairmont

TOMBSTONES ON GRAVES OF SHOT MINERS, GRANT TOWN, WEST VIRGINIA

MINERS' BAND AT MINERS' DEMONSTRATION, MONONGAH, WEST VIRGINIA

and a very able representative in the person of Mr. Van A. Bittner, but the plain fact is that the competition of the non-union operators of West Virginia is more powerful than the union in influencing the rates of wages.

The struggles of the United Mine Workers, and it is difficult for an Englishman to realise how heroic they have been, have revolved mainly round the question of wages. In 1894 and in 1897 attempts to maintain wages and secure a uniform wage agreement resulted in a general strike. Following the strike of 1897 and the renewal of the interstate agreement which had been discontinued in 1899 the United Mine Workers entered upon a period of rapid expansion which spread its influence into all parts of the United States. The bitter opposition encountered caused many strikes, the most important of which occurred in Maryland in 1900, in Alabama in 1908, and in Westmoreland County, Pennsylvania, in 1910 and 1911.

At the outbreak of the war the coal-mining industry passed under the control of the Fuel Administration which immediately altered the wage scale made under the interstate agreement. All future appeals for a wage increase were, however, rejected and the consequent general dissatisfaction found expression in the strike of 1919.

The refusal of southern Ohio and Pennsylvania to renew the interstate agreement in 1922, due largely to their inability to compete with non-union West Virginia and Kentucky, resulted in the first general strike throughout both anthracite and bituminous fields in the history of the industry. This strike, though effective in limiting the production of coal, failed to unionise West Virginia. Injunctions, gunmen and the "yellow-dog" contract (a form which a miner applying for work at a mine must sign, undertaking that he will not join the union) have proved too much for the United Mine Workers. The following excerpt from the author's diary may convey an idea of the hostile atmosphere breathed by union organisers in the Fairmont district of West Virginia

"*Tuesday, February* 19, 1929. Called on V.B. in morning.[1] Introduced to others, including Ulysses A. Knapp, attorney,

---

[1] Van Bittner was Head of the United Mine Workers at Fairmont, specially appointed by the President, John L. Lewis, a shrewd judge of the requirements of a situation, to take charge of this difficult outpost.

Teti, who organised building of barracks for evicted families, Aiello, V.B.'s field representative, C. F. Davies, of Welsh descent, and P. C. Moran of Irish descent, V.B.'s secretary. In afternoon Aiello drove Knapp and me in his Graham Paige to see some of the mining camps, Knapp narrating incidents connected with the various places. He has acted for the United Mine Workers throughout the strike (past four years) and so knows a great deal that has never been published. The route was through Barrackville, Farmington (Buffalo Creek), Grant Town, Baxter and Dakota (Pawpaw Creek). Snowing heavily the whole time, but one got an idea of the beauty of the setting—lovely hill country, some of the hills quite imposing, the whole scene surpassing in loveliness any of our South Wales mining valleys. At Barrackville I had my first sight of a fenced-in mine (Bethlehem Steel Company, Schwab)—wire netting with barbed wire on top. No admittance to a fenced-in mine or even to an ordinary company mining camp without a pass, to be obtained from the company. Mine guards usually posted outside to challenge visitors. I did not see any mine guards but Aiello explained this was due to the snow and that they were inside alright: apparently he had spotted them out of the corner of his eye although he was driving. At Farmington the fence was as high as a tennis court outside wire netting. Grant Town full of dramatic interest—scene of killing of John Kello (redneck) and a mine guard named Tobin. Knapp said Wagner (another mine guard) was guilty of the offence of killing Kello but was never arrested or indicted. Fourteen union members were kept in jail for many months on suspicion of the murder of Tobin, but were eventually got out, largely I suspect owing to the efforts of Knapp who struck me as a very able and courageous lawyer (major in the American Army—eleven months in France, only a week or so in England.) Knapp said that evidence of a boy ('an idiot') who swore that he was on the spot was mainly responsible for the freedom of Wagner, though his mother testified that her son could be persuaded to believe anything and that he was actually at home in bed when the murder occurred. 'Nobody troubled about Kello—he was a redneck!' At Grant Town a member of the United Mine Workers was ordered by a mine guard ('yellow dog') to give up a list of new members. On refusing he and three others were severely 'beaten up,' but on complaining later to the State's Attorney about their treatment, charging 'highway robbery,' they were told by the attorney 'Well, you should keep out of Grant Town.' Also the case of Bobby Reed—beaten up by a mine guard named Tenney apparently because he was 'smarty' in replying to Tenney. Reed kept in prison ten days without a charge but finally charged with contempt of court. Fined, but case dropped. Knapp described and pointed out scene of a picketing line at Grant Town which had been marked by armed mine guards, state police and deputy sheriffs. Knapp himself and eleven others arrested on a charge of intimidation—in jail for about three hours. I got a valuable insight into the administration of justice—sheriffs, justices, etc. Case of Judge Lazelle owning stock in mines and trying cases arising out of disputes at those mines. Saw company stores also at Grant Town, barracks at several points (built by the United Mine Workers to house families evicted in middle of winter of 1924), company houses—without baths or inside toilets (except those of officials, built close to the mine and overlooking road)—searchlights, boarding rooms and boys and girls returning from school. An interesting and quite valuable outside view of an isolated, ununionised mining community."

No apology is made for the inclusion here of another diary entry two days later, for it contains material of value to the student and of human interest to the general reader.

"*Thursday, February* 21. Read reports etc. in morning. In the afternoon Studdert[1] drove me to Monongah. He bought his Buick, he told me, with 'two pays when times were good.' Introduced to a group of the men, most of them Italians. Looked over the Hall, built by United Mine Workers in 1924. Fine theatre, used as cinema on Saturdays and for meetings of locals, etc. Studdert and I taken by Pete Andia to his barrack house. Here we found his wife, a handsome Italian, looking very ill (under medical treatment by a Fairmont doctor who doesn't press for payment of bills) and a daughter of about sixteen, who was ironing. House heated by two coal stoves, one in living room, which also had a gas stove for cooking, and the other in one of the two bedrooms—three other children, then in school, one boy and two girls. Italian views on walls. No bathroom or inside toilet, but clean house—wooden structure, warm enough to-day despite six inches of snow—good fire—but was told it was almost

[1] Another field officer of the United Mine Workers.

insufferably hot in the summer. Pete has been on strike for four years and although worried about his wife's illness seemed to be adamant. Very charming fellow. He told me his wife was of a good family—both from same town near Naples though they didn't meet till they came to West Virginia. We next visited a little store at a neighbouring camp called Watson, kept by a former miner who had been on strike and been arrested. Here was an interesting group, something like a group, except for racial differences, one might see in the local shop of a Welsh mining village—a man of about sixty-five, of quite gentlemanly bearing (had two daughters teaching); a Slavish-looking man of about fifty (truculent in speech and style); a kindly, firm little fellow of about forty-five; a youngish man, not more than thirty, born and bred in West Virginia, a fine, handsome type with just a dash of the negro about him, very bitter about the 'yellow dogs'; and the storekeeper himself, affable, though rather glib. All these men were strikers, most of whom found some other work in connection with building, road work, etc. The talk was mainly about the company union and incidents of the struggle, each man describing incidents in which he had been involved. A little shy of me at first but the shyness gradually wore off and the talk got more and more 'free.' I was with them for about two hours. Young boys kept dropping in and I learned a little about the local school. Got quite a bit of 'atmosphere.' The men of remarkable spirit, indomitable, yet like our Welsh miners fond of a joke and a yarn. They were obviously impressed by what I told them of the position in South Wales and were not too much obsessed by their own troubles to express their sympathy with the British miners and their families. Later Pete Andia drove me to visit his cousin Joe Andia who lived in a company house and belonged to the company union. He had been a striker for two years but had returned to work. He gave me a pretty clear idea of the company union. The house was quite a good, five-roomed house, though having an outside dry toilet and no bathroom. The wife, a buxom Italian, seemed to be very proud of her family, one boy at the High School, plays the clarinet, and four daughters, the eldest a stenographer earning 100 dollars a month (£5 a week) in Fairmont, one delicate, one at High School and the youngest attending the grade school—three of the girls unusually pretty. (All the men I met who were Italians were also good-

looking and had particularly fine teeth). The rent of the house
was 10 dollars a month, coal and electric light extra. The house
normally tenable only during employment under the company.
Andia said that the company would let you stay on during sickness.
He showed me his pay docket, net earnings 42·50 dollars for
the fortnight, after deducting 1·50 dollars for doctor, hospital,
etc., and 95 cents for the Miners' Association (the company
union, head of which was the Superintendent). There was a
native courtesy about this family that was very charming. The
mother expressed a longing to pay a visit to Italy, but dreads the
sea voyage and besides 'it cost a lot of money.' The father and
mother spoke English with quite an Italian accent and not very
fluently, though they came over in 1907. Mrs. Andia said that
three of her brothers were killed in the explosion at Monongah
(six months after her arrival here) when 361 men were killed—
the biggest explosion in the history of the United States. Joe
Andia was at home sick that day and Pete happened to 'lay off'
or they would almost certainly have been killed as there was
only one survivor. One of the most interesting things I saw
during the day was the following, printed in good style, evidently
by a skilled man, in large size across the length of a United Mine
Workers' hut at Watson:

'The home of locked out miners who are fighting for American
standards of living and for humanity. They signed the contract,
but oh! how they lied!' "

This last statement was apparently a reference to a breach of
agreement made by a number of operators, including the coal
interests of the Bethlehem Steel Company. The Jacksonville
agreement was signed in 1924 and was to be in force till April 1,
1927. It removed the possibility of interruption by strike, and
improvements of transportation service eliminated the shortage of
cars. It established a day rate of 7·50 dollars for inside men
throughout the Competitive Field—Illinois, Indiana, Ohio, and
West Pennsylvania. On August 10, 1925, the Pittsburg Coal
Company posted notices at its mines requesting its employees
to return to work at a lower wage rate. The cut in wages for inside
men was from 7·50 dollars to 6 dollars—1·50 dollars a day.
The employees refused to return and in six months almost all
former employees were evicted. A steady flow of strike-breaking

labour was shipped from cities like Chicago, Detroit, Cleveland, St. Louis and many southern cities as well, the bulk of the strike-breakers being coloured. According to a statement prepared by Mr. Philip Murray, International Vice-President of the United Mine Workers, strike-breaking (non-union) miners under the Pittsburg Coal Company in February, 1928 (shortly before the author interviewed Mr. Murray), numbered about 7,000, a very large percentage being negroes from the Southern States—Alabama, Georgia, Kentucky and Tennessee—having little if any previous experience of mining. The author has a vivid recollection of the sight of these imported negroes herded together in specially constructed huts, built by the company, living in a closely regimented encampment suggestive of military discipline. He is convinced, incidentally, that the importation of negro "scabs" into this field is responsible for a good deal of the "prejudice" of white miners in the north against the negro race. It is true that the United Mine Workers does not exclude coloured workers from membership, and one may see negro delegates at the annual conference, but the vehemence with which certain highly intelligent and otherwise liberally minded coal-diggers, active union workers, inveighed against "the bloody niggers" in the course of a private conversation came as a surprise and something of a shock. This attitude is largely explainable on economic grounds.

Since the formal expiration of the Jacksonville Agreement, the United Mine Workers has had to be content with the best terms obtainable by negotiation with the operators' organisations in various parts of the competitive field. In the Pennsylvania anthracite district, John L. Lewis has met with some success in direct bargaining with the operators and this remains the most highly unionised area in the States.

The partial unionisation of the large scattered coalfields of America has not been achieved without sharp conflicts. The early records of organisation are eloquent of many a struggle on the part of the men for recognition and a higher standard of living. Even where the union has obtained a foothold and proved its value, not only to the miners, but also to the tradesmen and business men of a mining community, the price of integrity has been constant vigilance and resistance against attempts to lower wages. The United States Coal Commission, 1923, recognised this by stating in substance that "the history of the past thirty years affords conclusive evidence that the United Mine Workers of America has been the potent agency in the betterment of the miners' working conditions, and it is necessary to-day for the protection of the standards that have been attained." Not more than twelve years ago the miners of Southern Illinois were put to the test. Reference has already been made in the discussion of the policy of wage-cuts in Chapter II, to the incident that has made Herrin famous in American economic history. A short account of that extraordinary occurrence will serve to illustrate the excesses of feeling and action that in the United States turn on the issue of Unionism.

Herrin

The author spent a month in the Illinois coalfield towards the close of 1928. As Herrin was the scene of one of the most dramatic industrial struggles in the history of any country in the world he looked forward with keen interest to his visit to the town. He was hoping to glean particulars on the spot which, as he had been informed by one in a position to make such a statement, it was impossible to get from official reports. Fortunate in his approach, being aided by one of the best experts on the history of the coalfield and himself formerly a miner, by local officials of the United Mine Workers, a well informed attorney, a local schoolmaster, and a working miner who escorted him to the tragic field, he yet failed to ascertain anything importantly new. The fact is that even after six years the local people are extremely reluctant to indulge in anything more specific than general observations about what happened. The supposition is that some of the miners themselves were so closely "mixed up" with the killings that they and their relatives deem a quiet tongue the best way of burying the dead and preserving the living!

The scene of the massacre was a new strip-mining operation, called the Leicester mine, just outside the town of Herrin, in Williamson County, Illinois. In 1928 Herrin seemed a flourishing and well-governed little community. It is said that the residents of Williamson County own more automobiles than those of any other county in the State of Illinois except Cook County, which includes the city of Chicago. One was impressed by the number and types of cars in the town itself. The schools were of a high

standard—good teachers, well-nourished-looking pupils who asked intelligent questions, and excellent equipment. On the day of the author's visit the local press gave great prominence to the success of a former Herrin High School boy who had just been awarded a Rhodes Scholarship, and conversations with some of the townspeople revealed great pride in the achievement. One got the impression that the residents were deeply religious, there was no evidence of communist activities and there is practically no socialist vote in the whole county. But the power of the union was strong, and even the tradespeople gave it their unqualified support. This loyalty of the town to the union is an important consideration in any review of the facts as they are now generally accepted.

The company that owned the mine at the time—the Southern Illinois Coal Company—had obtained the permission of the union to continue removing the earth overlying the coal during a stoppage in the State, promising in return that it would not mine any coal. When this work was completed the superintendent discharged the union men who had been engaged on it, imported a number of non-union men, together with a force of armed guards supplied by a Chicago detective agency, and started mining coal. For a week or so there were minor hostilities, the miners establishing pickets at the mine and persuading many of the imported non-union men to return. The mine guards in the meantime had made themselves obnoxious to the community by challenging people on the road, insulting women, etc., and at one time it was reported that the local sheriff had been killed while attempting to suppress their unlawful activities. An effort was made to call out the State troops and the sheriff visited the mine. He did not, however, interfere in any way. The reason given for his inaction is that he was at this time a candidate for the office of County Treasurer. In any district where the union was weak the probability is that the State troops would very soon have been brought into action against the local miners.

Matters continued comparatively quiet until Wednesday, June 21, 1922, when a party of non-union miners who were being brought in on a truck was ambushed. The casualties were one killed and three injured. Following this the miners raided hardware stores at Herrin and the neighbouring town of Marion, taking all the firearms they could find and telling the proprietors

DEMONSTRATION OF WIVES AND CHILDREN OF MINERS IN FAVOUR OF THE UNION, U.M.W.A., FAIRMONT, WEST VIRGINIA

to send in the bill to the local union. They then surrounded the mine and in the course of the afternoon three of the union men were shot and killed: one of these was a favourite character in the union and it is said that he was shot while attempting to negotiate with the non-union miners for a parley. On the following morning firing was resumed. The non-union men claimed that the miners fired on a white flag but the miners allege that the guards were firing from under the flag. A parley was soon arranged, however, and it was agreed that if the non-union men and the guards would leave their arms at the mine they would be given safe conduct out of the county. It appears certain that this promise was made in good faith but in the meantime hundreds of new recruits from the surrounding country were arriving and the rumour spread that the State troops were on their way to the scene. As a result of this report and others that were circulating the crowd soon got out of hand and before the party of non-union men had proceeded a mile from the mine the superintendent was taken out of the line and killed. Shortly afterwards the forty to sixty prisoners in the party were lined up against a fence and told to run, taking their chance of being shot. A number escaped, some of whom were hunted down and killed later: of the others, six were tied together with ropes round their necks and marched through the streets of Herrin to the cemetery where they were either shot or had their throats cut; one of these six survived. The total number killed is not known exactly, the most reliable estimate being twenty-five.

The sentiment of the local people was shewn in significant ways. The quiescent attitude of the Sheriff was endorsed by his election as County Treasurer by a very large majority. The verdict of the coroner's jury was that "the deaths of the decedents were due to the acts, direct and indirect, of the officials of the Southern Illinois Coal Company." And although different aspects of the affair must have been witnessed by hundreds of persons, many of whom undoubtedly represented the most responsible elements in the community, it was not possible to secure a single conviction of any of the miners. That it was condoned by the union is evidenced by the active part it took in defending those accused of complicity in it. It is not to be inferred, however, that the whole plan was premeditated or even contemplated: the United States Coal Commission made an exhaustive investigation into the

M

matter and recorded that "although the tragedy might have been prevented it finds that the union officials never anticipated it would happen."

There is ground for the view that the great majority of the people believed the existence of the miners' organisation was threatened. Many undoubtedly thought they saw in the attitude of the Company the initial step in a campaign that would ultimately crush the union and bring about a resumption of the pre-union conditions when men worked ten hours a day in gas-filled rooms, frequently in water half-way to their knees, for a wage of from 1·25 dollars to 2 dollars (5 shillings to 8 shillings) a day. The tradespeople had no wish to see the men's wages reduced, the preachers and teachers supported the union on humanitarian grounds, and the miners who belonged to the union were prepared to fight to the death for it as indeed some of them proved when put to the test.

NOTE.—For the main facts relating to the Herrin "Massacre" I have drawn on the summary made in Chapter V of *The Coal Industry*, by A. T. Shurick.

Colorado

The bitterest struggles in the non-union fields have been in Colorado and West Virginia. Life in Colorado mining communities, not alone in coal camps, was decidedly "raw" at the turn of last century. The cinema-goer of to-day may get a vivid if somewhat exaggerated idea of such life from word pictures of groups of "tough" miners—hard workers and hard drinkers, singing, dancing and gambling, with the inevitable Sheriff and the inevitable gun! Gold digging was on the decline in 1878 and many mining towns were being deserted when it was discovered that silver and lead might be extracted from the masses of carbonates discarded by the gold seekers. Immigrants flocked to Leadville and soon the yield of the lead and silver exceeded that of gold. Serious strikes broke out among the miners in 1894, 1896–97 and 1904, and recourse was had to military force to restore order. The greatest disturbance was that of 1904 when the strikers blew up the railway station at a place called Independence, killing fifteen non-union men and injuring several others. As usual severely repressive measures followed. Suspected persons were deported from the State, attempts were made by the military to intimidate the courts and the writ of *habeas corpus* was suspended by the Governor. These measures, which aroused much criticism throughout the United States, were largely inspired by the Citizens' Alliance, an organisation formed with the avowed purpose of exterminating the Western Federation of Miners.

It does not need much imagination to realise something of the difficulties encountered by pioneers in the work of unionisation among the miners in these remote Colorado settlements. The difficulties were no less formidable in the coalfields. To this day collective bargaining on a union basis in the Colorado coalfield is unachieved. There is one Company, the Rocky Mountain Fuel Company, which has a contract with the United Mine Workers, but this is an exceptional case, as we shall see later. In the meantime the union has waged a struggle against almost overwhelming odds. One episode in that struggle calls for more than a passing reference. In 1913–14 an exceptionally violent strike shook the Southern field with its centre at Trinidad, where the strike was called on September 23, 1913. The vital principle involved was recognition of the union, the United Mine Workers of America, but the miners formulated specific demands including their own checkweighmen, the abolition of certain abuses of the truck system, the reduction of the ten-hour to an eight-hour day, and advances in wages. Concessions in respect of the employment of checkweighmen and of hours and wages were made but on the principle of recognition of the union both parties to the dispute were adamant. A conference was called by the leaders of the union but this was ignored by the operators, not one responding, and when the strike was called about 85 per cent of the men came out. Something like guerilla warfare ensued. The operators aimed at resuming normal production by importing into the coal camps sufficient numbers of men to take the place of the striking miners. The leaders of the union organised the strikers. A notable feature of their organisation was the housing of the men and their families in a tent colony. During October and November there were several sanguinary conflicts between the strikers on the one hand and the militia and mine guards on the other. During the winter months nothing serious happened but in April, 1914, occurred the so-called "Ludlow Massacre" when the strikers' tent colony at Ludlow, a small mining town not far from Trinidad, was fired, six men were killed and two women and eleven children were suffocated. The men were now dangerously roused and the struggle became so violent that it passed beyond the power of State authority to control. Federal troops were called in and they remained on the scene till 1915, though the strike had been finally declared off at a meeting at Denver, on December 10, 1914.

During the author's visit to this coalfield in 1930 he had several talks with the leader of the men throughout the strike. Though made famous by the nation-wide publicity given to his case—he was condemned first to be shot, later to life imprisonment—John Lawson is an unusually modest and gentle man and as he spoke of what had happened at Ludlow it was difficult to realise that here was the man who had acted as a sort of commander-in-chief of the men's army. But as he said, in reply to a question, "We were forced into doing certain things."

Early in 1915 reports from various sources were made on the Colorado Coal and Fuel strike, as it was called after the name of the Company which dominated the southern field. A final report was presented after an investigation of the case by a sub-committee of the House Committee of Mines. According to this report both sides were prepared for battle. Political conditions in the mining regions were found to be particularly bad and the manner of selecting juries was declared illegal. The companies were in supreme command in the mining villages by virtue of their control of the land and of the stores and as a result of their extensive employment of imported workers. Various persons connected with the management were severely criticised and a more reasonable attitude on their part in dealing with their employees was suggested. As an alternative stringent Federal interference and control was proposed and the report declared: "If these strike troubles continue to break forth it will be plainly necessary to consider whether some method of regulation shall not be adopted with reference to the business as carried on in inter-state commerce as is now done with the business of transportation." A deduction made from the Hearing before the United States Commission on Industrial Relations alleged that the Rockefellers, owning 40 per cent of the stock of the companies, were responsible for what happened in that they could have prevented its happening.

A long controversy followed between the critics, who attributed the affair to the evils of absentee capitalism with its abuse of power, and the companies, which denied these allegations.

The leading Company, however, the Colorado Fuel and Iron Company, evidently realised that "something must be done about it," and John D. Rockefeller, Jr., seems to have taken the initiative in instituting a more benevolent plan as a substitute for the blood-and-iron policy which culminated in the "Ludlow Massacre." The motive behind the plan was to establish better relations with the employees, but to leave the operators and their employees free from the restrictions of joint agreements governing areas larger than that covered by the plan; in other words, to keep out the union. Mr. Mackenzie King, who later became Premier of Canada, was called into consultation as an expert in the field of industrial relations and a scheme was fashioned which has become widely known and copied as the "Rockefeller Plan" or the Colorado Fuel and Iron Company Plan or the Colorado Industrial Plan or more briefly the Colorado Plan. In the words of J. D. Rockefeller, Jr., the plan was formulated for the purpose of seeking "some means of avoiding the possibility of similar conflicts arising in the future."[1] In the revised version in 1921 it was stated that the plan was "for the purpose of maintaining and developing harmony and right understanding" between the Company and its employees. The plan was initiated by the Company and was submitted to a meeting of delegates elected by the employees. After receiving the sanction of the delegates it was submitted to a referendum vote of the employees. Seventy-eight per cent of the employees voted[2] and 84.4 per cent of those voting were in favour of it.[3] The plan merits a somewhat detailed description. For a full account the reader is referred to a most careful piece of research by Ben M. Selekman and Mary Van Kleeck, undertaken under the auspices of the Russell Sage Foundation—"Employes' Representation in Coal Mines."

The Colorado Coal and Fuel Company Plan

Certain rights are accorded which were intended to give employees a new status in their daily employment and to facilitate

[1] Rockefeller, J. D., Jr., *The Colorado Industrial Plan*, p. 16.
[2] *Ibid.*, p. 94.   [3] Rockefeller, *Brotherhood of Men and Nations*, p. 12.

the adjustment of disputes and grievances. These rights may be stated under six heads:—

1. The right to hold meetings outside working hours on the Company property or elsewhere, though meetings during working hours may be held at the mines only with the consent of the local management.
2. The right to freedom from discrimination for membership or non-membership of labour or other organisations.
3. The right to purchase goods at independent stores.
4. The right to caution and to a hearing before suspension or discharge except for one of a list of offences for the commission of which an employee may be dismissed without notice.
5. The right to appeal to the president and superior officers of the Company against unfair conditions or unfair treatment by the management, and
6. The right to employ checkweighmen to verify the weight of the coal produced by the men.

There is an elaborate organisation for the application of these principles.

1. *The Annual Election of Representatives.* Representatives are elected annually from each division and subdivision of the Company's properties. All employees, except salaried officials and those having the power to engage and discharge, who have been in the employ of the Company for the preceding three months are entitled to vote. Representatives are elected for one year. They must be citizens of the United States, be twenty-one years of age or over and must have been continuously employed by the Company for a year. In general the basis of representation of employees is one representative for every 150 wage-earners or major fraction thereof.

Nominations and elections are made by secret ballots under conditions that ensure freedom of choice and an impartial count. Any twenty-five employees who are dissatisfied with the election may demand and sign a petition for a recount. The tellers must preserve the ballots and surrender them to the president of the Company for recount. If after the recount and consultation with the local Committee on Co-operation, Conciliation and Wages the president is of opinion that the nomination and election have not been fairly conducted he may order a new election.

Meetings of employees or conferences of representatives may be held at times which will not interfere with the work of the mine to consider and make representations on matters affecting employment, living and working conditions which the employees may wish to have considered by the joint conferences. The president or other officers of the Company may also refer questions to such meetings or conferences.

2. *The District Joint Conferences.* The mining communities are divided into six districts in which joint conferences are held at least three times a year. The purpose of these conferences is "to discuss freely matters of mutual interest and concern to the Company and its employees, embracing a consideration of suggestions, to promote increased efficiency and production, to improve working and living conditions, to enforce discipline, avoid friction, and to further friendly and cordial relations between the Company's officers and employes."

3. *The Joint Committees.* The district conferences select joint committees on Co-operation, Conciliation and Wages; Safety and Accidents; Sanitation, Health and Housing; and Recreation and Education. These committees are entrusted with duties assigned by the district conferences, and are available for consultation with an Advisory Board on Social and Industrial Betterment, the president of the Company, the President's Industrial Representative or any other officer of the company.

The joint committee on Co-operation, Conciliation and Wages may on its own initiative bring before the district joint conference or if referred to it by the officers of the Company, consider any matter "pertaining to the prevention and settlement of industrial disputes, terms and conditions of employment, including wages, hours, and working conditions, maintenance of order and discipline in the several camps, company stores, etc."[1]

4. *The Annual Joint Meeting.* An annual joint meeting is held in each district. It is composed of all the representatives of the employees and of the management, and includes the members of the various joint committees. Reports are presented by the joint committees, and the meeting considers "matters of common interest requiring collective action." As Mr. Arthur Suffern

[1] Rockefeller, *The Personal Relation in Industry*, p. 132.

points out in the chapter on "Employe Representation Plans" in his excellent study *The American Coal Miners' Struggle for Industrial Status* the phrase "matters of common interest requiring collective action" may be all-inclusive or decidedly limited in meaning and practice. It is true the joint meeting provides opportunity to raise general considerations regarding the clause in the agreement pertaining to wages, hours and working conditions. This agreement, "subject to revision upon 90 days notice by either of the parties," regulates the price of rent for dwellings, electric lights, water, prices of powder and domestic coal, fencing employees' homes, removal of garbage, bath and club houses, hours of work, semi-monthly wage payment, and adjustment of wages and working conditions. But what bargaining there is over wages, hours and working conditions seems to go on in the committees on Co-operation, Conciliation and Wages in each district. There is no annual joint meeting which gives general consideration to wages in all the districts. However, special joint meetings of any two or more districts may be called upon request to the president of the Company of a majority of the employee representatives or upon the initiative of the president, and this provision would permit of such general consideration of wages if the management so desired.

A State Law of Colorado provides that no change affecting conditions of employment with respect to wages and hours shall be made without giving 30 days' notice. The parties to the plan agreed to abide by this provision, though critics of the company allege that it did not do so when it declared a cut in wages in some of its mines during the depression of 1921. The company contended that a reduction was necessary if the men were to have work and that they had signed a petition for a reduction. The State Industrial Commission apparently attached little importance to the men's claim that they had not voluntarily signed a petition for a reduction and upheld the company in its contention.

The Company promised to increase wages in proportion to those granted in competitive districts but it is free to adjust its wages, hours and working conditions without participating in joint conferences representative of competitive fields. There is no pressure of opinion from competing operators or union representatives seeking general improvement in wages, hours

16.—1ST PRIZE GARDEN AT HOUSE NO. 115. STANDARD. 72812

PRIZE GARDEN IN COMPANY VILLAGE, COLORADO

and working conditions in the industry as a whole. It is a self-contained plan, and the market supplied by the company is so different and distant from that of the competitive field that wages in the Colorado field are not materially influenced by those ruling in Pennsylvania.

The plan provides procedure for the prevention and adjustment of disputes. Although the Company definitely retains the right to engage and discharge, the machinery by which grievances may be settled puts some limitation on the autocratic use of this power.

1. *Local Settlements.* Employees or their representatives are required first to take up their grievances with the foremen or superintendents of the mines. In the event of failure to adjust their differences they confer with the "president's industrial representative." This officer is required to visit all mines at least once every three months to confer with the representatives of the employees and with the management regarding working and living conditions, observance of Federal and State laws and of the Company's regulations, and to report the results to the president of the Company.

2. *Appeal to Higher Officers.* If the president's industrial representative fails to adjust a dispute satisfactorily the employees may appeal to the divisional superintendent, assistant manager or manager, general manager or the president, preferably in consecutive order. As a matter of practice the consecutive order is not rigidly adhered to.[1] The employees must exercise their right of appeal within two weeks after their failure to agree with the industrial representative. The appeal to higher officials is intended to safeguard the employees against the arbitrary use of power by the local management.

3. *Adjustment by Joint Committee and Arbitration.* If the employees fail to agree with the higher officers the dispute may be referred at the request of the employees or on the initiative of the president to the joint committee on Co-operation, Conciliation and Wages. If the committee can give a majority decision the case is settled. When the committee cannot render a majority vote its members may select an umpire to sit with them, if a majority of the members so agree. If the committee cannot agree

[1] Selekman and Van Kleeck *Employes' Representation in Coal Mines,* p. 176.

upon an arbitrator or refuses to accept one or more appointed by the Colorado Industrial Commission the dispute is investigated by the Commission in accordance with the provisions of the Statute regulating its powers. The findings of the Commission are final, only provided that both sides have agreed in advance that they shall be. In case the employees are dissatisfied with the award their only remedy is to strike, which would be a rare occurrence.

An employee representative who believes himself to have been discriminated against because of his efforts on behalf of the employees has the right of appeal to the superior officers of the Company, to the joint committee on Co-operation, Conciliation and Wages and finally to the State Industrial Commission. If the representative is upheld in his contention the Company must make such reparation as the Commission may deem just.

The plan also provides for a consideration of social and industrial betterment and establishes a personnel which is responsible for improvements in this sphere. A vice-president or other executive officer to be known as the Industrial Relations Executive is given supervisory power in carrying out the Company's policies of social betterment. He confers with the various joint committees, is chairman of the "Advisory Board on Social and Industrial Betterment" composed of officers of the Company, and exercises a "general supervision over the sanitary, medical, educational, religious, social and other like needs of the different industrial communities."

Such is a brief description of the Plan. In considering its economic and social value one is driven to the conclusion that its real purpose is to prevent the development of trade unionism, in the traditional sense of that term. In essence it is a form of Company unionism. The term "Company Union" has been used very widely and very loosely. Any organisation from a mutual benefit association to a rival trade union has been called a Company Union. Many people are apt to think that a Company Union is simply a benefit society, to pay out sick and death benefits. Others think of it as being concerned with welfare activities. True that it may combine the functions of a benefit society and a social club. But a Company Union is more than this. Its distinguishing feature is that it is supposed to have a voice in the management of the plant, factory or mine; it is at least consulted concerning some of the working conditions and activities in the plant.

The various stages in the evolution of the relations of the company with its workers have been clearly traced. In the first stage the employer's word is absolute law: he does not explain his orders to his workers or even pretend to consult them about conditions affecting their welfare in the factory. Another stage is reached when the employer uses posters, bulletin boards and perhaps a Company magazine as means for securing the workers' approval and loyal support of the Company's policies. Later he may call the workers into a general meeting or assembly to explain certain policies, as for example the necessity for accepting a wage cut. In the next stage he may go so far as to choose a few of the more loyal workers on a very informal committee to consult with the management occasionally. But the Company Union stage is reached only when the employer sets up a definite machinery for electing committees, serving usually in some sort of joint council with the representatives of management, to consider certain grievances. Beyond this there are the various stages within the company union itself, depending upon the degree of consultation, responsibility or power, if any, which the management may care to grant to the committees.[1]

In this sense the Colorado Plan, like other employee representation schemes, is a form of Company Unionism. It is initiated by management and does not, like genuine collective bargaining, come as the result of pressure from workers who have organised themselves into a union. Mr. Arthur Suffern, in discussing such plans, says:

"It is questionable whether they (the employes) could muster the necessary unity to oppose the Company if they disagreed strongly with the Company's policies. The effectiveness of the voice of the employes is entirely dependent upon the breadth of interpretation which the Company gives to the principles it has agreed to and the consistency with which it seeks to establish a real and increasing basis of co-operation. The employe representatives, except in the case of the labor commissioner of the Davis Coal and Coke Company, are also entirely dependent upon the Company for their salaries and for their security of

---

[1] I have made this summary of a Company Union from the first chapter of Robert W. Dunn's valuable little study: *Company Unions.*

status, except as they are protected against discrimination by the procedure for appeal."[1]

The United States Coal Commission emphasised the view that employee representation plans cannot be used to cope with the competitive nature of the industry. The way was still open to competition in the undercutting of wages and in establishing relatively unfavourable working conditions which might give operators having employee representation plans an advantage in costs of production. The fact is that in their negotiations regarding wages, hours and conditions of labour the employees, not belonging to an organisation covering competing districts, cannot expect any help in bringing up the level of their wages or in resisting cuts. Being members of a self-contained Company organisation they are largely dependent upon the Company's good-will and the extent to which it follows an enlightened policy.

The Colorado Plan has now been operating for eighteen years and has been closely studied by many experts, European as well as American, in the field of industrial relations. There seems to be general agreement that the workers are afraid to submit their grievances to appeal, and fear discrimination and discharge in spite of the paper promises of the plan. Their representatives, though immune from discrimination under the plan, made the investigators for the Russell Sage Foundation give them a solemn promise that they would not betray them to the Company. Without a genuine trade union behind them even the best intentioned and honestly elected worker representatives expressed themselves as feeling like petty generals without an army. The investigators who talked with them wrote:

"It did seem to us that many of the miners' representatives were timid, untrained, and ill-prepared to present and argue the grievances of the miners, and that their experience as representatives was not developing initiative or leadership in them. The representatives themselves were of the same opinion, and so were most of the miners whom we interviewed." (*Employes' Representation in Coal Mines*, p. 188.)

Again: "When we asked the men why they did not take their grievances to the representatives, they answered with even greater indignation that it was useless, the representatives did

[1] Suffern, *The American Coal Miners' Struggle for Industrial Status*, pp. 300–301.

not amount to anything; they would not risk their jobs or antagonize their foreman; they had no power, and so on."

It is also generally believed that the plan has been used from the start as a bulwark against the United Mine Workers and to effect wage reductions. Mr. Suffern writes:

"The history which lies behind the industrial relations of all the companies has undoubtedly established deep-grained suspicions that they are mainly concerned in forestalling the development of unionism. And in all probability the memories of the past, and the pressure of union men or men who formerly belonged to the Union, keeps alive a spirit of suspicion of the motives of the companies. This spirit of suspicion is not allayed by attempts to reduce wages when the company has promised to pay a scale equal to its competitors who are paying the union scale."[1]

It is also alleged that the workers had no voice in drafting the plan and are still, for the most part, indifferent to it.

On the positive side, it is claimed that the plan has been successful in settling disputes, that the limitations imposed upon the arbitrary power of discharge gives the employee a better status and that the arrangements by which the representatives can present the men's grievances open the way to better understanding and encourage both sides to cultivate co-operative attitudes and practices. It is also generally admitted that the plan has done much to improve living conditions and social life in the mining communities, though some critics maintain that such improvements might have been granted directly without the elaborate machinery of representation. The fact remains that the houses are well built and not ungenerously provided with garden space.

While the author was in the Colorado coalfield he had opportunities of discussing the plan with mine superintendents and other officials of the Colorado Fuel and Iron Company, with some of the workmen and with former employees who are now working for a different company. Before and after his visit to Colorado he discussed the merits and defects of the scheme with many experts, including Miss Mary Van Kleeck. The general impression left upon his mind is that while it is an interesting

[1] Suffern, *The American Coal Miners' Struggle for Industrial Status*, p. 303.

experiment in industrial relations and has certain minor merits, such as the promotion of co-operative attitudes and practices, it is at best merely a plan by which the management can ascertain and settle certain grievances arising from the daily conduct of industry and a more civilised substitute for the arrogant despotism of the "Ludlow Massacre" days. But in so far as the men have no real share in the management, to say nothing of the financial control of the undertaking, they are still working under a benevolently despotic régime. The scheme was initiated by the company; the workers are given an opportunity to help run the machine but it is essentially an opportunity to remain unequal. They win nothing for themselves as men do by genuine trade union collective bargaining; what benefits they have are bestowed upon them by the company.

The plan may continue to operate for some time because of the indifference of most of the workers about it and because of the remoteness of the influence of the United Mine Workers, but one cannot escape the feeling that it is a temporary device and that it cannot permanently keep out the union. Apart from a sense of grievance about such a thing as the discharge of older men lest they add to the burden of funds for pensions, which some men complained of directly to the author, there appeared to be a strong, if suppressed, feeling of discontent on the question of wages—"the committees don't seem to make much difference" —and an underground current of general dissatisfaction with their lot among the more intelligent workers that threatened to grow into a wide river of revolt. The strikes of 1919, 1922, 1925 and 1927–28 on the properties of the company can hardly be regarded as evidence of satisfaction on the part of the employees or of the efficacy of the plan from the standpoint of the company.

. . . . .

Another interesting experiment in the field of industrial relations is being pursued in the Colorado coalfield. It may be described as a form of co-operation between the company (the Rocky Mountain Fuel Company) and the union (the United Mine Workers of America). So far as the author is aware, it is unique in the coal industry of any country and as it has a close bearing on the organisation of the coal workers, a brief account of it may fittingly be included in this section.

Union-Management Co-operation

The Rocky Mountain Fuel Company is the second largest coal concern in the Colorado field. In years past it was a consistent leader, along with the Rockefeller interests, in mining warfare in that State until the reorganisation of the company, when Miss Josephine Roche secured financial control in 1927. Miss Roche, with whom the author had the pleasure of discussing the scheme in considerable detail on several visits to the office and to mines, is the daughter of the leading director of the company under the old régime. Their views on the conduct of industry were widely divergent, and when her father died, leaving her almost 50 per cent of the stock, she obtained sufficient funds to give her the controlling interest in the company. Miss Roche had been a social worker in Denver and in New York and had liberal ideas about the running of industry. Since 1922 there had been no general agreement with organised miners in the northern Colorado coalfield, and the United Mine Workers had virtually ceased to exist. Miss Roche immediately set to work to promote conference between the operators and the miners, but the operators were not interested. Indeed, the operators all along have been hostile; they have regarded Miss Roche as something of a "blackleg" and the local banks have been financially antagonistic. So the Rocky Mountain Fuel Company went ahead and dealt with the Union alone.

On September 1, 1928, an agreement went into effect between the company and the United Mine Workers of America. The following entry from the author's diary may be of interest here:

"*June* 21, 1930. Joined Miss Roche, Lawson, Merle Vincent (President of the company, formerly well-known Attorney), Costigan (General Counsel of the company, champion of miners, now running for Senatorship), and McGuire (Superintendent of all the mines). After lunch went with Vincent and Miss Roche for a run round some of their properties. Visited the Columbia mine at Lafayette (18 miles from Denver). Here I met a young Welshman, born in Rhondda Valley, named Morgan (chief clerk), Henry Thomas, the pit foreman, native of Swansea Valley, a Spanish Mexican, and other officials. We descended the shaft (330 feet) but did not explore the mine. Much struck by the extraordinarily friendly relations between the officials and men and Mr. Vincent and Miss Roche. Quite the most remarkable instance of happy industrial relations between employers and employed I have seen either at home or in the States. Later visited Vulcan Mine. Superintendent—Harry R. Unwin—mixture of English (Durham University) and South African. Unusual habit of addressing Vincent and me as 'sir.' Learnt a good deal about the aims of the company during the afternoon. The purposes are set out in the Agreement between the R.M.F.C. and the U.M.W. of A., District 15, for the period beginning September 1 1928, and ending August 31, 1930:

" 'To promote and establish industrial justice.

" 'To substitute reason for violence, confidence for misunderstanding, integrity and good faith for dishonest practices, and a union of effort for the chaos of the present economic warfare.

" 'To avoid needless and wasteful strikes and lockouts through the investigation and correction of their underlying causes.

" 'To establish genuine collective bargaining between mineworkers and operators through free and independent organisation.

" 'To stabilise employment, production and markets through co-operative endeavour and the aid of science.

" 'To assure mine-workers and operators continuing mutual benefits and consumers a dependable supply of coal at reasonable and uniform prices.

" 'To defend our joint undertaking against every conspiracy or vicious practice which seeks to destroy it; and in all other respects to enlist public confidence and support by safeguarding the public interest.'

"I had heard a good deal in various parts of the country about Miss Roche and the reorganisation of the Rocky Mountain Fuel Company, so it was of great interest to meet her and get first-hand information about the company's experiments. Miss Roche strikes one as being an unusual combination of idealism and practicalness. She obviously has the welfare of the miners at heart and is wishful to prove that it is possible to make a commerical success of coalmining while paying relatively high wages and giving the men a considerable measure of self-government. At the end of the first year of operation under the Agreement with the U.M.W.A. the following gains were noted:

The output in 1928 was 600,000 tons.
The output in 1929 was 800,000 tons, an increase of over 30 per cent.
The output per man increased $\frac{7}{10}$ of a ton.
The cost of production decreased 19 cents per ton (app. 9½d.).
The average earnings per man in 1928 were 1,661·01 dollars.
The average earnings per man in 1929 were 2,104·30 dollars, an increase of 443·29 dollars per man (app. £88 12s. 6d.) or a gain of 27 per cent.
The number of working days per man increased from 178 to 216, or 38 days—an increase of 21 per cent.
The average number of working days for all coal-miners in the State in 1929 was 159, 'which the R.M.F.C. bettered by 47 days or 30 per cent.' "

Mr. Merle Vincent, in his article on "Employment and Wage Security" in the 1930 *Official Year Book of the Colorado State Federation of Labor*, writes:

"The Rocky Mountain Fuel Company has not attained, but has taken only a first step toward effecting, the purpose of its policy. The past year has, however, witnessed an increase in working time, an increased production per man per day and substantially increased average annual earnings for all workers."

When the new labour policy of the Rocky Mountain Fuel Company was announced, specifically recognising the right of collective bargaining through independent organisations of the miners' own choosing, organised labour in Colorado immediately became interested; it was felt that here was a sincere effort to correct the injustices of the past in the State's coal-mining industry. The State Federation of Labor pledged its unqualified support in its annual convention of 1928; the Denver Trades and Labor Assembly and the Denver Building Trades Council quickly followed and combined in a campaign for the purpose of assisting in the marketing of union-mined coal, produced only by the Rocky Mountain Fuel Company in the northern field. At a gathering of more than sixty representative trades unionists, a Central Coal Committee of five was formed and this Committee in turn organised local Union Coal Committees, each consisting of three members for the purpose of enlisting the purchasing power of the entire trade union membership in the city. In May, 1930, there were seventy-four local union Coal Committees functioning under the direction of the Central Coal Committee. The Secretary of the Central Committee was giving full-time direction to the selling campaign

The women's auxiliaries have co-operated, and when the author was in Denver in June, 1930, they had just completed a telephone campaign among their members, urging them to support the marketing scheme. The 'phone method is frequently used in America in connection with drives and campaigns for various objects. Before long it will probably be adopted in England as one of the inevitable consequences of the Americanisation of Europe.

Another novel method of enlisting the purchasing power of the community, more particularly of the Churches, may be indicated by the publication of "A Statement by the Committee on applied Christianity of the Colorado Congregational Conference concerning Coal Mining," a copy of which was given to the author at Denver. This statement was widely circulated. After noting the results of the first year's operation under the agreement it proceeds:

"In view of these gains we commend the Rocky Mountain Fuel Company's economic and industrial efficiency to the public attention. It appears greatly to have lessened the likelihood of industrial strife where such strife has been notoriously and tragically prevalent in the commonwealth.

"We suggest that the State Industrial Commission make a study of the progress achieved by this company, and direct the attention of other coal-mine operators in the State to this successful industrial experiment.

"We further urge the patronage of Rocky Mountain Fuel Company products, in view of its service to society. The Company produces every grade of coal east of the mountains as follows:—

Good Coal (Frederick District) Grant Mine.
Very Good Coal (Lafayette District) Columbine and Standard Mines.
Best Coal (Louisville District) Vulcan and Industrial Mines.
"It also operates the Alpine Mine on the Western slope.

"No other company, at the present time, is operating under a U.M.W. of A. agreement.

> Committee:
> Rev. Alfred W. Swan, Greeley.
> Rev. O. R. Warford, Pueblo.
> Mr. D. W. Working, Denver.
> Miss Nellie L. Butler, Longmont."

The author was credibly informed that a certain pastor in Denver from the pulpit exhorted his congregation to buy Rocky Mountain coal! If American readers will pardon the English exclamation, "Isn't it lovely?"

There has been a persistent belief in reactionary business circles in the Denver district that the methods of the Rocky Mountain Fuel Company, which they regard as radical because of their challenge to traditional business ethics, would be disastrous. The author himself met business men in Denver who resented the intrusion of Miss Roche with her new-fangled notions and predicted early disaster. But it is significant that the operators of the northern Colorado coalfields recently formed an association and adopted a code of business ethics which had been the policy of the Rocky Mountain Fuel Company for nearly two years. All the principal operators are in the association and they asked the President of the Union Company to head the new group. Mr. J. O. Stevic, the Secretary of the Central Coal Committee, wrote in 1930:

"Labor here is congratulatory in its attitude towards this first step, but there still remains the question of the complete unionisation of the northern field mines, in which labor is vitally interested and which it believes will follow if the non-union members of the producers' Association will make a careful study of the union management co-operation program now operating between the Rocky Mountain Fuel Company and Organised Labor."[1]

It certainly would be an interesting development if this field became unionised as the result of the example set by the Rocky

---

[1] "Union Management Co-operation," in the 1930 *Official Year Book of the Colorado State Federation of Labor*, p. 35. I had fruitful talks with Mr. Stevic and have drawn freely on his article.

Mountain Fuel Company. Much will depend on whether the early success of that Company can be maintained. If it continues to thrive without jettisoning any of its principles and the other operators lose ground it is not perhaps too optimistic a belief that its methods will be generally adopted by the non-union operators, and this would mean unionisation throughout the field. At the moment, however, such a prospect seems rather remote, for it must not be forgotten that the Rocky Mountain Fuel Company is itself experiencing difficulties as a result of the general depression in the coal industry.

Recently the Organised Labor Central Coal Committee sent out to a large number of the working miners a *questionnaire* in order to get their reaction to the changed conditions. Under the union contract grievances and complaints are quickly settled with apparent satisfaction and fairness. We are told that in the twenty months after the contract went into effect only two cases passed beyond the pit committee stage; these were carried to the Executive Officers of the Company and a settlement was promptly made. Conferences are held between the Executive heads and the miners direct. At these conferences matters not ordinarily handled under the contract are openly discussed. Methods of operation, markets, finance and various business and labour problems form the topics for the interchange of ideas. Suggestions and criticisms are encouraged and the miners feel free to express themselves without fear of jeopardising their jobs. Suggestions have developed in these meetings which have been immediately applied and proved valuable to all concerned. The agreement with the union stipulated for a basic daily underground work scale of 7·00 dollars, the second highest wage scale in the United States for this class of work. In Illinois, the best organised soft coal district in the country, the scale in 1930 was 6·10 dollars. The replies to the *questionnaire* appear to prove conclusively that the miners are benefiting by the new relationship between themselves and the Company. Monetary returns, security of the job, freedom of expression, the right to board, live and trade where the men and their wives please are all contributing to a change for the better in the coal camp life, according to the testimony of the miners.

The following reply will be of more than passing interest to all who are interested in industrial problems. It is written by an actual coal miner who was in 1930 employed at the Industrial

Mine of the Rocky Mountain Fuel Company. The writer of the letter was educated in England before entering the mines, where he has spent the major part of his life.

"ORGANIZED LABOR'S CENTRAL COAL COMMITTEE,

"DENVER, COLORADO.

"Answering your letter of the 24th requesting the facts on how the labor policy of the Rocky Mountain Fuel Company is working out from the miners' point of view, I will give it to you as I see it and in the order requested on your blank, with a few extra conclusions that may help you or may not, but, in any case, should be known.

"1. *Has any improvement resulted in your working conditions since Rocky Mountain Fuel Company mines are under contract with your union?*

"I should say emphatically Yes. It is a mighty nice feeling to have, when you go to work, and to realize you won't be fired or harassed, cussed, etc., for no reason other than the boss being somewhat out of sorts, in many cases through his own excesses. Material is plentiful; we have a checkweighman, and last, but not least, we are being transported to work in a man trip to our working places underground, which are in some cases nearly two miles from the bottom of the shaft. I should estimate conservatively that we have been saved over 100,000 miles of weary tramping in the mine during the time this contract has been in force. In addition, over 20,000 cans of powder, from ten to twenty pounds each in weight, have been carried for us that we formerly carried ourselves, in addition to many thousands of picks and other tools that have to be taken out and sharpened daily. The trip also lessens the risk of being run over by the motors pulling the cars, both loads and empties to and from the bottom of the shaft—and as a safety measure is invaluable. We also have made a couple of examinations of the mine, in company with the mine officials and the State mine inspector, and have been accorded full facilities to state our points of view on the many intricate situations met with. Our suggestions were considered and in many cases acted upon. The scales on which the miner's coal is weighed have been examined by us on numerous occasions to satisfy us as to their correctness. Further, the men are not crowded together in their working places as they were before the contract was signed. Also many changes for the better were made—changes that were not in the contract, but negotiated locally, and with commendable willingness on the part of the Company. So you will readily see that conditions are immeasurably better, as these changes have taken place since the contract was signed.

"2. *Have the miners' monthly earnings increased? If so, about how much per man?*

"Wages have been stabilised at 7 dollars per day and I have no hesitation in saying but for this policy no less than two and possibly three dollars per day would have been lopped off without any corresponding benefit to anybody. This applies to day men. Piece men are making anywhere from 10 to 40 per cent more, and, by the way, low wages in these mines bring a bigger loss to the business people in Denver than their so-called cheap coal would benefit them, as many of the miners trade mostly in Denver. If this point could be driven home to the bigger business houses in Denver, we would get more help from them and less catering to the other fellow.

"3. *Are adjustments of grievance under the union contract method proving satisfactory to the miners?*

"The very fact that we can meet together and discuss our grievances, and then take them to people of the caliber of the officers of the Rocky Mountain Fuel Company, is sufficient guarantee of their being settled satisfactorily, and I don't know of any other method that would improve this.

"4. *What is the attitude generally in regard to the Rocky Mountain Fuel Company labor policy? Do the miners think it any improvement over the non-union mines?*

"The miners don't think this is an improvement—they know it and are more satisfied than they have been for years past.

"5. *Is the mine where you are working operated more regularly than in former years?*

"This mine, the Industrial, seems to me to have worked between two and three hundred per cent more than previous years, and I assume no small measure of this is due to the assistance rendered to the company and ourselves by your central Coal Committee and the organised workers of this State.

"6. *Are the men permitted any greater freedom under Rocky*

Mountain Fuel Company union conditions than they were under former non-union conditions?

"Ye Gods! freedom was unknown up here in the mines from 1910 until contract was signed. The chief requirement to get a job in these mines previous to this time was inability to speak English and be unmeltable in the American melting pot. You were not supposed to know anything, had to board in the company boarding house if single, and if married, live in a company shack and trade in the company store. If any jobs were left, after these kinds were supplied, then, and not till then, were the home-owners of the camps given other jobs. The *Denver Post*, Arthur Brisbane, and others, always stress the fact of their desire to see everybody in this country own their own homes, in addition to an automobile and a radio. Owning something like that up here in these coal mines kept you from a job! Before the strike of 1910, probably 80 per cent of the miners in Lafayette owned their own homes, spent their money in Colorado and were an asset to the State. Since then the home-owner has been discriminated against to much that he now is in the minority to such an alarming extent that the type referred to above can outvote him on almost any question that is put up. However in the Rocky Mountain Fuel Company mines, a man can live where he pleases, board where he pleases, and nobody asks him whether he has an auto or a radio. I believe the company would be pleased to see their miners get these things. Home-owners are once more coming into their own in these camps and freedom has returned.

"7. *What do you know about working conditions in non-union mines which may be stated as a fact?*

"Having been boycotted for a long time in the non-union mines, I can't say much definitely about them, but this I do know, you do as you are told, right or wrong; no buts and ifs and ands about it—you just do it or you have no job. If they want you to work nine hours, you do it; if they want you to work Sundays, you also do that. Conditions in some of them are so bad, so I am told, that conditions just ain't! That's all.

"I will close, hoping this may be of some use to you. These are my personal impressions and you have full liberty to use them as you see fit.

Yours fraternally,
JOHN GREEN."

It is not easy to estimate the prospects of the continued success of this experiment. The depression in the industry generally and the particular financial difficulties of a company attempting to apply liberal ideas in a hostile economic *milieu* tend towards pessimism; on the other hand, the financial and moral support of organised labour, not alone in Colorado, but of progressive people all over the country promises success. The most advanced radical groups in America regard the whole experiment with suspicion and are quite unconcerned about its success apparently. To European miners, who have long formulated demands for nationalisation and seriously discussed workers' control, it does not appear to go very far. But, having regard to the comparative isolation of the field, the weakness of union organisation in the State and the almost lawless arrogance of the operators in the past, one cannot withhold one's admiration of the gallant attempt now being made by Miss Roche and her associates.

Reference has already been made to Merle Vincent, the President of the company, who, in addition to being an able lawyer, is an astute business man and is well versed in the economics of the coal industry; and also to McGuire, a man of wide experience on the technical side and apparently more interested in efficiency than in social ideals. But John Lawson is deserving of a chapter to himself. His official position is Second Vice-President of the company, but his real value in the scheme derives from the fact that he is the same John Lawson who organised the miners in their struggle against the Colorado Fuel and Iron Company in 1913–14. That in itself is a sufficient guarantee to the employees of the Rocky Mountain Fuel Company that their grievances will be sympathetically considered and their general interests safe-guarded. But seventeen years later he impresses one as a man of transparent honesty, sincerity of purpose and genuine sympathy with the working miners. His reply to the Judge when he was sentenced to imprisonment for life in 1915 has more than a personal interest; it is a record of historical importance and is, therefore, quoted here in full:

"The Court has asked me what, if anything, I have to say why sentence should not now be pronounced against me.

"During two days of argument on that very question, through which I listened, not in a personal way, but so far as possible as a citizen of our common country, I had supposed that many and unanswerable reasons supporting my view had been given to the Court.

"Therefore, in the Court's interest at this moment, I must recognise a mere formality. It is plain that nothing I can say will change your fixed determination so far as you have the power to start me down the dark path of imprisonment for life.

"It is proper that a man so situated, especially when, as in my case, he is the victim without fault of an utterly unscrupulous persecution, should be permitted to enter his protest against injustice, however much that protest may appear weakened by its relation to individual experience.

"Fortunately, what I have to say is warranted by bigger considerations than any personal to me. So far-reaching are they that I feel I have a right to ask you to hear my views with the same courtesy I have used during my trial through your rulings and remarks.

"About to be condemned by you to prison for life, I will, therefore, make answer to your question in the following way:

"First of all, in the name of the Courts of my country, which I respect, I protest against your right of power to pass any judgment against me. It is undenied in this case that you were appointed to the Bench this spring for the trial of myself and my associates, fresh from the employment of the very coal operators of Colorado and the country, including the Rockefellers, who have pressed and engineered these prosecutions.

"Yourself a coal company attorney, engaged to assist as a practicing lawyer in the trial of cases arising like mine out of industrial disturbances of 1913 and 1914, you had no right, when challenged, to sit as trial judge in the case of any striking miner.

"You were so deeply prejudiced against me that my case was a travesty of justice from the start. Notwithstanding the affidavits of reliable citizens who have sworn to your prejudice, you have persisted on the Bench. To-day the Supreme Court of Colorado in Denver is reviewing your conduct, and yet you refuse to wait another twenty-four hours for the guidance of that Court's decision. Such unseemly haste in the exercise of such a jurisdiction to thrust me into prison should not be passed without a protest.

"Second only to the resolution with which you hold your seat upon the Bench, was the method adopted by you for selecting

a jury to try me. You refused to permit the jury to be drawn
from the regular jury box provided by law, and you ordered an
open venire.

"This method was exactly adapted to procure what none
were surprised to discover—a hand-picked jury of coal company
partisans. After you had removed the coroner as a summoning
officer, over my protest, you selected your own instruments to
pick this jury. And the jury so chosen was naturally subject to
the self-same coal company influences which with hue and cry
now seek to drive me to the penitentiary.

"It matters not that I was utterly guiltless of the charge against
me. It matters not that the prosecution was forced to abandon
its claim that on October 25, 1913, I fired a shot or did other
than seek to avoid the violence which menaced the cause dearest
to my heart.

"It matters not that it became necessary for the prosecution
to invoke legal doctrines of conspiracy, which, if applied im-
partially, would convict the leading coal operators of Colorado
and the country for the deaths of men, women, and children
at Ludlow on April 20, 1914.

"Perhaps this seemed immaterial, because none of them have
been informed against, much less tried, and none of them fear
our Courts or prosecuting officials.

"It matters not that the only evidence, on which the prosecution
was forced to rest, was the testimony of two disreputable Baldwin-
Felts detectives, employees of the coal operators' association,
with whom you yourself were formerly professionally associated.

"Nothing was to be permitted to stand in the way, and it is
significant that even a jury so selected refused to convict me
until a bailiff selected by you, according to affidavits on file in
this Court, tortured a juryman with manufactured reports of
the dangerous illness of the juror's wife, and as a final stroke
warned the jury that under your orders, the jury would have
nothing further to eat until they rendered their verdict.

"In the face of this sworn charge, which Courts everywhere
have held sufficient to undermine the whole structure of jury
trials and to destroy the integrity of such a verdict, your bailiff
has remained silent and this Court impassive. May I ask whether
judicial travesty is not the right description of such proceedings?

"Such practices, however astonishing to our people in general, do not surprise one who has observed our industrial history. From long experience I recognise the power of wealth, the magnitude of our industrial problems and their effect on our existing social system. I can understand, for I have seen how men who seek a living realisation for the workers of the world of the old ideals of justice and equality; who endeavour to open the eyes of their fellows to the true economic conditions that surround them as they seek their daily bread, are persecuted, defamed and even, in exceptional instances, hounded to the gallows by those who control the wealth and privileges of our generous country.

"I have seen some masters of finance within and without this State using the full powers of government to divide the workers, to crush the hopes and aspirations in their breasts, and to extinguish the kindling light of intelligence in their souls in full realisation of the fact that understanding brings the fixed desire for the higher and nobler things of life, including a dream of equality of opportunity some day for the children of rich and poor alike.

"And it is not overstatement to say that I am here to-day because, with others, I have patiently, without bitterness, yet persistently, for years sought these things—a wider chance in life for those who toil, a higher type of democratic citizenship and a social system of industry which gives promise to mankind and denies autocratic power over the lives and liberties of the great mass of workers to the masters of millions who have usurped governmental authority itself.

"Such usurpation has reached its most finished expression in Las Animas and Huerfano counties, in this State, and those who, like myself, have continued none the less to worship at the ancient altars of human liberty and justice in this country have been marked for annihilation.

"But let no one think we have not seen through years this very possibility.

"In receiving sentence of life imprisonment at hard labor from this Court, I can do so with the knowledge that I have broken no law and committed no crime, unless it be that I am a coal-miner, honored by my fellow workers, with their years of confident faith that my devotion will stand even this acid test for the maintenance of their principles.

"In a word, the reason this Court should not pass judgmen as I see it, is that by so doing it will openly violate every principl of justice for the promotion of which our Courts exist.

"Solemnly facing iron bars and prison walls, I assert my lov for justice and my faith in its ultimate triumph—not a justic of theory, but of reality extending to men, women and childrei whose proper equality of opportunity it embraces; and witl utmost earnestness I want it understood that my one satisfactio in my lot—separated though I be from those who are deare to me than life—lies in the belief that this, my undeserved experi ence, may help awaken others to the living wrongs in our world calling to-day as definitely as in the past for remedy.

"IT IS A PRIVILEGE AND A DUTY EVEN BY SACRIFICE TO ADVANC OUR PRICELESS CAUSE. I AM, THEREFORE, READY TO RECEIVE TH SENTENCE THIS COURT SHOULD DECLARE ITSELF WITHOUT EITHE AUTHORITY, RIGHT OR JUSTIFICATION TO IMPOSE."

MINING WARFARE IN WEST VIRGINIA

And now it is time to transfer the scene to West Virginia, which of the non-union States, shares with Colorado, Alabama and quite recently, Kentucky, the distinction that comes of resor to civil war in mining disputes. Wherever the author went ii the States and discussed this feature of American coal history h was met with the somewhat defensive attitude, "Ah, yes, Wes Virginia, but that's our blackest spot." He met, among others Winthrop D. Lane, a journalist, who has made a special investi gation of conditions in that field and written a little book unde the title, *Civil War in West Virginia*, to which the reader i referred for what seems to be a faithful account of the violenc characteristic of the southern part of the State.

"In this untamed section of West Virginia," says an *Atlanti Monthly* article, "two tremendous forces have staked out a battle ground. They are the United Mine Workers of America and th most powerful groups of non-union coal operators in the country It is a battle to the bitter end; neither side asks quarter, neithe side gives it. It is a battle for enormous stakes, in which money is lavished; it is fought through the Courts, through the Press with matching of sharp wits to secure public approval. But more than this, it is actually fought with deadly weapons on both sides; many lives have already been lost; many may yet be forfeited."[1]

Clearly there is something unusual behind a struggle of such intensity. Let us examine first some of the fundamental issues at stake. There are certain reasons why it has seemed necessary to the United Mine Workers to organise the non-union fields, especially West Virginia. The operators of the central competitive field (Western Pennsylvania, Ohio, Illinois, Indiana) contended, before the United States Coal Commission of 1923, that owing to freight differentials the real competitors of these States were the fields of West Virginia and Eastern Kentucky, which were outside the central competitive field. It would be to the interest of the union operators therefore to weaken the competition of the non-union operators of West Virginia. One way of doing this would be to reduce the wages of their own employees but this they could not do because of the strength of the union. Any policy therefore which would raise the wage-scale in the non-union fields they were disposed to support. The extent to which they actually assisted the union in attempting to organise their competitors' mines is difficult to determine but the point is definitely mentioned in one of their early agreements.

Here is an interesting situation, unparalleled in the British coalfields. Operators in one section assisting the union against the operators in another section! But of course it is explained by the difference in the conditions. In Great Britain the coalfields are almost uniformly organised; in the American fields organisation is piebald, patchy.

Apart from this pressure of the union operators to get the non-union fields organised the United Mine Workers have realised that the unorganised fields are a menace to the very existence of the union. The union operator chafes under the restrictions implicit in his marriage with the Union and would be glad of any excuse for a divorce. Further, the very large production which the non-union mines can put on the market whenever there is a strike in the union fields offsets the efforts of the union officials to paralyse the productive capacity of the country. Other conditions also tend to make the unorganised fields a constant problem for the union officials, such as the increased

[1] James M. Cain, "The Battleground of Coal," *The Atlantic Monthly*, October, 1922.

profits of the non-union operator, the higher wages of the non-union miner when there is a strike in the union fields, and the indirect benefit enjoyed by the non-union worker through increases in the union scale which are usually made the basis for payment in the non-union fields also.

It is obvious therefore why the union officials attach such importance to the necessity for effecting the organisation of the non-union fields.

The principal stronghold of the non-union operators lies in south-western West Virginia and eastern Kentucky, a picturesque mountainous country, inhabited by a primitive class of back country people more or less accustomed to taking the law into their own hands, the whole setting being admirably suited for the bitter guerilla warfare that has characterised the efforts of the United Mine Workers to secure a foothold in the district. The operators own or control the lands in the affected territory to such an extent as to make it virtually impossible for an outsider to enter any of the fields without becoming a trespasser within the definition of the law. It is difficult for an Englishman who has not explored this district to realise the tremendous difficulties that union officials have to face. The author was told by one of the leading officials of the United Mine Workers that on one occasion when he was obliged to visit a mining town in southern West Virginia he had to have an armed body-guard, and he himself carried a pistol. On another occasion the Mayor, who was the tool of the local operating Company, ordered him out of the town and in spite of his protests and threats, out he had to go.

The system of "mine guards" has been extensively employed in this section. It appears to have arisen out of the demand for more officers than the meagre taxes of the relatively poor sections would support. When abnormal conditions developed over labour controversies the supply of deputy Sheriffs to protect the mine properties was considered inadequate. Consequently the operators hired "guards" and undertook to relieve the civic authorities of any financial obligation by paying the bill themselves. This roused a popular protest and the operators then agreed to lend the necessary money to pay these "guards" to the county and this is now the practice. There is no evidence that any of these loans have ever been repaid or that the operators are pressing for payment.

Even in normal times nearly every camp has its duly authorised deputy sheriff, who usually also serves in some minor official capacity at the mine. His chief duty is to keep informed about any stranger who may put in an appearance in the vicinity and to ascertain his business; if this is found to be in any way objectionable he is expected to find ways of discouraging the newcomer's presence, which can usually be readily done by bringing a charge of trespass against him. Under such conditions a union organiser has little chance of even starting his activities. It is no wonder that the whole system of deputy sheriffs and "guards" has evoked the most bitter criticism from the United Mine Workers.

The operators have also secured a favourable interpretation of the law governing evictions from the company-owned houses. This has done much to hamper the activities of the union organisers. The courts of West Virginia have ruled that the relation of tenant and landlord does not exist in the case of these houses since they are used exclusively for the housing of company employees, and the relation is, therefore, more that of master and servant. Occupancy of the house is thus contingent upon continued employment in the service of the Company, as in the case of a servant in the house, so that when the miners went on strike they automatically dispossessed themselves of their domicile. Under these circumstances it was necessary for the miners to move out into tents, if any land not owned or controlled by the Company were available. But the law was weighted against them even under canvas. For instance, a temporary injunction restrained the miners "from further maintaining the tent colonies of Mingo County or in the vicinity of the mines of the plaintiffs"; and representatives of the United Mine Workers were further restrained from "furnishing to the inhabitants of said tent colonies or to those who may hereafter inhabit the same, any sum or sums of money, orders for money, merchandise, or orders for merchandise, or any other thing of value. . . ."[1]

In other instances miners are required to sign leases for their houses which provide, in substance, that the occupant will allow no one on the property other than members of his family,

---

[1] Felix Frankfurter and Nathan Green, *The Labor Injunction*, p. 100. A most erudite work, giving overwhelming evidence of the use of the injunction against the interests of organised labour in all branches of industry in the United States.

physicians, draymen to move him in and out, and the undertaker. The rights of property, both inside and outside the houses, are jealously guarded. A young miner told the author that on one occasion he took his "girl" home in his automobile, which he parked outside the house. A policeman ordered him off the property and when he explained that his companion's father worked for the Company he was told that he had no right to be on the Company's property though his friend, of course, had. Nor did the daughter's protestations avail and the love-sick swain had to depart, muttering curses, doubtless, on the whole institution of Company ownership.

In discussing this matter of the organisation of the mine-workers it should be realised that the non-union operator regards the union as a monstrous impudent challenge to his right "to do as I like with my own" and that he considers himself fully justified in resorting to any methods available to nullify the efforts of the union organisers. He regards himself as a public benefactor and in support of this he emphasises the point that he is the only source of supply when there are strikes in the union fields. Regarding the power of the union as dangerous he warns the public of the consequences of the complete unionisation of all the fields. He contends that the rules established by the union greatly impair the efficiency of his operations. This charge is made also by certain union operators. Colonel W. M. Wiley, vice-president and general manager of the Boone County Coal Corporation of Sharples, West Virginia, in his testimony at the "Hearings before the United States Committee on Education and Labor" in 1921, said:

"Now, a union operator in my condition—our mines have run ever since last October with a union contract—it is difficult for us to meet the competition of the gentlemen in the Guyan field, who are able to adjust their wages and meet the present conditions. But the wage adjustment is the least of our troubles. The gravest trouble we have is: We can pay the wages and compete with the Guyan field, but we cannot meet the inefficiency that comes from the union, preventing us from rewarding the good workman and punishing the poor workman in order to get efficiency. It is the lack of efficiency in our mines that seriously handicaps us."

The union has made many desperate and partially successful

MAIDSVILLE BARRACKS, WEST VIRGINIA, BUILT TO HOUSE EVICTED MINERS

efforts to organise the non-union sections of West Virginia and the surrounding country, and in spite of the handicaps it is working under the indications are that it will persevere. John L. Lewis, the president of the United Mine Workers, assured the author that his policy was to maintain outposts in the difficult fields and bide his time till the conditions were favourable for intensive "drives." He seemed quite confident that one day even West Virginia would be wholly unionised. On being pressed as to what conditions might be favourable he indicated that when the industry recovered from the present slump the operators would need the union for purposes of wage agreements, etc. The author ventured to express his doubts that the coal industry would ever attain to the level of its former prosperity and the discussion rode off from the prospects of unionisation to the possibilities of new uses of coal, markets, etc. The author can only record his impression that John L. Lewis was more optimistic as to the prospect of the unionisation of all the fields than the present economic trends would appear to warrant.

The reader will now be in a position to appreciate some of the deep-rooted issues that lay at the back of the struggle in West Virginia.

Unionising efforts that began on an active scale in 1902 have resulted in some of the severest industrial conflicts in American history. As a result of these efforts the union gained recognition in a small area in the Kanawha field. There a two-year district agreement was signed with the operators. This agreement included an increase in pay with a semi-monthly pay-day, reduction of the working day to nine hours, the right to employ a checkweigh-man, the right to buy elsewhere than at a company store, and reinstatement of strikers without discrimination. The operators also agreed to "check-off" the union dues. The "check-off" is a system by which the contributions of the men to their union are deducted from their pay by the Company and handed over to the union.

For twenty years the Kanawha district remained a union strong-hold in West Virginia. Union officials hoped that in time other operators would see the smooth working of the Kanawha agree-ment and adopt a more friendly attitude towards the union. But the southern counties were just being opened up, largely by companies allied to the interests which had fought to a finish the unions in the steel industry. So instead of bargaining with the United Mine Workers' Union they began to sharpen their weapons against it. The holding of meetings "at or near the mines of the Companies was prevented by an injunction, the legal right to organise was curtailed by the West Virginia Supreme Court in 1906, the 'yellow-dog' contract was gradually introduced and some Companies with the help of State officials specialised in importing under contract foreign workers who were kept in a state of peonage until they had worked out their 'indebtedness' to the Company."

The system of private armed guards was developed as a continuous routine, even when there was no strike brewing. The notorious Baldwin-Felts agency at Bluefield built up a business of supplying spies and gunmen to the operators. Private mine guards had roused protests which led to the Governor of the State in 1907 to refer to them in his message to the legislature:

"They (mine guards) are used at some of the collieries to protect the property of owners, to prevent trespassing, and especially to prevent labor agitators and organisers of a miners' union from gaining access to the miners. . . . Many outrages have been committed by these guards, many of whom appear to be vicious and dare-devil men who seem to add to their viciousness by bull-dozing and terrorising people."

But the mine guard system remained.

In 1912 the struggle between the striking coal-miners in Cabin Creek, Paint Creek and other West Virginian fields and the armed guards acting for the operators produced a state bordering on civil war. Governor Glasscock ordered out the militia and issued a proclamation of martial law. This was later cancelled but shortly renewed. In a case involving "Mother Jones" (a doughty champion of American miners, a remarkable old lady in many ways) and others who had been arrested for helping to conduct the strike, Justice Robinson gave this dissenting opinion:

"Petitioners were arrested in the city of Charleston on a warrant of a Justice of Peace, a civil court, charging them with civil offences, that of a conspiracy to inflict bodily injury on persons whose names were unknown and other offences. They were taken before the Justice in sight of the Court House, where the civil courts of the county were open and in exercise of their powers Instead of giving the accused preliminary examination, and upon the finding of probable cause holding them to answer the grand jury, the Justice directed the special constable having them in charge by endorsement on the warrant to deliver them to the military authorites in the so-called military district. They were so delivered and were about to be put on trial before a military commission . . . for the same offences charged before the civil court . . . that court in absolute disregard of their rights and the law governing it, sent them to the military authorities in a distant part of the county. . . . This illegal procedure alone entitled the petitioners to be remanded to the civil courts. . . . Yet it simply illustrates the extreme to which disregard of the Constitution and legal procedure has run. Instead of recognising the true order of the statute whereby a militia is to aid the civil authorities, the law is reversed and the civil authorites used to aid the military power. Verily, indeed, has the military power been made absolutely independent and dominant in West Virginia."[1]

The strike of 1912 was a long and bitter struggle. A peculiar feature was that some evicted strikers could not get their mail (correspondence) from post offices on company property, and it is on record that at least once mail was deliberately burned by a store manager.[2] The roads up the creeks were guarded by machine guns and no stranger or known union organiser was allowed to pass. Stirring tales are told by Mother Jones and others of wading and driving up the creeks to encourage the strikers and assist in organising the men. The author has explored these creeks in normal times; it does not need a highly developed imagination to visualise the scene in times of industrial war. The governor sent in the State militia but the presence of the militia did not prevent a trainload of Baldwin-Felts guards, with machine guns and rifles, from shooting at a tent colony at a place called Holly Grove, killing a miner and a woman and wounding sixteen others. A military commission took over the administration of justice and arrested and detained scores of strikers without regard to the State laws. They worked in consulta-

---

[1] Quoted by Leon Whipple in *The Story of Civil Liberty in the United States*, pp. 246-7.

[2] Anna Rochester, *Labor and Coal*, p. 195. A valuable piece of work, highly critical of the United Mine Workers of America from the left wing angle and containing information difficult to find elsewhere. I have drawn freely on Chapters X, XI, and XII.

tion with the Governor and later admitted that they were keeping
certain miners out of the way until they "had peace and order
in that territory." Meantime they were aiding the mine guards
to protect imported "scabs."

After more than a year of struggle and suffering a compromise
settlement was secured. The union gained a foothold in the Paint
Creek, Cabin Creek and New River fields though in none of them
were conditions brought up to the standard of the Kanawha
agreement.

Until the war boom the paid-up union membership in West
Virginia was barely one-tenth of all the coal-mine workers in
the State. In 1916 and 1917 the union was strong enough to gain
recognition in the Fairmont field (in the northern part of the
State), and in spite of the operators' terrorist tactics workers
were organising in the wild mountain regions about Logan and
south of the Kanawha district.

The struggle reached a climax in 1921 in what is known as
"The Armed March of West Virginia." Two years earlier, in
September, 1919, three thousand union miners from the Kanawha
field assembled armed with rifles at a place called Marmet, to
march over the mountains to unionise the mines at Logan, and,
if necessary, to do battle with the operators. The Governor and
Mr. Keeney, the President of the Union district, pressed them to
disband. The Governor promised a full investigation of the miners'
grievances in Logan county and the men heard that Federal
troops, which they believed would enforce fair play, were on their
way to Logan. So they yielded and returned on the train provided
for them by the State.

During the following spring (1920) a number of operators in
Mingo County tried to break the attempt to organise by locking
out their miners and bringing in strike-breakers. At Matewan,
the Mayor and the Chief of Police (Sid Hatfield) protested that
the eviction of union members by the Felts brothers and a band
of their gunmen was illegal. Albert Felts tried to arrest Hatfield
and in a five-minute battle ten men were killed, including the
Mayor and the two Felts brothers. Troops were brought in and
stationed about the mines while nearly three thousand striking
miners and their families spent the winter in tent colonies.

The conflict continued through the summer of 1921 and reached
a climax in "The Armed March." In May of that year, as a

result of disorders arising from the stoppage in the mines, Mingo County had been placed under martial law by Governor Morgan. The whole situation was charged with electricity. On July 31st there occurred an event that inflamed the fighting spirit of the union miners in the Kanawha field. On that day Sid Hatfield, the Chief of Police, who was regarded as a good friend of the Union, and his friend Ed. Chambers were shot on the steps of the court house at Welch, in McDowell County, by an ambushed gang of Baldwin-Felts men, led by a "stool pigeon" or renegade who had once been active in the union. The killing of Hatfield caused a great deal of unrest and aroused intense indignation. When the author was in the district he was often told about the shooting of Sid Hatfield and that it was the chief cause leading up to the armed march. This is hardly borne out by all the evidence. Colonel Wiley, who in his evidence before the Senate Investigating Committee, alleged that the purpose of the first and second marches was to get newspaper publicity, admitted that the object of the third march (the famous so-called "armed march") was that "they wanted to unionise the mines at Logan." There is little doubt however that Hatfield's death was a big factor in bringing matters to a head. Three weeks later between five thousand and seven thousand men (the estimates vary within this range) gathered again at Marmet for the purpose of marching over the ridge of mountains to Logan and Mingo Counties. This ridge, known as the battle line, was about 25 miles from one end to the other and separated the union part of the county from the non-union part of the county.

It is difficult to ascertain the extent to which the miners were armed. Colonel Wiley speaks of every man "making good with his high-powered rifle and his pistols, and with six thousand to back him—six thousand armed men to back him up." (This estimate he later modified to between five thousand and six thousand.) Others informed the author when he was on the spot that many of the "army" were unarmed and merely marched to swell the numbers. At any rate there appears to have been a fairly elaborate organisation. The men wore a uniform of blue overalls and a red handkerchief round the neck. They had a commissary, passes and a small band of nurses to care for the wounded. Colonel Wiley said: "I saw automobiles with nurses in them with Red Cross uniforms on, except in place of the cross on the cap was 'U.M.W.' and they had thoroughly established field hospitals and they had commandeered the doctors into them." They were evidently set on winning Logan county for the union and they knew this meant war.

Federal troops in considerable numbers were brought in, largely as the result, according to Colonel Wiley, of the "very drastic action taken by the Logan Operators' Association and the equally drastic action taken by the Charleston Chamber of Commerce."

"THE CHAIRMAN: About how many troops were brought up there?

MR. WILEY: Some stopped at Madison before they came there. I think about 200 got off at Jeffrey. The second train brought 135 to Sharples, and the third train took about 500 to Blair.

.   .   .   .   .

THE CHAIRMAN: Now, against these 25 miles of men, who was shooting?

MR. WILEY: Do you mean against the miners?

THE CHAIRMAN: Yes.

MR. WILEY: The officers and officials of Logan county who were trying to protect themselves against being raided.

THE CHAIRMAN: They were deputies, I suppose?

MR. WILEY: I imagine so, sir. I do not think I am the first authority on that.

THE CHAIRMAN: I was wondering what it was that took care of the 25 miles of battle line. What stopped it? There must have been some force that stopped it.

Colonel Wiley "passed the buck" to other "authorities"; in other words he referred the Chairman to others (mentioning two by name) for the desired information.

Again the Governor of the State and District President Keeney tried to hold the men back and John L. Lewis, the International President of the United Mine Workers of America, attempted to stop the trouble by pressing President Harding to arrange a conference of union officials and the operators of Mingo County. The miners had gone half way to Logan when they actually began to disperse, but they heard that the miners' outpost near Sharples had met the State troopers and that three miners had

been killed. Once more they headed southward with reinforce-
ments. They swarmed over the mountains in several divisions,
but the delay had given the operators time to increase their
forces. Gunmen, business men and militia, with rifles, machine
guns and aeroplanes lined up to resist the marching miners.
The battle lasted nearly a week—there were more than fifty men
killed altogether on both sides—and the miners were breaking
through the lines when Federal troops arrived and turned the
tide against them. Martial law continued in force and little by
little the strike was smothered.

This reverse was only the beginning of withdrawal and defeat
throughout the State. In 1920 the United Mine Workers was at
its peak of membership, with a paid-up enrolment in West
Virginia of nearly half the 100,000 mine-workers in the State.
By 1929 there were barely 600 paid-up members in West Virginia.

Early in 1922 most of the Kanawha and New River operators
tried to force a district agreement without waiting as usual for
the outcome of negotiations in the Central Competitive Field.
When the Union refused this the operators announced a wage
cut and open shop operation. The miners struck, independently
of the nation-wide strike call of 1922, and stayed out in the
Kanawha field long after the big northern strike was over. In
spite of hunger and suffering many were still refusing two years
later to work in non-union mines. A few Kanawha operators
had signed up separately in 1922 but by 1924 the union had lost
its foothold in the field. Then the wave of destruction swept
northward to the Fairmont field where most of the operators
had signed an agreement after the 1922 strike. A smaller group
went through the form of an agreement in 1924, only to break it
in the following year. Again a strike with evictions, barracks,
tent colonies—and defeat. The determination of the operators
on the open shop policy and the failure of the United Mine
Workers to withstand it practically destroyed the union throughout
the State.

Difficulties in Alabama

A month spent in this coalfield—the author chose Alabama
as being typical of the south-western extension, comprising
Kentucky, Alabama and Tennessee, of the eastern or Appalachian
field—is sufficient to make an Englishman realise the difficulties

in the way of unionisation. The whole field seems to be dominated by the power of the United States Steel Corporation through its subsidiary the Tennessee Coal, Iron and Railroad Company (T.C.I.). The ramifications of the financial and political influence of this economic domination are not easy to trace but one has the sense that it controls the entire life of the population in this area. And when the coal interests of this octopus, whose tentacles stretch over a vast territory outside Tennessee and Alabama, are determined to destroy the union they succeed almost completely. They have certainly done so in Alabama. The United Mine Workers' organisation is shot to pieces and the economic interests of the coal-miners seem to be in the hands of a lone outpost of the American Federation of Labour.

Yet Alabama has had its spurts of unionism. Thirty years ago there was an eager response to the United Mine Workers organising campaign. In 1902 and 1903 several thousand miners were out in short local strikes. They secured an arbitration award with a slight increase in pay and some improvement in working conditions but the Tennessee Coal, Iron and Railroad Company refused to pay the scale of the arbitration award and in 1904 some 10,000 men employed by the T.C.I. and other "furnace" operators went on strike. Both Federal and State courts issued injunctions against the strikers. "The climax . . . came when the governor ordered the state militia to cut down the tents used to shelter the evicted mine workers and their families. In addition to this order, the soldiers were directed to take possession of the tents, and orders were issued that public meetings could not be held. The governor also threatened to call a special session of the legislature to repeal the vagrancy law of Alabama, so that every striking miner could be arrested and sent to prison."[1] Two years later all union agreements in Alabama had been broken and membership steadily declined.

During the war boom the union was revived and in May, 1920, when Alabama operators refused to accept the award of the Bituminous Coal Commission, a strike was called which spread throughout the coalfields of the State. But the coal interests, headed by the United States Steel Corporation, secured from the governor the use of the state militia which proceeded to break

[1] "United Mine Workers of America *Proceedings of the Twentieth Annual Convention*, 1909, p. 66.

WE ARE ON STRIKE AGAINST A REDUCTION IN WAGES.
AND FOR AN AMERICAN STANDARD OF LIVING.
FILL YOUR TANK WITH
UNIONISM AND.
STEP ON THE GAS.
WE STAND
FOR
ORGANIZED
LABOR
IF A MAN OWN'S HIS OWN SOUL.
HE WILL "DIG" UNION PRICE COAL.
SIGN UP
AND BE
A MAN
JOIN THE UNION
WHILE YOU CAN.
DEMAND
THE
UNION
LABEL.

IRONA BARRACKS, KINGWOOD, WEST VIRGINIA

up the picket lines and prevent all meetings and speeches, even including regular business meetings of union locals inside their own halls. The old story of evictions, tent colonies and imported strikebreakers was repeated. Even peaceful picketing was strictly prohibited. John Northcutt, who had persisted in leading a picket line, was shot at sight by one of the militia. The soldier who killed him was shot in his turn, and a miner named Will Baird, a son-in-law of Northcutt, was accused. Baird fled into the woods, but later gave himself up to the Sheriff. A gang of soldiers broke into the jail at midnight and carried Baird off for a lynching. His body was found in the woods, pierced by twenty-two bullet holes. The lynchers were known and the grand jury indicted them but they "got off."

In February, 1921, the United Mine Workers agreed to arbitration of the strike by the governor. He ruled against the union on every point. All recognition was refused and every miner who had been an active leader in the strike was black-listed by the operators. Van A. Bittner, John L. Lewis's chief assistant, was sent in to take charge of the weakened district, but the union has never regained its foothold.

Some idea of the backwardness of this State may be had from the fact that convicts continued to work in Alabama mines until after the war. In both Alabama and Tennessee there have been bitter strikes against the use of convict labour in the mines. In Tennessee especially the fight for its abolition has been protracted and severe. The miners in that State had been organised in 1888 and in the following year began a series of local strikes. In April, 1891, armed miners took the convicts out of the mines at Coal Creek and escorted them back to the prison in Knoxville. They then called on the governor of the State who promised to summon a special session of the legislature to pass laws against the use of convict mine labour. But the convict-leasing companies brought political pressure to bear and prevented the governor from implementing his promise. Convicts were returned to the mines and militia were stationed at Coal Creek. Miners made friends with the militia and succeeded in releasing 1,500 convicts. More soldiers were sent in and some were permanently stationed near the convict mines. In August, 1892, the miners renewed the struggle, first at Tracy City, then at the iron-mines at Inman and the coal-mines at Oliver Springs and Coal Creek. At first the miners were successful in battling the militia. "In several instances entire train loads of militia were taken captive and disarmed, but the final victory was with the militia. The mines were retaken from the miners and the prisoners were put back to work."[1]

With less notable conflicts in other states, a total of twenty-two strikes against convict labour in coal-mines are reported for the years 1881 to 1900. They were all defeated. To-day, however, convict leasing is a thing of the past.

The following entry from the author's diary may be of interest:

"*January* 16, 1930. . . . After looking at some of the houses we proceeded to Docena, where we stopped off to look at a class in First Aid which was being conducted by one of the Company doctors devoting all his time to First Aid instruction. Two other doctors are employed in the field for medical service. An interesting feature of the First Aid Class was that it was being held in the building which housed convicts who until 1925 were forced to work in the mines in the state of Alabama. The general feeling was one of satisfaction that this social stigma had at last been removed and I was interested to hear the opinion expressed that the convict labour in this field had never been efficient anyway."

One of the most interesting features of the Alabama field is the preponderance of negroes in the mining population. Estimates of the proportion of negroes to the total number of miners range from 53 per cent to 75 per cent. The lower estimate may be relied upon. In the industry as a whole negro miners are the only group which has actually increased in size. During the war years there was a change in the composition of the mining population. Thousands of miners were drawn into the army but the coal industry was expanding and tens of thousands of new workers entered the mines. In 1916–17 however, the great influx of immigrants was cut off and by 1920 American miners born of native white parents outnumbered the foreign-born; the number of foreign-born workers had fallen to less than 40 per cent of all workers in the industry. To-day fewer miners are employed than there were in 1920 and the foreign workers are a smaller percentage in this smaller total. But many more negroes were

[1] J. R. Commons *et al.*, *History of Labor in the United States*, Vol. II, pp. 498–499.

working in the mines. In 1920 there were about 60,000; to-day there are nearer 70,000 or more than one in ten, taking the industry as a whole. But in the Alabama coalfield about three miners out of five are negroes. There is a majority of negroes in the general population of this state but there is one special element in the increase of negro miners. In times of strikes negroes are often imported as "scab-labour" even as far north as Pennsylvania. The same policy has been pursued in Alabama. During the bitterly fought strike of 1920 many of the white and negro strikers were black-listed, and hundreds, if not thousands of strikers were replaced by negroes brought in from the surrounding country.

The following diary excerpts contain references to the negro miners in the Birmingham, Alabama, section:

"*January* 16, 1930. Taken by Mr. McHugh, a jovial old Irish-Scotsman, head of the Coal Division, out to the company's mine at Edgewater, some 15 miles from Birmingham. Birmingham is remarkably fortunate industrially. In the Red Mountain, stretching some miles on the one side, it has rich hematite iron ores; on the other side, not more than 20 miles distant, it has abundant supplies of coal, specially suitable for coking purposes; and between the ore and the coal are beds of limestone which is used as flux in the manufacture of iron. This juxtaposition of three valuable raw materials, together with geographical factors such as comparative flatness which facilitates railroad construction and the Warrior River which is linked up with the Mississippi and thus with the Gulf of Mexico, explains the extraordinarily rapid growth of Birmingham. Seventy years ago there was no Birmingham, Alabama; to-day there is indeed a 'Magic City' (as it is called), boasting a population of 300,000 people and believing it will at no distant date outstrip Pittsburg itself. A city of more recent development, Birmingham is better planned than Pittsburg and as I have been driven round the residential sections of both cities I can express the view that Birmingham has, on the whole, more lovely houses, more beautifully situated than Pittsburg has; nor did I see slums as deplorable anywhere in Birmingham as I saw in the heart of Pittsburg.

"On the way out to Edgewater, we stopped at one of the smaller collieries to see coal hoisted automatically on an electrically driven belt up the slope from the pit bottom—the first time to see this method. At Edgewater I spent some time at the school before proceeding to the mine. At the mine Mr. Flynn, the manager, took charge of us. After donning overalls, miner's cap and lamp we went inside, descending in a car down a slope to the first level, there being two levels as the result of a fault. After exploring some of the roads we came to a face where a few men were cutting by machine. It was noticeable that the machine was being worked by a negro and as I had understood that the skilled jobs were confined to the whites I asked the manager about it. He said that it did not require much training to work the machine and that a number of the more intelligent coloured men were now machine workers. I asked if the coloured and whites 'mixed' underground. He said that they were segregated even on the job. As nearly 60 per cent of the miners in this field are coloured it is difficult to understand how the separation can be complete. I laughingly suggested that it would not be easy to distinguish them underground anyway but my companions were not disposed to treat the matter lightly. On being told that the coloured miners were good workmen (I had heard the same testimony in West Virginia) I ventured to inquire in what sense they were good workers. The reply was that they are good-humoured, docile and accept orders without question or criticism, unlike coal-diggers who have worked in European mines.

"I was next taken to the other level, the car proceeding under the fault. The ventilation, lighting, roofing and engineering generally impressed me as being remarkably good. The manager was evidently a first-rate official, of the quietly efficient type. Lunched at the company restaurant. After lunch we inspected the workshops and bathhouses. A remarkable feature was that the bathhouse for the coloured men was very much larger than the one for the whites They were both well equipped. . . .

"Before leaving the Edgewater mine Mr. Flynn presented me with a cap and lamp. Mr. McHugh then drove me to the coloured school. I was taken over the school and had the pleasure of hearing the children singing several 'spirituals.' As far as one could tell from observation they seemed as intelligent as the children I had seen at the White school, though I got the impression that they were not so intelligent as the white children I had seen in the schools of Illinois and the Pennsylvania anthracite region."

Incidentally, the author had given three talks a week earlier to groups of negro women students at the Laura Spelman College at Atlanta, Georgia; after each talk there was an animated discussion. In the evening he saw three one-act plays, excellently done by the students, assisted by some of the men of Moorhouse College (for coloured men). Later that night a number of the women students quite spontaneously sang some of the beautiful "spirituals." The author has never heard more delightful folk singing anywhere in Europe, and Europe includes Wales! His considered view is that these students compared very favourably in point of intelligence with the students he has addressed in a considerable number of American universities.

"*January 16th (continued)*. One of the main characteristics of this coalfield is the preponderance of coloured workers in the mines. The percentage is the highest to be found in any coalfield in the world. Analysing the list of fatal accidents in this field in the year 1928 I found that of the total of 67 men killed 44 were coloured—65·7 per cent. Coloured schools, bathhouses, churches, cemeteries, etc., are all much bigger than the corresponding white. To anyone visiting from Great Britain where there is practically no negro problem this preponderance of negro coal-miners is very striking."

The demand for equality of white and negro workers rouses specially vindictive hostility throughout the southern fields and this hostility complicates the problem of unionisation. It is a difficulty even in sections where the mines operate under a union agreement for the United Mine Workers, although admitting coloured miners to membership, has apparently never taken a strong line in opposing race discrimination on the part of operators, landlords and storekeepers in such sections. It would require far greater courage and determination to do so in districts where there is no contract with the union. The whole industrial and social structure of the South is weighted heavily against the negro, and this is one reason why the organisation of the southern miners is so weak.

The American Federation of Labor recently embarked on a campaign for the unionisation of the workers in the South. Its chief concern was with the cotton operatives and it appears to have derived its inspiration from happenings at the close of 1929 at Gastonia, a rapidly developing cotton manufacturing

town in South Carolina. On January 8th the author stopped off
at Gastonia on his way south and has this entry in his diary
under that date:

"Explored Gastonia, scene of recent industrial disturbances,
including killings. Saw the court-room where seventeen men
were tried in connection with death of Aderholt, chief of police.
Seven officials were to be tried in the same court on the following
Monday in connection with death of one of the strikers—a woman
—in the cotton dispute over reductions of wages. Went through
Loray Mill (factory) where some of the strikers had worked."

"Gastonia" caused a great stir throughout the country and
stimulated a demand for greater attention to the needs, not
only of the cotton workers, but of all industrial workers in the
South. In response to this demand the American Federation of
Labor organised a "drive" in the South. The author happened
to be in Birmingham, Alabama, where the inaugural meeting
was held, and made the following entry in his diary:

"*January* 20, 1930. Called at office of American Federation
of Labor. In the evening heard William Green, President. Good
speaker. Speech was largely a plea to the operators and business
men to support the drive for organising labour in the district
and he made a point of appealing for their support on the ground
that the A.F. of L. would keep out the Communists. Had a few
words with Green at close of meeting."

A "push" for labour in such a "backward area" was something
of an event in the industrial history of the South and one felt
that it was quite an important meeting. It was held in a hall
capable of accommodating a seated audience of about 8,000
people, the audience on this occasion numbering about 5,000,
composed for the most part of working men and women and
including also a considerable representation of the business
element. The press gave it a good deal of prominence. One of
the most important economic changes taking shape in the United
States to-day is the increasing industrialisation of the South.
The manufacture of cotton goods is rapidly developing at the
expense of the New England States, capital from which is being
attracted South by offers of free or cheap land, lower rates, by
the supply of raw cotton on the spot and by an abundance of
cheap labour. The mineral resources are also being exploited
All this development provides the opportunity if not the necessity

for vigilance and action on the part of organisations designed to raise and protect the standard of living of the industrialised workers. Whether the American Federation of Labour will prove equal to the occasion is a matter of surmise; at any rate it sees the opportunity and recognises the necessity.

REASONS FOR BACKWARD STATE OF ORGANISATION OF AMERICAN MINE-WORKERS

Considerable attention has been given to the warlike character of the struggles towards unionisation in the bituminous fields of America because it is one of their most distinctive features and because it presents a striking contrast to the history of trade unionism in the coalfields of Great Britain and other European countries. It is not easy to furnish an adequate explanation of the contrast. Perhaps the key is to be found in the fact that in European coalfields the process of unionisation has been linked up with the political arm of the labour movement—in the past thirty or forty years with avowedly labour or socialist political parties. In the United States the various mine-workers' organisations have had no political arm—they have held out their hand for favours from the two traditional parties—and consequently they have been very much at the mercy of the operators. It has been, so to speak, more of a straight industrial fight between the employers and the miners in America than in Great Britain. And as the gun has played a big part in the pioneer and later stages of American civilisation it is perhaps natural that the pages of American history should be illustrated with pictures of pitched battles in the coalfields.

The reader is now in a position to understand that the United Mine Workers has encountered resolute, bitter opposition in its attempts to organise the non-union bituminous fields and to retain its foothold in the unionised fields. From the standpoint of membership the results must be disappointing to the officials. The membership in the bituminous fields has dropped from 386,000 in 1920—nearly two-thirds of the workers then employed —to about 80,000 or barely one-sixth of the total employed in 1929. Canadian membership also fell from 20,600 to 12,900. Illinois was in 1929 the only important bituminous district in the union, with more than half the bituminous membership of the country. Barely 30,000 members were scattered in other bituminous fields, and only in Illinois, Wyoming, Michigan and Montana were the organised miners as much as 80 per cent of the total in the State.

Economic conditions governing the industry and the determination of operators to keep out the union have been factors in this serious decline in membership. Reputable American economists with whom the author discussed the question as well as industrial workers who are left-wing critics of the union ascribe a considerable proportion of the decline to the character of the leadership of the union. They maintain that John L. Lewis, for example, works "hand-in-glove" with the employers, cannot therefore be militant enough and that when he declares a strike he does not "stick it out," being too much disposed to compromise. For his part, the author is reluctant to offer any critical comments on the policy of the president of the union, based upon two years' experience as a visitor in the American coalfields, but while sympathising with him in all his difficulties, he certainly formed the impression that John L. Lewis is the embodiment of business unionism, that he regards the union in much the same light as the president of a large commercial corporation looks upon his enterprise and that he is essentially a bargainer. One of the ablest coal experts in America told the author that he was greatly impressed by the contrast between Robert ("Bob") Smillie, whom he visited in his modest cottage in Scotland when he was president of the Miners' Federation of Great Britain, and John L. Lewis, whom he likened to a successful business man, drawing a big salary, possessing a fine home and accustomed to all the comforts of American life. The contrast was very decidedly in favour of the "refined and honest Scotsman." What impressed the American visitor most was Smillie's collection of books, his knowledge of them and the quality of his conversation on topics unrelated directly to the coal industry.

In reference to the question of leadership it is to be remembered that Lewis is merely continuing the American tradition. Practically all the United Mine Workers' officials have been "capitalists at heart." The careers of some of the past leaders are illuminating. President Ratchford of the United Mine Workers in its earlier days left the union to become a "labor commissioner" for the operators in Illinois. In 1904 D. C. Kennedy passed from the presidency of District 17 (West Virginia) to become "commissioner" for the Kanawha Coal Operators' Association. John Mitchell,[1] president of the union for several years, left the union to take up an important appointment with a patriotic organisation called the National Civic Federation. When he died he left a fortune of 250,000 dollars, largely in coal, railway and steel company securities. Tom L. Lewis, who succeeded Mitchell as president of the union, became himself an operator in West Virginia and secretary of the anti-union New River Coal Operators' Association. John P. White who was successor to Tom L. Lewis is now attached to the Union Pacific Coal Company in Wyoming as a labour arbitrator. A number of district officials and organisers have followed these examples, leaving the union to become operators or the servants of operators.

The history of the careers of British miners' leaders is not without instances of men like the Right Hon. William Abraham ("Mabon") who died worth far more than is expected of a miners' leader—the comment of the men at the time was that his friendly association with the employers enabled him to "feather his own nest"—or a man like Frank Hodges, a brilliant young miner who became secretary of the Miners' Federation of Great Britain, but is now a director of various commercial concerns and more or less, in the language of miners, "on the bosses' side." Such cases however are rare in Great Britain. Occasionally, a man who has reached high office in the union is appointed on the permanent staff of a government department where his experience is valuable to the government in the handling of coal disputes, as in the case of the Right Hon. William Brace. What is more characteristic in Great Britain is that miners' leaders enter the House of Commons and exert considerable political influence as members of Parliament. Even then, however, the politician retains his office in the union usually as a miners' agent unless, as in the case of the late Right Hon. Vernon Hartshorn, he reaches Cabinet rank. The fact is, defections from the union in Great Britain are very exceptional. Some of the author's American friends have suggested that if the temptations in England were greater, the loyalty of miners' officials might not be so firm. Who shall say? And yet "the union" does seem to be far more

---

[1] John Mitchell appears to have been one of the greatest leaders the Union has had. The reader is referred to *John Mitchell: Miners' Leader,* by Elsie M. Glück—an excellent biographical study.

of the warp and woof of the lives of British than of American
miners' leaders.

In the Report of the United States Coal Commission, 1925,
the union and non-union bituminous areas are broadly defined
on page 1050. They may be summarised as follows: The oldest
organised territory, as will be readily understood from the foregoing historical sketch, is the Central Competitive Field, embracing
the Pittsburg region and adjacent parts of Western Pennsylvania,
Illinois, Indiana and Ohio. A second centre of unionism is the
South Western Interstate Field, lying between Iowa and Northern
Texas and consisting of Arkansas, Kansas, Missouri and Oklahoma.
Directly north of the South Western Interstate are the Iowa
mines, thoroughly unionised. In the south is the partially organised State of Texas. In the Rocky Mountains the union fields
are located in Wyoming and Montana. North and south of the
Central Competitive Field are some organised districts in Michigan
and Western Kentucky; east of it lie the vast coalfields of Central
Pennsylvania, estimated by the United Mine Workers at the
time to be from 50 to 60 per cent organised.

The non-union areas, and in this group are included districts
that are partially organised but predominantly non-union, lie
around the union fields in a "broken crescent." The northern
end of this "crescent" juts up into the Pittsburg district and
Central Pennsylvania. This non-union portion of Pennsylvania
comprises the Connelsville coke region, the Irwin gas, Greensburg,
Latrobe and Ligonier regions in Westmoreland County, and the
Somerset Meyersdale field in Somerset County. These areas have
long resisted all the unionising efforts of the United Mine Workers.
From non-union Pennslyvania the crescent extends towards the
south. It includes practically all of Maryland, West Virginia
(except the Fairmont district, part of the Panhandle and the
upper half of Kanawha), Virginia, most of Eastern Kentucky
and Tennessee, and all of Alabama. West of Mississippi River
the second half of the "broken crescent" begins with the lignite
areas of Eastern Texas, passes around the partially unionised
bituminous mines of Texas to New Mexico and extends northward, taking in most of Colorado and all of Utah. In so far as
the operations representing half of the tonnage of the State of
Washington changed to a non-union basis in 1921, this State
may be included in the group.

The problem in the anthracite field differs from that in the bituminous fields because in the anthracite field the industry has been very largely a monopoly, concentrated in the hands of a small number of railroad companies. Owing principally to the competition of oil the monopoly shews signs of crumbling, but this is a comparatively recent development.

An active campaign of organisation carried on by the United Mine Workers led to a general strike in 1900. This was followed by a more decisive contest in 1902. The award of the Anthracite Coal Commission appointed at the close of the strike marked the beginning of an era of collective bargaining which has transformed the industrial relations of the industry. In 1906 and 1912 suspensions occurred. These were the only serious breaks in production following 1903, up to and including the time of the war. Difficulty in reaching an agreement in 1920 led to the appointment of a Commission of investigation whose award was to become the basis of a new contract. The findings of this Commission were accepted under protest and a strike occurred in 1922, when the time came for renewal. Governor Pinchot, acting as mediator, secured acceptance by both parties of an agreement which expired in 1925.

Anthracite workers demanded an increase in pay when this agreement expired. The operators insisted that wages must be reduced. The resulting strike lasted until the operators had sold off at high prices the coal stocks which they had been accumulating during the summer. The operators intended to renew the agreement and therefore made no attempt to import labour to run the mines.

In 1926, after conferences between John L. Lewis and Richard F. Grant, then head of the Hanna anthracite interests, an agreement was signed to run till 1930. The miners' demands were scrapped and the operators withdrew their threat of a wage cut. This was the longest joint agreement in the history of American coal-mining.

In spite of this agreement, however, there has been a good deal of unrest among the anthracite workers. As a part of the policy of rationalisation a number of collieries have been closed down, throwing thousands of workers and their families into hopeless poverty. While no formal reduction of wages is permissible under the agreement the men are convinced that their earning capacity has been reduced and their work speeded up by various changes introduced by the operators and connived at by the union. Various officials within the United Mine Workers have exploited this unrest for their own advantage, trying to build up a separate anthracite union but the Lewis machine has proved too strong for them.

Early in 1930 Lewis began bargaining with the operators for a renewal of the long-time agreement. Negotiations included another conference with Richard F. Grant, who now links up the Hanna interests with one of the strongest Morgan anthracite companies. Finally another agreement, to run for five and a half years, was signed. The operators' demand for a lower wage scale was withdrawn but another joint body for the fixing of terms and conditions to promote efficiency was set up. This will help operators to keep "peace" in the industry but at the expense of throwing more thousands out of work and speeding up those who retain their jobs. One concession made to the union was that the operators, for the first time in the anthracite field, agreed to a modified "check-off" of union dues. This means that the operators collect the union dues from their employees and this assures a steady revenue for the United Mine Workers' treasury in spite of the workers' increasing restlessness.

The anthracite field may be generally regarded as a unionised area.

The working philosophy of the United Mine Workers of America may be understood from the following quotation from a statement presented by Mr. Philip Murray, International Vice-President, to the United States Coal Commission.

"The United Mine Workers of America have no desire to injure the operators, for they realize that the interests of the operators and mine workers are identical. They respect the right of the operators to organize but on the other hand they insist that the operators must respect the right of the mine workers to organize without being subjected to discrimination. We say to the operators 'Come, let's reason together!' There is nothing radical or revolutionary about that. We know that this controversy will never be settled until it is approached in a spirit of common co-operation and good faith and we are now, and always have been, willing to meet them halfway in that spirit. Progress in industrial relations is defined in terms of betterment, namely to change from a given condition to a better condition. That has been the keynote of the United Mine Workers of America from the very beginning."

The Springfield United Mine Workers of America

While the United Mine Workers has had to face fierce opposition on the part of operators, some of whom still attribute the ills of the industry to "John L. Lewis and his union," it has not been free from family quarrels. As a result of this internecine strife there have been insurgent movements, two of which call for some attention.

One of these issued in what is sometimes described as the "Illinois Split" or more officially as the "Springfield U.M.W.A."

On March 10, 1930, a convention of 450 miners was held at Springfield, Illinois, for the purpose of reorganising the United Mine Workers of America. "The direct reasons for the present outbreak" writes Mr. Louis Stanley in *The Nation* (American) March 26, 1930, "concern the feud that has existed for years between the officials of Illinois District 12, the richest district in the United Mine Workers of America, and the international administration headed by Lewis." The convention was opened by President Fishwick of District 12 but the delegates chose Alexander Howat as chairman and later as President of the "reorganised" union. Howat had fought the industrial court law of Kansas State and had been expelled from the union by Lewis. John H. Walker, president of the Illinois State Federation of Labor, was elected secretary-treasurer. Adolph Germer, secretary of the Socialist Party during the war, was preferred as vice-president to Powers Hapgood, the Harvard graduate miner who has shewn a determined opposition to Lewis and to the operators for some years. Louis Stanley says "His youth, his attack on Farrington and his advanced ideas were against him." He was, however, elected to the policy committee. John Brophy, once president of a District and driven from the union by Lewis, was apparently one of the organisers of the convention though not elected to any of the chief offices. Stanley writes: "Almost all of Illinois, Kansas, and the South-west are with the 'reorganised' union and that means most of the bituminous coal miners in the United Mine Workers." And again: "The constitution commits the union to advocate the six-hour day, the five-day week, unem-

ployment insurance and 'The full social value of their (the workers')
product.' "

Whether this "reorganised" union will succeed or not—there
are legal difficulties and there is the possibility of a compromise
between the old and new unions—the Springfield Convention
of March 10, 1930, is interesting as a manifestation of dissatisfaction with the United Mine Workers and a bold challenge by
an important body of influential miners and officials to its very
existence. But the challenge does not appear to be at all revolutionary. It is backed by progressives like Brophy (who impressed
the author by his sincerity and ability: though convinced that
he was defeated for the international presidency in 1926 by
thousands of votes from "dead" locals he did not appear to be
animated by personal hatred of Lewis but he was strongly dissatisfied with the union), Hapgood, Howat and Haywood, but
Fishwick's secession seems to be largely a personal matter,
arising out of Lewis's removal of the Illinois district officials on
charges of corruption. Fishwick appealed to the courts and
prevented the provisional district officers from functioning. The
policy of this union does not appear to differ materially from that
of the Lewis machine so far as relations with the operators are
concerned. It approved the wage reduction of 1928 and even
blamed Lewis for not having yielded sooner. The author heard
Fishwick speak at a meeting of miners at Belleville, Illinois, at
the close of 1928: the burden of the speech was a justification for
accepting the wage reduction. From a talk the author had with
him later he is inclined to think that his industrial and political
views, like his Lancashire accent, had been considerably modified
by years spent in American coalfields.

The National Miners' Union

The other insurgent movement was essentially revolutionary
in character. It arose out of so-called "Save-the-Union" activities
of progressive and left-wing miners of all groups who wanted to
compel the United Mine Workers to adopt a more militant
organising policy. Differences as to policy within the Save-the-
Union movement produced a split. On one side was the group
headed by Brophy and Hapgood, who believed that the miners
were too discouraged for any tactics except a slow campaign of
education and a gradual driving out of "old-time" officials,

thought that the old union was still worthy of support and held to the tradition that bargaining is better than fighting. On the other side were the left-wing leaders, who believed that the rank and file were ready for an immediate policy of uncompromising struggle against the operators and that this could not be carried out within the framework of the United Mine Workers. The intensified crisis in the coal industry had sharpened the conflict of interest between the employers' drive for speed-up and profits and the workers' right to jobs and a living wage, and they felt that a new fighting union was now necessary. In September, 1928, under left-wing leadership, rank and file miners from eleven States organised the National Miners' Union. Its basic principles may be understood from the following excerpt from the preamble to the union constitution:

"Our organization declares that the interests of the employers and those of the workers have nothing in common but are diametrically opposed to one another. The history of the Coal Miners, as well as all the workers of the country, is that of an incessant struggle between these two classes—the class struggle. . . . We will proceed on this basis to wage a militant struggle for our rights against the employers. Simultaneously we will strive to educate our members and the workers of other industries to recognize the need of independent working-class political action as an additional weapon in this struggle. . . . We declare we will not only organize the Negro miners in every field but also draw them into full participation and leadership in our organization. . . . Our organization shall ever remain truly class-conscious. It will render support and show its solidarity with all workers in their struggles in other industries as well as with the working class internationally. . . . It shall by the use of all the power at its command, vigorously carry out its mission to secure for its members shorter hours, higher wages and better working conditions and proceed as an organization of the class struggle for the final abolition of capitalistic exploitation."

Salaries of officers and organisers were to be limited to "the average wage earned by the miners when fully employed." The final word in the calling of strikes was to be left, not with the officials of the union, but with the rank and file workers themselves.

Six months after its organisation the National Miners' Union, in accordance with its principles of international class struggle, affiliated with the Red International of Labour Unions.

Several local strikes against drastic wage-cuts were led by the National Miners' Union in northern West Virginia, Western Pennsylvania, Ohio and Kentucky.

Organisers had also been sent among the metal-miners, and at the second national convention of the National Miners' Union at Pittsburg, July, 1930, the union was placed on a broader industrial basis and the name was changed to Mine, Oil and Smelter Workers' Industrial Union. The constitution was amended to make even more emphatic the class struggle basis of the union.

"This industrial union is organised to unite all workers in the mining, oil, smelting and refining and quarrying industry and to lead them in their struggles against the capitalists for better working conditions and living and for ultimate abolition of wage slavery. This industrial union is founded on the principle of the class struggle . . . which must continue until the working class has conquered political power and abolished capitalism as a system, replacing it by a socialist society. . . .

"For this reason our industrial union does not limit itself to narrow craft or occupational interests, or even to the far wider interests of all the workers in our industry, but considers itself always as an integral part of the forces of the working class."

The major immediate demands of the reorganised union (M.O.S.W.I.U.) include the following:—

A minimum wage of 35 dollars a week (app. £7).
Union checkweighman elected by rank and file.
Abolition of the check-off.
Five-day week, six-hour day.
Workers' Social Insurance Bill, including work or full wages for all unemployed mine workers.

The union also demands recognition of a mine committee elected by the rank and file to lead in local struggles over daily grievances. Local union committees are responsible to district and national committees but responsibility of the central leadership to the will of the rank and file is a basic principle.

A women's department is organised to bring the wives, daughters and sisters into the union on a basis of full equality with the mine-workers, and a youth section is devoted to the special problems of the younger miners.

The formation of unemployed councils by the unemployed mine-workers is stressed as a major task.

"Since permanent mass unemployment is characteristic of present-day capitalism, the M.O.S.W.I.U. declares for the unity of employed and unemployed workers in all struggles."

Special importance is attached also to the solidarity of white and negro miners.

It is difficult to appraise the influence of this new union and the author has been unable to obtain statistics of membership but his general impression, based on a visit to its headquarters in Pittsburg, talks with some of its leaders, with rank and file miners and with economists and specialists in labour problems, is that it is not yet at any rate a very powerful organisation.

ASSOCIATIONS OF OPERATORS IN THE UNITED STATES

The organisation of the operators in the coal industry in America is looser and more diversified than that of the coal owners in Great Britain. The mine-workers of the States are less nationally and uniformly organised than the miners of the British coal-fields, but the operators are to an even greater extent split up into groups—union and non-union, State associations (e.g. The Illinois Coal Operators' Associations), Interstate groups (e.g. the Southwestern Interstate Coal Operators' Association), Bituminous Operators' Associations and an Anthracite Operators' Association and a federation of bituminous associations known as the American Federation of Coal Operators. There is no comprehensive national organisation for dealing with the union, corresponding to the Mining Association of Great Britain. There is the National Coal Association formed in 1917 when war conditions indicated the need of centralised administration of matters affecting the industry as a whole, but this is essentially a trade association. All these differences from the character of English organisation are due to a variety of causes—the huge geographical area, the comparatively recent development of the industry, the division of union and non-union, the separateness of the anthracite industry and the relative lack of federal political control over the coal-mining industry as a whole.

The United States Coal Commission, 1923, was sufficiently impressed by the lack of a united front on the part of the operators to suggest a more comprehensive organisation and a common policy in dealing with the union. Perhaps the chief hindrance to this has been the difference in attitude to the problem of the two factions within the National Coal Association. One faction regards the union as a permanent feature of the industry while the other expects "the union will be permanently kept out of or some day be uprooted from, at least, their section of the industry." The Commission suggested that a national organisation among the operators would not only be in a better position to negotiate with the union, but it could very profitably devote itself to such matters as the economic situation in the various districts, "the inequities in the system of wage differentials, the problems of irregular production and employment, and of car supply." It also suggested "that some plan for jointly providing for systematic supply of unemployed miners to mines needing men might be undertaken as one small factor to lessen gradually the number of excess men in the industry. . . . Such problems . . . are in the main, problems of national scope, which cannot be left to the districts to solve. Some day they will have to be solved for the good of all parties concerned. But such a step requires national organisation of union operators." As Mr Arthur Suffern pertinently asks, in his chapter on "The Operators Associations" in *The American Coal Miners' Struggle for Industrial Status*, should not this last recommendation apply also to the non-union fields?

Historically, the organisation of operators into effective working bodies is of comparatively recent date. The early associations were loosely organised groups, obviously formed to meet situations arising from the necessity of meeting competition from other fields or of co-operating during strikes and wage arbitration proceedings where the union offered effective opposition.

The formation of the Illinois Coal Operators' Association in 1897 indicated that the operators realised the importance of organisation to deal with competitive conditions affecting the whole State and to negotiate with the union. The Indiana Bituminous Operators' Association was formed in 1900, the Southwestern Interstate Coal Operators' Association in 1903, while most of the other associations have been organised since 1908.

The same process of subdivision and organisation of diverse interests has gone on between and within coalfields such as brought about subdistrict and district groups among the miners. There were in 1925 forty-one operators' associations.

There are two types of operators' associations. The first bargains collectively with the union. The second confines its activities to trade matters. The associations that bargain collectively with the union also concern themselves with the technical and commercial aspects of the industry, and except for the provisions dealing with labour both types are very much alike in their organisation. About fifteen of the associations deal with the union, and in general it may be said that all the associations deal with the union where the union is thoroughly organised.

The operators in the union fields enter into the negotiation of collective agreements, provide for the interpretation and enforcement of agreements and see that miners who strike in violation of the agreement are penalised.

The operators' associations in the non-union fields confine the statement of their purposes to such matters as the conservation of resources; methods of preparing and cleaning coal; advertising the merits and extending the market for their coal; investigating freight rates and discriminations by the railway companies; establishing rules for the prompt and accurate weighing of coal by the railroads; devising methods for conserving and marketing by-products; developing uniform cost-keeping methods and systems of accounting; the compilation of data bearing upon conservation, production, transportation and marketing; the establishment of bureaus of information, credit, publicity and sales extension; promoting safety measures for the protection of employees; improving sanitary and other conditions affecting the efficiency of employees; and co-operating with State officials in the enforcement of laws pertaining to coal-mining. It is probable that these associations devote a good deal of attention to the problem of keeping the union out of their mines but it is difficult to determine the extent of their activities.

The National Coal Association

Although the operators have not organised a national association to deal with labour, they have formed a national trade association called the National Coal Association. The membership includes operators who deal with the union and those who do not. Members may also be classified as individuals or groups (firms or operators' associations). But though it is primarily a trade association the percentage of production produced by its membership is probably not more than 60 per cent. It is of interest to note the recent tendency of the association to become predominantly non-union; since 1922 the percentage of production produced by the membership which deals with the union has steadily fallen off.

The association makes no statement of labour policy. The non-union operators belonging to it would strongly oppose collective bargaining on a national scale. Yet during a general strike the operators who deal with the union, and those who do not, might well find themselves acting on a concerted policy in the matter of labour policy. It is no secret that many of the operators who deal with the union would be glad to break the effectiveness of the union and be free to bargain with their employees individually. Failing that, they would at least like to have the union subject to prosecution for monopolistic labour control, to make it liable to suits for damages for breaking contracts and to have limitations imposed upon the right to strike. The National Coal Asociation is supposed to look after the interests of the industry as a whole in connection with legislation affecting such matters as ownership and commercial and technical operations.

The Association maintains a Market Research Institute which keeps its hand on the pulse of the trade and from time to time undertakes investigations based on figures privately supplied by constituent companies. Similarly, constituent associations maintain bureaus of information. For instance, the Anthracite Bureau of Information, sponsored by the Anthracite Operators' Association, is a well-equipped organisation which can give the research student a mine of valuable commercial and technical information relating to the anthracite industry. Mr. Edward W. Parker, the able and courteous Director, formerly Director of the United States Geological Survey, has a most intimate knowledge of the coal industry and gave the author considerable assistance in his investigation of the anthracite field.

NOTE.—I have drawn freely on Chapter 7 of Mr. Suffern's *The American Coal Miners' Struggle for Industrial Status* (London: George Allen and Unwin Ltd.).

SECTION G

HOUSING CONDITIONS

A comparison of the housing standards of mining communities in the two countries must necessarily be lacking in complete reliability. Considerations of site, methods of disposal of excreta, water supply, facilities for washing (clothes and the body), size and aspect of rooms, quality of materials and workmanship, spacing, security of tenure—these and other considerations can hardly be reduced to terms of exact comparison. Moreover, the geological, geographical and civic conditions in the two sets of coalfields are very different. For instance, subsidences or "cave-ins," as they are termed in America, are much more of a housing problem in the Pennsylvania anthracite field than they are anywhere in Great Britain. Nowhere in Great Britain are there such remote, isolated mining communities as those of West Virginia or Colorado. And local authorities play a much more important part in connection with housing in colliery districts in England than in America.

The comparison is further complicated by the fact that the average life of the mine is longer in Great Britain. One reason for the extremely low standard in certain coalfields in America is that the mine gets worked out in so short a time that expenditure on the provision of good houses, involving considerable capital, would be uneconomic unless rents were raised to a high level, and it is hardly to be expected that an individual operator or a private company will build houses to be let at uneconomic rents unless a low-rented or rent-free house is regarded as part of the wage. The author has seen a mining settlement in West Virginia composed of derelict shacks; the coal had been worked out in fifteen years and the settlement abandoned—veritably a deserted village. In mining the houses are built where the undertakings are situated, that is if travelling by the mine-workers is to be avoided. There is much to be said for the housing of miners working at different mines in a neighbouring town where they could live in municipal houses and enjoy the amenities of town life, travelling to and from the mine. But in the new, rapidly developed mining areas of the United States no such planning has been made.

Even in Great Britain, where the industry is much older, the comparatively short leases that have usually been granted in the past by the mineral owners to the mine-owners have hardly been long enough to promote good building. In England and Wales the period has been fifty to sixty years as a rule; in Scotland the custom has been only thirty-one years, which largely explains the relatively lower standard of construction in the Scottish coalfields.

The housing conditions of colliery workers, alike in Great Britain and the United States, shew great diversities but the range of variation is very much greater in the American coalfields. In the older established, unionised fields such as the Pennsylvania anthracite and Illinois, or even in some sections of newer, un-unionised fields like West Virginia or Colorado, one may see housing standards that compare very favourably with the best to be seen in British coalfields. But one may also see mining settlements of shacks where the conditions are far worse than the worst in Great Britain. And between the two extremes there is an extensive range of varying standards. Always the much greater size and the different stages of development of the American coalfields have to be borne in mind.

AMERICAN COALFIELDS

The following excerpt from the author's diary includes some observations on housing in the southern West Virginia Coalfield and illustrates the diversity shewn even in one mining area. It should be explained that Mr. Glen White, after whom the Glen White settlement was called, was something of a "housing enthusiast" and the author had been advised to "look over his Colony, since you are interested in housing and want to see about the best that's going in a mining section."

"*Thursday, March* 7, 1929. Left Charleston at 9 a.m. by train to visit the Glen White Mining Camp. Route, through Cabin Creek, Deepwater, Page, Oak Hill, Pax and Eccles, the whole journey through lovely hill country. Got off at Lester and went by bus, 2 miles, to Glen White. No one in at the colliery office who could give me facilities so I went to the school and had a useful talk with the principal, Miss Cavendish. About 170 pupils, boys and girls (majority native-born). Staff of six. Returning to the office I found Mr. Tom Morgan, Manager, and his brother, more of the commercial type but interested in living conditions. Tom of the practical, technical type, dressed after cowboy style— tall, striking fellow. John offered to shew me round. Went inside the Amusement Hall, very large, the ground floor being used for billiards (several tables) and at the far end there was a refreshment bar, the upper floor having a cinema, one room for classes in mining and another for instruction in first-aid. Every man qualifies in first-aid and is given a State certificate. The school also teaches first-aid. We went over the house of an English-woman, Mrs. Hilton, who despite thirty years' residence in this country retains her Lancashire accent. She and her husband hailed from Dobble, near Bolton. Good, five-roomed house, two bedrooms, two sitting rooms and the kitchen. Rent $2 per room per month (the rents varied from $1·50 to $2·50 according to situation and type of house). Nice lot of lawn round the house. We next visited the bathhouse, one section for white men, one for coloured men and a small one between for foremen and officials. Excellent arrangements for showers, drying of clothes, etc. Every man obliged to use the bath and charged $1 a month. Morgan said the men got to like it and quoted instances of men getting work elsewhere but returning because of the bath. Inspected the machine shop, blacksmith shop and the power house—very powerful engines. Shaft mine, 350 feet deep. Top of mine remarkably clean and buildings substantial. Company garages (100 in all, 27 in one block) a special feature—charge $2 a month. Each garage self-contained. Next visited, at my request, school for coloured children. The principal, a charming and intelligent woman who gave us a most cordial welcome—evidently pleased with our visit (Morgan had told me he had never entered a coloured school and was a little reluctant to accompany me though later he said he was glad he had done so). About 120 children. Half a dozen boys and girls read stanzas of *The Village Blacksmith* for our benefit. Reading quite good for youngsters of that age (about thirteen) though one or two were not easy to follow on account of their accent. Saw the coloured church and the pastor. Returned to the office and met Mr. C. R. Stahl, General Superintendent of the Company which has changed from E. E. White & Co. to the C.C.B. Smokeless Coal Company (Castner, Curran and Bullitt). Number of men employed at this mine 450. Number of houses 220, all painted in yellow and blue. A very imposing house on a hill built by Mr. White for himself. Other features were a Club House, where some of the teachers live together, the Union Church (undenominational) and doctor's 'office.' The whole village, surrounded by hills, in a beautiful setting. While waiting for the bus to Beckley we entered the stores, where Morgan shewed me scrip coins of $5, $1, and 50, 25, 10 and 5 cents, stamped G.W. (Glen White). The coins serve as currency throughout the district. A young English boy came in whom I had spoken to at the school and on Morgan's suggestion he took me to see his mother in "Little England," an apartment house containing three English families. Mrs. Bent, also from near Bolton (Chequerbent), has a daughter in the Beckley High School (bus transportation provided by the Authority), the boy and a little girl of about five. She seemed very contented and had no wish to live in England. Left by bus and arrived in Beckley about five.

"*Friday, March* 8. Rev. Roy Hashinger, on Staff of West Virginia University Extension Department, called to take me in his car along the Winding Gulf. We passed through several mining villages as far as Mullems and returned by a different route through Tams, a Gulf Smokeless Coal Company model mining camp. Variety of colour in housing scheme. Most of the villages however in Winding Gulf Valley appallingly bad—houses the worst I have seen, especially at Lillybrook and near Vanwood. Later in evening Hashinger took me to Cranberry where I had an interesting chat with a Scottish miner and his wife. We discussed the question of prices at the company stores and those at independent stores in the neighbouring town of Beckley. The wife gave me the following prices which she said she had herself paid:

	At Company Stores	At Beckley
Tea, per lb. ..	$1.20 (app. 5s.)	60c. (app. 2s. 6d.)
Butter, per lb. ..	65c. (app. 2s. 8½d.)	50c. (app. 2s.)
Coffee, per lb. ..	60c. (app. 2s. 6d.)	31c. (app. 1s. 3½d.)
Oranges	15c. (app. 7½d.) for 2	30c. (app. 1s. 3d.) a doz.

She told me that she had bought a week's groceries in Beckley at a saving of $3.50 (app. 14s.), including the taxi fare.

BEST KEPT GARDEN IN COMPANY VILLAGE, HOLDEN, WEST VIRGINIA

"*Tuesday, March* 12. Went in morning by bus to Holden, Island Creek Coal Co. Soon got in touch with Mr. W. A. Hunt, General Superintendent. First, talked for half an hour or so about coal situation generally and about Holden mining camp in particular. He showed me some extremely interesting photos of Safety Club Meets and Health 'stunts' such as a 'Drink more Milk' pageant. He said the health of the children had been greatly improved as the result of bigger consumption of milk. I cynically asked him if this was done to increase profits of dairy and he laughingly admitted that profits had been materially increased though they were interested in improving the health of the children. He then took me round in his car. Houses not so neat looking as those at Glen White, but the whole camp was one of the best I have seen. A special feature was the dairy of 50 cows of various breeds, including Guernseys, of high productive capacity. The man in charge, a Scotsman named Kilgour (delightful fellow), told me that 47 cows were now yielding 675 quarts a day—about 15 quarts per cow per day. The cattle sheds remarkably well kept. Feed a heavy item. Returning, we entered the store, where Mr. Hunt allowed me to choose some picture postcards and told the assistant to add others. Mr. Hunt was most reluctant to shew me over one of the houses that contained a bathroom, because he thought that I might be taken for a prohibition enforcement officer! Lunched at the Club House. People lunching were officials, doctors, teachers, stenographers, etc. Hunt impressed me as an ideal man for his job and shewed a pretty keen appreciation of the importance of human engineering. He drove me into Logan in time for me to catch a bus to Omar, ten miles out. At Omar I found that Mr. Bischoff, General Manager of the West Virginia Coal and Coke Co., was out of town, so I asked for Mr. Sheridan, General Purchasing Agent, whom I had met in the train between Fairmont and Charleston. He welcomed me most cordially and arranged to take me round their properties. Mr. Thomas A. Stroup, Chief Engineer of the Company, drove us in his car but before starting Sheridan took me into the Omar Store, the largest I have seen. As we approached the store we met three State Police Officers, who looked very military, one of them a huge fellow who, as Sheridan remarked, would take some 'disturbing!' First stopping place was Stirrat, which had one of the largest and most substantial buildings I have seen in any mining camp. Sheridan called it the Pennsylvania Hotel! It contained a big store, barber's shop, drug stores, amusement rooms, etc. On getting back to Omar Sheridan and the chief store manager left us in order to continue with a special inventory they were making. The Company is in the hands of the Receivers, the explanation given being that the mines had been badly financed and badly engineered, technically and socially. Stroup then drove me along a hard paved road, built by the company, for twenty miles through a number of camps and lovely scenery as far as Earling and Taplin. We had a most interesting conversation, he shewing as much interest in the social aspects as I tried to shew in the technical side of mining. He is specially interested in the relation of mechanisation in the mining industry to the system of wages and in the effects of mechanisation on the problem of fatigue. He said he would send me a copy of a paper he had prepared. (Note: Later I received a copy of his paper: it impressed me as being quite a valuable piece of work.) He is certainly one of the best engineers I have met anywhere, keenly interested in Economics and Psychology, and he said he was planning to spend a year sometime in study in England. I told him something of the National Institute of Psychology and of the Work of Dr. Myers and his Staff. He spoke of the possibilities of future development in West Virginia and gave me a deal of valuable information about the distillation of oil, low temperature carbonisation, hydrogenation, hydro-electric power, the conversion of coal into electricity at the pit-head (difficulty of power plants at tipple because of lack of water), pulverisation, etc. Some of the houses in the camps we passed through were certainly pretty bad, as he sorrowfully admitted. I told him of my vision of mining settlements in which every house, surrounded by lawn and garden, would have a bathroom and inside flush toilet. He seemed greatly interested and believed that mechanisation socially applied would make the realisation of such a scheme more feasible. He was also keenly interested in my idea that all workers in the coal-mining industry should be put on the same basis as regards earnings with the professions—a regular weekly or monthly salary, holidays with pay, etc. He drove me to Logan where we had a further interesting talk over the teacups. (Note: It is possible to get a cup of tea in America, even in the coalfields!)"

The next entries give some idea of social conditions in the West Pennsylvania field.

"*Friday, March* 29. Nunn and I left (Pittsburg) early by train for Tarentum—22 miles away. Met at Station by one of his students named Reiter who placed himself and his car at our disposal for the day. We drove to Curtisville—mining camp of the Ford Collieries Co. Found only eight families living in barracks built by the U.M.W. in autumn of 1927. Had a talk with a Welshman named Solman, in charge of lamproom. He hailed from Swansea and could speak Welsh but I could get no information from him about social conditions: he was interested only in lamps and technical aspects of mining. Rather a conceited, self-satisfied fellow—very different from 'my' type of South Wales miner. Had an interesting talk with a group of Czechoslovakians about the union, strike, prospects of work, etc. One of them said he had been on strike for seventeen months. Had $1,500 at the beginning and nothing at the end. Being a single man (strong chap of about fifty, with big moustache), he had had no relief. Got work at the Kinloch mine, scene of recent explosion. (Note: A week or so earlier, on March 21, I had spent the day at the Kinloch mine after reading accounts in the Pittsburg morning papers of an explosion there. The scenes at the tipple—rescue parties, dead bodies being brought out on stretchers, factory inspectors, newspaper men and photographers, solemn men, weeping women and puzzled children—were reminiscent of scenes at the pit-head of a South Wales mine on a similar occasion. Except for the variety of languages spoken by the men and women in the crowd one might have imagined oneself at a mine in the old country.) Dissatisfied with U.M.W. but not enthusiastic about N.M.U. At Barracks, built by U.M.W., at No. 2 mine (Curtisville) talked with an Englishman, suffering from cancer, and his wife, Mrs. Hickman, native of Rotherham, Yorkshire. She shewed us inside of her house which was remarkably clean and not badly furnished, containing a refrigerator and cooking stove (coal). Paid no rent. Would prefer to live in a company house and keep boarders, but company had refused permission. (Note: The Pittsburg *Post-Gazette* of April 4 published an interview, accompanied by a photograph, which an enterprising reporter had with this couple: stress was laid on the fact that the husband was a striker, and the world, including the said striker, was informed that he was dying of cancer!) Drove on to Russelton. Only five families living in barracks here. Talked with a Czechoslovakian. Similar case to the other, exhausted savings, single man, etc. Called at a drug store for refreshments. Had some interesting information from the waitress, daughter of a miner, who had attended the local High School, about the effect of the strike on business, magazines sold, etc. Extraordinary variety of magazines of the 'sexy,' war, adventure type. (Note: I hadn't time to make a list of the periodicals on the racks in this stores but the following list, which I made three months later in a newsagent's shop at Lansford, a mining town of about 10,000 population in the anthracite section of Pennsylvania, may be of interest to English readers: the list is representative though not exhaustive):

All the monthlies of the *Harpers, Atlantic, Forum* type.

Film Fun	*Ginger Stories*
Motion Picture	*Science Wonder Stories*
Auction Bridge Magazine	*World War Stories*
Correct English	*Love Story Magazine*
Farm periodicals	*Love Secrets*
Radio	*Stage Screen Stories*
Detective periodicals	*Romance*
Sea Stories	*Adventure*
Funny Stories	*Underworld*
Wild West Weekly	*Broadway Nights*
Far West Stories	*Paris Nights*
Zeppelin Stories	*Love Mates Stories*
Under Fire Magazine	*Real Story Book*
Western Trails	*Pep Stories*
Air Trails	*Physical Culture*
Battle Stories	*Tales of Danger and Daring*
Airplane Stories	*College Humor*
True Romances (biggest sale)	*True Story Magazine*
True Strange Stories	*Secrets—Love and Romance*
Dream World into the Land of Love and Romance	*True Love Affairs*
Screenland	*Screen Secrets*
The Red Book	*True Detective Mysteries*
American Magazine	*Psychology*
College Life	*Modern Girl Stories*
	Your Body

Child Life	*Style*
The Dance	*Motor*
Fashion periodicals	*Whoopee*
Whiz Bang	*Hot Dog*
Wise Cracks	*Jim Jam Jems*
Eye Opener	*Police Gazette.*

"Called at the office of the Republic Iron and Steel Co. Mine. The Superintendent (McVicker) arranged for us to go down the shaft, drop of 230 feet. Chief feature the remarkably fine rock roof. Six-foot seam. No 'live stock.' This is a 'Captive' mine. (Note: A "captive" mine is one owned by other than a Coal Company, in this case by an Iron and Steel concern, to ensure regular supplies of its own coal.) Caught train back to Pittsburg.

"Chief impressions—'deadness' of unionism of any sort among the men but operators maintaining certain union features, e.g. eight-hours shift, payment for 'dead' work. Housing conditions much better than in most of West Virginia I had seen though not so good as in Glen White or Holden. These mining camps not so isolated as those of West Virginia and not so entirely under the control of the companies, due partly to geographical conditions and partly to influence of recent unionisation.

"*Saturday, March* 30. With Nunn, visited Castle Shannon (Pittsburg Terminal Coal Co.—Taplin interest)—No. 2 mining camp. Got into conversation with Russian, living in Company house. Unemployed. Bitter about Company. Shewed us inside one of the houses. Rent $3 a room per month, $1 a room more than usual in West Virginia. Rooms in very bad condition, obvious leakage in roof. This man not interested in unions but didn't think U.M.W. would 'come back.' Next talked with an old German, living in U.M.W. barracks. Ardent U.M.W. man and had been in thick of fight—knew Mother Jones and John Mitchell —but didn't think there was any future for the Union. Over 60, a bachelor, living alone. Spoke to two miners returning from work, carrying picks on their shoulders. They said they were obliged to take them home every day for they would be 'pinched' if left in the mine. Native Americans, not interested in the Union. Walked on a couple of miles to Mollenauer. Saw headquarters of 'Coal and Iron' Police. Told me there was only one man on duty. Also saw the barracks ('bull-pens') that had been built by the Company for 'strike-breakers'—eight men to one room. Dining hall, latrines, &c. Whole scene suggestive of military camp. Housing conditions in some parts of the village extremely bad—water running under some of the houses. Had interesting talk with a Scotsman, living in U.M.W. barracks—wife and nine children. Black-listed and couldn't get into the mine at all.Worked occasionally on the road and at odd jobs. His eldest son earned something by selling papers. He seemed well dressed and said he was better off than many of the men who were working, whose average he estimated at $4 a day when they worked. Dour fighter and optimistic as to the return of the Union. He thought the men were ready for 'another fight' and that they could win. General impression of serious lowering of standards compared with Union days and of general if suppressed discontent. Many evidences of 'negro occupation'—'hangover' from imported strike labour."

One more diary entry, made while still in the Pittsburg area:

"*Wednesday, April* 3. Visited Harmarville—Consumers' Mining Co. ('Captive' mine of Labell Steel Co.). First camp where I saw brick and stone houses. They contained bathroom and inside toilet, but rents were high—five-roomed, $27 a month—water and gas (slot) extra; four-roomed, $25. About sixteen houses in a row—more like British row than anything I had seen."

It may be observed here that, with few exceptions, American miners live in semi-detached, wooden frame houses, whether they live in remote camps in West Virginia, Alabama or Colorado or in large towns like Scranton or Wilkes-Barre, and that British miners live in brick or stone houses, usually in long dreary rows, often on a hillside overlooking the colliery. It seems a fair general deduction therefore that whereas the American miner has the advantage in the matter of spacing, miners' houses in Great Britain are more substantial and durable.

The Coal Commission of the United States collected some valuable material on housing conditions in 1922 and 1923 in the course of its investigation into conditions of life and the cost of living of the coal-mine workers. For population Statistics it relied on the data originally secured by the U.S. Bureau of the Census in the course of its 1920 enumerations but its own agents made a comprehensive and thorough independent study of the cost of living and of living conditions. Fifteen hundred and seventy-eight mine-workers' families were visited personally by the Commission's agents in the course of its cost of living study, and information concerning living conditions was secured on a detailed schedule by Commission agents who made personal visits to 1,004 communities in which about 350,000 mine-workers lived. It was found that four-fifths of the total coal-mining population lived in the bituminous fields and the other one-fifth were employed in the anthracite mines. Approximately one-half were housed in company-owned dwellings in company-controlled towns—a fact which in itself, with some exceptions, indicates the remoteness of these families from independent urban centres. The exceptions are certain Pennsylvania coal-mining regions where, in spite of the fact that mining operations are within reach of the labour supply of independent towns, a considerable number of the mine-workers, who are chiefly foreign-born, are housed in company dwellings.

The enlightened coal operator recognises the importance of providing good living accommodation and attractive surroundings for his employees. Apart from humanitarian considerations, good housing facilities bring returns on the investment in the form of more efficient, more contented and more permanent workers. The typical mining community is laid out in much the same way as any other small town in rectangular blocks of suitable size and grouped round a central point where the mine office, company store, post-office and railway station are situated. In the modern, well-designed camp, there are, first, a few substantial, well-built houses, equipped with modern conveniences throughout and comparable with the better type of the modest town house, for the superintendent of the mine, the doctor, clerical staff and store manager. Next there is a larger group of similar though less substantial houses for the foremen, sub-foremen and some of the preferred class of men such as the electrician, master mechanic, etc. The remainder of the houses which make up the bulk of the camp are roughly divided into two general classes. The first of these will be of a fair standard, usually of four or five rooms and equipped with running water and possibly a bath and inside toilet. This type is designed for the more permanent miners with families and is usually plastered inside and equipped with some extras, such as a porch, that tend to lift it above the class below. The inferior houses may be built roughly along the lines

of the next class above but would be finished with wood ceiling
inside, have outdoor toilets and be dependent on an outside
spigot for its water supply.

The well-planned mining village however is exceptional. Let
us look a little more closely at the prevailing type. Wooden
houses, semi-detached, each house exactly like its neighbour, in
straight rows, small back yards cluttered with sheds and privies,
the houses with roofs of composition paper, usually without a
cellar and often supported only on posts with the wind sweeping
through under the floor—these are the prevailing type. More of
the houses in the North than in the South have solid foundations,
weather-proof walls and roofs of shingle or slate. Anna Rochester,
in *Labor and Coal*, says that in all the mining States together
about one house in four is of the flimsiest board and batten
construction, and that even in the northern fields nearly 10 per
cent of the company houses are board and batten. In the North
most of the weather-board houses are plastered inside but in the
South a rough-wood finish is more common. The composition
paper roof is almost universal in the southern villages.

Most of the houses have three or four small rooms. In the
better type of miner's house the living room and one of the
bedrooms as a rule would be 14 ft. by 14 ft., the other bedroom
and the dining-room 14 ft. by 10 ft. and the kitchen 13 ft. by
11 ft. 6 in. A few companies provide five or even six-room houses.
At the other extreme are hundreds of two-room shacks and even
one-room shanties. In the South, especially in Alabama, the
housing for Negro miners is extremely bad.

Since nearly half of the families consist of five or more persons
and thousands of families take in boarders or lodgers serious
overcrowding is common. When the Federal Children's Bureau
studied a section of Raleigh County, West Virginia, it found
that in one house out of seven from four to nine persons were
sharing each sleeping room.

In the bituminous fields the Commission made a survey of
approximately 71,000 company-owned family dwellings in 713
company-controlled communities, having almost 100,000 coal-
mine workers. Only two of the 713 villages were certified as
meeting the standard set by the Commission in both water supply
and disposal of sewage and other waste. One other village was
rated at 100 for housing but in this case the water supply and

INTERIOR VIEW OF MINERS' BATH HOUSE, PENNSYLVANIA

disposal of waste were below the standard. Only 23 were scored at 75 per cent or higher on all three points.

Water Facilities.

The results of this survey summarised as to water facilities for housing purposes shew that:

First.—Although over 60 per cent of the company-controlled communities had waterworks, less than 14 per cent of the family dwellings had any running water at all. Only 2·4 per cent of the homes had a bathtub or shower.

Second.—In over 85 per cent of the dwellings water had to be carried from outside the house. Driven or dug wells, usually equipped with pumps, but not infrequently "bucket wells," constituted the prevailing method of water supply.

Third.—In less than one-tenth of the communities was each family supplied with its own well or hydrant. In one-sixth of such communities there was a single water outlet for every two families. But in another sixth of these communities six or seven families used a single water supply point, and in still another sixth from eight to more than thirty-one families were dependent on one well or hydrant.

Fourth.—While the distances over which water had to be carried for household purposes are not given the agents reported members of mine-workers' families, including the wives, as carrying water over distances ranging from just outside the house to the equivalent of "an average city block." In the northern States the labour involved in carrying water was increased during the winter months by snow-drifts and ice-covered walks and paths.

Fifth.—Water service, of whatever nature it may be, was quite generally included in the rental charge for company-owned houses.

The water facilities in privately owned houses in the 167 independent towns in the bituminous regions scheduled by the Commission's agents did not differ materially from the facilities available in company-controlled towns. This is shewn by the fact that approximately 14·4 per cent of the 167 independent towns as compared with the 14·9 per cent of the company-owned towns, had water piped practically to all home premises (not necessarily to the inside of the houses), and 56·9 per cent of the independent towns had waterworks systems, as compared with 60·8 per cent of the company-owned towns.

In the anthracite field water facilities are much better. Over nine-tenths of the families live in independent towns and 96 per cent of these had public waterworks systems, as compared with about 83 per cent of the company-owned towns. Of the company-owned dwellings in the controlled towns, 80·6 per cent were equipped with running water, though only 5·4 per cent had either bathtub or showers. In approximately half of the independent towns having public waterworks systems water was piped to practically every house in the community.

"Running water in the house" meant usually one faucet in the kitchen, for which $6, $7.20 or $8 was the prevailing annual charge. For an additional faucet, regardless of whether the volume of water used was larger, an additional annual charge ranging from $1.50 to $4 was made. A bathtub entailed an annual charge of $4 to $4.80; a wash basin equipped with faucet, $2 to $2.50; stationary washtubs (not to exceed three) $3 to $4. The Commission published this scale as "the schedule of one of the water companies" and as one which did not differ substantially from that of any of the other companies in the matter of rates.

Plenty of hot running water, with shower or stationary bath, is more needed in a miner's house than in almost any other dwelling. But as we have seen less than 3 per cent of the houses in the company-controlled communities in the bituminous and less than 6 per cent of those in the anthracite field had a bathtub or shower. Mining laws in several States compel the companies to provide washhouses (pit-head baths) at the mine where the men may "wash up" and leave their working clothes. But as a matter of fact their actual use is confined to a minority of the men. Speaking of the restricted use of the mine washhouses in the anthracite region, where working conditions and facilities of life are regarded as much more adequate than in the bituminous coalfields, the report of the United States Coal Commission points out:

"Another matter pertinent to this discussion is the requirement of the Pennsylvania mining laws that mines provide washhouses for the mine-workers. Reports from the agents assigned to the living conditions study, as well as the reports from agents assigned

INTERIOR OF BATH CHANGE HOUSE, UTAH

to certain phases of working conditions, shew that practically all of the mines have such washhouses, but the reports from the same agents shew that, for one reason or another, thousands of men do not use these mine facilities. Indeed, the reports from agents describing family conditions for this study indicate that quite generally the mine-worker comes home 'to wash up.' This custom, whether enforced by inadequate facilities at the mine for the number of men employed or followed voluntarily, puts an added burden upon the domestic water service and upon the shoulders of the mine-worker's wife."

The reasons usually given for this restricted use are that the washhouse is often crowded and overheated when the men come pouring out of the mine, inadequate provision of lockers and that the miner's street clothes are hung in a messy bundle from the ceiling and unprotected from pilfering. And so the miner prefers to go home in his working clothes and use the tub of hot water which his wife or landlady is expected to have ready for him in the kitchen. It may be that the author saw only the better wash-houses in all the coalfields he visited but he is bound to say that from what he did see there appeared to be little ground for such complaints.

Water facilities as shewn for the majority of mine-workers' families do not represent the small minority at either end of the scale of equipment. Some families living in company-owned houses, like many miners' families living in well-developed independent towns, had hot and cold water and bathtubs or showers. This shews that adequate facilities are not an impracticable adjunct of coal-mining life. Some families, too, had most meagre and inconvenient water supplies, often perilously unprotected from pollution. This shews to what a level of drudgery daily living falls when a mining community's water resources are little more than nature has provided.

Toilet Facilities

The character of water facilities prevailing in the majority of coal-mine workers' families is a fair index of the other facilities which enter into the livability of home and community. Less than 4 per cent of the more than 80,000 company-owned family dwellings scheduled in the bituminous and anthracite regions had inside flush toilets; only five of the 811 company-controlled

towns in the two coalfields had all the houses connected with
sewers. Of the 283 independent towns in the two coal-mining
regions included in the Commission's investigation, almost
11 per cent were sewered throughout; about 45 per cent of such
towns and 60 per cent of the company-controlled communities
had no sewers at all. These communities depended entirely
upon privies, some of which were provided with cesspool and
septic tanks, but more of which, in the bituminous regions, were
merely surface privies. Concerning these facilities the report of
the Commission says:

"Manifestly, the best type of privy . . . will become a marplot
and health menace if left without care. The poorer types of
construction, namely, the surface, fly-exposed, loose structure
affairs, are inevitably unsightly and unsanitary at the start, and
without care, quickly become indescribably filthy and indecent."

That there was a general lack of adequate care, as well as of
adequate sewage-disposal facilities, especially in the bituminous
regions, is made plain not only by the Coal Commission's report
but also by the sanitation report incorporated in it, prepared by
the United States Public Health Service, which says:

"There can be no question as to the general backwardness
of the bituminous coal patches as regards satisfactory methods
of disposing of human excreta. In many mining camps and towns,
too, it is apparent that the importance of the subject is but partially
realised. Moreover, it is plain that little progress has been made
since the establishment of the towns.

"The average sewerage ratings in the anthracite coal districts
shew a slight superiority over those of the bituminous regions.
It is probable that the higher ratings . . . are due to the *relatively*
infrequent use of *surface privies*, the greater number of sanitary
sewers, greater size of the communities, better supervision of
excreta disposal and better economic conditions."

Lighting

An encouraging contrast to the standard of equipment maintained as to toilet facilities was the standard of lighting facilities
prevailing in both company-owned and independent towns.
Over 61 per cent of the 80,000 company-owned dwellings were
equipped with electric or gas light, and nearly 8·43 per cent of
the independent towns had electric street lighting. It goes without

saying that for the families and communities who were without
adequate lighting facilities, the depressing gloom was not relieved
by the fact that the majority of other mine-workers' families
and communities had the cheer and the protection afforded by
good light. And it is hardly necessary to call attention to the fact
that the women, especially those gainfully employed who had
to come home after dark, were particularly concerned about the
proper lighting of the streets of a community.

Community Planning

Apart from the achievements of the more enlightened operators
and companies, little has been done in the way of community
planning or the general improvement of the environment under
which the mine-workers live. The difficulty arising from a comparatively short life of the mine has already been referred to.
There are also in some cases physical obstacles. Speaking on this
point the Commission's report says:

"Difficulties of natural location frequently confront the operators
who must build towns in precipitous country. Sometimes they
are overcome; more frequently they are allowed to dominate."

The United States Public Health Service in its special report says:

"It is at once apparent that insufficient study and attention
has been devoted to the improvement of the general environment
in many mining towns. For one thing it cannot be expected that
grass, trees, flowers, and gardens will thrive on slate dumps,
where so many houses have been thoughtlessly located. Nor can
suitable streets, walks, or playgrounds be maintained under
such conditions. While not directly concerned with sanitation,
suitable environment is believed to exert a subtle yet nevertheless
certain influence upon the human mind. Moreover, it is felt
that a favourable mental reaction is reflected in increased happiness
and contentment, which in turn aids in the maintenance of health."

Upkeep

As to the general upkeep of company-controlled towns in the
bituminous regions the Coal Commission reports:

"Repair and general upkeep are as important in determining
the character of a community as are plan, construction and
equipment. The repair of company houses appeared to be a subject
of constant controversy between individual mine-workers and

254 COAL AND MEN

mine officials. Tenants contended almost uniformly that it was a difficult matter to get defects and dilapidations corrected by the companies without repeated complaints and insistent demands. On the other hand, there was general complaint by company officials that the tenants wilfully or carelessly destroyed company property. Unquestionably it is true of tenants in company houses —as of tenants in houses rented for twenty times the amounts they pay—that they do not take care of other people's property as they would of their own. Sometimes the mine-workers make repairs at their own expense. Sometimes the companies provide materials and the tenants do the work. Many exceptions were found to the prevailing neglect, but they were not so numerous as to constitute more than exceptions. In places where some pains were taken to keep the houses painted, it seemed to be done usually as a measure for preserving the property rather than to increase its attractiveness, for the colors were uniform, and frequently ugly, throughout the entire community. In this respect too, there were refreshing exceptions, expressing an appreciation that monotony of color has an irritating and unsettling effect, like monotony of sound, and affects the comfort and content of human beings.

"In the worst of the company-controlled communities the state of disrepair at times runs beyond the power of verbal description or even of photographic illustration, since neither words nor pictures can portray the atmosphere of abandoned dejection or reproduce the smells. Old, unpainted board and batten houses—batten going or gone and boards fast following, roofs broken, porches staggering, steps sagging, a riot of rubbish, and a medley of odours—such are features of the worst camps. They are not by any means in the majority; but wherever they exist they are a reproach to the industry and a serious matter for such mine-workers and mine-workers' families as are dependent upon the companies for living facilities."

One cannot help feeling that such conditions are not merely a reproach to the industry but a disgraceful feature of the social life of the country and a challenge to the American nation.

It is difficult to appraise the efficiency of the general upkeep of the mine-workers' homes, interspersed as they are with the homes of other wage-earners, in the independent towns situated in the coal-mining regions. There are some very black patches, e.g. in Pittsburg and Birmingham, Alabama. The general standard, however, is decidedly higher. It is to be realised that in such towns home and community standards are considered to be within the control of community members. A very considerable number, sometimes amounting to a majority, of these community members are the mine-workers themselves and their families.

In the anthracite region there are some important factors, entering into the physical environment of the miner's family, for which the companies are responsible. Chief among these are the huge culm piles, whose century of growth has marred the sky-line and scarred and charred the landscape. In addition these piles cover a great acreage of land much needed for houses. Secondly, the extraction of this culm, together with the hard coal sent to the nation's fires and furnaces, has left beneath the surface cavities that still further restrict home building. Caving-in is not uncommon, and the fear of suits for damage from settling surfaces has kept mining companies from selling the land near abandoned mines even though a land-hungry people and a shortage of housing make a responsive market for housing sites. Thirdly, the wet process of coal cleaning used in the anthracite field has turned the rivulets and creeks into black, muddy streams over acres of land—a coat of black silt which kills vegetation, destroys the comeliness of a naturally comely region and still further reduces the housing facilities for an already overcrowded region.

It may be that these evils are not avoidable by the operators but the conditions grow out of the industry and they exert a depressing influence, especially on the wives and children of the mining community. If not by the operators themselves then by the public authorities something might be done, in the interests of the community, to remove them. The operators are a powerful influence in framing public policies but the mine-workers, wives and adult sons and daughters constitute a considerable proportion of the electorate who by taking a more active interest in civic affairs could stimulate progress towards the solution of social problems arising out of the industry.

Home Tenure

A distinguishing feature of housing in American company-owned mining camps is the insecurity of tenure of the tenant.

The Coal Commission's report revealed that of all the coal-mine
workers studied 31 per cent owned their homes wholly or partially,
as compared with 46 per cent of the entire population; that for
West Virginia and some of the other newer bituminous States
the proportion was below 20 per cent; and that the proportions
of home ownership were highest for the States where there were
fairly well developed communities before coal-mining operations
were started. But where the company owned the mining town
there was, with one or two exceptions, no home ownership by
the mine-workers. A few companies have made the experiment
of selling sites and dwellings to the miners with a view to stabilising
mine labour, but the experiment has not been at all widely copied
It is true that the miner living in a company-owned house pays
relatively a smaller rent, usually gets heat and light at much less
cost, has water facilities, such as they are, at less expense, and
is assured of medical service at a much smaller outlay than is
available to the family living outside the company town; but when
a miner ceases to work in a company's mine he must, as a rule,
cease to live in the company's house. So essential is this rule
that the leases covering occupancy of company houses stipulate
that when a mine-worker ceases to work for the company for
any cause whatsoever the right to occupy the company house
terminates automatically. It should be borne in mind that this
termination of the lease with cessation of work in the company's
mine is not contingent upon the voluntary withdrawal of the
mine-worker from the employ of the company; the mine boss
may discharge the worker or the miner may be forced by circumstances to cease working for the company. Whatever be the
cause, he loses his right to the home both for himself and his
family when he loses or gives up the job. Naturally this stipulation
tends to keep him rooted to the spot and in times of industrial
disturbance especially men have not dared to seek work elsewhere
fearing that their families would be evicted if the companies
discovered that they had gone in search of other employment.

It is sometimes pointed out that the companies do not enforce
the stipulations when the miner is injured or too ill to work or
after the death of a miner who has been a victim of a mine accident
But these are measures of mercy and are as elastic as the social
sympathies of the operators. The important point is that neither
the miner nor his family has any protection in law that would

BARRACKS BELONGING TO THE UNITED MINE WORKERS OF AMERICA, BUILT TO HOUSE EVICTED MINERS, OSAGE, WEST VIRGINIA

secure to him notice of termination of the lease and days of grace in which to provide for the safe and orderly transfer of his family to another dwelling.

The overwhelming majority of British miners, whether living in their own houses or as tenants, are free from outside interference with their home life. In America this is true only of miners owning their own houses or as independent tenants. The mine-working tenant of a company-owned dwelling has to give up something of that dominion over his abode which is considered to make of every man's home a castle. Under a company lease he frequently agrees "that he has only the right of ingress and egress for himself and his immediate family," that he will not "entertain without the Company's consent persons objectionable to the company," and "that he will not take into his house without the operator's consent boarders or lodgers who do not work in the company's mine, and he grants to the owning Company the right of entrance to his house for purpose of inspection any hour of the day or night." The object of these restrictions is to prevent a tenant from harbouring or entertaining a union organiser and to enable officials of the company to enter the house to find and eject any visitor whom the company might consider "objectionable."

These leases, which strike European observers as being so remarkable by contrast, have proved a powerful weapon in the hands of operators. During every serious strike hundreds, in some cases thousands, of families are evicted from their homes and the union does what it can to house them in temporary "barracks." The companies and judges defend the evictions as reasonable since the worker has signed the lease and thus agreed that the dwelling goes with the job. When men go on strike they leave their jobs, the companies say, and they must expect to leave their homes also. Which sounds quite fair and very "legal." But the plain fact is that in coalfields where the majority of the mines are tied to company villages with no independent houses within reach of the mine the individual unorganised worker has no choice but to take the job and the house on the company's terms —or join the ranks of the unemployed. The miner's freedom is a sort of "Hobson's choice!" Evictions have an important bearing on the living conditions of miners' families in America. There is almost constantly, in one coalfield or another, a certain proportion of the mining population living in homes erected by the union but these "barracks," while they provide the essentials of shelter and freedom from interference, are unsubstantial affairs, and their very "temporariness" militates against an organised, established social life; each tenant feels himself an outcast in an inhospitable world and the evicted families constitute an isolated group instead of being happy units in a congenial community.

How long will it be before a home in an independent community will be as normal to the American miner as it is to-day to the British miner? How much longer is the company-controlled camp to be tolerated as a necessary evil? This is one of the most challenging social problems in America arising out of the conduct of the coal-mining industry. A necessary step towards a satisfactory solution would seem to be a much larger and stricter social control over the ownership of land, for in many cases the operating companies own all the land within convenient reach of the mine. Housing conditions in such communities are almost wholly dependent on the enlightenment and good will of operators and companies but this seems a precarious basis for a much-needed improvement in housing standards and for an enlargement of the area of freedom in the lives of coal-mine workers and their families. Obstacles there are undoubtedly but one may fully realise how formidable they are and yet be deeply impressed by the urgency of the necessity of getting rid of the whole institution —company houses, company police, company land, the company store, the company cinema, the company-supported school and church and all the other features of the American feudal, serf-like company-controlled mining community.

NOTE.—*Home Environment and Employment Opportunities of Women in Coal-mine Workers' Families*, Bulletin No. 45 of the Women's Bureau of the United States Department of Labor, is an excellent study, on which I have drawn freely in the foregoing section. Readers interested in the economic and social condition of the wives and daughters of American miners will find valuable material in it. *Houses for Mining Towns*, Bulletin 87 of the Department of the Interior (Bureau of Mines), contains very full details of types of houses, construction, measurements, windows, doors, lighting, heating, water and waste systems, together with plans and photographs. The English Department of Mines could with advantage take a leaf out of the book of the United States Bureau of Mines in respect of publications.

CHILDREN OF EVICTED MINERS, JERE BARRACKS, WEST VIRGINIA

BRITISH COALFIELDS

To establish an adequate comparison it would be desirable to treat of housing in the British coalfields along the same lines with those adopted for the American fields. Unfortunately no comprehensive survey of housing conditions in British coalfields has been made. Professor H. Stanley Jevons, who has taken a special interest in housing and was the virtual founder of the Cardiff Workers' Co-operative Garden Village on the outskirts of Cardiff, the chief port for the export of South Wales coal, devotes some attention to the problem in his book *The British Coal Trade*; Government Commissions have taken evidence on certain aspects of housing in mining communities; reports have been published by various Housing Associations and Government Departments; the reports of the Medical Officers of Health of the local authorities in districts where coal-mining is the main industry contain much valuable information; and in each coalfield there are individuals who know a great deal about housing conditions in their own field and are prepared to share their knowledge with others. But, so far as the author is aware, no attempt has been made to collate all the relevant material from these sources and to publish the results in a comprehensive report, covering all the British coalfields. Certainly no such attempt will be made here. The most that will be done for purposes of this study is to give a brief description of housing conditions in British coalfields in the hope that it will be sufficient to enable the reader to make a general comparison of the home environment of mine-workers and their families in the two countries.

Overcrowding

One of the worst features of the life of the industrial workers of Great Britain is overcrowding in the homes. Social investigators from other countries are usually impressed by this feature. True, different standards prevail in different countries. But judged by any civilised standard living conditions in this respect in the industrial districts of Great Britain fall far short. Contrary to general expectations, however, the colliery districts are not appreciably worse than industrial districts generally in this matter of overcrowding, except in certain counties and in Scotland.

The general test of overcrowding applied in England and

Wales is whether there are more than two persons per room living in five rooms or less. In the County of Northumberland 24·2 per cent of families were living under these conditions at the Census of 1921; the percentage of overcrowding in the mining districts reached 24·3 per cent in Newburn and 23·7 per cent in Ashington. In the County of Durham the percentage of families living in an overcrowded condition reached 25·9 per cent at Stanley and 21·9 per cent in the Rural District of Chester-le-Street, the percentage for the whole county being 22·2 per cent. It will be seen that only in the cases of Newburn, in Northumberland, and Stanley, in Durham, was the percentage greater for a mining district than the percentage for the whole county.

In Lancashire, with a county average of 5·9 per cent, overcrowding was worse in some and better in other of the mining towns. The individual figures were for St. Helens 14·5 per cent and for Wigan 10·8 per cent, but other mining towns, such as Farnsworth and Chorley, had less overcrowding than the county average.

In Yorkshire the Pontefract Borough and Rural Districts and Barnsley exceeded the percentage of overcrowding for the county as a whole (7·5 per cent). But two other mining towns, Ardwick-le-Street and Bentley-with-Arksey, were both below this percentage.

In Derbyshire, Chesterfield and the Rural District of Blackwell both had a greater degree of overcrowding than the average for the whole county (4·2 per cent), but Alfreton and Ilkeston were both below the county average.

In Nottinghamshire the percentages for the mining towns were very close to that for the county.

In South Wales there are few marked deviations from the county averages. In Glamorgan, Neath slightly exceeded the average for the county (7·7 per cent) but Merthyr, Mountain Ash and Aberdare had less than average overcrowding. In the County of Monmouth, Tredegar (10·7 per cent) considerably exceeded the county average (7·6 per cent) while Abercarn and Bedwellty were below it.

The extent of overcrowding in Scotland is considerably greater than in England and Wales. The method used in Scotland to measure crowding is to take the average number of persons per 100 rooms for the whole district. This average for Scotland was 142, as compared with 91 for England and Wales. In certain selected mining districts, where the mining population is known or considered to exceed 20 per cent of the occupied male population, this ratio is 178 to 100 rooms. The existence of severe overcrowding is evident in some mining communities, such as Cowdenbeath (226 per 100 rooms), Loghgelly (226), Hamilton (211), Kilsyth (212), Middle Ward of Lanark (215), Armadale (262), Whitburn (204) and Bathgate County District (219).

In Scotland 33·7 per cent of all families lived more than two persons per room in five rooms or less, compared with 7·5 per cent in England and Wales. In the mining districts referred to above the percentage is 46·7 per cent. In those of Lanark County, excluding Glasgow, 54·6 per cent and in those of Fife 42·5 per cent lived in this condition. In individual districts even higher figures are reached. The Middle Ward of Lanark County had a percentage of 58·8 and Armadale in West Lothian County reached 63 per cent.

It will be seen that in Scotland there is a much greater disparity than in England and Wales between the conditions of overcrowding of mining communities and those of the rest of the population.

In the absence of a method of measuring crowding common to Great Britain and the United States a comparison between them must necessarily be of a very general character but it would appear that overcrowding is more prevalent in the British coal-fields. There are some spots in America, e.g. in certain parts of southern West Virginia, which are more congested and over-crowded per room than the worst mining districts of Scotland, but taking the American coal-mining population as a whole one would be inclined to say that it is less overcrowded per room, less congested in large, populous mining towns and better spaced than the British mining population.

Condition of Houses

It is impossible to shew the condition of houses at all adequately on a statistical basis. Dilapidated and unweather-proof dwellings, the lack of decent sanitary arrangements, of proper footpaths and water supplies do not lend themselves to this kind of treatment. But records are available of the number of houses inspected by medical officers of health, the number found quite unfit for habitation and the number found not reasonably fit, together with the various steps taken to induce landlords to put their property in order. Comparison between different countries and even between different districts within one country may be invalidated by the different interpretations of the different medical authorities of what precisely constitutes unfitness for human habitation. A brief description of conditions in each country may, however, provide the reader with the means of forming a general comparative picture.

In Great Britain as in America the housing conditions of the miners shew great diversities though disparity between the worst and the best is more marked in America. They are often very bad in Great Britain, however; many of the old villages consist of poorly constructed cottages, small and frequently overcrowded, with sanitary arrangements primitive and inadequate, the general aspect being drab and dreary in the extreme. In some of the coalfields, e.g. in the West Midlands and Yorkshire there are still houses of the "back-to-back" type, with no doors or windows except at the front of the house, and consequently no through ventilation and, in many cases, no sun. Mr. J. C. Grant, in his recently published *Back-to-Backs*, gives a gruesome, almost terrifying picture of the effects of the social, including the housing, environment of a contemporary North Country back-to-back mining town. At the other extreme there are garden villages (built by some of the large new colliery companies) which are well planned, well constructed, generously spaced and well equipped—superior to the best housing settlements in any American coalfield. Between the two there is every gradation. In some of the districts, where the housing is generally poor, there may be found groups of excellent new cottages, built by colliery proprietors or by the Local Authorities. In other districts, where the general standard is fairly good, there may be found groups of old houses surviving from the days when the standard of construction was low.

Housing conditions in Great Britain appear to be worst in Northumberland and Durham, and in Scotland, though they are bad also in Yorkshire, Lancashire and South Wales.

In the Northumberland and Durham Coalfield large numbers of houses were declared by the Royal Commission of 1925 as being not reasonably fit for human habitation in Stanley and Hetton. In the Rural District of Auckland 229 houses were shewn as being quite unfit and 627 as being not reasonably fit for habitation.

In Yorkshire, Barnsley and Cudworth contained large numbers of houses not reasonably fit. Lancashire shewed some high numbers in the same category—Hindley 849 and Swinton and Pendlebury 887.

Wrexham, in the Denbighshire (North Wales) field, had 544 such houses. In South Wales very considerable numbers of houses were shewn as being quite unfit, notably in Pontypridd (266), Pontardawe (196), Abertillery (176) and Tredegar (160), and in addition very large numbers of houses in these and other towns were shewn as being not reasonably fit for habitation.

In Scotland 1,596 houses in the mining districts were considered unfit for habitation as the result of investigations made in 1924; 509 of these were in Lanark county.

Apart from the defective conditions of the houses themselves, much dirt and inconvenience are caused by the lack of proper roads and footpaths. In many places sanitary arrangements are exceedingly primitive. Attempts are being made wherever possible to insist on the introduction of indoor sanitation, to provide water closets instead of the prevailing privy, and to multiply them so that there may be one per house. But water supplies and the difficulties of proper drainage facilities have in some districts held up possible improvements.

Local authorities appear to be alive to the problems with which they are faced and some progress has been achieved. In many cases closing orders have been made and a considerable number of houses have been made properly fit for habitation as the result of either formal or informal action. The chief problem before the local authority is how to improve the standard of housing and the condition of existing houses without taking such drastic action that the shortage of houses and the extent of overcrowding are actually increased. The difficulties of the authorities are further complicated by the fact that in many districts where miners are employed rents are greatly in arrears and the property owners are not therefore stimulated to make the necessary improvements.

Provision of New Housing

Houses are being built in mining districts by local authorities, by colliery companies and by private enterprise with and without State assistance.

A survey of the need for houses made in 1919 revealed a shortage, in those districts of England and Wales where the mining population exceeded 20 per cent of the whole, of 186,000 houses if overcrowding was to be avoided, unfit houses were to be replaced and some provision made for industrial development. In these same districts about 59,000 had been completed by 1925. Of these about 36,000 were built by local authorities, about 18,000 by State-assisted private enterprise and about 5,000 by colliery companies and Public Utility Societies. A very large proportion of this last class were built by the Industrial Housing Association. This Association is a Company established for the purpose of encouraging the construction of houses in colliery districts, and possesses certain powers of borrowing from the Public Works Loan Commissioners.

Mainly inspired by Lord Aberconway this Association has made a notable contribution to the improvement of miners' housing conditions, especially in Yorkshire, North Derbyshire and North Nottinghamshire, and to some extent in the South Wales Valleys and in the recently developed Kent coalfield. After the war many new pits were sunk and Lord Aberconway persuaded the responsible heads of certain colliery groups to form the Association for the express purpose of building miners' houses on a large scale. These companies agreed jointly and severally to guarantee the capital and the interest on loans that might be advanced by the Government. A Sinking Fund was established under which, at the end of a given period, all the houses would become the unencumbered property of the various companies. Certain provisions were inserted in the Public Works Loans Act of 1922 which made it possible for loans to be given for housing under careful guarantees against any loss to the State or any profiteering on the part of individuals. It was decided that the Industrial Housing Association should trade without profit and that no dividend should be paid on the share capital. The houses built are leased to the various colliery companies on thirty years' repairing leases at a rent sufficient to cover all the interest and Sinking Fund charges, and as no dividend can be paid it has only been necessary to add to this rent a very small margin for administrative charges. The subsidy of £6 per house granted under the 1923 Act for a period of twenty years is passed direct from the Ministry of Health to the colliery companies, who lease the houses from the Association:

n this way it is possible to lower the rents charged to the tenants.

Much of the success of this experiment was due to the ability and energy of Sir John Tudor Walters who was chosen by the Association as the Chief Executive head of the enterprise. The full story of his achievement is told in his book entitled *The Building of 12,000 Houses*. The drawings in the book, numbering almost a hundred, shew the high standard that has been set up n these new mining villages, including recreation grounds for adults and children. The houses have been designed to meet the needs of the colliery workers and their wives. Generally there are three bedrooms and even in the non-parlour type there is always one large-sized living room. The houses, which cost between £450 and £500 each, including roads, sewers and all outlay, are each fitted with a bath, electric light and water drainage and are provided with garden plots and excellent roads. There are cupboards, sheds for cycles and perambulators and in some cases there has even been a demand for accommodation for a motor-car. When the author mentioned this point to an American audience it was "tickled to death" to think that a garage was hardly ever part of the accommodation of a British miner. Will the day come when provision for motor-cars will be as liberal in British mining districts as it is to-day in American mining camps? Perhaps when that day comes the majority of American miners will be flying to their work! That is, if any work there be in the coalfields!

As shewing a revival of company provision of community facilities it is interesting to note that co-operative stores, churches, chapels, schools, cinemas and institutes have also been built in connection with these mining garden villages by the colliery companies concerned.

NOTE.—For the section dealing with company provision of houses in Great Britain I have drawn mainly on *The Basic Industries of Great Britain*, by Lord Aberconway.

In Scotland a survey made at the same time shewed an estimated need for 17,635 houses in mining districts. By October, 1925, 4,714 houses had been built in these districts by local authorities and private enterprise with State assistance. Of these, 10,144 were built by local authorities, 2,927 by colliery companies and ,643 by State-assisted private enterprise other than colliery companies. These results compare very favourably with those achieved in England and Wales but the Royal Commission said that the standard aimed at in the estimates of Scottish housing needs was probably lower than that adopted in England and Wales and that the initial overcrowding was much greater.

From the following tables, kindly furnished at the request of the author by the Department of Health for Scotland, it will be seen that in the period from 1926 to July 31, 1931, 24,700 houses were completed in County Areas in the Scottish coalfield and in Burghs within those areas by (a) Local Authorities and (b) by private enterprise with assistance under the Housing Acts. Of these 19,981 were built by local authorities and 4,719 by private enterprise. It is noticeable that since 1928 there has been a rapid decline in both public and private building. This shews a marked correlation with the progressively worsening general economic conditions. In 1929 the colliery companies built only 70 houses in the County Areas, compared with 605 in 1926 and 202 in 1928. In 1930 and 1931 they did not build a single house.

It will be seen that far the greatest proportion of the shortage in England and Wales and in Scotland has been met by the Local Authorites. This offers a striking contrast to the position in the United States, where most of the houses occupied by mine-workers are built and controlled by the companies. It is a surprising fact, however, that even in Great Britain, between a quarter and a third of the miners live in houses owned by the colliery companies. In 1925, according to the Royal Commission, there were probably 180,000 such houses; 68,000 of these were let free of rent, almost all being in Northumberland and Durham, about 560 of the rest being in South Wales. In Northumberland and Durham it is the custom where houses are not provided free to pay an allowance as an addition to wages; allowances of about 4s. 8d. per week were made in 1925 to 70,000 workers. The free houses and allowances were given only to heads of families.

The average weekly rent, including rates, of colliery-owned houses let at a rental was, in 1913, 4s. 2d. and for houses owned by the same companies in 1925, 6s. 2d., an increase of 60 per cent. The average rent, including rates, of company houses built since the war was, in 1925, 11s. 2d. For colliery-owned houses of both classes, pre-war and post-war, the average rent, with

HOUSING IN SCOTTISH COALFIELDS

TOTAL HOUSES COMPLETED IN COUNTY AREAS WHERE COALFIELDS ARE SITUATED (a) BY LOCAL AUTHORITIES AND (b) BY PRIVATE ENTERPRISE WITH ASSISTANCE UNDER THE HOUSING ACTS

Local Authority	1926 (a)	1926 (b)	1927 (a)	1927 (b)	1928 (a)	1928 (b)	1929 (a)	1929 (b)	1930 (a)	1930 (b)	To 31/7, 1931 (a)	To 31/7, 1931 (b)	Totals (a)	Totals (b)	Grand Total (a) and (b)
Ayr County ..	61	156	282	53	504	52	186	31	238	11	159	14	1,430	317	1,747
Clackmannan County	12	2	56	4	44	1	48	—	4	—	48	—	212	7	219
Dumfries ..	—	112	—	—	—	11	—	1	—	10	—	4	—	138	138
Fife County ..	118	268	226	9	272	191	58	11	122	17	20	15	816	511	1,327
Lanark County ..	580	270	1,624	148	1,533	239	617	221	260	91	60	72	4,674	1,041	5,715
Midlothian County	—	86	—	152	52	102	—	60	—	66	—	6	52	472	524
Sterling County ..	104	102	235	58	284	44	153	36	228	39	30	9	1,034	288	1,322
West Lothian County	—	32	74	5	26	15	32	1	—	—	—	—	132	53	185
Total	875	1,028	2,497	429	2,715	655	1,094	361	852	234	317	120	8,350	2,827	11,177

TOTAL COMPLETED IN BURGHS IN ABOVE AREAS

Local Authority	1926		1927		1928		1929		1930		To 31/7, 1931		Totals		Grand Total
	(a)	(b)	(a)	(b)	(a)	(b)	(a)	(b)	(a)	(b)	(a)	(b)	(a)	(b)	(a) and (b)
Ayr County ..	538	295	660	134	529	117	456	162	452	30	148	41	2,783	779	3,562
Clackmannan County	84	5	118	3	—	—	—	—	—	—	—	—	202	8	210
Dumfries County ..	14	—	—	1	12	—	6	—	—	—	—	—	32	1	33
Fife County ..	752	113	579	74	522	75	306	39	74	23	230	12	2,463	336	2,799
Lanark County ..	634	81	898	39	1,010	52	400	32	214	61	212	12	3,368	277	3,645
Midlothian County	97	8	120	21	40	54	116	50	170	5	24	3	567	141	708
Stirling County ..	438	94	393	97	495	78	348	12	210	34	120	23	2,004	338	2,342
West Lothian County	57	9	57	2	30	1	24	—	24	—	20	—	212	12	224
Total	2,614	605	2,825	371	2,638	377	1,656	295	1,144	153	754	91	11,631	1,892	13,523

TOTALS OF COUNTIES AND BURGHS AS ABOVE

Local Authority	1926		1927		1928		1929		1930		To 31/7, 1931		Totals		Grand Total
	(a)	(b)	(a)	(b)	(a)	(b)	(a)	(b)	(a)	(b)	(a)	(b)	(a)	(b)	(a) and (b)
Ayr County	599	451	942	187	1,033	169	642	193	690	41	307	55	4,213	1,096	5,309
Clackmannan County	96	7	174	7	44	1	48	—	4	—	48	—	414	15	429
Dumfries County	14	112	—	1	12	11	6	1	—	10	—	4	32	139	171
Fife County	870	381	805	83	794	266	364	50	196	40	250	27	3,279	847	4,126
Lanark County	1,214	351	2,522	187	2,543	291	1,017	253	474	152	272	84	8,042	1,318	9,360
Midlothian County	97	94	120	173	92	156	116	110	170	71	24	9	619	613	1,232
Stirling County	542	196	628	155	779	122	501	48	438	73	150	32	3,038	626	3,664
West Lothian County	57	41	131	7	56	16	56	1	24	—	20	—	344	65	490
Total	3,489	1,633	5,322	800	5,353	1,032	2,750	656	1,996	387	1,071	211	19,981	4,719	24,700
	5,122		6,122		6,385		3,406		2,383		1,282		24,700		

NUMBERS OF HOUSES ERECTED IN COUNTY AREAS BY COLLIERY COMPANIES

(INCLUDED IN THE FIGURES SHOWN IN PREVIOUS STATEMENT)

Local Authority	1926	1927	1928	1929	1930	To 31/7, 1931	Total
Ayr County	89	—	8	—	—	—	97
Clackmannan County	—	—	—	—	—	—	—
Dumfries	102	—	—	—	—	—	102
Fife County	233	—	40	—	—	—	273
Lanark County	106	—	48	8	—	—	162
Midlothian County	75	126	88	62	—	—	351
Stirling County	—	—	18	—	—	—	18
West Lothian County	—	—	—	—	—	—	—
Total	605	126	202	70	—	—	1,003

TOTAL COMPLETED IN BURGHS IN ABOVE COUNTIES

Ayr County
Clackmannan County
Dumfries County
Fife County
Lanark County
Midlothian County
Stirling County
West Lothian County

NIL

rates, was, in 1925, 7s. 3d., an increase of 74 per cent above the pre-war figure.

In 1928 the rent for a non-parlour house with three bedrooms under the Industrial Housing Association Scheme in the Yorkshire, Derbyshire and Nottinghamshire fields varied from 8s. to 8s. 6d. a week. In the South Wales Coalfield, where the cost of building is higher, the average rent was 9s. 6d. a week. For a house with a parlour and three bedrooms the rent varies from 9s. to 10s. 6d. a week. These figures do not include rates, which are paid by the tenants, and in most cases there is a charge for electric light and other services. Since 1928 there has been little deviation from these rental charges, for the companies fix the rents on a long-term basis to cover the cost of building, administration expenses, etc., but owing to the reduced earnings of the miners the present tendency is towards lower rents.

It is difficult to obtain a reliable estimate of the average rent, with rates, of houses built by private enterprise and the local authorities in mining districts but from inquiries made by the author in various parts of the South Wales Coalfield it would appear that it is higher than the average for colliery-owned houses. The majority of the houses have been built since the war when building costs were high and they are of a more uniformly better type than the bulk of the colliery-owned houses, most of which were built before the war, when costs and the standard of construction were much lower.

American visitors sometimes raise the question whether miners living in colliery-owned houses in Great Britain are as much socially dominated by the company as are the mine-workers living in an American company mining village. The British company has the usual legal rights attaching to the ownership of houses and in comparatively small self-contained mining communities the local manager plays a rôle similar to that of a local squire in an agricultural village, but the power of the Miners' Union and the influence of political ideas have reduced that rôle to a minor part, albeit played in subtle ways, in the drama of village mining life. In the larger urban mining communities there is little attempt to interfere with the social freedom of the miner. The author has knowledge of a man living in a colliery-owned house in South Wales who takes a very active part in union affairs and is generally regarded as a "Bolshie"; never, he says, have his political or social activities jeopardised his position as a tenant. This may be an exceptional case and one has heard of other cases where a miner who has made himself "objectionable" to the management has been penalised, not only by being given a poorer "place" underground where his earnings would be less, but by being kept waiting for a house or by having to give up a house on account of rent arrears while other men, more docile, were allowed to remain as tenants in spite of arrears. But in general British miners living in colliery-owned houses enjoy a much larger measure of freedom as tenants than do the mine-workers living in the company mining camps in the United States.

In the past few years there has been a regrettable retardation in the rate of progress towards better housing standards in the mining areas of Great Britain. This is due to the serious economic plight of the industry which has imposed heavy burdens on the local authorities, working on reduced revenues, and resulted in restricted private enterprise.

The following extracts from an article by Mr. E. A. Charles, "Housing Position in Wales"—in *The Welsh Housing and Development Year Book*, 1931, give some idea, based on reports of Medical Officers of Health for the year 1930, of the position in one of these areas, the South Wales Coalfield:

"*Merthyr Tydvil.*—The report of the Medical Officer shows that with the exception of 20 houses built to replace a like number demolished to provide a tipping ground, the Council had not erected any houses since 1927. A report presented to the Ministry of Health showed that there are 19 tents and vans used as habitations, 123 cellar dwellings, 917 houses were in such a bad state that they should be closed, and that 1,450 houses needed extensive repairs to make them habitable. Overcrowding continues, and action can only be taken in a few of the worst cases, because of the lack of alternative accommodation. The Sanitary Officers have spared no effort to effect improvements, no less than 2,781 houses having been inspected during the year. Of the number 196 were found to be unfit for human habitation, and 891 were found not to be in all respects reasonably fit.

"*Rhondda.*—From the public health standpoint, housing accommodation remained unsatisfactory, and no active steps for the provision of new houses were taken by the Authority, whilst private enterprise resulted in the completion of only six houses during this period. The existence of overcrowding is indicated by the large number of houses which are occupied by two or more families, and though there is a considerable number of vacant premises in the district, the rents demanded or conditions imposed by the owners preclude their occupation by tenants with large families and proportionately inadequate incomes. It is not anticipated that the housing conditions in the district will be relieved until a revival occurs in the coal industry, as the long continued depression has seriously depleted local financial resources, both private and public. Closing orders were issued in respect of 33 ordinary dwelling-houses, and 5 closing orders and 2 demolition orders were determined after the houses had been rendered fit for occupation. Of the 1,345 houses inspected during the year, 33 were found unfit for habitation and 1,115 were classed as not reasonably fit. Although notices were served in all the 1,115 cases, defects were remedied in but 69 instances.

"*Monmouthshire.*—Further efforts have been made to improve the houses in the districts, some of which are of the very old type and with poor accommodation. Notices are served, and where possible repairs are effected, but in some cases it has been necessary to obtain closing orders under the Housing Acts, and several houses have been demolished as they were found to be totally unsuitable for reconstruction. In many of the districts the housing problem remains serious. More working class houses are needed, not only to alleviate overcrowding, which is very prevalent, but to replace the closing and demolition of unfit and dilapidated houses. It must be realised that this shortage of houses is one of the chief causes of overcrowding, and it is evident that this state of affairs is not conducive to good health or decent morals. At many of these houses where two families are accommodated, the accommodation is so limited that parents and children, some of whom have reached puberty, are compelled to sleep in the same bedroom, whilst as regards sex accommodation, it is not uncommon for members of both sexes, of advanced ages, to use a common sleeping room. Many of the older types of houses have the disadvantage that they have none of the facilities which tend to promote a healthy life, as most of the household washing, cooking, etc., have to be done in the one living room, which is often the only room on the ground floor. The bedroom accommodation in these houses is also very limited, and in quite a number of

s

instances comprised of one room, partitioned off by means of light, flimsy partitions or curtains. There are still a number of back-to-back houses in existence in the County, and every effort should be made to do away with this type of house. It is regretted that a number of houses erected by Local Authorities under the Housing Acts are doubly occupied. These houses are designed and erected for the accommodation of one family only, and are not in any way suitable for two families. The practice of allowing this double occupation should be discouraged as much as possible, as the houses will soon become little more than slum property."

These extracts could probably be paralleled from Reports of Medical Officers of Health in the mining areas of Scotland and England. It must be admitted that they shew a retrogression in the social life of British mining communities. They shew also how dependent the provision of social amenities is upon the general prosperity of industry. The three local authorities referred to above have a sense of civic development unsurpassed if not unrivalled in Great Britain but the industrial depression has almost paralysed their housing activities.

THE MINERS' WELFARE FUND OF GREAT BRITAIN

The past decade has seen a very marked and most pleasing improvement in the provision of recreational facilities in the British Coalfields. Desolate hills of slag have been made plain and blackened wastes have been transformed into delectable recreation oases—beautiful bowling greens, cricket fields, tennis lawns (generously supported by grey and red hard courts), open-air swimming baths, children's playgrounds, equipped with chutes, merry-go-rounds, ocean-waves, leap-frog courses, jungleyms and other devices to delight the minds and develop the bodies of kiddies. In their way the various pavilions, the children's shelters and the bandstands are quite an attractive feature for they are well-designed and suitably coloured. When one compares the Welsh mining valleys to-day with their pre-war appearance one is greatly impressed by the remarkable change. And the same kind of improvement is to be observed in all the other coalfields. Psychologically also these welfare schemes have been beneficial. Miners are no different from other people in feeling brighter after a game of cricket, tennis or bowls under pleasant conditions. And miners' children are no differnt from other children in their enjoyment of play. Employers have testified that the social benefits accruing from the Welfare Fund have tended to allay discontent in the coalfields. Some of the men indeed see in these Welfare Schemes a menace and have consistently refused to assist in their administration; their view is that by making the miners more contented the schemes postpone the realisation of complete workers' control of the industry. But that the provision of facilities for recreation is vastly better admits of no doubt; that it has promoted more content than discontent may be open to question but the author's firm belief is that if a vote were taken in the coalfields there would be an overwhelming majority in favour of its continuance and that any considerable restriction, which indeed is now a real danger owing to the depression in the industry and the clamant demands for "economy" on the part of an influential body of politicians, would create a considerable amount of hostile discontent.

One criticism may be made here. There is reason to believe that many of the miners are unable to enjoy the amenities provided owing to lack of money. This is particularly true in the case of lawn tennis. Many of the men cannot afford to buy the necessary equipment in the way of clothes, rackets, balls, etc., and although the playing fees are low compared with those of private clubs some of the miners who are quite useful players are too poor to pay them and have to rely for their games on friends or relatives, often brothers or sisters who may be clerks or teachers. Indeed one often hears the complaint that the courts are used to a far greater extent by women and men who are not miners than by the miners themselves. While it is true that the Fund is intended to benefit the sons and daughters of miners it seems a great pity that the miners themselves should be unable to take part more generally in the games. In some instances the difficulty of "making the tennis courts pay" is so acute that the grass courts have been converted into putting greens. The prevailing industrial depression affects athletic clubs of all kinds but it is to be hoped that a way may be found of keeping these Welfare clubs going.

The contrast between the American and British Coalfields in this matter of recreational facilities is very striking. In the American Coalfields they are provided almost entirely by the companies or individual owners and while in some cases the playing grounds and apparatus cost a considerable sum even the best of these private schemes compare unfavourably with the average Miners' Welfare Fund Scheme in Great Britain; in many cases there is no provision at all. There is nothing comparable to the Miners' Welfare Fund in America—nothing in the nature of Welfare work applicable to all the coalfields and administered under a unified plan by a Committee representative of employers and employees, with outside experts, and from a fund created out of the proceeds of the industry, all authorised by Acts of Parliament. Many people in the United States, including politicians important enough to influence legislation, presidents of coal companies, officials of miners' unions, economists, sociologists, students, social workers and government officials seemed keenly interested in what the author told them about the British Miners' Welfare Fund and some of them expressed their intention to press for something on similar lines in their own country. It is hoped therefore that a more detailed exposition of the whole scheme will be of interest to American readers while readers in the country of its origin may also find it informative.

The Miners' Welfare Fund was established by the Mining Industry Act, 1920, though its origin is to be found in one of the recommendations of the Coal Industry Commission of 1919. The Mining Industry (Welfare Fund) Act, 1925, extended the period during which payments might be paid by five years and provided for the addition of two members to the five who were appointed as the Welfare Committee under the Act of 1920. The Mining Industry Act, 1926, established a Royalties Welfare Levy at the rate of one shilling for every twenty shillings of the rental value of rights to work coal and of mineral wayleaves in connection with coal: it also provided for the addition of two more members to the Committee. And the Mining Industry (Welfare Fund) Act, 1931, extended the life of the Fund by a further five years.

The Acts of 1925 and 1931 may be described briefly as continuing or extending measures. The Acts of 1920 and 1926 are important because they stipulate the sources of revenue and define the scope of the activities of the Committee entrusted with the administration of the Fund. They are so important as to make it worth while to quote extracts from them.

The following are the salient clauses of the Act of 1920:

"(1) There shall be constituted a fund to be applied for such purposes connected with the social well-being, recreation and conditions of living of workers in or about coal mines and with mining education and research as the Board of Trade, after consultation with any Government Department concerned, may approve."

NOTE.—It will be seen that the fund is to be applied for certain educational as well as for general socio-recreational purposes but the educational activities will be dealt with later.

"(2) The owners of every coal mine shall, before the thirty-first of March, nineteen hundred and twenty-one, and before the same day in each of the subsequent five years, pay into the said fund a sum equal to one penny a ton of the output of the mine during the previous calendar year, and the sums so payable in respect of any mine shall be defrayed as part of the working ex-

penses of the mine, and shall be recoverable either as a debt
due to the Crown, or by the Board of Trade summarily as a civil
debt."

NOTE.—Until 1926 the whole income of the Fund was obtained from
this levy of a penny on every ton of coal raised and even since 1926
when the income was first supplemented by the royalties levy about
nine-tenths of the income has derived from the penny-a-ton contribution.
The receipts from the output levy in the period 1920–1930 amounted
to nearly £10 million whereas the receipts from the royalties levy from
1926 to 1930 amounted to £1 million.

"(3) The duty of allocating the money from time to time
standing to the credit of the said fund to the several purposes
aforesaid shall be vested in a Committee consisting of five persons,
appointed by the Board of Trade, one of whom shall be appointed
by the Board of Trade after consultation with the Mining Association of Great Britain, and another after consultation with the
Miners' Federation of Great Britain. The Committee shall have
the assistance of three assessors, appointed by the Minister of
Health, the Board of Education, and the Secretary for Scotland
respectively; the Assessors shall have the right of attending
meetings of the Committee and of taking part in the deliberations
thereof, but not of voting; and different persons may be appointed
by the above-mentioned departments to act as Assessors in relation
to different matters: Provided that the Committee shall allocate
for the benefit of the several districts mentioned in Part I of the
second schedule to this Act sums equal to four-fifths of the
contributions from the owners of coal mines in those districts
respectively.

"(4) The Committee may invite a local authority to submit
a scheme for any of the purposes to which the fund may be
applied, and, if such scheme be approved by the Committee,
they may make such grants in aid to the said local authority out
of the fund and upon such conditions as may seem to them
desirable:

"Provided that in no case shall any grant be made out of the
fund for the building or repairing of dwelling houses."

NOTE.—It will be observed that housing in the ordinary sense is ruled
out entirely. This Clause has operated mainly in the granting of financial
support to local authorities to enable them to build and equip educational

institutions of the type of mining schools, mining departments of university and technical colleges, senior and advanced centres for Mining Education, etc. It need hardly be said that such support is most welcome to the harassed local authorities of the distressed mining areas.

The most important Clauses of the Act of 1926 are:

"(1) Any person liable to pay mineral rights duty on the rental value of rights to work coal and of mineral wayleaves in connection with coal, or who would be so liable but for any conception by common law or statute, shall be liable to pay for the financial year ending the thirty-first day of March, nineteen hundred and twenty-seven, and for every subsequent financial year a levy (hereinafter referred to as 'the royalties Welfare Levy') at the rate in each case of one shilling for every twenty shillings of that rental value.

"(2) The number of the Committee constituted under section twenty of the Mining Industry Act, 1920, as amended by the Mining Industry (Welfare Fund) Act, 1925 (hereinafter referred to as 'the Miners' Welfare Committee'), shall be increased by the addition of two members appointed by the Board of Trade, of whom one shall be appointed after consultation with the Miners' Federation of Great Britain, and one after consultation with such Associations or Bodies as may appear to the Board to represent persons liable to pay the royalties welfare levy, and the said section twenty shall have effect accordingly."

NOTE.—The Act of 1925 had increased the number of the Committee from five to seven: since 1926 the number has been nine. It may be appropriate here to mention the fact that the Chairman of the Committee throughout the lifetime of the Fund, except for a short period at the beginning and during the time he was a member of the Labour Cabinet in 1924, was Lord Chelmsford. In 1931 he retired from the Chairmanship to the regret of all sections of the industry, but he accepted the chairmanship of the Committee set up in 1931 to report on the future of the Fund and retained the Chairmanship of the Selection Committee of the Scholarship Scheme up to the time of his death. His name will always be associated with this development of the social side of the industry if only by virtue of the description of the activities of the Fund which he wrote as Chairman in 1927: the report is obtainable from H.M. Stationery Office. The present Chairman of the Committee is Lord Noel-Buxton.

"(3) It shall be the duty of the miners' Welfare Committee to secure as far as reasonably practicable the provision at all

Coal Mines to the satisfaction of the Committee, of accommodation and facilities for workmen taking baths and drying clothes."

NOTE.—It is under this Clause that such a remarkable improvement has taken place in the provision of pit-head baths in Great Britain in the past seven years.

Any group or community of miners can apply for a grant from the appropriate district fund to finance any scheme covered by the definition in the Act.

One of the main principles laid down by the central committees for the guidance of district Welfare Committees was intended to secure the co-operation of both sides of the industry in the control of all schemes established by the Fund. Joint control is held to be essential to the successful development of welfare ideals, and just as the district welfare committees themselves consist half of workers' and half of owners' representatives, so also should the bodies of local trustees and the local management committees. Management committees consisting solely of workmen are discouraged except in cases where it is impossible to find owners' representatives able to serve on them, for it is believed that the splendid potentialities of the Fund can only be fully realised as the result of whole-hearted enthusiasm and co-operation within the industry itself. The system of Joint Management Committees is accordingly the general rule in all local schemes and each committee is known as the local welfare committee; it may represent a pit or a group of pits or a mining village or in some cases and for some purposes it may represent the whole of a district, according to the nature of the scheme. In the case of areas where the mining population forms only a portion of the whole, the mining community, by entrusting their scheme to the District or Parish Council, run the risk of losing control over it, as the local authority cannot bind itself to give proportionate representation on the Committee of Management to any particular interests.

The local committees submit their proposals to the district joint committees but the final decisions and the allocations of grants lie with the central Miners' Welfare Committee. Some trouble has been experienced by the central committee in dealing with cases involving anticipation of its decisions on recommendations submitted by district committees, which have frequently advised local Committees that they may proceed with their schemes without waiting for the central Committee's notification of an allocation. The Miners' Welfare Committee, in its tenth Annual Report, 1931, touching on this point, says:

"But it might save misunderstandings in future if local Committees were not communicated with until notification of the actual allocation could be conveyed to them. Since the average time spent in dealing with district committees' recommendations is so short, the interests of expedition provide no excuse for the anticipation of our decisions."

Apart from this difficulty the machinery appears to have run smoothly enough.

The tendency towards increased co-operation between the district welfare committees and the central committee was assisted in the second period by the appointment of two additional district organisers, making seven in all, and by the holding of annual conferences of these organisers in various district centres.

The year 1931 marks the end of the second statutory period of the Fund, and in the following general summary of its activities it will be convenient to proceed on the lines of a contrast between the two five-year periods.

The income from the output levy, with interest, for the first period was £5,855,469; in the second period it was £4,891,670. The difference is to be explained by the facts that the first period included an extra half-year at the outset and that it was less severely affected by the stoppage of 1921 than the second period was by the stoppage in 1926. The total of bad and doubtful debts in respect of the levy for the second period was estimated at about £96,000, as compared with only £13,000 in the first period, this considerable increase being due to the straitened financial condition of the industry, which is also reflected in the greater difficulty experienced in collecting promptly what is due. This difficulty also affects the Fund by reducing the amount of interest earned on its unexpended balances. The interest was in fact £48,286 less in the second period than in the first. It is creditable to all concerned however that the bad and doubtful debts represent only 1 per cent of the total sum collected.

It is remarkable also that although the sum collected in the second period was substantially less than in the first, the amounts allocated were approximately the same, namely £3,623,095 from the district funds as compared with £3,701,093, and £974,572 from the general fund as compared with £868,142, and the un-assigned balance at the end of the year was also much the same as at the end of 1925.

The number of allocations from the district funds was nearly double the number in the first but the average amount of each allocation was very much less because so many of them took the form of supplementary grants for schemes previously established. In the second period 339 new recreational schemes and 106 new health schemes were established and the need for new schemes is by no means yet exhausted.

The most prominent feature in connection with district schemes in the second period was the movement towards a greater expendi-ture on schemes connected with health than on those connected with recreation. In the first period, out of every hundred pounds allocated from the district funds, 64 were classified as recreation and 31 as health; while in the second period the amount of the recreation group had dropped to 51 and the health group had risen to 41, the percentages for the whole period of the Fund being 58 and 36 respectively. There was a substantial increase in the amount granted to hospitals though the allocations for nursing services and ambulances were somewhat lower, but the real reason for the great expansion in the total sum allocated for health purposes was the fact that allocations for convalescent schemes, at over £1¼ millions, exceeded the total for the first five years by over £300,000.

Allocations from the district funds for education, while still only little more than 1 per cent of the total amount, were more than double in the second period what they were in the first, while allocations for pit welfare (baths, canteens, drinking water underground, etc.) remained at almost exactly the same figure (about 3½ per cent). The chief development in the second period under the head of education was the encouragement given to district welfare committees to recommend grants for the assistance of students, particularly in those cases where a student of more than average ability had entered on a course of study which he was unable, as the result of unforeseen circumstances, to continue without financial assistance. Since 1927 fourteen different com-mittees have made 208 grants to 148 different individuals entirely from the district funds. Some of the author's own students have been assisted in this way. Financial support has also been given for the establishment of non-vocational lecture schemes and in 1928 a grant of £500 was made from the general fund to the Industrial Health Education Society which organises the provision of health lectures.

Some particulars of the activities of the Fund in the year 1931 may be of interest.

Recreation

From the District Funds 665 allocations were made for recreational purposes. This number included 63 for the establishment of new schemes, the total of separate schemes in this category being thus increased to 1,256 in all. The total number of allocations under this head since the inception of the Fund had by the end of the year reached the figure of 5,100.

In South Wales active steps were taken by the district committee to encourage still further the provision of boys' clubs, a form of activity in which this district is considerably in advance of others. During the year the South Wales district committee formed an organisation known as the South Wales Federation of Miners' Boys Clubs, for the purpose of encouraging the establishment of new clubs in the coalfield, besides assisting those already in being. It is interesting to record that this organisation was successful in securing a grant of £5,000 from the Harkness Trust in furtherance of its objects, and that the Director of the Trust in Great Britain, Dr. Thomas Jones, C.H., was born and bred in the Rhymney Valley, one of the Welsh industrial valleys, and has played an important part in the amelioration of the social conditions of the industrial workers of South Wales. The boys' club movement in that district derives much of its impetus from the boys' seaside camp at St. Athan, which was established in 1925; this seaside camp has become a notable feature of the boys' Welfare movement of Great Britain.

Pit Welfare

The number of allocations during the year for purposes falling under the heading "Pit Welfare" was 22, making a total since the inception of the Fund of 130. One of the allocations was a contribution of £625 towards the cost of erecting a pit-head waiting-room, to be used for ambulance training, at South

Leicestershire Colliery, the balance being met by the colliery owners. Another was for the completion of the pit-head cycle sheds in the South Derbyshire district. Seven cycle-sheds have so far been provided in connection with pit-head baths, three in Durham, two in Warwickshire, one in South Staffordshire and one in Cumberland, the district funds having paid for five and the colliery owners for the other two. One-third of the new pit-head baths put in hand by the end of 1931 had been or were being equipped with canteens from various sources, mainly from the district funds.

Health

Seventy-one allocations were made for purposes connected with the health of miners. Among these were 29 for new schemes making a total of 224 separate schemes. By the end of the year the number of allocations under this head had reached a total of 530. The amount allocated was expended on ambulance services, hospitals, nursing services and convalescent treatment. The convalescent homes in the various coalfields are one of the finest features of the health services of the Fund and are greatly appreciated by the miners. They are worth enumerating and are mentioned in the order of their upkeep costs, beginning with the lowest, the name of the home being given after each area which it serves

Derbyshire at Skegness, Cannock Chase (Weston-super-Mare), South Yorkshire (Scalby), Lancashire (Blackpool), West Yorkshire (Lytham), Ayr (Troon), North Staffordshire (Rudyard), South Wales (Talygarn), Warwickshire (Higham), Mansfield area (Berry Hill) and Ayr (Kirkmichael). The cost of upkeep per patient per week, exclusive of patients' travelling expenses, ranged from 24s. 10d. for the Derbyshire home at Skegness to 54s. 1d. for the Ayr home at Kirkmichael.

Education

During 1931 a sum of £11,129 was allocated from the district funds for educational purposes. The number of allocations was 119. Most of these allocations were special grants for students. Ninety such grants were made entirely from the district funds. In addition, eleven special grants were made from district funds to supplement grants from the general fund, in accordance with recommendations made by the Scholarship Selection Committee. Nine allocations were made for various forms of non-vocational lecture schemes, including three for the continuation of the health lectures in the districts of South Wales, Lanark and the Lothians, three for the continuation of the general cultural lectures in the districts of Nottinghamshire, Derbyshire and the Forest of Dean, one for similar lectures in the North Staffordshire district for the continuation of the work of training young miners preparatory to emigration. Another allocation was made in the North Staffordshire district for the provision of small bursaries to courses of non-vocational lectures and week-end or Summer Schools held under the auspices of the Workers' Educational Association.

Other allocations made during the year included £100 for libraries for mining students in Warwickshire, £50 for the mining students' society at the Nuneaton Mining School, £100 for books for the mining library at the Castleford and district technical institute, £175 for Studentships at evening and part-time mining Classes in North Staffordshire, £36 and £24 for safety-first badges for young students in South and West Yorkshire, and £21 for a lantern for use in connection with lectures at Chirk, in the North Wales Coalfield. In this connection it is interesting to note that a new film is now being prepared which will tell the story of the activities of the Fund.

Administrative Expenses

The expenses incurred by the district Committees in administering such large grants must necessarily be considerable but it is a remarkable fact that the sums allocated for administration work out for the year at approximately 1·2 per cent of the total allocations made from the district funds. The proportion is slightly higher than it was at the end of the first five years, when it was rather less than 1 per cent, but the difference is chiefly accounted for by the larger number of district organisers. Few, if any, can reasonably complain of such a low percentage of administration cost.

THE GENERAL FUND

The amount credited to the general fund during the year 1931 was £199,749, making a total of £903,200 for the second period.

A sum amounting in all to £211,580 was transferred to the bath
fund. Forty-nine allocations were made to a total amount o
£98,610, of which £40,550 was for research, £49,444 for education, and £8,616 for administrative expenses and other miscel-
laneous services.

As will be seen, research and education are the two main
objects stimulated by grants from the general fund.

Research

During the first five years it provided £500,000 for the purpose
of promoting research into the health and safety of mine-workers
Of this sum approximately £71,100 was spent on the provision
and equipment of the research stations, and approximately
£169,400 on financing the work in progress. The research stations
were not actually completed, however, until the second period
the large-scale one at Buxton being opened in 1927 and the
small-scale laboratories at Sheffield in 1928.

During the second period the amount allocated for research
was £208,094, of which about £14,000 was for capital purposes
and £193,024 was for current work. The scope of the work
was considerably extended during that period, first by the adoption
of various measures under the head of "safety instruction" for
bringing the workers in the industry in close touch with the
purpose, value and results of the work, and secondly by the
wide extension of the field of work undertaken with a view of
reducing the high accident rate arising from haulage dangers and
falls of ground.

Much of the actual safety research work is done by the Safety
in Mines Research Board. This Board submits estimates to the
general fund which allocates substantial grants after approving
certain estimates. In 1931 a sum of £38,550 was thus allocated
from the Fund, with an additional sum of £2,000 for safety
instruction. The approved estimates included a sum of about
£10,600 for the new work on haulage and falls of ground dangers,
of which £5,500 took the form of grants-in-aid to investigators
not on the Board's staff. They also included £1,700 for health
researches and £2,570 for other grants-in-aid to outside investigators. The grants for safety instruction provided for the continuance of the usual arrangements for promoting popular lectures
on safety subjects, and for the visits of parties of miners to the

Buxton research station; in addition the Board published during the year a further paper, in the series entitled *What every mining man should know* about the safe use of explosives in coal-mines.

In furtherance also of the Safety instruction work additional expenditure was authorised for the provision at Buxton of more suitable accommodation for the proper exhibition and demonstration to parties of visitors of Safety appliances and models; it included the erection of an exhibition hall for diagrams, pictures, models and specimens of various kinds, and the construction of a full-scale model of a short section of a modern mine roadway, with a gate-end and a portion of a longwall face, to demonstrate modern methods of roof support and underground lighting.

A summary of the total allocations for research work since the inception of the Fund, together with a list of the main subjects of research on which work was done during the year, will be found in Appendix IX of the Tenth Report of the Miners' Welfare Committee. A full account of the activities of the Safety in Mines Research Board is published in their annual reports, to which reference should be made for details of particular researches.

Education

During the second five-year period considerable progress was made with the provision of buildings or equipment for mining education and only £85,612 of the sum of £750,000 set aside for this purpose remained unallocated at the end of it, as compared with £316,911 at the beginning. At the beginning of the period allocations had been made for new buildings or extensions for four university mining departments and fifty advanced or senior-course mining centres, but only five of these buildings had been actually completed. During the five years all the remaining forty-nine were completed except six, and in addition allocations were made for seventeen new buildings or extensions, of which three are completed; one of these was a university mining department.

During the year 1931 a sum of £56,850 was provisionally allocated to new schemes for the provision of buildings or equipment, bringing the total grants from the sum of £750,000 up to £664,388. Allocations amounting to £48,160 were confirmed (i.e. definitely granted on approval of schemes in detail) during the year, bringing the total of confirmed allocations to £537,990.

For educational purposes the whole country is divided into the following Groups, though no description will be made here of the developments during the year in each group:

Group   I   (North-Eastern Area)
Group   II   (North-Western Area)
Group III   (North Midland Area)
Group IV   (South Midland Area)
Group   V   (Western Area)
Group VI   (West Scottish Area)
Group VII   (East Scottish Area)

In view of the author's special interest in the South Wales Coalfield he is tempted to describe the developments in Group V (Western Area) during the year. The senior centres at Bridgend and Neath were opened during the year and the original programme for the provision of mining education centres in South Wales and Monmouthshire was almost completed. Only two of the centres contemplated remain to be provided, the advanced centre at Swansea and the senior centre at Pontardawe, and these were both under construction in 1931. In addition, provisional allocations were made for two new centres in Monmouthshire, at Tredegar and New Tredegar, and for one in Carmarthenshire at Llanelly. The Glamorganshire Education Authority contemplate enlarging and improving the advanced centre at Treforest and it was agreed to make a substantial contribution to the cost, provided that the authority is able to come to an agreement with the University of Wales for the use of the centre for the applied science part of the mining degree course at Cardiff University College. By the terms of a provisional agreement which has been come to by representatives of the College, the local authority and the general fund, a mining student at the College would spend two years in Cardiff doing pure science, and two years at Treforest doing applied science, and a professor of mining would be appointed who would be in charge of all the mining work at Treforest, while any other work done there would be under the control of a person appointed by the authority. It is to be hoped that the negotiations will eventually meet with complete success and that South Wales will be provided with the facilities for mining degree work to which its importance as a coalfield entitles it.

An interesting feature of the educational activities of the general fund is the system of Scholarships and special grants.

The Miners' Welfare National Scholarship Scheme was established at the end of the first quinquennium, and the past five years saw the first operations of the scheme. In the first year there were over 2,000 applications for Scholarships, but this was partly due to the nature of the scheme not then being properly understood, and in succeeding years the number has varied between 618 and 689. The number of scholarships awarded each year has varied between 11 and 15, the total for the five years being 61. Of these 33 were awarded to working miners and 28 to the children of miners, ten of the latter being girls. Of the miners, 11 have completed their scholarships satisfactorily but 5 were unable to complete their courses, being unsuccessful in passing necessary examinations. It is well known of course that the majority of the adult miners are handicapped by the lack of a secondary school training and it is not surprising that a proportion of them fail to clear all the hurdles in the Examination course. The astonishing thing is that 11 out of 16 should have been successful, none getting lower than second-class honours. Of the children of miners 9 have completed their scholarships, all of them taking degrees.

Each scholarship includes an outfit allowance (up to £50 in the case of Oxford or Cambridge, up to £40 elsewhere), a maintenance allowance (up to £200 at Oxford or Cambridge, up to £150 elsewhere) and the cost of all fees for tuition, examinations, etc. The scholarships can be held only at Universities which grant their own degrees or at constituent colleges of such universities.

The endowment scheme was increased by £10,000 to £260,000 in 1930.

In 1931 the number of applicants for scholarships was 672, an increase of 54 on the figure for 1930. This increase was in the applications from working miners as well as in those from children of miners.

The applicants for the scholarships are in two categories, "A" candidates being workers in or about coal-mines, "B"

T

candidates being the sons or daughters of such workers. After a sifting process a number of candidates are selected for personal interview. In 1931, 20 "A" and 33 "B" candidates were interviewed. The Selection Committee, who are appointed by the Trustees of the Scholarship Fund, in their Fifth Report (1931) say that the quality of the "B" candidates interviewed was very high but although some of the "A" candidates were very good the general standard was not so high as they would like to see it and that they were obliged for the first time to recommend more "B" awards than "A," 9 as compared with 6.

It is an interesting fact that the Miners' Welfare district which supplied the largest number of candidates, both "A" and "B," was, as usual, South Wales and Monmouthshire, with 283, or 42·1 per cent of the whole entries, though the proportion of the awards going to Wales was not so high as in previous years, only 4 scholarships being secured by the principality—all from the County of Glamorgan. Of the remaining scholars, 4 were from Derbyshire, 2 from Northumberland and 1 each from Leicestershire, Somerset, Lancashire and Stirlingshire.

The total number of girl candidates, all of the "B" class, fell from 94 in 1930 to 83 in 1931.

The average age of the working miner ("A") candidates was 23·9 years, a further reduction on that of the last two years. The oldest candidate was 42 years of age. Only 84 "B" candidates were over 20 years of age and only 52 over 21. The oldest "B" candidate was aged 36.

Of the "A" candidates 109 had attended elementary schools only and 56 or nearly 34 per cent had attended secondary schools —a slightly higher proportion than in 1930. Of the "B" candidates all except 33 had attended secondary schools.

Of the 140 "A" candidates not already at a university, 9 were attending residential colleges, 56 were attending technical colleges (mainly for part-time or evening work) and 16 were attending other evening classes held by local educational authorities. Of the 339 "B" candidates not already at a university or university college, 7 were attending other residential colleges, 231 were still at school, 28 were attending technical colleges and 14 were attending other evening classes held by local education authorities, while 50 were not attending any place of education.

Three of the "A" candidates wished to do post-graduate work, 1 in education, 1 in metallurgy and 1 in mining. Of those who wished for scholarships for degree courses, 42 aimed at degrees in mining engineering, 37 in arts subjects, 32 in pure science, 18 in engineering other than mining engineering, 9 each in economics and commerce, 4 in music, 3 in fuel technology, and 1 each in medicine, metallurgy, biology and divinity, while 4 asked for courses not leading to degrees. The percentage of the candidates wishing to study mining was over 25—rather more than in the previous year but less than in previous years. It seems somewhat surprising that so few candidates from this class wished to pursue degree courses in economics. Of the "B" candidates, 22 wished to do post-graduate work, 7 in education, 6 in chemistry or physics, 2 each in metallurgy, fuel technology and economics, and 1 each in law, biology and history. Of the candidates for degree courses, 199 wished to take degrees in pure science, 188 in arts subjects, 20 in medicine, 15 in engineering other than mining engineering, 9 in economics, 5 in music, 4 each in mining engineering and commerce, 3 each in dentistry, fuel technology and law, 2 in pharmacy, and 1 each in metallurgy, theology, forestry and agricultural chemistry. Five did not mention any degree subject and 5 asked for courses not leading to degrees, while 1 candidate wanted the Scottish double degree in arts and science.

Of the "A" applicants 132 were last employed underground and 33 on the surface. Of those in employment in the "B" class 21 were teachers (13 student teachers, 4 uncertificated teachers, 2 certificated teachers and 2 music teachers), 12 were clerks or book-keepers, 9 were fitters or mechanics, 7 laboratory assistants, 6 apprentice chemists, and the remainder included persons following the occupations of articled surveyor, errand boy, postal worker, motor driver, shop assistant and dairy worker.

The choice of occupation made by the candidates is a matter of considerable interest. Of the "A" candidates 67 wished to become teachers or lecturers and 32 proposed to remain in the industry as mine managers, mining engineers, inspectors of mines or mines officials; 14 wished to become research workers in mining, metallurgy, engineering, fuels, chemistry and physics, and another 14 wanted to become engineers other than mining engineers, while 9 aimed at becoming ministers of religion.

Among the remaining 29 candidates there was a great diversity of aims, including the occupations of doctor, civil servant, politician, trade union official, journalist, industrial or analytical chemist, and clerk. Of the 492 "B" candidates no fewer than 328 wished to become teachers—a strikingly high proportion, while the other occupations that were named most frequently were civil servant (21), doctor (17), industrial chemist (16), engineer (13), and minister of religion (13). Research work attracted 36, in chemistry (12) and in other branches of science (24). One each proposed to follow the occupations of mine manager, mining engineer and inspector of mines. The other occupations mentioned included biologist, lawyer, archaeologist, journalist, geologist, dentist, fuel technologist, metallurgist, librarian, pharmacist, accountant, musician, veterinary surgeon, public administrator and clerk.

As many as 13 scholars completed their work at the University in 1931. Two obtained first class honours—1 in English at Oxford (Balliol College), the other in natural philosophy at St. Andrews (Dundee University College). Both are sons of miners. Four obtained second-class honours, 3 took third-class honours, 1 obtained a B.Litt. at Oxford, 1 qualified to take his degree in mining engineering, while another completed a second year of post-graduate work in geology, partly at Manchester and partly at Cambridge, and has done some very valuable research work for the Safety in Mines Research Board in connection with their investigation into the causes and prevention of falls of roof and sides in mines; he has now entered the employment of the Board, for whom he is continuing the work. One of the scholars who obtained second-class honours was 32 years of age on commencing his course and had to work during vacations to support his wife and three children. This method of "working their way through College" is quite a normal thing among American students but there are a surprising number of cases even in Great Britain, especially in Scotland and Wales.

As regards the quality as well as the number of the two classes of candidates the Selection Committee report that, generally speaking, the "B" candidates have now for some years been superior to the "A" candidates, although individuals among the latter have been exceptional. This might not appear remarkable in view of the fact that very few of the "A" candidates have had the advantage of a secondary education. When, however, it is considered that about 800,000 miners are in employment and a great many are unemployed and that there are now very wide facilities provided in every coalfield for evening or part-time studies for those who desire to further their education, then it does appear surprising, so the Selection Committee feel, that only about a hundred "A" entries should be received each year and that the greater part of these should not be at all exceptional compared with the average adult evening class student. The Committee say they are unable to suggest any explanation but feel that the matter is one worthy of further consideration. It may be that low wages, unemployment and depression in the industry have a paralysing effect on the educational aspirations of a certain sensitive type of intelligent miner instead of acting as a spur to acquiring the necessary equipment for higher posts or other occupations, though the author's own experience has been that, despite the industrial depression, his classes have increased in size and the students have been of a better calibre. The following suggested explanations are offered as throwing some light on a difficult problem. First, a number of the more intelligent men are more concerned with an understanding of the social and economic fabric and of contemporary problems than they are to improve their own economic position in life: they constitute a fine type of disinterested student. Secondly, some of the men, able and sincere students, regard the universities with a certain degree of distrust and suspicion: they say that the universities are "a pillar of the capitalist system," are largely dependent on wealthy supporters who are intent on preserving the existing social system which the students wish to change and that they have an undesirable influence on the miners' sons and daughters, who enter them with a certain degree of class consciousness but leave them without a trace of it, if not, indeed, with a bias against "their own class" and a desire to get out of it into "cushy jobs." This may seem an intransigent attitude but it exists and is a factor to be considered. Then there is the difficulty that arises in the case of married men who cannot or will not undertake the enterprise of leaving or supporting their wives and children while they take to the life of the student. For every case where this is done there are dozens where the men do not even send in applications.

These explanations are suggested in the hope that they may be of some assistance to the Selection Committee.

Another departure in the second five-year period was the decision by the central Welfare Committee in January, 1927, to set aside a sum of £500 a year for the purpose of making special grants to individual students in exceptional circumstances and it was later decided to restrict these grants to persons recommended by the scholarship selection committee, that committee having found that among the applicants for scholarships there were always a number of cases where a comparatively small sum would enable a student to complete a course on which he had already embarked, or would enable a student to enter a university for which he already held a scholarship or had resources of some kind, but who needed additional assistance to make up the sum required. A good standard of intellectual merit is always required in addition to these circumstances before a grant is made. Altogether, during the five years, 77 special grants from the general fund were made to 54 different persons, 46 of the grants being supplemented by an equal sum from the district fund concerned. The number of special grants made in 1931 was 19, amounting to £576, and 11 of these were supplemented by grants amounting to £140 from the respective district funds.

The names and particulars of candidates who were awarded Scholarships and, in certain cases, special grants, are set out in Appendix I of the Tenth Report, pp. 102, 103. Those readers who may not see this report may be interested in the following particulars of two candidates, the first being of the "A" class (workers in or about Coal Mines), the second a "B" candidate

"*Joseph Jones*, aged 34, formerly employed as a haulier at Ynysfais Colliery, Glamorganshire. Had private tuition in Latin, Greek and English 1917–22; attended classes in philosophy at Maes-yr-haf Educational Settlement 1927–28; and spent two years at Harlech College 1928–30 on a course of English, economics, philosophy and logic, with a bursary from the College and a special grant from the Miners' Welfare Fund. Awarded a Scholarship to enable him to take an honours degree in economics at the University College of Wales, Aberystwyth.

"*Eunice Rees*, aged 21, daughter of a coal-cutter machine-man at Rock Colliery, Glamorganshire. Attended Cyfarthfa Castle Secondary School. Obtained the Higher School Certificate in

1928 and entered the University College of South Wales and Monmouthshire with a State scholarship and a Caroline Williams open scholarship. Took a first-class honours degree in Zoology, 1931. Awarded a scholarship to enable her to remain at the College to do research work in Zoology."

To those who wish to know something of the achievements and present occupations of Miners' Welfare scholars whose scholarships have been completed Appendix III of the Tenth Report, p. 105, will be of interest.

The foregoing sketch will give some idea of the varied beneficent activities of the Fund. There remains one other and that not the least important activity to be described, namely, the provision of pit-head baths.

Pit-head Baths

It is not proposed here to dilate upon the benefits gained by the miner and his family from the facilities at the pit-head for bathing and changing into clean dry clothes before the journey home. The advantages of such a practice are now too generally recognised to require further emphasis. In most of the coalfields of Europe the provision of washing and drying accommodation is compulsory but this is not so in those of either Great Britain or the United States. In the States the author saw many very fine "bathhouses" but in that country there is nothing corresponding to the Baths Fund administered by the Miners' Welfare Committee in Great Britain. A year or two before the war an effort was made to encourage the provision of pit-head baths in Great Britain by making it compulsory if a sufficient majority of the workmen were in favour and were prepared to pay half the cost of upkeep but the effort was nullified by a proviso that the provision could not be enforced if the total cost of upkeep exceeded 3d. per man per week. At the end of 1920, therefore, before the establishment of the Miners' Welfare Fund, the only pit-head baths then existing in Great Britain were the fruits of voluntary effort on the part of certain progressive colliery owners. The actual number of installations at that time, not including those reserved for officials, was only 10, equipped with 407 shower-bath cubicles with accommodation for some 5,300 men.

In the section of the Act which established the Fund, pit-head baths were specifically recognised as one of the purposes to which the Fund might be applied. But the Miners' Welfare Committee realised that considerations of cost prohibited anything in the nature of attempting their general establishment during the first five years. While, therefore, they welcomed such recommendations as were submitted by district Welfare Committees for the erection of baths at those places where local committees desired them, their general policy was confined to the encouragement of such schemes as examples in the hope of stimulating construction from other sources on a more extended scale. Even this policy was temporarily suspended in 1924, when a Bill making the provision of pit-head baths compulsory was before the House of Commons; but this Bill lapsed when Parliament dissolved in the autumn of that year and the Committee at once reverted to their previous practice.

The Mining Industry Act, 1926, untapped a new and fruitful source of income in the form of a 5 per cent royalty levy. The income from the royalties levy for 1931 alone amounted to £220,000 and the total receipts from this source for the first five years (1926–31) reached exactly £1,000,000. This sum was £250,000 short of the total which the Samuel Commission (1925) expected to be received. The Commission aimed at a total revenue of £400,000 per annum, of which £250,000 was to be derived from the royalties levy and £150,000 from the Fund's other resources. To make up this £150,000 the Committee hoped to get £100,000 a year from interest on the invested balances of the output levy and they proposed to contribute the remaining £50,000 from the general fund. The interest in the five-year period amounted to £382,420 or £117,580 less than the sum anticipated, but the Committee made up this deficiency by increasing the contribution from the general fund, which has thus provided £367,580 for baths instead of the sum of £250,000 originally promised. Besides this, the investment of the baths fund balances has earned interest to a total of £138,693, so that the gross total of the baths fund reached a figure of £1,888,693 by the end of 1931—an imposing sum though somewhat short of the £2,000,000 which the Samuel Commission thought it desirable to make available for baths in that period.

In the same period a sum of £1,797,891 was allocated for approved schemes and expenses, leaving an unallocated balance of £90,802, which will enable the Committee to maintain a constructional programme somewhat in excess of the normal for one more year. Thereafter, unless other sources of revenue become available, they will have to reduce the rate of progress to conform with the actual revenue of each year.

When it is considered that the first two years were occupied with experimental installations and that the main constructional programme was not begun until the autumn of 1928 one feels that the Committee have every reason to be satisfied with the progress made in the first five years. In that period they made allocations for 127 schemes, of which 113 were new schemes, 6 were extensions of schemes established prior to 1926, and 8 extensions to schemes which they had themselves initiated since that date. These schemes, when completed, will provide accommodation for 150,396 men and 196 women, and will include 44 canteens.

In addition to allocations amounting to £1,721,326 from the baths fund, these 127 schemes have involved contributions of £103,639 from various district funds and £34,348 from the colliery owners; the total contract value of the work thus amounted to £1,859,313. In the same period the actual expenditure on technical staff was £69,652. The technical costs, therefore, in spite of including the cost of a considerable volume of unproductive work on schemes that have been dropped or temporarily deferred and of preliminary work on schemes that have not by the end of 1931 reached the stage of going out to tender, represent less than 3·75 per cent of the value of the work actually put out to tender by that date. The Committee estimate that on these services they have saved a sum of nearly £100,000 by employing their own staff for the purpose and have thus been able to build at least six more installations than would otherwise have been possible. This estimate of savings, moreover, takes no account of the value of the improvements effected by centralisation, nor of the economies which have resulted from the placing of bulk orders in large quantities for standardised items of equipment. The latest type of locker, for instance, although a decided improvement on the early types, is no less than 30 per cent cheaper in consequence of the number for which orders can now be placed, and this alone represents a saving of something approximating to £25,000 per annum.

The following particulars of the average cost of these pit-head baths should be of interest to a number of readers. The author has been questioned on the point by many people in America and at home. Excluding from the total cost the amount spent on special accommodation, such as canteens, cycle-sheds, officials' baths, covered ways and the like, but including the technical costs and the cost of essential extras such as boilers, sewage plants, water supply and so on, the cost per head for all the schemes approved in the first five years was approximately £12 4s. This average may, however, be misleading, because the cost per head of an individual building depends on so many factors, including the size, the proportion of cubicles to lockers, the extent to which special extras are necessary and the building conditions and general price levels of different districts. The average for the two York-shire districts, for instance, barely exceeded £10 10s. per head, while that for Scotland was over £14, chiefly owing to the relatively smaller size of the collieries, and that for South Wales is nearly £16 per head, largely because of the difficulty of the sites. The highest figure per head yet recorded is £23 6s. for the scheme at Kinghill No. 2 Colliery in the Lanark district, which accommo-dates 432 men, while the lowest is £8 for the scheme at Parsonage Colliery in the Lancashire district, accommodating 1,400 men.

The total contributions from the district funds include a sum of £66,676, which was applied towards the cost of the baths themselves. Further contributions amounting to £36,963 and all the sum of £34,348 from the colliery owners referred to above were devoted to the provision of special accommodation which is not provided by the baths fund. Of the 44 canteens, for instance, 4 will have been provided by the colliery owners, 1 by the owners and workmen jointly, and the remaining 38 by the district funds. Thirteen of the 23 possible districts have recommended grants for the provision of canteens, the most notable being Lanark (13) and North Staffordshire (6). Lancashire, South Wales, Ayr and Somerset have hitherto definitely refused to recommend any grants for canteens in spite of applications made to them by the local baths committees. Cumberland, North Wales, Leicestershire and South Derbyshire had not been asked for grants for this purpose, and Kent has had no money to spare. The cost of the canteens provided up to 1931, including their furniture and equipment, is approximately £38,866. The cost depends mainly on the floor area, which in turn is dependent on the number of men likely to be in the building at any one time. This is the same factor as determines the number of bath-cubicles, and the basis for estimating the size for a canteen is at present an allowance of 8 square feet of floor space for each bath-cubicle in the building. The average cost per cubicle of the 44 canteens already provided is approximately £13.

Pit-head baths in Great Britain are broadly of two designs, which for purposes of convenience may be described as the old and the new, the old being that followed by the baths existing before the Act of 1926, the new having been generally followed since. The old design follows very closely in its details the practice in France and Belgium and in many of the American coalfields. The building consists of a large and lofty hall surrounded by shower-bath cubicles of the enclosed type. The hall is used both for undressing and for dressing and is equipped with a system of ropes or chains by which either the clean or dirty clothes may be suspended in the roof of the building. This design is objectionable because the men who have had their bath have to come back into the common hall in order to dress and thus again get soiled by the men who are still undressing and by what has fallen and is falling during the hoisting up of the pit-clothes. The clean clothes also are apt to get soiled through hanging side by side with the dirty clothes and in the coal-dust laden atmosphere.

Among the minor disadvantages of the old type are the following:

(1) The baths have not been constructed in such a way as to facilitate rapid and effective cleaning; some of them are deficient in lavatory accommodation;

(2) Ventilation and lighting are inadequate.

Moreover, efforts to economise in the cost of construction have resulted in the hall being overcrowded and thus being deficient in seating accommodation and in general comfort, while the necessity for a lofty building means a high cost. Finally, the various fittings require frequent replacement and this, coupled with the time spent on cleaning, increases the cost of upkeep.

The new design consists essentially of three sections, one for pit-clothes, one for bathing and one for clean clothes. These sections may, of course, be placed in any convenient position relative to one another according to the nature of the site.

The bathing section of the new design consists of shower-bath cubicles, similar to those generally in use, but so designed as to be as economical as possible in the use of material and the consumption of water. The pit-clothes and clean clothes sections (often referred to as the "dirty" and "clean" sections) are each equipped with lockers, one for each man, the principle being that a man, after coming to the surface, leaves his pit-clothes in his dirty locker, has his bath and then resumes his clean clothes previously left in his clean locker, so that clean clothes and clean men never come into contact with dirty clothes and grimy men and are in a separate section of the building from those parts where coal-dust is likely to collect. The dirty lockers are constructed so as to dry and fumigate the pit-clothes as well as to confine the dirt to a controllable area, while the clean lockers are capable of drying clothes if wet owing to a rainy day. There is always sufficient seating accommodation because each man has the space in front of his own locker and there is ample ventilation and lighting. Adequate lavatory accommodation, a first-aid room for dressing minor injuries, arrangements for boot cleaning and greasing and for supplying drinking water to fill water bottles, and also a special hot-air drying chamber for dealing with very wet clothing, are included as a matter of course; there is no difficulty in adding provision for a canteen, cycle sheds, laundry, the repair of clothes and boots, etc., if desired.

Special accommodation for officials may involve either the screening off of a row or two of lockers for the minor officials or the erection of a special annexe, usually equipped with slipper baths, for the higher officials. In either case the cost has to be borne by the colliery owners, as the Committee do not recognise the need for separating the minor officials, and do not think it proper to provide accommodation for the higher ones at the cost of the Fund. In 1931 there were thirteen examples of such facilities.

Reference has been made to the provision of a first-aid room and as many people have a confused idea of its function it may be well to make it clear. Every pit-head bath is provided with a small first-aid room, the purpose of which is to ensure the immediate antiseptic treatment of minor injuries which manifest themselves during bathing. It is not intended to take the place of the fully-equipped ambulance room, which the colliery owners are bound by statute to provide for the treatment of accidents of all kinds. If, however, the colliery owners desire to rebuild their ambulance room as part of the pit-head bath the Committee are prepared to undertake its planning and erection under the main contract, and to charge the owners only with the difference in cost over and above what would have been the cost of the normal first-aid room. In 1931 there were seven of these cases, two each in South Yorkshire and South Wales, and one each in Lanark, North Staffordshire, and South Staffordshire.

The question is often put: What use do the miners make of the pit-head baths? The Committee have some interesting evidence as to the extent of the use made of some sixty-six installations which had been opened before the middle of December, 1931. The figures shew that on the average 82·7 per cent of the workmen employed at each colliery were actually making use of the facilities provided. In no less than 45 of the 66 cases the figure was 80 per cent or higher, and there were only 11 below 75 per cent. When these percentages are compared with the results of the ballots which were held at some of the collieries before the schemes were put in hand, it is found that such a ballot is quite unreliable as an indication of the probable popularity of the scheme. None of the preliminary ballots gave a percentage in favour exceeding 84 per cent, and the average figure was only 58 per cent. This bears out the contention of the Committee that once a bath has been provided it is only a matter of time before the great majority of the workers use it, whatever may have been their views before they had a practical opportunity of appreciating the advantages of bathing at the pit-head.

It is because of this that in a number of cases the Committee have had to extend the accommodation shortly after the opening as it was their practice at the outset to provide accommodation for only about 80 per cent of the numbers employed or likely to be employed by the time the baths were complete. This limitation so frequently proved inadequate that for some time the Committee have been basing their plans on the full numbers as it is relatively cheaper to erect the whole building in one contract, apart from saving time that can be devoted to the erection of baths at other collieries. The popularity of the installations already completed is also beginning to have its effect on the general demand for similar facilities from other collieries. In many instances the early offers found the owners and workmen doubtful and inclined to defer a decision. It should be explained that the Committee have devised a system by which the circumstances of all existing collieries can be reviewed and pits classified according to their relative priority so that definite proposals to the owners and workmen may be made on the basis of a long-period plan. Both parties are shewing an increasing tendency to make up their minds definitely in favour of accepting the offer and in the case of offers made more recently there is, generally speaking, less delay before it is accepted, while there is a steadily increasing demand for installations from collieries which had previously rejected an offer or which are too low on the priority lists yet to have received offers at all. Already more than forty such applications have been received, some of which unfortunately have little chance of being dealt with for a number of years. There is every indication that the demand will soon be much in excess of the rate at which the available revenue enables installations to be provided.

The demand is more keen in some districts than in others and apparently there are still some owners who are inclined to put difficulties in the way; but at any rate there is no doubt that the demand will be far from satisfied when the £4,000,000 recommended by the Samuel Commission has been spent. Such a sum (on the figures of cost which they had in mind) would have provided accommodation for about 360,000 men. The Committee believe that baths will be required for at least double that number.

The average size of the new schemes approved in 1931 was 1,422 pairs of lockers and 86 cubicles, as compared with averages of 1,288 and 79 (including extensions) for the whole of the preceding period. In 1931 forty-three collieries were visited for the purpose of preliminary investigation, and 47 separate sketch plans were prepared and approved.

The cost of upkeep is an important consideration. There are necessarily variations in individual cases according to the local conditions, and the cost per head is bound to be relatively higher in the smaller installations than in larger ones. As a broad generalisation, based on the twenty-four schemes for which the Committee have figures, it may be stated that the small installations (below 400 users) cost about 8½d. per head per week, the medium-sized ones (400–1,000 users) about 7½d., and the large ones (over

,000 users) about 5½d. The principal items in which these figures vary are the attendants' wages, the reserve for repairs or renewals, and the cost of heating, the figure for each of these three being much less per head in the larger installations than in the smaller ones. In each case about 40 per cent of the upkeep costs goes in attendants' wages.

In the majority of cases for which figures are available the colliery owners contribute towards the upkeep costs either in the form of a cash contribution or by providing some or all of the essential services free of charge or at specially low prices. In three of the twenty-four cases they make no direct contribution but the average for the total number represents a contribution of about one-third of the costs. The men's weekly contribution varies from 9d. a week in the smallest installation to 3d. in some of the larger ones. There are ten cases of 6d., one of 5d., six of 4d. and five of 3d. Ten of these schemes have been equipped with canteens, on which the gross profit varies from 15 per cent to as much as 33 per cent on turnover, and there was only one instance in which the profit was insufficient to leave a surplus after meeting the share of charges attributable to the canteen.

In many cases it appears that all the workmen pay the agreed contribution, whether they actually use the baths or not. This is generally the result of a voluntary arrangement between themselves and the colliery owners which no individual workman could be compelled to accept. It has been explained to the author that many men who do not want to use the baths willingly pay the weekly contribution because it puts them on the same footing with those who do use them in the matter of holding or getting jobs. A contribution can only be made compulsory on an individual workman if it forms part of his contract of service or conditions of employment; some colliery owners have included, or propose to include, such a condition in the contracts of new entrants.

Improvements continue to be made both in design and in equipment and fittings. The general planning of the pit entrance hall, for instance, was modified during the year 1931, one of the chief improvements being the isolation of the boot-greasing facilities in a separate room, which can be cut off when not required. The boot-cleaning machines also were remodelled so as to be both cheaper and more efficient. The question of dust extraction from pit-clothes was also under consideration, and plans have been prepared for the erection of an experimental laundry in which pit-clothes and towels could be washed. It was decided during the year to provide drinking fountains at the clean entrance instead of at the pit entrance, and it was decided also to drop the provision of wash-basins for surface men. In special cases, however, a trough can be installed at the pit entrance for enabling men with greasy hands to cleanse them before going into the locker-rooms.

During the year it was also found possible to effect considerable improvements in the lockers without increasing their cost, and the latest pattern includes a door with rounded corners and with a new type of handle incorporating a lock, a continuous top facilitating cleaning and a coloured number-plate corresponding to the colour grouping of the bath-cubicles.

In July, 1931, an installation was opened at Haunchwood Colliery in Warwickshire in which some of the cubicles are made of stainless steel.

It was found as a result of experience gained at the Women's bath at the Maypole (Lancashire) installation that various modifications would be desirable in the general planning of baths for women, owing to the special conditions which apply to such installations.

It comes as a surprise to many people to know that women are still employed in the coal-mining industry in Great Britain. They are employed on the screens (large movable riddles for sifting the coal) at some collieries, chiefly in Lancashire, where they are called "pit-brow lassies," and also in Scotland. The total number employed does not much exceed three thousand, and the number at any one colliery is usually quite small. The Committee have accepted the principle of providing special accommodation for women employees if they desire it and if their numbers are sufficient to justify it. Unfortunately, the small numbers and the relatively increased space necessary make the cost per head very high.

Baths for men at the Parsonage Colliery in Lancashire were opened in 1930 but no provision was then made for women though a number are employed there. A women's scheme was to have been erected in the 1931 programme but the experience gained at Maypole led to a revision of the plans. In planning the new scheme consideration has been given to the fact that all the women cease work simultaneously and are therefore all in the building approximately at one time, instead of being spread (as in the case of men) over several shifts, each of which in turn is spread over the length of the winding time. This involves a much higher proportion of washing facilities and an increase of seating accommodation between the lockers to avoid waiting and congestion. On the other hand, it is improbable that all the women will desire to take a complete bath every day and accordingly it is unnecessary to provide spray-cubicles on the full scale that daily bathing would necessitate, provided equivalent space is available for washing their faces and hands. It has been decided to calculate the provision of cubicles on the basis of one to every ten women, and of hand-washing space on the basis of approximately one to five, while the extra seating accommodation between the locker rests (which are similar to those provided in men's baths) is secured by installing a double seat (with a back rest) between the rows, in addition to the seat normally fixed to the lower tier of lockers. This enables all the women to be seated simultaneously. The usual provision is made for boot cleaning, attendants, first-aid and lavatories and, in addition, a comfortably furnished rest room is included.

On a lovely summer Sunday in June, 1932, the author paid a special visit to see the pit-head baths at the National Colliery at Wattstown, in the Rhondda Valley. The way from the main road lay through a narrow, steep, stone-flagged lane, dignified by the name "The Avenue"; one suspects the local mining folk of an ironical sense of humour! On the left, high up, is a forbidding row of ugly houses; on the right lies the colliery. We walk through the yard, which is heavily coated with coal-dust, on to the cheerful-looking building that houses the baths. In response to our knock the attendant is soon upon the scene, a trim little figure in white shirt sleeves—off duty really but eager to shew and explain everything. We enter by way of the pit entrance, clean our shoes on the electrically propelled brushes and take note of the wash-bowl and arrangements for the greasing of boots, including a bed of sawdust for catching stray drops of grease.

First we are led to the section where the men strip themselves of their pit-clothes and put them in a locker, each having a numbered key for his locker; on having his attention drawn to the fact that many of the lockers looked as if they were never locked the attendant explained that some of the men did not use their keys at all, either for their dirty or clean clothes locker.

Next we found ourselves admiring the cubicle shower-baths. Rows of cubicles, the first in each row having painted on it the numbers in the row. Eighty cubicles in all. The shift system makes the number adequate. An impression of white cleanliness. Rather warm for a hot summer's day, though as it was a Sunday the temperature was below the week-day normal, but the splash of the water as the attendant turned on a jet made one feel almost cool. The author's thoughts "reversed" for twenty-five years when he lived in a miner's home in this very district and frequently talked with a collier as he rubbed himself down, standing in front of the blazing kitchen fire while his family busied themselves in preparing his meal in the same little room. What a contrast! One wonders that the harassed wives of the mining areas do not "down" their household tools and demand that all their menfolk clean themselves up at the pit-head. As a matter of fact the great majority of the wives are in favour of pit-head baths but there is a minority of the men who are prepared to risk a household "strike." The attendant told us that seven in one family use the baths—the father and six sons. They each pay 6d. a week, but think what it means to the housewife, to say nothing of the comfort, convenience, enjoyment and health of the men. It seems that about 66 per cent of men—800 of the 1,200 employed —make use of the baths now, though about four years ago the result of the ballot was unfavourable. Our guide was emphatic on the point that the early opposition among the men, even the most "advanced politically," to the pit-head baths and indeed to Welfare Schemes generally had almost disappeared—"it's more and more of it they want now. I suppose you know the latest is, they're after pensions from the Fund!" Even after the baths were built, however, the men were slow to use them at first, starting at about 200, jumping up to 600 in one year and increasing at an average of 100 a year in the last two years. Our attendant who for impersonal reasons seemed very wishful that all the 1,200 men should make use of the baths told us a surprising thing. He said that the young men were more shy than the older men of stripping before others. The explanation may be that the older men have already been accustomed for many years to standing about naked in their homes but one would have thought that modern youth was free of this kind of self-consciousness outside the home. At this colliery, at any rate, there is a larger proportion of young men than of older among the 400 non-users. On being pressed our attendant admitted that the weekly contribution, especially with wages shewing a downward tendency, of 6d. a week was a factor against the full success of the scheme. We suggested that some of the younger men might be paying 3d. a week to belong to the Institute and that some played tennis, for which the charge was 1s. an hour for the court. Yes, those things were factors, no doubt a "big factor," but nothing could shake our guide in his interesting opinion that the young men are "kind of timid and shy."

We leave the cubicles and pass to the clean clothes section, as the men do after their "shower." More numbered lockers and the same aspect of cleanliness. A glance over two or three special baths for disabled men, one of whom we later saw hobbling out on his crutch after having his "shower," and a peep into the spotless first-aid room, and we return to the attendant's room where we drift into a general discussion of the whole scheme after he has answered numerous questions with quick intelligence, patience and a sense of humour. A few more facts. A number of men from other collieries where there are no baths use these and pay 6d. a week. "Outsiders," i.e. tradespeople, clerks, teachers, etc., may also use them at a charge of 2d. per bath. The water is heated by steam from the colliery—a saving of expense. The upkeep cost, our attendant estimated, is between 6d. and 7d. a week per head. The author told him that the Committee's report pointed out that 40 per cent of the cost of upkeep of the baths generally went in attendant's wages. His instant comment was "Well, *we* don't think we get enough, you know!" In the Institute there are reading, billiards, and games rooms, a concert room accommodating 300 and a wireless set. A suggestion was made by the attendant which might be worth considering seriously —that there should be a recreation fee "covering the lot," i.e. the baths, the Institute and tennis, bowls, etc. To the objection raised that many of the men might not wish to use all these facilities he replied that "plenty of the men pay for the baths now and don't use them." A composition fee is common enough in colleges and other institutions and it might prove satisfactory in a Welfare Scheme—it would certainly put the finances on a more definite footing.

Before we left we discussed with our intelligent and well-informed guide the reparations conference at Lausanne, industrial conditions in the United States, unemployment, amalgamations in the coalfields and the general prospects of economic recovery. On the previous day in the dressing-room of a tennis club the author had been reluctantly drawn into a discussion of much the same questions and had listened to an amazing display of ignorance and prejudice on the part of a young public-school man, especially about reparations and Germany's economic condition. One could not help contrasting the two men—the one young (though there are hundreds of equally young miners who are far better educated than this youth), dogmatic, unconcerned about national economic problems except as they affect his own job, ignorant of international problems and steeped in prejudice; the other, a mature family man who had worked underground for many years before being made the baths attendant after a prolonged spell of unemployment, remarkably well-informed on economic and political questions, concerned about keeping his job certainly but also keenly anxious about the world.

A hearty hand-shake and we parted. But he represents a type that is well worth further description—the educated coal-miner. This opens up the whole question of the provision of education facilities in the coalfields. This we shall describe in Section I.

SOME POSSIBLE DEVELOPMENTS OF THE RECREATIONAL SCHEMES

It is an interesting point whether there is any clear line of demarcation between the recreational and educational sides of life. Recreational activities are now normally included in the course of training in most educational institutions. And it is good to find that the Miners' Welfare Committee regard all their recreation schemes as part of the whole problem of improving the social environment of mining communities. The Committee is fortunate in having as Chief of its Advisory Staff a man of big vision in the person of Commander B. T. Coote. After his visit to the Wattstown pit-head baths the author called to see him at his office in the Mines Department in London. For two hours we talked "welfare" and it did not seem a minute too long. It was an inspiration to listen to the Commander as he described the growth of the work, explained the various schemes, outlined new possibilities, and gradually revealed his glorious vision of mining areas peopled by full-breathed, bright-eyed and happy-hearted human beings. Now and then he would get up and illustrate a point by reference to the fascinating maps that studded the walls, by turning up reports, by fondling architect's plans of children's playgrounds or by describing some of the numerous films, neatly arranged in a frame, of photographs which he himself had taken of baths, pavilions, institutes, swimming pools, tennis courts, cricket grounds, bowling greens, children's playgrounds, etc. The Commander laid great emphasis on the necessity of catering more for the children. In the case of most welfare schemes chief consideration is given to the demands of the grown-ups, especially the men who want to play tennis, cricket or bowls—the specialists. A swing and a chute in the corner sufficed for the kiddies. Commander Coote has already done much to redress that balance and is out to do much more. He realises that the children are not only entitled to the best recreational facilities that can be provided for them as children but that they will soon be the adult population and he wants to see a steady and continuous improvement in the type of people living in the coalfields. The following quotation with which he introduces his Paper No. 2 on "Outdoor Recreation for Children up to 10 years of age," gives some idea of his approach to the problem:

> "Give them a chance for innocent sport,
>   give them a chance for fun,
>   Better a playground plot,
>   than a court and gaol when the harm is done.
>   Give them a chance, if you stint them now,
>   to-morrow you'll have to pay—
>   A larger bill for a greater ill,
>   so PLEASE give them a chance to play."

He asks the question "Why is it that Children's Playgrounds do not hold first place for importance with every mining community?" and continues:

"To me it seems almost superfluous to write about the need for such things, because it is so obvious, travelling in every part of the coalfields as I do, and seeing the children all the year round playing in the streets, more often than not. Apart from the danger to these little ones of the ever increasing amount of traffic, and the continual anxiety to the overworked mother who cannot spare the time to be always watching them, it is a national disgrace to think that this great sporting country of ours should spend vast sums of money yearly on adult recreation, while the majority of children are without 'fully equipped' playgrounds."

This is Commander Coote's idea of the equipment of a modern children's playground:

Barrel of Fun

Boards (Rocking)

Boats: Rocking
      Flat
      Paddle

Caves

Cement Tables for Hopscotch and Top Spinning

Cement tracks for Bowling Hoops, Running, Scooters, Roller Skating, etc.

Climbing and Sliding apparatus

Drinking Fountains (jet type)

Flower Beds

Giant Strides

Ground Teeters

Jungleym

Leap Frog Courses

Merry-go-round (Boys' type)

Merry-go-round (Girls' type)

Merry-wave Stride

Ocean Wave

Overhead Teeter

Ponds, with or without islands, boathouses, etc.

Sand-pits

See-saws: Centre Balance
      Pendulum

Shelters for Boys and Girls, with or without lavatory accommodation

Sliding Chutes

Swings: Children
      Infants
      Babies
      Plank

Whirl-over.

What possibilities are opened up by this list! Imagine the results if such facilities were provided and used by all the children in the country.

The problems of leadership, supervision, maintenance and all that is involved in securing the best use of the playground have been carefully considered. Commander Coote is most wishful to have the co-operation of the School authorities and of the teachers. The local authorities are not often in a position to provide adequate facilities but their co-operation with the district welfare committees would not only contribute to the success of the welfare schemes but would add to the effectiveness of their own educational activities. In some cases the sympathy of the school authorities is obtained by co-opting members of the education committees on the welfare committees. Some schools issue to each child under 10 a special tally which has to be presented by the child before it can gain admission to the playground. The possibilities of this form of co-operation are immense.

Commander Coote considers welfare activities for mining communities in four sections:

I   Children up to 10.
II   Boys and girls from 10 to 16.
III Adults over 16.
IV   Specialists, e.g. footballers, cricketers, athletes.

His approach to the problem is indicated in the following quotation from his Paper No. 3, referred to below:

"I am attempting to reconstruct recreational activities from the bottom, so as gradually to build up healthier ideals in regard to games, for we are now seeing the result of a drifting policy which caters only for those who are born to excel—a 5 per cent minority. My suggestions apply to the 95 per cent majority. Leave existing methods (or lack of method) to work out their own salvation (it won't help to make this world better, morally or physically), and build up something which, in virtue of its own superior moral and physical value to the community, will eventually not only predominate, but supersede it throughout the country."

He has written a series of valuable though brief articles in accordance with this general plan. They are:

Paper No. 1.   Indoor and Outdoor Welfare Developments.
Paper No. 2.   Outdoor Recreation for Children up to 10 years of age.
Paper No. 3.   Outdoor Recreation for Young People from 10 to 16 years of age.
Paper No. 4.   Outdoor Recreation for Adults from 16 years of age, upwards.
Paper No. 5.   Outdoor Recreation for Specialists.
Paper No. 6.   Maintenance and Upkeep of Outdoor Recreation Schemes.

The reader is referred to these Papers, which are issued by the Miners' Welfare Committee. These Papers, the Annual Reports of the Welfare Committee and the descriptive report written by Lord Chelmsford should give any interested student a fairly comprehensive knowledge of the aims and achievements of the Fund. The general reader will perhaps be specially interested to know that the Film illustrating the growth of the work is in preparation.

Two problems seemed to the author to be exercising Commander Coote's mind. One is the problem of leadership. He is concerned about the lack of people in the local mining districts who will take the right initiative when schemes are formulated, guide them on desirable lines and link them up with the general social life of the district. In some cases there are district organisers but in many there are not and he feels a crying need for men and women who have this capacity for wise direction and for inspiring others to co-operate. He says: "Voluntary effort and private enterprise are excellent where there is no possibility of anything better to take their place. In the case of the Miners' Welfare movement, however, we have a unique opportunity to set up a college of training for leadership. In it selected men and women would be trained to promote a high condition of body and mind in the general mass of children and young people, so that they may find an incentive to increase social usefulness in their better understanding and enjoyment of life."

The other problem is how to get what Commander Coote calls the "spirit of welfare" behind and into all the schemes. It is not easy to define this "spirit" or to explain its connection with the question of trained leadership. The Americans call it "community spirit," and the essence of it is that in Commander Coote's words it "must be made a real living force in every phase of communal life." The Commander has also visited the United States, concentrating on recreation schemes, so that we were able to compare notes. He seemed to incline to the view that there is more of the spirit of welfare over there than in this country. He agreed that there is nothing in America to compare with the Miners' Welfare Fund and that all the recreational facilities provided in the American coalfields are dependent on the good-will of individual employers or companies but he was emphatic that while our machinery was more social in its character there is

CHILDREN'S PLAYGROUND IN MINING TOWN IN PENNSYLVANIA, PROVIDED BY COLLIERY COMPANY

a finer community spirit in the States—more care for the general
mass of non-specialists and especially for the children. The
recreational activities of some of the big coal companies in America
are certainly more varied than anything to be seen in a British
coalfield. In West Virginia for instance, the author met a lady
who was employed by the company to teach the children of the
miners all kinds of dancing, including the Old English dances,
and to act in plays and pageants; she was most enthusiastic
about her work and believed that it was the means of introducing
lots of fun and colour into the drab life of the community. And
wherever in the States provision for recreation is made it is done
systematically; in this country there is the organisation but a
lack of trained experts to make it work. Indeed, perhaps the whole
contrast may be summed up by saying that in America there is
systematisation without social organisation whereas in Great
Britain there is organisation without systematisation. It may be
that we can "learn something" from the States by importing
more of the American community spirit into our welfare schemes
and the author believes that the mining communities in America
would in ten years be greatly benefited socially if something on
the lines of the British Miners' Welfare Fund were established
in that country: he hereby publishes the banns of marriage
between spirit and organisation!

What the future of the Fund in this country will be it is difficult
to predict. It is generally agreed that it has been an excellent
thing. But like other good services it is likely in the immediate
future to be curtailed. The industry is suffering from economic
anaemia and the pressure of the employers to have the output
and royalty levies reduced seems likely to be effective. The
Committee now investigating the position are considering evidence
from various sources but one fears that while the report will
speak favourably of the achievements of the Fund it will recommend that owing to the economic depression there must be a
"slowing down" of progress and that new developments must
be "postponed." It is too much to expect that in the circumstances
the Committee will say "Go ahead full steam; carry on with your
good work." And yet that is what everyone who has at heart
the welfare of our mining communities would wish them to say.
It is during depressed times that the need for a brighter environment is greatest. But as a matter of mere prediction one ventures

to say that the next five years will see a considerable curtailment of the activities of the Fund. The unpleasant fact must be realised that social progress depends to a large extent on economic conditions.

It is now time to leave the Miners' Welfare Fund and proceed to consider another aspect of the social environment of mining communities—what may be briefly described as the educational aspect.

NOTE.—In 1933 a Bill was presented to the House of Commons reducing the output levy of a penny a ton to a halfpenny. This Bill will most probably become an Act of Parliament before 1934 has run half its course. The bulk of the reduced revenue will be devoted to the provision of pit-head baths. Thus unfortunately will our fears of retardation of development materialise.

EDUCATION OF THE WORKERS, INCLUDING COAL-MINERS, IN GREAT BRITAIN AND THE UNITED STATES

I

BEGINNINGS IN ENGLAND

We have considered the physical, political, economic, ethnic, organisational and social conditions of the mining population in the two countries. We have now to survey the provision of educational facilities in the two sets of coalfields. There are people who regard educational institutions as agencies of training intended to counteract the effects of the physical and social environment. We take the view that while they may exercise a modifying influence on the environment they are essentially a part of that environment itself and function within it.

In Chapter III a very general comparison was drawn between the two types of miners and some reference was made to their education as adults. The time has come to trace this development in greater detail. It is proposed to describe the growth of workers' education generally in the two countries before considering the position in the coalfields more particularly. The terms "workers' education" and "adult education" are often used undiscriminatingly, and it seems to be necessary to distinguish between them. The author has a vivid recollection of a talk he had in 1929 with a brilliant young student at the Experimental College of the University of Wisconsin on this point. He said he was "bemused" by all the loose talk of workers' and adult education as if they were one and the same thing, which as he said "they couldn't be."

Theoretically, adult education should mean the education of adults, whether in a university college or a Labour College Class, in a technical college class in Engineering or an Extension Class in Music. But in practice its purpose "is to satisfy the dual educational demand of the workers, first for training specifically directed towards rendering themselves better fitted for the responsibilities of membership in political, industrial and social organisations;

second, for education for fuller personal development."[1] It looks on education not only as an end in itself, but as a means of equipment for the rights, duties and responsibilities of citizenship. It puts the emphasis on the "spiritual" aspects of life and on the importance of training citizens for community service, and distinctly affirms a complete class neutrality. It appears to have had its origin in the desire of a group of Oxford "intellectuals" to help the working-man to become "better educated" and to hasten the approach towards an enlightened democracy.

The workers' education movement was initiated by working-men or groups in which working-men have exercised the controlling influence and proposed to give the industrial workers the desire and ability to share in social control, to become masters of their own industrial fate.[2] The content of instruction in agencies for workers' education is not dictated by love of knowledge for its own sake. It is a discipline for a specific purpose, the purpose being that the workers should seek to use knowledge, especially of the social sciences, for class advancement. The emphasis is on class action, for which special knowledge and a peculiar technique are necessary, rather than on community service or personal development.

In the following brief historical sketch it is proposed to pursue workers' education as the main theme, with variations on the phases of the growth of adult education. The history of workers' education, at least in Great Britain, may be divided into three periods. During the first, prior to 1830, the workers interested in education were poor, illiterate and inarticulate, both economically and politically. The initiative in educating the poor was assumed by the ruling classes under the leadership of the Established Church, the Methodists and certain charitable organisations. In the next period, between 1830 and 1900, they were skilled artisans less illiterate and more politically conscious. The initiative shifted from religionist to philanthropist. The objective of education was definitely political under the Chartists

[1] Greenwood, Arthur, "Labour and Education" in *Cambridge Essays on Adult Education*, ed. by R. St. J. Parry, pp. 123–124 (Cambridge University Press, 1920).

[2] Hodgen, Margaret T., *Workers' Education in England and the United States*, pp. 3–4 (London: Kegan Paul). A fine piece of research. The author had a valuable talk on this subject with Miss Hodgen at the University of California, Berkeley.

out grew less defined with each new effort. Under the Christian Socialists and in Toynbee Hall economic and political motives were blended with aesthetic and humanitarian impulses. In the third period, after 1900, they had become organised working-men, with an elementary education, the vote and powerful trade union affiliations. The initiative was gradually assumed by organised labour. The educational objective of the working-class became more clearly defined as control over the political and economic aspects of its existence. Broadly, its method was educational enterprise administered by trade union organisation.

In the United States, although the same general periods of development may be traced, the earlier acquisition of the political franchise and the establishment of the public (elementary) school diminished the interest of labour in education for purely working-class purposes. It was not until after all the free land had been taken up and the immigration of streams of foreign-born workers that American labour realised that the American worker needed special and peculiar training for his function in the labour movement. Indeed it is doubtful if this is realised in America even to-day. During his stay in that country the author was much struck by the faith of labour leaders and educationists in the self-sufficing achievements or potentialities of their public schools—grades, junior high, and high—and universities. There seemed to be a fairly general reliance on these agencies and a feeling that there was not the same need for workers' education there as in Great Britain.

Passing over the repressive attempts of the Established Church in England to educate the poor, the missionary schemes of evangelical educators like the sisters Patty and Hannah Moore, and the educational experiments of the manufacturers like those conducted by Robert Owen in the school at his New Lanark Mills, we may conveniently begin this account with the work of Dr. George Birkbeck, a physician, who may be regarded as a pioneer of popular education. His intercourse with the artisans of Glasgow "discovered to him such evident indications of latent genius in the minds of workmen, accompanied with so much anxiety for the acquisition of knowledge, that the spontaneous feeling of regret excited by their want of scientific information, was instantly succeeded by the benevolent wish that the means of obtaining this information could be placed within their reach."

As a teacher Birkbeck had further opportunities of watching the
intelligent curiosity of "unwashed artificers." He observed such
strong indications of the existence of the unquenchable spirit of
inquiry that he asked himself the question: "Why are these minds
left without the means of obtaining the knowledge which they
so ardently desire; and why are the avenues to science barred to
them because they are poor?" He was moved to devote a portion
of his time to the teaching of mechanics and in the autumn of
1800 he organised a Mechanics Class with an attendance of
seventy-five members. Saturday evening was chosen for the
lectures and the first gave such satisfaction that at the next meeting
there was a gathering of two hundred workmen, at the third there
were three hundred listeners and one month after the course was
started Dr. Birkbeck talked to five hundred artisans.

The idea of instructing working-men in the rudiments of
science was ridiculed as visionary and absurd by the doctor's
colleagues and was not revived till after a lapse of about twenty
years. Thomas Hodgskin and Joseph Robertson, editors of the
Mechanics' Magazine, published in London, secured the support
of Birkbeck, who in the meantime had moved to the metropolis
to practise medicine, and in November, 1823, a meeting of two
hundred artisans was held at the Crown and Anchor Tavern.
Dr. Birkbeck, Francis Place, Mr. Bailey and the two editors
were appointed members of a sub-committee. Place drew up
the rules and the London Mechanics' Institute was formed,
though some authorities trace the more remote origin of the
Institute to a small society established in 1817 by Timothy
Claxton called The Mechanical Institution. The reader will find
the point discussed in Godard's biography of Birkbeck, p. 35.
The purpose of the Institute seems to have been to enable mechanics
and artisans to become acquainted with science, to give them an
intellectual interest in the exercise of their art and to qualify
them to make improvements and even new inventions. Dr.
Birkbeck was elected President.

The movement inaugurated by the establishment of the London
Institute was attended with popular success. Other cities followed
the example of London. An Institute was established in Leeds
in 1824, Liverpool in 1825, Bristol in 1826. The plan increased
in popular support until no town of any size could maintain its
civic self-esteem without one. The financial success of the

Institute was guaranteed from the first day by the "princely contributions of the well-to-do." Money was subscribed by Lord Brougham, Earl Spencer, Wilberforce, James Mill, Ricardo, Grote, Cobbett, Bentham, and Place. Working-men quickly shewed their approval of the project. The first to "send their adhesion" were members of a small society consisting of working mechanics, tradesmen and radical reformers. The "first five hundred names enrolled . . . consisted almost entirely of master mechanics, shop-keepers, and dealers in hardware with their workmen, cabinet-makers and house-painters." In addition to class instruction and lectures on various sciences, including mechanical philosophy and chemistry, libraries were formed and instruments and models were collected for experimental purposes. Francis Place saw eight hundred artisans attending one lecture on chemistry. An interesting insight into the motives of some of the influential supporters of the work of the Institute is to be had from what Lord Brougham said in giving it his blessing: "It affords me pleasure to think what a mass of natural intellect this will call into action; if the plan succeed, . . . the ancient aristocracy of England will be secure for ages to come."[1]

The Mechanics' Institute underwent a period of popularity succeeded by failure. Dr. Birkbeck's purpose had been that of a teacher whose wish was to inspire a love of knowledge: he chose the field of science because it was his own hobby and served also to explain objects in the everyday life of the average workman. When the Institute was adopted by the Society for the Diffusion of Useful Knowledge the motives were less disinterested. Its members wished to improve workmanship and increase production and profits, and also to make the Institute a credit to themselves. It definitely asserted that no kind of knowledge was necessary for the operative except science or the practice of his art or that did not tend to make him a better workman and more useful to his employer.

The movement flourished, however. In 1831 there were 55 Institutes with 7,000 members. By 1850, 610 Institutes had been established throughout the country with a membership of 102,050 and an annual book distribution of 651,000. But the Institute of 1850 was not the same as the Institute of 1820. The emphasis

[1] Dobbs, A. E., *Education and Social Movements*, 1700–1850, p. 67 (London: Longmans, Green, 1920).

had shifted from the task of teaching working-men the fundamentals of science to the more showy one of making the Institute a going concern. The men claimed that the courses were desultory and that the library was deficient in technical works. The number of lectures dwindled from more than fifty per course covering only one branch of science to one per evening covering every branch of science. The Institutes had become not only mere training schools for local industries, but poor training schools at that. It is interesting to note that the first cause of dissatisfaction among working-class members of the London organisation was occasioned by the poor quality of instruction offered. In this respect working-men students are extremely critical. It is a mistake to offer them anything short of the best quality of teaching. The author has observed the case of a young tutor who soon after obtaining his master's degree for a thesis on Foreign Exchanges, took over some successful classes in September: by the end of December the classes had collapsed; the majority of the students were miners, iron and steel workers and railwaymen, and they merely showed their opinion of the teaching by ceasing attendance. Ability to learn is one thing: ability to teach and conduct discussions with working-men students is another. The tutor was lacking in the latter kind of ability.

The dissatisfaction of the Mechanics' Institute students was increased by what amounted to taxation without representation. In order to make the Institutes appear successful in the generally accepted sense of the word, contributions were spent in the purchase or erection of extensive premises in central sections of cities. The administration of large sums of money invested in city property occasioned much financial anxiety and led to friction among directors. Different groups of financial supporters asserted rival claims to control. But they were agreed upon one point, the exclusion of working-class students from everything except attending lectures and paying fees. Not only were the students denied a voice in the control of funds and the arrangement of curricula, but they were called upon, first, for quarterly or half-yearly dues and, second, to make up deficits incurred by the ambitious schemes of wholesale education inaugurated by donors. The first recourse of directors in the chronic financial embarrassment which beset the Institute was to ask students to increase their fees.

Under these circumstances working-class students moved out and the directors surrendered to the financial competence of the middle-class. Prosperous shopkeepers, however, had little use for science: they wanted an introduction to those branches of learning which had acquired reputability as the peculiar adornment of the gentry. The Institue accordingly substituted literature for mechanics and chemistry, and became the tradesman's finishing school. When Lord Brougham visited Manchester in 1835 there were three times as many merchants, manufacturers and clerks on the rolls as mechanics or operatives. In Birmingham conditions were similar. Only one-half of those enrolled at the working-class subscription were receiving weekly wages. It was generally acknowledged that only one-twentieth of the students of the Mechanics' Institute in Great Britain belonged to the artisan class. The Institute continued its corporate existence for over a hundred years but it lost the confidence of the working-class movement soon after it began.

The story of the Adult School movement in Great Britain has often been told. It may be described as an attempt to attract the poorer workers to religion by teaching them the rudiments of education. The first Adult School was opened in 1812 in Bristol by a working-man, William Smith, who occupied a "rank in life no higher than that of a door-keeper of a Dissenting Chapel"; with the assistance of an influential Quaker, Stephen Prust, and a Bible Society, he found a room and organised an "Institution for Instructing Adult Persons to Read the Holy Scriptures." Two students enrolled. One was William Wood, aged sixty-three, the other was Jane Burrance, aged forty. The numbers steadily increased. At the end of a year, as a result of unwearying exertion in securing teachers and rooms for assembling classes, there were thirteen classes with 432 men and women. The reception accorded the Adult Sunday Schools in Wales had been even more remarkable. After 1730 Griffith Jones was instrumental in establishing 3,495 Sunday Schools with an attendance of more than 158,000 mature persons. In East London the number af adults attending Sunday Schools in 1816 was estimated at 600. In Bristol during the first year classes more than doubled and others were established in twenty surrounding towns. Whole villages attended. In 1849, 250,000 persons had been taught to read. Adults also attended the early Ragged

Schools. About 100 persons of all ages between 16 and 35 attended the Marylebone Ragged School.

Between 1814 and 1834, however, a decline in attendance at Adult Schools began to set in. The enthusiasm which had swept over the country receded. In Bristol, for instance, between 1812 and 1834, Adult Schools increased from one school to 136. In 1849 they had decreased to 18. Other records indicate that although new students were admitted to the number of 510 in 1811, the number had decreased four years later to 49.

The educational results seem to have been somewhat meagre. Apparently only one out of every three adults who attended an Adult School learned to read. One government report said: "The number who say they read an easy book is three-fourths; this commonly includes all who can spell their way through words."

Since those days the Adult School has made very considerable progress and is now a feature of the social life of Great Britain of some importance. Its annual handbook is an eloquent testimony of a remarkable expansion in the scope of its activities, especially those of an educational character. But while it is true that numbers of working-men and women attend these Schools the emphasis is still on their religious activities and they do not count for much in the modern working-class educational movement.

The fact is that neither the Mechanics' Institute nor the Adult Schools offered instruction useful to the poor in solving their economic difficulties. The self-taught among them, therefore, began to preach self-instruction and to organise groups for mutual improvement. Mutual Improvement Societies sprang up in every town and village. Compared with the Mechanics' Institutes in large industrial centres these little societies were very modest. But they were self-governing and self-instructing in the sense that they formed their own committees, relied on their own fees, varying from one half-penny to threepence per week, and that the teacher was always one of the operatives.

Many observers testified to the solid character of the information acquired in these societies. Engels, for instance, reports having heard many a British working-man, whose fustian jacket scarcely held together, speak on geological, astronomical and other subjects with more power than the educated German of the time possessed, and that the epoch-making products of modern philosophy and politics were read by working-men. Many a coal-miner in the Tyne Valley would have several of Scott's novels on his shelf, a volume on mathematics or English History and a few Methodist classics. There were other artisans who knew Milton, Byron or Shelley and could repeat portions of Shakespeare by heart. In politics Blackstone, Bentham and Godwin were read. There were also botanists and entomologists, "practical, shrewd, hard-working men, who pored over every new specimen with real scientific delight."

Self-education was the only form of instruction open to leaders of the British working-class movement for a hundred years, and its quality may be judged by the type of leadership produced. Francis place, the breeches maker, Thomas Cooper, the shoe-maker, Lovett, the Chartist, and Holyoake, the co-operator, were all well-educated men of great power. In addition to producing exceptional men for prominent positions in the working-class movement, self-education trained many an obscure weaver, cotton operative or coal-miner as the less known leaders of the second line of defence. The habit of debate in Mutual Improvement Societies tended to direct the most promising workmen into oratory, lecturing and politics; others became publishers, pamphleteers, preachers and teachers.

II

CHARTISM AND WORKERS' EDUCATION

The next phase of educational development affecting the industrial workers is bound up with the Chartist Movement, covering a period of some fifteen years between 1832 and 1848. Though the points in the Charter were essentially political in character—the demand for the ballot being the most popular—they were part of a sustained effort on the part of the working-class in England to obtain a measure of economic security. And the Movement had a strong educational trend. The workers' dissatisfaction with the conduct of the Mechanics' Institute and their distrust of the Society for the Diffusion of Useful Knowledge was a cause of this trend. This Society assisted the Institute in its repressive policy by supplying the workers with what it considered sound economic doctrine. One interesting way in which it did so was by the creation of an economic literature expressed in simple language. In this work two women writers played an important part.

Mrs. Jane Marcet's *Conversations on Political Economy in which the Elements of that Science are Familiarly Explained*, written in 1821, reads very quaintly to the eye of a modern economist. The author had already written a popular exposition of the laws of chemistry. She certainly had the gift of narrative ability and apparently she exercised considerable influence on popular thinking on economic questions at the time. Her purpose in helping to educate the labouring class was to make them industrious, frugal and sufficiently interested in their future to prevent overpopulation. Indeed, all the economic tractarians of that day based their theory on the Malthusian idea of the causes and control of poverty. Mrs. Marcet enlarged upon the blessings of inequality of wealth on the ground that the rich and poor are necessary to each other. In her *Conversations* occurs this illuminating judgment: "It is precisely the fable of the belly and the limbs; without the rich, the poor would starve: without the poor, the rich would be compelled to labour for their own sustenance."

Miss Harriet Martineau's influence was more far-reaching. She knew the taste of her public and fed it with what the Diffusion Society wanted it to digest. Starting with a tract entitled *Illustrations of Political Economy* she wrote a series, while Brougham wrote a few thumb-nail treatises which filled a long-felt want for text-books more or less adapted to the previous educational preparation of working-class students. It became the fashion to read Miss Martineau, and her writings are said to have been a common topic of conversation over the tea-cups in London drawing-rooms. They were industriously circulated in Mechanics' Institutes and widely read by the workers. But though, judged by modern standards, the workers were in the main ignorant men they felt instinctively there was something false in the doctrine preached by Brougham, Miss Martineau and members of the Diffusion Society, that the security and freedom of the working-class depended upon upholding the right of property. This instinctive distrust became so great that even Miss Martineau, who seems never to have grasped the significance of the Chartist Movement, finally admitted that the surest way not to reach the people was to address them through the Diffusion Society.

It is always difficult to appraise the influence of individuals in the social process but three men, at this juncture, helped to change the attitude of the workers towards education—Robert

Owen, Thomas Hodgskin and William Lovett. Owen was out of sympathy with the political aspirations of the Chartists but he believed in education as a means of liberating personality and he seems to have inspired the working-class to some extent in its efforts to educate itself for political responsibility and a more abundant life. Hodgskin was at once more practical and more of an economist. Moreover, his relation with the working-class was more intimate than Owen's. His interest in education was coloured by what he conceived to be the task of political and economic reform, namely the creation of a new social order. He believed that the education of the people would always be directed most effectively when under their own control. William Lovett, the most important personality among the Chartists believing in education, was a man of action as well as of thought. From the time of the organisation of the First London Co-operative Association in 1829 to the last days of the National Association for Promoting the Social and Political Improvement of the People in 1859, Lovett was in the thick of it, organising, promoting, inspiring. A methodical and careful man, he was the universal secretary. But in every job, cabinet-making, running a coffee-house, drafting a charter or serving a jail sentence, the education of the working-class was his chief preoccupation: under his influence the various organisations adopted a more and more definite educational purpose. He deprecated the tendency of the poor to look up to leaders and urged the workers to supplant those supplied to them by the class whose control they sought to break. He exhorted them to follow great principles rather than great men. He emphasised education as the most important single factor in the achievement of political liberty. He was a perfectionist, for whom education was the solvent of all social inequality. Even the Charter became not an end in itself but a means for training working-men in political responsibility. Unlike Hodgskin, Lovett was not opposed to co-operation with sympathetic members of the middle and upper classes. He realised that there was a great difference of opinion "as to where the line should be drawn." But he emphasised the importance of independent educational action on the part of the workers. "While we might be anxious," he said, "for the co-operation of good men from all classes, we should mainly rely on our own energies to effect our own freedom."

The first Chartist organisation to profess an educational purpose was the Metropolitan Trades Union, formed in 1831. Lovett, representing the cabinet-makers, succeeded in effecting a reorganisation under the name of The National Union of the Working Classes and Others. This Union divided into discussion groups where political subjects, articles from the newspapers and the standard political works were read and commented upon. Class leaders were appointed at public meetings in the proportion of one for about every thirty or forty members. It appears to have spread to different parts of the country but under the impact of Owen's comprehensive scheme of the Grand Consolidated Trade Union of 1833 and 1834 it dissolved. In 1836 a group composed of many of the same people took the name of the London Working-men's Association, dropping the phrase "and Others," together with all it had signified. Working-men had begun to want to organise by themselves and for themselves. Lovett said of this second enterprise, "We wished to establish a political school of self-instruction among them, in which they should accustom themselves to examine great social and political principles." The London Working-men's Association met with some success, organised more serious class instruction and even drew forth a favourable comment from Francis Place, now a disillusioned old man. But it did not last long and in 1840 Lovett made his third and most determined effort to commit the adherents of the Charter to a programme of political democracy based upon self-education. In collaboration with John Collins, a tool-maker, he wrote a book called *Chartism; a New Organisation of the People embracing a plan for the Education and Improvement of the People, Politically and Socially*. This little book is significant because it advocated the education of the children of working-men, not only for political initiative and responsibility but also for the enjoyment of a fuller life, and as being the first attempt made by a representative of the working class to indicate what it considered should be the content and purpose of popular education.

Lovett proposed to divide the country into districts in each of which were to be erected Public Halls for use during the day as Infant Schools and during the evening for the instruction and entertainment of the industrial workers. The plan included normal, agricultural, industrial schools and circulating libraries accessible to every man, woman and child. Lovett also formed a new organisation called the National Association for Promoting Political and Social Improvement of the People. In London a model District Hall was opened. Man of action as he was, how-ever, the task of financing a nation-wide enterprise was too much for Lovett. He fondly imagined that the million signers of the Charter Petition would subscribe a shilling per quarter and that with the amount thus produced the Association would be enabled to build 80 schools, establish 710 libraries, distribute 20,000 tracts and support 4 missionaries. As a matter of fact the money failed to arrive in small regular amounts from a large number of people and Lovett was forced to fall back upon the expedient of accepting a few large gifts from a small group of donors. In addition to financial stringency there were difficulties in connection with the management of the London Hall, the head-quarters of the Association and the central feature of the original plan. The Hall was to be devoted to the usual lectures, classes and public meetings. Owing to enforced modification of Lovett's original plan of control the management was vested, with the concessions usual in such cases, in the hands of those guaranteeing financial support. Independence of thought was denied by an agreement to use the Hall neither for socialist purposes nor for theological controversy. Lack of money and these restrictions prevented the development of most of the features which Lovett considered of value to the workers. After a few years it lost its essential working-class character and became a day school for children in which Lovett continued to teach and invent new educational methods. In 1849, one year after the official death of Chartism, the minute book of the National Association was closed and the school was handed over to Lovett and his friends.

The contribution of Chartism to workers' education was not the creation of permanent educational institutions but rather the enunciation of a few fundamental principles and the gallant attempts of a group of penetrating pioneers to put them into practice. It showed the workers that they would not get the edu-cation they needed until they provided it for themselves. With the withdrawal of working-men from the Mechanics' Institute and their perception of the motives underlying the efforts of such organisations as the Society for the Diffusion of Useful Knowledge an end was put to one phase of patronising educational endeavour. From that time on the working-class movement was never without leaders interested in workers' education. It was clearly established also that the universal working-class adult education was not "practical politics." Lovett found that more could be achieved through a small nucleus of ardent workers than through an army of the half-convinced. Chartism revealed the connection between workers' education and a definite working-class philosophy. Lovett's efforts would have been impossible had education for self-improvement been his only aim, but the desire of the workers for a share in the government of the country by means of the ballot gave his educational pleas political meaning and purpose. The Chartist programme of education thus became a part of the long struggle of subject classes for political and economic emancipation.

III

THE UNIVERSITIES AND WORKING-MEN

The third phase of the development of workers' education in England is closely associated with the Universities, especially Oxford and Cambridge. A group composed of teachers at these ancient seats of learning and professional men recently trained there were concerned to find a Christian solution to the social problem and interested themselves in supplying that type of knowledge which would remedy what they felt to be defects of working-class character. The modern system of university extension work, extra-mural classes, etc., may be said to have its had roots in the activities of this group of Christian Socialists. They felt that Chartism had made the mistake of emphasising legislative rather than moral reform. Their early activities took the form of experiments in co-operation, and a number of workshops owned and operated by working-men were established. The workshops failed but their advocates believed that co-operative enterprise would make use of working-class talent and at the same time permeate the workers' movement with a spiritual purpose.

The two outstanding men of the group were J. M. Ludlow and Frederick Dennison Maurice. Ludlow was a lawyer. He was educated in France where he became familiar with the socialist and co-operative enterprises in which the French working-men were pioneers. He was democratic and wanted the privilege of the few to be widened to admit the many. Maurice was a clergyman and a University teacher. He believed in the authority of the upper classes over the lower but, like other men of his group and profession, felt uncomfortable about the growing breach between them. His views on social questions were derived from fundamental religious rather than political ideas. Government was best administered, he felt certain, by men who were set apart by birth for the work.

The desire of Maurice to educate the working class took tangible form in the Working Men's College founded in London in 1854. Some years earlier what was known as the People's College movement was developed in response to the failure of previous educational enterprises to reduce illiteracy. For in spite of all the Adult Schools and Mechanics' Institutes could do the state of education in England in the middle of the century was very unsatisfactory. In 1845, 33 per cent of the adult men and 49 per cent of the adult women were unable to write their names. The first People's College was founded in Sheffield. Here the Rev. R. S. Bagley, a nonconformist minister who had been influenced by William Lovett's address on National Education, opened rooms in a white-washed, unfurnished, unwarmed garret. By 1848 attendance reached the figure of 462 men and 104 women. The fee was ninepence and control was vested in a committee of students by whom the constitution was drafted. Nottingham People's College was established a few years later in 1846. Classes and lectures for working-men were held in People's Hall. The constitution was drafted by Lovett. Other Colleges were opened in Norwich in 1847–48, in Cambridge in 1855, in Wolverhampton and Ancoats in 1857, in Liverpool in 1860 and in Leicester in 1860.

Maurice's Working Men's College differed from the People's College mainly in its reliance upon University affiliations. He regarded the enterprise as a union between "labour and learning" which would assist professional men to acquire a new sense of their relation to the working class, and the working class in turn a knowledge of the conditions which kept it weak. The education offered was to be humane rather then technical, because the workman was "a person, not a thing, a citizen and not a slave or even a wage-earning animal." It was to be not merely a system of instruction but a way of life shared by teachers and students. Emphasis was to be laid on the ethical rather than the practical.

Although the discussion of social and political subjects was not forbidden, emotional detachment in argument was to be encouraged. Men were to be trained not as partisans but as citizens.

The educational machinery of the Working Men's College was put in operation by a most unusual group of men. After the College got under way Maurice was joined by prominent undergraduates from Oxford and Cambridge and by men whose reputations were already made, such as John Ruskin, Charles Kingsley, Dante Gabriel Rossetti and C. Lowes Dickinson. Classes were conducted in the Gospel of St. John, Shakespeare, English History, Geography, Drawing, Modelling, Public Health, Arithmetic, Law and Grammar. For recreation Thomas Hughes (author of *Tom Brown's Schooldays*) held sparring classes and Dr. Furnival, the distinguished philologist, led Sunday walks.

The example of these men had a far-reaching effect upon educated opinion, especially in the universities. Kingsley held the Chair of Modern History in Cambridge from 1860 to 1869. Maurice was Professor of Moral Philosophy in the same institution from 1866 to 1872. Ruskin taught at Oxford from 1870 to 1878 and again in 1883 and 1884. Such authority in the nation's intellectual centres greatly strengthened the appeal of the idea of cultural democracy. With the achievements of the Working Men's College before them the students of neither University could remain indifferent to the new field of endeavour. The following half-century was to be devoted to attempts by college groups, either official or personal, pedagogical or religious, to bring the educational agencies of the country within reach of the poor.

The first of these attempts was made officially by the University, in the form of University Extension work. The idea was advocated first by Mr. William Sewell of Oxford in 1850. But the practical initiative was not taken till seventeen years later in 1867 when Mr. James Stewart, a Fellow of Trinity College, responded to an invitation of a group of ladies in the north of England to deliver some lectures. Others followed later for railway men in the Mechanics' Institute at Crewe and for co-operators at Rochdale. Stewart was led to consider the possibility of a "peripatetic university" for working people. In 1873 Cambridge adopted his proposal and a course of twenty-four lectures was arranged at the request of groups in three towns. In Nottingham the initiative was taken by the Trades' Council. This was followed by the organisation of the London University Extension Society in 1876 and by Oxford and other Universities soon after.

Not long after extra-mural education became a regular function of University instruction a group of University bred clergymen interested in education took up residence in the East End of London. Among them was Samuel A. Barnett who secured the intellectual and financial support of a group of teachers and students in Oxford, bought a house in East London, adopted the College Missions idea of the desirability of residence by University men among the poor and opened Toynbee Hall in 1884 as the first University settlement. Many British Universities have since established Settlements and the author visited several similar institutions in America, including Hull House in Chicago and Kingsley House in Pittsburg. These Settlements have done a good deal of valuable educational as well as more general social work in working-class districts.

In spite, however, of youth, zeal, sincerity, social purpose and personal integrity none of those who pioneered the founding of the Working Men's College, University Extension or the University Settlement Movement lived to see those institutions carry out their programme of educating the working class. Ambition outdistanced accomplishment. It was the intention of Maurice, for instance, to establish branches of the Working Men's College in every large town in England, with at least half a dozen more in London. His hopes were realised to the extent of seeing twenty, some of which belonged more properly to the People's College Movement. Of these, however, none survived in their original form. Some collapsed. Some lost their working-class character, either by becoming the nuclei of large institutions of higher learning or, as in the case of the London Working Men's College, by succumbing to the inroads of clerks and other middle-class people.

When Toynbee Hall was opened Canon Barnett hoped with the co-operation of the University Extension Movement to make it the nucleus of an East End University for artisans and factory hands. And in 1888 Barnett's vision seemed far from extravagant. One hundred lectures were given to 400 listeners. By 1891 two Halls had been built to house the students. As year followed year, however, the enterprise began to develop signs of failure. Among the first students teachers and clerks had predominated but it was believed that the number of artisans would increase until they formed the majority. Instead, the number of students in 1898, regardless of occupation, began to decrease. And in 1902 attendance was so small that it was suggested that the lectures be given up altogether. Its more recent history, however, reveals increasing activity and steady progress. Under the inspiration and energetic direction of its present Warden, J. J. Mallon, it has been a live educational centre for many years where Classes of a high standard in a wide variety of subjects are attended regularly by a large number of students.

The same fate attended the early efforts of the University to educate the workers. The first Extension classes were arranged with the intention of meeting the educational demand of three groups of people: first, ladies and persons of leisure; second, young men of the middle class; third, artisans. In the beginning it seemed as if the enthusiasm and earnestness of the working-men would be the life of the movement. One early class in Nottingham was composed of 31 men and 27 women. Among the men, 4 were students, 5 artisans, 4 packers, 9 clerks, 6 factory owners, and 1 was a teacher. Among the women, 7 were daughters of factory owners, 2 of ministers, 12 of tradesmen and there were 6 milliners. North Cumberland miners were particularly responsive to all Extension efforts. When the University of Cambridge began its work, crowds of students streamed in. Extension became the fashion. Money was plentifully supplied and miracles were expected of the movement. A great response was hoped for from working-men. But it did not come. In one centre only twelve out of four hundred students were manual workers.

The movement for working-class education which derived its influence from the Church and University represented the educational wing of mid-century liberalism. Mid-century liberalism, in spite of a genuine concern for the suffering of the people, relied on middle-class rather than working-class leadership. Consequently, fellowship between labour and learning meant one thing to Christian Socialists, University teachers and Canon Barnett and quite another thing to leaders of the working class. And in actual practice working-class students had no real voice in the conduct of the Working Men's College, Toynbee Hall or University Extension Classes.

EDUCATION OF CO-OPERATORS

The second half of the century was a period of great expansion, not only in popular education but also in labour organisation. The workers gradually developed a power which enabled them to organise their own educational enterprises on a small but vigorous scale. After the revolutionary period of Chartism working-men with a certain sober resignation adopted the policy of making the best of every opportunity, however indirect, and contented themselves with modest, unheralded efforts. These were sporadic and short-lived. They usually possessed but one common administrative characteristic, namely, the desire to keep free of church, philanthropic or University domination. The educational initiative among the workers shifted from political sources to economic. And of these the organisations of consumers seemed for a time to possess a more practical grasp of the needs of education than those of producers. Several early groups of co-operators organised schools in accordance with Owen's preaching that education was the basis of all reform. The most notable experiments were those made in Manchester, Brighton and Sutton-in-Ashfield (Notts) but it was the Rochdale "Equitable Pioneers" in 1844 who gave the co-operative movement a definitely educational character. They declared it to be their object "to arrange the powers of production, distribution, education and government," and their store soon became an educational centre where religion and politics were common subjects of discussion. A few years later $2\frac{1}{2}$ per cent of the quarterly profits, assigned for division among the members, was set aside for an educational fund, and the mental improvement of the members was promoted by the establishment of a reading-room, library and a School for young people. This was a deliberate avowal of the principle and policy of developing co-operative character by using the business profits of the stores for purposes of instruction. The Pioneers, inspired by Robert Owen's educational theory, believed that given suitable conditions human nature could be modified indefinitely for the better and the ideal they had in view was no less than the creation of a new society. As the movement has become more and more of a practical economic success, however, it is to be feared that it has lost much of its earlier idealism and that its conception of the part to be played by education in working-class emancipation

has become more limited. Since the 'eighties the educational
objective of the movement seems to have shifted from Owen's
idealistic purpose to the more or less humdrum detail of training
employees for co-operative enterprises or, at most, reformers
within the existing order. It has been well said that co-operators
have become co-operator conscious, not class-conscious. In
recent years the movement has developed its educational activities
on a big scale, every district having its scheme of classes, lectures,
etc.—all under the able direction of a full-time official in the
person of Mr. F. Hall, M.A., M.Com. The educational aims of
the movement may be summarised as (1) the training of experts,
whether they be managers or assistants, in the principles and
methods of the movement; (2) the provision of a liberal education
for members in a co-operative atmosphere; (3) the development
of the co-operative spirit. These aims are carried out in classes
organised by the movement itself, by co-operation with the
Workers' Educational Association, with Ruskin College and
other educational movements for working-men. A certain degree
of dissatisfaction is expressed by a group of co-operators on
account of the orthodox theories of economics taught in the
classes but on the whole care is taken to prevent criticism on
the part of the much larger number of co-operators who are
themselves orthodox.

The working-class producers' organisations adopted a policy of
compromise after the collapse of Chartism. The trade unions
shed revolutionary, Utopian aspirations and concentrated on the
protection of the vested interest of the craftsman in his craft
and on the financial and administrative reform of their organisations. While they did not repudiate the necessity for education
they formulated no programme.

The only exception occurred among the coal-miners. The
earliest form of instruction among the miners was determined
by religious and economic conditions, the first teachers in the
mining villages being preachers of the Primitive Methodist Church
who were themselves workers and wage-earners. These men
found time before and after working hours to go from village
to village with their message. They took the lead in all movements
for the improvement of conditions surrounding the lives of
their parishioners. Circles of Methodists in quiet hamlets studied

the *Age of Reason* and the *Rights of Man*. They were especially interested in adult education and introduced the Methodist system of Sunday and Adult Schools. In 1860 a law was passed permitting the miners in each pit to elect a checkweigher or checkweighman from among themselves. This proved a stimulus towards educational improvement. In the 'seventies Student Associations were formed in some mining localities similar to the Mutual Improvement Societies of the early industrial towns. In these, some member was appointed to introduce a subject by reading a paper, lecture or book. Discussion followed. When every point was mastered by every man, new subjects were introduced. In 1879 University Extension lectures on Political Economy were held in Newcastle and other mining towns. The interest of the miners was enthusiastic. They formed a committee which made a repetition of the course possible. In the 'eighties the Northumberland Miners' Union asked their organisation to grant financial support to the movement. It is interesting to see the grounds of their appeal. They said . . . "the greatest battle in which your class has been engaged is yet to be fought . . . the battle against intellectual darkness. The attention and consideration which your grievances receive from the public and the legislature depends upon the ability with which you plead your case through the newspapers and on the public platform. The amount of wages you receive depends on the ability of those who represent you in the arbitration court or on the sliding-scale committee. Thus your very wage questions are really educational ones. If you do not want this higher education, surely you will aid in educating the men in whose brains your wages and your position in the estimation of the public and the legislature depends."[1] The miners were virtually the only group of workers among whom University Extension work was successful at this time. And it is in the mining districts that subsequent developments in workers' education have been most significant.

Two other institutions derived from the University movement for the education of the workers remain to be considered—Ruskin College and the Workers' Educational Association. The founders of both of these enterprises went back to Maurice and Ruskin for their inspiration. They relied mainly on the equipment and

[1] Picht, W. R. V., *Toynbee Hall and the English Settlement Movement*, p. 169 (London: Bell, 1914).

teaching staff of the University. But enough had been done by working-men in co-operative and trade union circles to warn them of the dangers of educational action divorced from the official labour movement. Both therefore at the very beginning provided for some form of co-operative regulation with the trade unions and other working-class organisations.

RUSKIN COLLEGE

Ruskin College, the first embodiment of the new spirit, was established under rather unusual circumstances at Oxford in 1899, by two American admirers of John Ruskin—Mr. and Mrs. Walter Vrooman. Their tribute took the form of a residential college in which working-class students might study and live together. Although not a constituent part of the University it drew to some extent upon the University staff for its teaching. Speaking of the purpose of the college at the inaugural meeting, Mr. Vrooman said, "We shall take men who have been merely condemning our institutions, and will teach them how, instead, to transform those institutions so that in place of talking against the world, they will begin methodically and scientifically to possess the world, to refashion it, and to co-operate with the power behind evolution in making it the joyous abode of, if not a perfected humanity, at least a humanity earnestly and rationally striving toward perfection."[1]

Mr. Vrooman added the conviction that the future of working-men was bound up with the future of the working class. The students were to be taught to regard education not as a means of personal advancement but as a trust for the good of others. They were to be trained in subjects essential to working-class leadership; they were not to rise out of their class but to raise it.

At first Ruskin College was practically owned by Mr. Vrooman. He himself selected the students. The first class, including engineers, miners, weavers and railwaymen, numbered twelve.

After a short interval the founders returned to America, withdrawing their support. The College had then to appeal to labour and charitably disposed individuals for support. In 1907 the Trade Union Congress issued an appeal to constituent unions. "The

---

[1] Pamphlet, *The Burning Question of Education*, p. 3 (Oxford: Fox, Sons & Co.).

time has now come," it read, "for the Labour Movement itself to take the College in hand and make it an assured success. There can be, therefore, no better investment for our money." As a result, several unions subscribed regular sums for upkeep and scholarships. The Amalgamated Society of Engineers raised the annual sum of £2,000 and sent six scholars; Amalgamated Society of Railway Servants, £300 and two scholarships; Northern Counties Weavers' Association, £90 and three Scholarships; Amalgamated Union of Co-operative Employees, one scholarship; subscriptions from London Society of Compositors and Scottish Co-operative Wholesale Society.

It is now supported by a large number of working-class institutions. In 1931 the following organisations made financial contributions to the College Funds (General Fund, Scholarship Fund, Bursary and Maintenance Fund):

Trades Union Congress General Council.
General Federation of Trade Unions.
Working Men's Club and Institute Union, Ltd.
Transport and General Workers' Union.
London Society of Compositors.
London Co-operative Society, Ltd.
Royal Arsenal Co-operative Society, Ltd.
National Society of Operative Printers and Assistants.
Union of Post Office Workers.
Yorkshire Mineworkers' Association.
Workers' Travel Association.

The Cassel Educational Trust contributed £1,000 and the Noel Buxton Trust and the Thomas Wall Trust made donations of £50 and £60 respectively. It is interesting to note that the Glamorgan, Durham and Kent Education Committees subscribed to the Scholarship Fund. Individual subscriptions, ranging from £60 to 2s. 6d. amounted to £393 2s. od.

The first Principal of the College was Mr. Dennis Hird. In the first few years the curriculum was scrappy and disconnected, consisting mainly of short courses of lectures on widely divergent subjects, attended by students who might chance to be staying for a week, a month, three months or a year. Later a number of one-year scholarships were established by trade union and other bodies. Progress was disturbed, however, in 1909, when recurring

differences between Principal Hird and the Executive Committee
came to a head and the Principal retired on a pension. Many of
the students took umbrage at what they considered to be unfair
treatment of Principal Hird and the "strike" occurred of which
much was made in the press at the time. This was over in a few
weeks but the internal difficulties to which it gave rise did not
disappear till an entirely new set of students came with the year
1910. Meanwhile a College, known as the Central Labour College,
of a more definitely Marxian character, had been established in
London by some of the malcontents and only came to an end
in 1929.

With 1910 came also a new constitution. The whole control
was vested in representatives of working-class organisations.
Three consultative members of recognised educational standing
were also to be appointed on the Governing Council; in 1931
the three consultative members were Canon Carlyle, Mr. A. D.
Lindsay, Master of Balliol College, and Dr. R. H. Tawney.

Under the new régime Dr. Gilbert Slater became Principal.
The College, however, lost the services of Charles Sydney Buxton
who had been appointed as Vice-Principal in 1908; he left to
concentrate on the welfare of the agricultural labourer, and his
father, now Earl Buxton, established the Buxton Scholarship
for Agricultural Workers in his memory. The new buildings,
opened in 1913, were made possible largely by his generosity
and the main lecture hall is known as Buxton Hall. Under Dr.
Slater, the College gained in prestige. One reason for this was
the large proportion of successes obtained by students year by
year in the examination for the University Diploma in Economics
and Political Science, side by side with University graduates
and undergraduates. These have continued to the present day.
In June, 1931, seventeen students sat for the Diploma Examination and fifteen were successful—a record number in the history
of the College.

In 1914, the College was thoroughly inspected by five of His
Majesty's Inspectors and from this inspection finally arose the
Board of Education regulations allowing *per capita* grants to be
made to the College and later to other residential colleges providing adult education for working-class students.

During the war residential work closed down but the work
of the Correspondence Department continued. A scheme for

tuition by post had been set up in the old Ruskin Hall days and, with recurrent revision and improvement, has been carried through without a break to the present time. Some 14,000 students have benefited by it and more than 500 are at work in correspondence courses to-day. In 1915 Mr. Sanderson Furniss, Tutor in Economics at the College, was appointed Principal, Dr. Slater having left to take up a post in India. Under the new Principal the full programme of work was re-established in 1919. Mr. Furniss (now Lord Furniss, whose recent book, *Memoirs of Fifty Years*, is full of interest to workers in this field of work) steered the College through the difficult period to 1925, keeping up all the while the high standards set in 1919. He had finally to retire because of ill-health and was succeeded by the present principal Mr. A. Barratt Brown, M.A., a well-known member of the Society of Friends. Under Mr. Barratt Brown's statesmanlike direction and stimulating enthusiasm the College continues to flourish in spite of adverse economic conditions.

The College has always stood for non-vocational adult education, non-sectarian and non-partisan, and has aimed at giving to working-class students a course of training designed to arouse independent thought untrammelled by dogmas and catchwords either orthodox or heretical. The main field of studies is in the social sciences but a wide horizon is encouraged and courses in history, literature and modern languages are provided. More importance is attached to provide tuition and written work and to discussion in class or seminar than to set lectures. The aim of the teaching staff is to promote habits of careful study, hard thinking, a standard of judgment and a sense of proportion and of values.

More than thirty-two years have passed since a public meeting to inaugurate Ruskin Hall was held in the Town Hall of Oxford. One of the outstanding figures then present, Mrs. Walter Vrooman, maintained an active connection with the College up to the spring of 1932 when she died. In recent years she was known as Mrs. Anne L. Grafflin. The Founder's Scholarship for Miners is only one of the many gifts to ease the way of working-men to the use of the institution which she helped to establish. She left an endowment for an additional scholarship for miners and it is probable that the total amount of her endowment will enable three miners to be in residence at the College in the future by this means in addition to any who may succeed in entering the College with Trade Union Congress or other scholarships, e.g. Durham and Glamorgan Education Committees.

THE WORKERS' EDUCATIONAL ASSOCIATION

Four years after the establishment of Ruskin College another attempt was made to found an educational enterprise in harmony with the spirit of independence abroad in the labour movement. This attempt was of purely English origin. Indeed the Workers' Educational Association is a modern expression of the humanitarian tradition of England. It represents the most recent and the most successful effort of the influential classes, functioning through the Universities, to raise the intellectual level of labour. The new movement seems to have derived its inspiration from Albert Mansbridge. He was raised in a working-class family and knew the problem of education from that angle. He was a clerk in a co-operative store and had led classes of fellow-employees in the history and principles of co-operation. He had assisted in the work of Toynbee Hall and agreed with Toynbee that the educational task of the workers was to train themselves for the complicated duties of modern citizenship. His experience as an instructor in the Co-operative Movement had convinced him that the teaching of Economics, Industrial History and Citizenship could be carried on much more effectively in affiliation with University Extension[1] than in isolation. For although he was well aware of the past failure of the Universities to capture the loyalty and imagination of working-class students, he felt certain a way could be found to remedy the situation. He believed scholarship divorced from labour to be artificial and ingrowing, and labour divorced from scholarship to be handicapped and hindered.[2]

After publishing three articles in the University Extension Journal expounding this theory he summoned assistance in the task of perfecting an organisation. With the help of Dr. Holland Rose and a group of working-men, who were accustomed to meet

[1] Mansbridge, Albert, *An Adventure in Working-Class Education, Being the Story of the W.E.A.*, pp. 10–11 (London: Longmans, 1920).

[2] Mansbridge, Albert, "The Workers' Educational Association," p. 353 (*International Labour Review*, September, 1922).

at his home as the "Christian Economic Society," Mansbridge and his wife took action by becoming the first members of an 'Association to Promote the Higher Education of Working Men." On July 14, 1903, a small temporary committee began work. A few weeks later it was succeeded by a larger and permanent one. The Association immediately received public recognition from nearly all the Universities and a large number of labour organisations. The name was changed three years later to the Workers' Educational Association.

Little happened during the first year. At the beginning of the second year, however, a working printer was instrumental in establishing a pioneer local branch in Reading. After this branches spread with great rapidity. By 1906 branches had been formed in eight towns. By 1907 records of forty-seven branches were presented. The same year is important in the history of workers' education for the publication of that epoch-making report— *Oxford and Working Class Education: Being the report of a Joint Committee of University and Working-Class Representatives on the Relation of the University to the Higher Education of Working People.* This report is an interesting and brilliant piece of work and should be read by everyone interested in the movement. From that time on growth has been remarkable and continuous.

In 1907 a new Constitution was adopted which defined the Association as consisting of the Central Authority, Districts and Branches, thus giving it a form which it has since retained. Various changes in the machinery and management were made, all in the direction of local autonomy and democratic government, which is the goal towards which the Workers' Educational Association has always worked.

In 1908 there were only three districts (including South Wales) and twenty-three of the fifty branches were attached to the Central Office; but the next few years saw the division of England into districts almost completed and a large increase in the number of officers who were giving their full-time services to the Association. By the session of 1913–14 district organisations were operating in every part of England with the exception of the Cornish peninsula; subsequent changes took the form of the subdivision of districts into more workable areas.

A dominating feature of the expansion of the Association during the pre-war period was the rapid growth of Tutorial

Classes. Class work in the Workers' Educational Association i
conducted on what is known as the tutorial system. Each clas
is composed of not more than twenty-four men and women who
have pledged themselves to attend for two hours each week
during twenty-four weeks a year for three years. The first hou
is devoted to a lecture, the second to discussion. Essay work i
a part of the course. Affiliation with the University occurs in the
administration of the Classes. Local management is in the hands
of the students themselves. But the central administration is
located in a Joint Committee consisting of an equal number of
representatives from the University and working-class organisations. When the Tutorial Class system was first devised the only
authority that would undertake such classes was the Oxford
University Extension Delegacy. It was the Delegacy that appointed
R. H. Tawney as the Tutor of the Rochdale Class, which may be
regarded as the first Class of its kind. Apart from the value of
his writings, particularly *The Acquisitive Society* and *Equality,*
and the inspiration which his teaching has given to a host of
students all over the world, Dr. Tawney will always have an
honourable place in the history of adult education as the Tutor
of the Rochdale Class. He had a rare combination of qualifications
for the work. He was a scholar, having had a distinguished
academic record at Balliol College, Oxford; he had the power
of teaching—at that time he was Assistant Lecturer in Economics
at the University of Glasgow; he was in sympathy with and had
some understanding of the working-class, having had experience
of working-class conditions, chiefly in the East End of London;
and he was an active member of the Association. He proved a
model for the long line of Tutors who have succeeded him.

While the arrangements for the Rochdale Class were under
consideration events were moving towards the creation of a
special authority for Tutorial Classes. As the result of a Conference held at Oxford in 1907 a Joint Committee was formed
consisting of seven persons nominated by the Vice-Chancellor
of the University of Oxford, and seven persons nominated by
the Executive of the Workers' Educational Association. It was
this Committee that produced the Report on Oxford and Working-
class Education. The importance of this Report lay in its recommendations, one of which asserted the principle that the body
responsible for the provision of Tutorial Classes should be

composed of an equal number of University and working-class representatives. This proposal—that working-class representatives should be associated with the actual administration of a part of the work of the University—was without precedent, but it was accepted by the Vice-Chancellor, and on October 27, 1908, a statute was promulgated in Congregation giving power to the Extension Delegacy to set up such a Joint Committee. The precedent being thus established by Oxford, similar Joint Committees were set up by other universities undertaking Tutorial Classes and became the recognised machinery by which University teaching (other than University Extension lectures) was made accessible to the work-people.

There was rapid growth. In the autumn of 1908 Oxford commenced six additional classes and by the following year the Universities of Cambridge, Manchester, Liverpool, London, Leeds and Sheffield had also undertaken Tutorial Class work; in the session 1909–10 there were thirty-nine classes running. When in 1913 Mr. Mansbridge described the inception, aim and work of Tutorial Classes in his book, *University Tutorial Classes*, he was able to write of a firmly established movement which, though but five years old, had already come to be recognised as a normal and necessary part of the work of a university. By the end of the session 1913–14 fourteen joint Committees had been formed and 145 classes, with 3,343 students, were at work.

Three developments accompanied this growth. A Central Joint Advisory Committee on Tutorial Classes was set up; Summer Schools were established; and a Central Library was founded to supplement the local libraries in the supply of the more expensive books of reference required by Tutorial and other Workers' Educational Association classes. For particulars of these developments the reader is referred to *The Story of the Workers' Educational Association, 1903–1924*, pp. 46–55, by Mr. T. W. Price, himself a member of the first Workers' Educational Association Tutorial Class, and now Warden of Holybrook House, Reading, where students are trained to conduct classes. Among the earlier activities of the Association it is interesting to note the publication in October, 1908, of the first number of its monthly magazine, *The Highway*. The purpose of the magazine was to focus the spirit and experience of the Association, to provide a means for the interchange of views, and to be a channel whereby information of important events in the educational world might be brought to the notice of members of the Association. The Book Room was a gradual development arising out of the distribution of *The Highway* and other publications of the Association, and the growth of a demand for books consequent on the progress of the Tutorial Classes. As time went on it became necessary to set up a special department to deal with this side of the work.

The years 1914–18 were a severe testing time for the Workers' Educational Association, but although the regular class work had to be curtailed the organisation stood the test. Indeed, war conditions were immediately responsible for a widening of the field of educational interest of the Association. The action of agricultural interests early in the war in demanding the release from school of children of school age in order to work on the farms and the readiness of some Education Authorities to fall in with this demand brought the Workers' Educational Association into the field in defence of the children. The new Constitution, adopted in 1916, widened the objects of the Association so as to include that of assisting "the development of a national system of education which shall ensure to all children, adolescents and adults such education as is essential for their complete development as individuals and citizens." It took a very active and effective part in the campaign that culminated in the passing of the Education Act of 1918. By its agitation in 1922 against the recommendations of the "Geddes Committee" it was in no small degree responsible for the checking of the retrograde educational policy of the Government at that time which was threatening to disintegrate the educational system of the country. It was active in connection with the Report of the Committee on Adult Education which was set up in 1917 to "consider the provision for, and the possibilities of, Adult Education (other than technical or vocational) in Great Britain, and to make recommendations." The Final Report of this Committee, issued in 1919, was the most comprehensive survey of adult education in Great Britain that had ever been made, and the Executive of the workers' Educational Association, in addition to drafting its own recommendations, issued invitations to the Club and Institute Union, the Educational Committee of the Co-operative Union, the National Adult School Union, the Y.M.C.A. Universities Committee, Ruskin College, the Labour College and the Scottish Labour College to send representatives to a Round Table Conference to discuss with its own representatives the proposals contained in the Report. As a result of three meetings a set of proposals was drafted and submitted to the respective organisations.

Subsequent to the publication of the Report the Board of Education set up an "Advisory Committee on Adult Education," with a view to simplifying the relations of the Board with the Bodies engaged in adult education and also to provide means whereby these bodies could discuss common interests. The Workers' Educational Association was represented on this Committee, the President of the Association, Dr. Temple, being appointed Chairman.

The Association busied itself also in connection with the Royal Commission on the University of Oxford and Cambridge. Important results of this Commission were the allocation of Treasury grants to extra-mural education and the formation of Extra-Mural Boards. These changes have meant a further extension of University teaching to working men and women throughout the country.

Side by side with all this activity in educational reconstruction went on the development of the ordinary work of the Association. Even before the end of the war the Workers' Educational Association was recovering the ground it had lost, and with the coming of peace its growth became more rapid than ever in its history.

With the cessation of hostilities the membership of the Association and the numbers of classes and students rose in a remarkable manner and in the session 1919–20 there were 20,703 members, 229 classes and 5,320 students. In the session 1922–23 there were 24,360 members, 363 Tutorial Classes, with 7,434 students, and, in addition there were 624 One-Year Classes and Study Circles, with 15,314 students.

In spite of the economic depression which set in about 1921–22 and has continued, with varying degrees of acuteness, up till to-day it may be said broadly that the last decade has been a period of extraordinary expansion. No attempt will be made here to give the relevant statistics year by year: they are published in the Annual Reports which are easily obtainable. Facts and figures taken from the twenty-eighth Annual Report, for the year ended May 31, 1931, will be sufficient indication of this remarkable development.

The total number of students was 53,538. Of these 47,270 attended grant-earning classes. Truly an astonishing growth. The following statistics relate to the various kinds of classes, some of which are new since 1921

Advanced Tutorial Classes

These classes are in the main small groups of from nine to fifteen students who must have passed through Three-Year Classes or possess equivalent qualifications and be capable of more advanced work that than which is pursued in Three-Year Classes.

1929–30	..	..	5 Classes:	55 Students.
1930–31	..	..	13 Classes:	144 Students.

Three-Year Tutorial Classes

1929–30	..	..	591 Classes:	10,012 Students.
1930–31	..	..	607 Classes:	10,231 Students.

The figures for 1930–31 include 17 classes in their fourth year and 1 in its fifth year.

Preparatory Tutorial Classes

These classes, as the name indicates, are organised with a view to preparing students for a Three-Year Course and must continue for not less than twenty-four weeks during a year, each meeting lasting two hours. The number of students in each class must not exceed thirty-two.

1929–30	..	..	71 Classes:	1,353 Students.
1930–31	..	..	87 Classes:	1,657 Students.

University Extension Courses

This description is correct for the year under review but modifications of the Adult Education Regulations, affecting Extension, Terminal and Short Courses, came into effect in August, 1931.

These courses consist of eighteen meetings of from one and a half to two hours' duration. The meetings may be divided into a lecture and class period. Only persons who are prepared to attend for both periods and to do written work may be entered on the roll of students. Persons not entered on the roll may, however, attend the lectures. The majority of Extension Courses are organised independently of the Workers' Educational Association, but a certain number of Joint Committees have been responsible for the following courses

| 1929–30 | .. | .. | 78 Courses: 1,444 Students. |
| 1930–31 | .. | .. | 106 Courses: 2,024 Students. |

One-Year Classes

These classes are a kind of half-way house between the Terminal Course and the Three-Year Class and are arranged mainly for those who find it difficult to pledge themselves to a full Three-Year Course. The Class must meet for not less than twenty weeks, each meeting lasting not less than one and a half hours, and the standard of education must be comparable to that of a Preparatory Tutorial Class. The number of students must not exceed thirty-two. One-Year Classes of much the same standard are also arranged by the Workers' Educational Association in conjunction with some of the local Education Authorities. These classes are included in the figures given below

| 1929–30 | .. | .. | 634 Classes: 14,899 Students. |
| 1930–31 | .. | .. | 766 Classes: 17,642 Students. |

Terminal Courses

These courses are specially useful for pioneer work and aim at stimulating students to attend the more intensive and consecutive types of classes dealt with above. Written work is not an essential condition of all Terminal Courses but it is always encouraged. Groups of not less than twelve meet for not less than twelve weeks during the year, each meeting lasting for not less than one and a half hours. Similar courses are run in conjunction with certain local Education Authorities. These Courses are included in the figures given below

| 1929–30 | .. | .. | 749 Courses: 13,602 Students. |
| 1930–31 | .. | .. | 808 Courses: 15,572 Students. |

Short Courses and Study Circles

A large number of short courses have been given. Prior to August, 1931, these were non-grant earning courses but under the new regulations some short courses are grant-earning. Another type of less formal course is the study circle, which may consist of from six to twenty people, meeting either in a student's house

or in a more public meeting place. The informal nature of the
study circle often adds to its value for very elementary students.

1929–30	.. ..	266 Short Courses: 5,662 Students.
		73 Study Circles: 1,074 Students.
1930–31	.. ..	208 Short Courses: 5,427 Students.
		60 Study Circles: 841 Students.

In addition to these regular winter classes and courses a considerable number of Summer Schools, Week-end and One-Day
Schools are now held every year. In August, 1932, the author
visited a Holiday School in the Gower Peninsula, South Wales.
It was in the nature of an experiment and as it appeared to be
an unqualified success it is likely to become a permanent feature
of Workers' Educational Association Summer programmes.
Ten Summer Schools were held in 1931 under the auspices of
the various Joint committees at Bangor, Bristol, Cambridge,
Chester, Durham, Abbotsholme, Stratton Park, Oxford, Hereford
and Saltburn-by-the-Sea. Three Workers' Educational Association
Districts held Summer Schools on the Continent—at Brussels,
Liége and Frankfurt. Two Summer Schools were conducted at
Coleg Harlech under the joint authority of the Council of the
College and the Extension Board of the University of Wales.
Coleg Harlech is not a Workers' Educational Association institution though it appears to work in close collaboration with it.
Founded in 1927, largely as the result of the inspiration and
organising ability of two men who have always been actively
associated with the Workers' Educational Association, especially
in Wales—Dr. Thomas Jones, C.H., and Sir Percy Watkins, LL.D.
—it is probably the most beautiful residential college for working-
men in the world. Situated on a broad sweep of the Welsh coast
it commands a magnificent view of sea and mountains while the
building itself is a fine modern mansion which has been admirably
adapted for use as a college. During the winter months systematic
courses, mainly in the social sciences, are pursued by working-
men students from all parts of Wales; in the long vacation it is
the home of a number of Summer Schools, Week-end Schools
and Conferences organised under the auspices of various educational and social institutions.

The post-war period has been one of expansion in the Workers'
Educational Association overseas as well as at home. It is in

Australasia that the movement is strongest but considerable progress has been made in Canada and South Africa and in 1920 a branch was formed in Madras. The influence of the Association has extended to the United States also and may be traced in the foundation of the Workers' Educational Bureau of America in 1921. The Bureau has developed more exclusively in relation to the organised labour movement than the Workers' Educational Association has in Great Britain, but its ideals and methods are similar. Both Professor H. W. L. Dana, who was instrumental in forming the Bureau, and Mr. Spencer Miller, Jun., its General Secretary, have first-hand knowledge of the work of the Association and the two movements maintain a close contact with each other. Mr. Dana has however departed considerably from the ideals of the Bureau and has interested himself in recent years in educational activities of a more specifically working-class character. There are not many phases in the development of adult or workers' education in the United States with which Mr. Dana, always ready to give a welcome and information to interested visitors from other countries, has not been actively associated.

The policy of the Workers' Educational Association in making use of the universities has been criticised by certain sections of the Labour Movement on the ground that University teaching is of necessity biassed in favour of the *status quo*, and that in consequence it is not merely useless to the working-class student but actually hampers his efforts to equip himself for service in the working-class movement. The Workers' Educational Association holds the view that any possibility of reactionary bias in teaching can be safeguarded by giving to working-class organisations an effective control in working-class education. When the Constitution was revised in 1922 the principle of the original Constitution, that there should be definite provision for the representation of the most important working-class bodies on the Committee, was restored, and representatives of the Trades Union Congress, of the Co-operative Union and of the Club and Institute Union were once more given places on the National Executive Committee, independently of election by the Central Council. At the same time a statement of Workers' Educational Association policy was issued in which the Association emphasised its conviction that the success of working-class education depended upon the working-class movement through the freedom of trade unions, co-operative societies, clubs and similar bodies to build up and control their own educational organisation in co-operation with the universities and other educational institutions.

In the meantime a new step had been taken in 1919 in the development of working-class education in direct relation with organised labour when the Workers' Educational Association entered upon an experiment with the Iron and Steel Trades Confederation to organise educational facilities for its members. The facilities proposed included the remission of class fees of members of the union; the provision where necessary of special classes and the organisation of lectures in branches of the Confederation; the provision of scholarships to Summer Schools and Week-end Schools; and the arrangement of facilities for the borrowing of books. All these facilities were actually arranged and Week-end Schools and special Trade Union courses at Summer Schools were organised. The scheme was controlled by the Workers' Educational Trades Union Committee, which was an organisation set up jointly by the Workers' Educational Association and the Confederation, and consisted of a central committee, divisional committees and, where practicable, local committees, on all of which the Confederation had a majority of representatives. The machinery of the Workers' Educational Association was placed at the disposal of the Committee for the arrangement of the facilities and so far as new expenditure was incurred the cost was met by the Confederation. Provision was made for the inclusion of other unions and the first year of work was so successful that the committee was encouraged to seek the extension of the scheme.

In 1921, the Union of Post Office Workers, the Railway Clerks' Association and the Association of Engineering and Shipbuilding Draughtsmen joined the W.E.T.U.C. Their inclusion made it necessary to enlarge the organisation so as to make the area of operations of the W.E.T.U.C. co-extensive with that of the Workers' Educational Association. The scheme has proved highly successful and by the beginning of 1931 the number of trade unions included in it had increased to thirteen. During 1930 199 Summer Schools Scholarships were taken up; 34 week-end Schools, attended by 1,099 students, were held; and there were 47 one-day schools, attended by 2,260 students.

It is of interest to classify the students of all the Workers' Educational Association Classes according to occupation. The 12,032 students attending Tutorial and Preparatory Classes in 1931 were distributed as follows:

Clerks, Secretaries, Typists, Telegraphists ..	2,089
Teachers	1,656
Colliery workers, miners and checkweighmen..	908
Housewives, Domestics, etc.	1,889
Metal, Machine- and Tool-Workers	472
Engineers, Mechanics and Fitters	581
Shopkeepers and Shop Assistants	523
Railway Servants	320
Textile Workers	301
Civil Servants	606
Professional Workers	272
Carpenters and Woodworkers	195
Food Workers	186
Tailors, Dressmakers, Cutters, Milliners ..	312
Printers, Engravers, Bookbinders	143
Overlookers, Foremen, Managers	104
Builders, Brick and Stone Workers	192
Insurance Agents, Travellers	154
Boot, Shoe and Leather Workers	172
Miscellaneous Factory Workers	159
Postmen, Tram and Policemen	203
Warehousemen	89
Draughtsmen and Designers	81
Municipal Employees	163
Electricians	57
Labourers	159
Blacksmiths	27
Potters	50
Miscellaneous: Gardeners, Caretakers, etc. ..	489

The occupations of the 35,238 students attending Extension, One-Year and Terminal Courses were:

Manual Workers	9,518
Domestic and Home Duties	7,524
Clerks and Shop Assistants	5,556
Teachers	2,955
Professional Workers	1,538
Postal Workers	576
Foremen	473
Miscellaneous and Unspecified..	7,098

The occupations of the 6,268 students attending non-grant-earning classes cannot be given here but it is clear that of those attending the grant-earning classes there was a large proportion of students who can hardly be regarded as "working men and women," e.g. professional workers, civil servants, teachers. Is there not some danger of a departure from the ideal proclaimed by Mr. Mansbridge in his book *The Workers' Educational Association*?

"The Association is open . . . to every person and to every institution interested in the development of the education of working people. It has never been in any sense a 'class' movement, but it was recognised from the outset . . . that if the proportion of working men and women in the Association fell below . . . 75 per cent, the Association would not only become vitiated but scholars would cease to take an interest in it."

It is also significant that 25·87 per cent of the classes studied Literature and Drama, whereas only 12·71 per cent pursued courses in Economics. Is the Workers' Educational Association entering upon a period of disintegration as an agency catering for the educational needs of working-men similar to that which followed a period of success in the case of The Mechanics' Institute about a hundred years ago? It will be recalled that the Institute substituted literature for mechanics and that the proportion of artisan students sank as low as one-twentieth. There is a deal of nonsense talked about "history repeating itself" but the reasons why the Mechanics' Institute lost the confidence of the working-class movement would appear to be in the nature of a warning to the Workers' Educational Association to-day.

In all the industrial districts, particularly the coalfields, there are other agencies providing one form or another of educational facilities for adults. The Young Men's Christian Association has made quite a notable contribution by conducting systematic courses in economics, sociology, religion, philosophy, history, literature, music, etc., as well as popular lectures, discussion groups and Institutes and Clubs carrying on a considerable amount of informal work in the way of Physical Training and Hobbies. The Club and Institute Union is another organisation that supports and organises educational enterprises for working-men. And in each coalfield there are special agencies at work. In the

South Wales coalfield, for instance, in addition to all the organisations that have already been described, there are bodies carrying on work of a special and local character. In 1929 the National Council of Social Service set up a Joint Committee for the Promotion of Educational Facilities in the South Wales and Monmouthshire Coalfields to operate for the purpose of providing support for the educational work conducted by the bodies already functioning —the University Colleges, the Workers' Educational Association, the National Council of Music and the Young Men's Christian Association—and of developing less formal and more recreative forms of education in the present condition of unemployment. The funds for all these purposes have been provided by the Carnegie United Kingdom Trustees. Mention must also be made of the establishment in recent years in the coalfield of Educational Settlements with their associated classes, craft workshops, training centres, clubs, etc., and of Boys' Clubs and Holiday Camps.

IV

INDEPENDENT WORKING-CLASS EDUCATION

Ruskin College and the Workers' Educational Association disowned anything in the nature of independent working-class education. No one wishing to appraise the educational influences operating on the lives of the industrial workers, especially the coal-miners of Great Britain, can afford to neglect the Independent Working-Class Education Movement.

As we have seen Thomas Hodgskin had raised the issue of working-class self-instruction and control at the time of the foundation of Birkbeck College in 1823. While the "extensionists" were engaged in bridging the gulf between the classes the Socialist Movement was being reborn in England. The early eighties saw the foundation of the Social Democratic Federation and the Fabian Society. Ten years later came *The Clarion* and the Independent Labour Party. Inevitably the revival of Socialist propaganda paved the way for a rebirth of the idea of independent working-class education. The books and pamphlets in which H. M. Hyndman, for example, sought to popularise Marxian economics raised doubts in many minds as to the correctness of orthodox political economy. The Fabian Society undertook a

z

certain amount of definitely educational work. It arranged a system of "book boxes" which were loaned to Workmen's Clubs, etc., and it organised lectures and classes in economics, industrial history, local government, etc., for members of Socialist societies. William Morris emphasised the need for an education which should be based on a recognition of antagonisms existing in a class society and believed that a mere "extension" of education as ordinarily understood was of no use from the working-class point of view. After the unemployed riots of 1886 he wrote in *The Commonwealth*: "At the risk of being misunderstood by the hot-heads, I say that our business is more than ever Education. . . . Education towards Revolution seems to me to express in three words what our policy should be; towards that New Birth of Society which we know must come, and which, therefore, we must strive to help forward so that it may come with as little confusion and suffering as may be."

But it was not until 1908 that the issue raised by Hodgskin once again became prominent. It arose in connection with the revolt of certain students at Ruskin College to which reference has already been made. The Trade Union Congress in 1907 had called on the Labour Movement to "take the College in hand and make it an assured success." A number of the students then in residence felt the anomaly of an appeal to the workers' organisations for financial support for an institution whose curriculum was certainly not based upon anything approaching a working-class point of view. In October, 1908, they formed themselves into an organisation called the Plebs League, the aim of which was to "bring about a more satisfactory connection between Ruskin College and the Labour Movement." But the new organisation had not been long in existence when its founders realised that a bigger issue than that of control was involved: a demand was growing for a different *kind* of education. In February, 1909, the disaffected students established a monthly Journal, *The Plebs*, and in the first issue there is the following paragraph in an article on "The Relation of Ruskin College to the Labour Movement":

"The number of attempts to impose education from 'above' are legion. Prominent among them stands the University Extension Movement, with its powerful ally, the Workers' Educational Association. While probably the intentions of the promoters of these movements are of the most benevolent character, few will deny that the effect of their success would be to militate against the self-reliance of the workers in their own educational movement."

In the editorial, in this same issue, the aim of the Plebs League is expressly defined as "the education of the workers in the interests of the workers." And the following month's editorial asserts: "Education cannot be imposed from above, it cannot be handed down by a superior class to an inferior class. The working class must achieve its own salvation."

All this implied a criticism of the actual tuition given in Ruskin College. The result was some friction between the College authorities and the students organised in the new League; and this came to a head in the forced resignation of the Principal, Mr. Dennis Hird, and the students' strike.

The result of this direct action was the foundation, a few months later, of a new college, the Central Labour College, which was supported by several districts of the South Wales Miners and by the Amalgamated Society of Railway Servants. It was established in premises in Oxford and it remained there for two years but in 1911 it was removed to London, "largely owing to the opposition of University landlords."[1]

With the foundation of the Central Labour College the movement for Independent Working-Class Education had at last definitely begun. In the first few years the new College had an uphill fight. The number of residential students holding Trade Union Scholarships varied from twelve to twenty and their fees were scarcely sufficient to meet the necessary expenses of the institution. But rank-and-file interest in the educational aims and policy of the College steadily grew, and a strong movement in the South Wales Miners' Federation and the Railwaymen's Union was at work pressing for official union support. This movement was successful in 1914 when the two unions, at their respective annual meetings, decided jointly to purchase and control the College. By 1916 certain necessary alterations in their Constitutions were put through and the two unions took over the College as the Labour College, London.

The pioneers of the new movement had never limited their aims to the establishment of a college for residential students. The first number of *The Plebs* called for the formation of branches

[1] *Working-Class Education*, J F. and Winifred Horrabin, p. 46.

wherever possible. "As soon as a branch is formed efforts should
be made to start classes in sociology, history and economics."
In various industrial districts, notably in South Wales, in the
West Riding of Yorkshire and in Lancashire, classes conducted
under Plebs or Labour College auspices began to appear. These
classes, of course, received no Government grants nor any subsidy
from University funds; nor did the Union control of the London
Labour College involve any financial support of the provincial
classes. These had to depend on donations from local Trade
Union branches or from Trades Councils. The tutors were
almost invariably unpaid. Every class was a practically autonomous
unit, the only common bonds being the Plebs League, in which
the active spirits enrolled themselves as members, and *The Plebs
Magazine*, which has filled a similar function in this movement
to that of *The Highway* in the Workers' Educational Association.

In this class-work men and women of every section of the
Labour Movement took part—Independent Labour Party members, Socialist Labour Party members, "plain Trade Unionists,"
and members of various Left Wing and "minority" movements.
The years between the formation of the Plebs League and the
outbreak of the war were years of industrial unrest, and in such
an organisation as the League many of the active spirits who
were seething with ideas, more or less revolutionary, found a
common ground for discussion and argument. The classes themselves were almost invariably in economics and industrial history
and these subjects naturally lent themselves to keen debating on
all those problems which lay closest to the everyday life of the
workers.

During the years of the war this class movement made great
headway. In Scotland especially the idea of independence in
workers' education was taken up with enthusiasm and the Scottish
Labour College came into being. The Plebs League, during the
same period, made a start in the provision of text-books and
pamphlets for the classes in response to the need that was felt
for the publication of literature expressing the working-class
point of view. At Text-Book Conferences, convened by the Plebs
League, plans for further developments were elaborated and a
scheme was evolved for a series of text-books which were to be
drafted by one or two hands and then discussed by a committee
of Tutors and students.

In October, 1921, representatives of the classes in various parts of Great Britain met in conference at Birmingham to discuss the desirability of organising the class work on a national basis and decided on the formation of the National Council of Labour Colleges. The Council comprised the numerous non-residential provincial Labour Colleges, the London Labour College, the Scottish Labour College and the Plebs League; and its Executive included a representative from each Trade Union which arranged an educational scheme for its members through the National Council of Labour Colleges. The provincial or District Labour Colleges are not colleges in a physical sense—there are no college buildings: they are essentially district centres for the purpose of organising classes; some of the Colleges conduct about sixty classes per year. The following table shews the number of District Labour Colleges and Class groups (nuclei of future Colleges):

1922–23	..	.. 27	1927–28	..	.. 106
1923–24	..	.. 91	1928–29	..	.. 94
1924–25	..	.. 132	1929–30	..	.. 93
1925–26	..	.. 120	1930–31	..	.. 93
1926–27	..	.. 117			

The annual report of the National Council of Labour Colleges for 1931, which carries the significant title *Education for Emancipation*, ascribes the recent drop in the figures to the fact that many of the smaller Colleges and Class groups have been amalgamated into larger and more effective units.

The first union to inaugurate an educational scheme with the National Council of Labour Colleges was the Amalgamated Union of Building Trade Workers. The number of organisations which have adopted the schemes increased from 9 in 1923 to 22 in 1924 and now stands at 30. A full list of the organisations is given on page 23 of the annual report for 1931. The schemes usually provide free access to all National Council of Labour Colleges classes and free Correspondence Courses. Under such schemes the Union, as a rule, pays a sum of about 3d. per member per annum, although no hard-and-fast line has yet been drawn. The Union is entitled to a representative on the National Executive, to another on the National Council and to one on each of the Divisional Councils, while every Branch is, as a rule, entitled to send a representative to the local College catering for its area.

The typical National Council of Labour Colleges scheme provides the following facilities for the whole of the members:

(*a*) Free access to Classes.
(*b*) Free Correspondence Courses.
(*c*) Occasional Branch Lectures.
(*d*) Free access to Non-Residential Day and Week-end Schools.

The local Labour College also provides facilities for local Trade Union Branches, Co-operative Societies and Labour and Socialist bodies. These local bodies in return for a payment of 2d. per member per annum, receive free access to Classes for all their members and are entitled to representation.

The membership of the thirty organisations with National Council of Labour Colleges schemes is 1,700,000. It is claimed that the National Council of Labour Colleges has more Trade Union educational schemes than all the other working-class organisations put together and that these schemes, as a rule, are more comprehensive.

The outstanding feature of the work in 1930–31 was the enormous increase in correspondence course students, who numbered 6,595 compared with 2,715 in the previous year. The Correspondence Department is helping to overcome the difficulty of increasing the proportion of students willing to do written work.

In addition to Day and Week-end Schools (165 in 1930–31 with 8,941 students) one or two National residential Summer Schools are held, the students receiving scholarships from trade unions, co-operative societies and other bodies, while some pay their own fees.

The table on page 359 shews the numbers of classes and students.

It will be noticed that since 1927 the students have decreased in number. This is attributed to the increasing apathy which followed the National Strike and Miners' Lock-out in 1926. Another factor is that these classes depend entirely on the financial support of Trade Union and Labour organisations and it is well known that the economic depression has seriously depleted their funds.

The tutors and lecturers conducting National Council of Labour Colleges classes are mainly working men, self-taught or trained at the London Labour College or in its own evening classes, though these have been augmented in recent years by an increasing number of University trained men and women, professional teachers, etc., whose experience has convinced them of the need for the working class to take in hand its own educational work. A great deal of this teaching is done voluntarily but the financial support of large Trade Unions has made possible the division of the country into districts and the appointment in each district of a whole-time paid tutor-organiser.

What of the content of the educational work of these classes? As the purpose of the National Council of Labour Colleges is

Year	Number of Classes	Students
1922–23	529	11,993
1923–24	698	16,909
1924–25	1,048	25,071
1925–26	1,234	30,398
1926–27	1,201	31,635
1927–28	1,102	27,147
1928–29	931	20,520
1929–30	816	19,275
1930–31	846	18,393

to assist Trade Unionists and members of the Working-class Movement in general, the subjects taught are chosen with a view to helping the students more effectively to carry on work in the Trade Union, Labour and Co-operative Movements. The principal subjects taught are:

Biology
Bourgeois (Orthodox) and
   Marxian Economics
Class Tutoring
Conduct of Meetings
Co-operation
Economics
Economic Geography
English Grammar and Article
   Writing
Esperanto
Evolution
Evolution of Capitalism
Finance
History of the Family
History of the British Working-
   class
History of Trade Unionism
History of British Socialism
History and Theory of Socialism

Imperialism	Psychology
Industrial History	Public Speaking
Labour Journalism	Revolutionary Periods in History
Literature and Social Conditions	Social History
Local Government	Sociology
Marxism	Science of Reasoning
Modern Problems	Theory of History
Modern European History	Trade Union Law.

It does not appear to be generally known that the Plebs League and the Residential Labour College in London no longer exist. The League may be described as the father of the Labour College Movement. As we have seen it began publishing *The Plebs* in 1909; in the same year it was responsible for the foundation of the Central Labour College, afterwards the Labour College, London. From then until 1921 it encouraged the formation of local colleges and classes, just as it had previously helped to keep the residential college going till it was taken over by the South Wales Miners' Federation and the National Union of Railwaymen. In 1921 the League called the conference that formed the National Council of Labour Colleges. In 1927 it handed over its publication work to the National Council of Labour Colleges and consequently by 1928 it appeared to have no national function left. It was closed down in 1930 after a career covering more than twenty-one years.

The last few years have been very difficult for all Labour organisations, especially Miners' Unions. During 1928 and 1929 four Unions dropped their national educational schemes. In addition, the Maesteg (Glamorgan) Miners' Union and the Rhondda Miners' Union had to discontinue local educational activities, and the South Wales Miners' Federation had to decide to give up its half control of the residential Labour College at Earl's Court, London. It will be recalled that in 1916 the South Wales Miners' Federation and the National Union of Railwaymen purchased the college jointly. In consequence of the financial position of the South Wales Miners' Federation the two controlling Unions closed down the College in 1929. At the Swansea Trade Union Congress in the previous year they had offered to hand it over to Congress but the offer was not accepted, many of the delegates feeling apparently that they had no power to commit their Unions to additional expenditure. It should be mentioned that both the Unions that controlled the College have maintained their interest in the Movement. The National Union of Railwaymen has adopted a National Council of Labour Colleges scheme and the South Wales Miners' Federation has come to a similar decision, though in point of fact the coal-miners, who have played such a big part in the independent movement, are now represented by only one Union—the Mid and East Lothian Miners.

The National Council of Labour Colleges, therefore, remains the only national organisation functioning in the movement for independent working-class education. In its annual report for the year 1930 occurs the following paragraph:

"By 1925 the N.C.L.C. became the most powerful trade union educational organisation in the country, and the largest educational body of its kind in the world. Although in 1929 the residential Labour College was closed as a result of the financial position of the South Wales Miners' Federation (one of the two joint owners), the National Council of Labour Colleges itself was by 1930, in consequence of increased support from Trade Unions, in a stronger position than it had ever been."

V

LOCAL EDUCATION AUTHORITIES AND ADULT EDUCATION

In addition to the various voluntary organisations already described the majority of local education authorities have made provision for adult education. The educational administrator operating under a local authority is concerned not only with boys and girls attending day schools and evening classes: he is concerned also "with those who have hitherto been for thousands of reasons outside the pale, or in whose lives there has been a long period of hibernation, at the end of which they wake up to the realisation of a want unsatisfied. They cannot be put back into school desks. The lecture and the study group are what they need."[1]

In 1922 the Board of Education announced that "in their

[1] W. A. Brockington, "Adult Education and the Local Education Authority" in *Journal of Adult Education*, Vol. I, No. 1, p. 94.

scrutiny of local education authorities' statements of expenditure
upon further education" they had observed the occasional
appearance of items other than the ordinary items of technical
education. There were university tutorial classes and preparatory
classes, and university extension courses; and other lecture courses
(including lectures of a popular character) organised sometimes
by the authority or sometimes by another body. And, finally,
the Board had observed that assistance was being given to the
general expenses of bodies conducting educational work and not
expressly related to particular courses. In fact, what the Board
had observed were all the stirring activities of adult education,
as distinct from the systematic instruction of young persons in
technical schools.

The local authorities had been realising very acutely that in
addition to the class of student who was treading the narrow
pathway of technical knowledge they had to meet the needs of
another class who had already passed into manhood or womanhood
along the highway of life and experience. They had become
conscious of the special bargain which the Board of Education
had made with the Workers' Educational Association; and in
the light of that bargain, they had extended their own administration. Their policies had not merely been thought out in the
abstract; they had already been tried out. And the Board of
Education amplified, extended and codified local practice.

The progressive stages in the development of the policy of a
local authority are marked first by the creation of an Adult
Education Committee as the gathering ground for all local needs.
In co-operation with the extra-mural department of a neighbouring
University or University College, University Tutorial and
Preparatory Classes are organised. These courses are either
assisted by grants or they are conducted by tutors appointed by
the authority. In course of time there is invariably a growing
inclination towards the employment of Staff tutors, and assisted
courses diminish in direct ratio. A County Rural Library is
established or, if already established, is linked up with the Classes
because one object of such a library is to provide books for students
in the village classes. Through the Central Library for Students
in some cases by arrangement with the public library of some
central town and, in Wales, through the National Library of
Wales, reference and text-books are made available so that no

serious and systematic student has to ask in vain for any book which is essential to his studies.

Following the successive reports of the Departmental Committee on Adult Education a further codification was made in 1924. The Board indicated the lines along which adult education should be developed as part of the public educational system. They would be prepared to recognise a programme which included single lectures and short courses. They authorised a grant for University Extension Courses and so made possible pioneer work which would lay the foundation of more systematic and continuous study. They encouraged the local authorities to appoint full-time tutors to Tutorial Classes. All this possibly increased the danger of overlapping and has perhaps intensified the Local Education Authorities–Workers' Educational Association controversy, but it is significant as indicating recognition of the development of this kind of adult education as *part of the public educational system.*

In addition to classes organised by Local Education Authorities in co-operation with voluntary organisations a number of local authorities conduct courses in the social sciences quite independently, and in one instance at least, the Glamorgan County Council, a whole-time Travelling Tutor conducts classes at various centres in the administrative area and picked students from each centre attend the authority's own Summer School for three weeks annually. The Warwickshire and Lancashire authorities also have appointed full-time tutors for adult education work. The West Riding of Yorkshire and Sheffield authorities have both set up special committees for the purpose of fostering and co-ordinating adult education. Some provincial authorities have established institutions devoted entirely to non-vocational adult education. Leicester and Manchester each conduct one centre and Edinburgh two centres, exclusively for adults, the Manchester centre being for men only. With these exceptions the provision of special institutions appears to be restricted to London. The London institutions in all number more than sixty and are of three types—literary institutes, men's institutes and women's institutes. The literary institutes, established in their present form in 1919, provide classes in a variety of subjects, including social science, history and languages, for students, numbering more than 10,000, who have received a good elementary education followed in many cases by some secondary or commercial education. The men's institutes constitute a successful endeavour to deal with another side of the adult education problem. They cater for a different type of student—men who, for the most part, have remained untouched by any educational influence since leaving the elementary school. The subjects taught include physical training, handicrafts, hobbies and music. The women's institutes supply instruction in a wide range of practical subjects appertaining to the conduct of the home. It may be assumed that about twenty thousand adults attend these men's and women's institutes.

There is reason to believe that all these types of institutes and institutions justify the enterprise of local authorities in making direct provision of adult education and that they appeal to sections of the public which have not been attracted by the voluntary bodies.

A large number of authorities offer assistance to students for non-vocational adult education. Generally the awards are of three kinds: firstly, senior scholarships which enable a student to enter upon a full-time course of study at a University; secondly, scholarships which are attached to a particular non-University institution such as Ruskin College, and Hillcroft College for Women; and lastly, scholarships for part-time study (generally used by students for attendance at evening classes). Other authorities, without having any special scheme, are prepared to consider applications and to give grants in particular cases. The Glamorgan authority annually makes 150 awards tenable at the Glamorgan Summer School in educational handwork; in addition that authority provides another 25 scholarships to students, the majority being miners, to enable them to attend the Social Science Course at the authority's own Mining, Engineering and Social Science Summer School, usually held at University College, Swansea.

In 1928, a Joint Committee appointed by the British Institute of Adult Education and the Tutors' Association conducted an inquiry into the problems of the supply and training of Tutors in Adult Education. The Carnegie United Kingdom Trustees undertook the publication of the Report which is a valuable and altogether admirable piece of work. In Chapter XI on "The Work of Local Education Authorities in Adult Education," the Committee say:

"In conclusion, we desire to emphasise the growing importance of the work discharged by Local Education Authorities in adult education, both by direct provision and by aid to voluntary bodies. More and more it will be necessary to look to them for funds for the further development of adult education, while the effectiveness of their work will largely depend upon the success achieved in devising schemes for co-operation with voluntary bodies. Various suggestions have been made from time to time, but we feel that no one method can be uniformly applied. Each area must be given freedom to frame its own scheme in the light of its own special difficulties."

In the foregoing account an attempt has been made to describe the history and activities of the principal organisations catering for the educational needs of working men and women in Great Britain. None of these agencies specialises in the education of coal-miners but each coalfield is a network of classes conducted under the auspices of the various organisations. These classes have been carried on sufficiently long for the results to be noticeable and there is no doubt that they have exercised a marked influence on the life of the mining population of the country.

ADULT AND WORKERS' EDUCATION IN THE UNITED STATES

I. Historical Survey

The American working-man has for several generations been less interested in self-education than the British, and Workers' Education is a more recent development in the States than in England. Wherein lies the explanation? In the first place, the American public school system is an important factor. Long before 1870, when the foundations were laid of the British elementary school system, America had its free public (elementary) schools, and everybody knows that the high (secondary) schools in America have always been free. The American people are naturally proud of this feature of their educational system, and the pioneers of it and of the free State Universities that followed it believed the products of all these institutions would be well-educated adults, including working men and women, and that therefore it would be unnecessary to concentrate on the education of the workers. For a long time even the working class itself had a proud if somewhat pathetic faith in the public school system as a solvent of its economic and political difficulties. Even to-day one may meet trade union leaders in America who have no use for adult or workers' education in the European sense.

Another factor is that the American people were enfranchised politically before the British. Although the Chartist movement was essentially economic in character the Chartists concentrated on the ballot—it was one of the Six Points in the Charter—as a means of political education. In America there has been no Chartist uprising and the vote was obtained without a long, pugnacious clash between the working class and the landed and manufacturing interests like that which preceded the winning of the franchise in England. With the vote and the public school system come by so easily why should the American workers agitate for "extension" or "emancipation"? And there was surely no reason why the Church or the University or the social settlement, which had been so active in England, should undertake to educate the working class in America.

The explanation is still inadequate. The nineteenth century was a period of tremendous agricultural and industrial expansion in America and as the cotton, coal, iron and steel, transport, farming, building and numerous other industries developed there arose the need for an increasing army of workers. The normal growth of native-born population was totally inadequate. The necessary supply came from other countries, mainly from Europe. In 1820 the number of foreign-born set ashore in the United States was only 8,385. Between 1847 and 1857 no fewer than 200,000 arrived each year. Those who came prior to 1825 were largely English, Scots, Protestant Irish and Protestant German. After 1848, owing to the failure of the potato crop in Ireland, Irish immigration reached a very high point. Of these more than one-half were unable to read and write. Later came the millions of immigrants from eastern, central, southern and south-eastern Europe—a huge mass of physically strong but intellectually undeveloped human beings, for the most part peasants and labourers accustomed to a very low standard of life. The new immigrant population was absorbed by the hungry, rapidly-growing industries. America presented to the world a picture of he biggest and most variegated transplanted working class ever known. From whatever country they had been transplanted they thrived in the new soil. They worked hard and long but they received high wages and enjoyed a standard of physical comfort far superior to anything they had experienced in Europe. They found they could send their children to school and to the University; their daughters became teachers or social workers and they were able to boast that their sons had become doctors or attorneys. On becoming naturalised citizens of the United States of America they could vote Republican or Democrat. A great and wonderful country—a country of opportunity! It is not difficult to appreciate the problem, from the standpoint of those interested in workers' education, created by this inert mass of semi-literate immigrants, satisfied with the flesh-pots of American civilisation.

Nevertheless, Trade Union Colleges, Workers' Universities, Labour Colleges, People's Colleges and similar agencies have finally appeared. The story of their slow and belated development is full of interest but it cannot be traced in detail here. Something in the nature of a summarised narrative will be attempted, however.

Reference must first be made to a political organisation bearing the name of the Working Men's Party, established about 1828. It was the chief instrument of the founding of the American public school system but it did not establish a system of education for the working class as such. It did not even formulate a working-class educational tradition. For in spite of its name and of efforts to improve wage and hour conditions the Working Men's Party was primarily a middle-class movement and its educational purpose was to erase all political and social barriers.

With the decline of this organisation in the early thirties industrial society in the United States began to undergo certain changes of great importance to the development of education as a working-class problem. Here and there groups of working-men asserted the need for special education. In Boston, in 1833, a committee on education appointed by a working-men's convention, recommended the arrangement of lectures for adults in political economy. In 1834 another group called attention to the lack of knowledge among adult workers. In 1837, after a stormy period within the ranks of the National Trades' Union, working-men announced that their ultimate hope lay in self-education. They proposed to organise trade associations, not only to protect their trades, but first of all to improve their moral and intellectual condition But the official labour movement did not share the educational doubts of some of its members. Changes in industrial society, warnings of illiteracy figures and the unfavourable comments of friendly foreign visitors like De Toqueville and Harriet Martineau passed unnoticed. During the middle years of the century Labour was completely absorbed in the task of adjusting structural revolutions within its own organisations.

When the Federation of Organised Trades and Labour Unions was reorganised into the American Federation of Labour in 1886 all references to education in the Constitution were deleted. The Officials of the American Federation of Labour accepted the educational tradition developed by the Working Men's Party. The Federation refused to enter politics as a separate party and distrusted all the devices, among them education, by which the working class elsewhere had endeavoured to combine economic and political protest. Not that this policy went uncriticised and unchallenged but those vigorous spirits of the Federation who were dissatisfied with educational practice were forced into withdrawal.

The path of educational orthodoxy for the Federation, however, was not always smooth notwithstanding the remarkable personal influence of its leader, Mr. Samuel Gompers. In 1900 Walter Vrooman, the same American who was mainly responsible for founding Ruskin College, Oxford, sought the assistance of the Federation in establishing a similar institution in Trenton, Missouri, to be called Ruskin Hall. No support materialised. The Federation obviously recognised no need for such an institution which somehow savoured of socialism.

Towards the end of the nineteenth and at the beginning of the twentieth century the voices of local unions especially in the West were heard at every convention urging a modification of the Federation educational policy. As early as 1891 a resolution was introduced instructing all State federations of labour to follow the example of the trade unions of Seattle, Washington, which had established a library of labour literature so that the members of unions might have the opportunity of being kept informed upon the general labour movement and become educated in trade union principles. From 1902 on, resolutions of a similar character were of annual occurrence. One delegate recommended a lecture campaign for education among non-unionists in trade union principles. Andrew Furuseth, of San Francisco, and Victor Berger, of Wisconsin, called the attention of Convention delegates to certain books such as Ward's *The Ancient Lowly*, Rogers's *Six Centuries of Work and Wages*, and Webb's *Industrial Democracy*. In 1905 a delegate from Missouri proposed the immediate establishment of a lecture bureau. The United Mine Workers asked that lecture courses be held under the auspices of central bodies "throughout the United States, Canada, and insular possessions." And Paul Scharrenberg, of San Francisco, urged upon labour the necessity of bringing the work of State Universities more in conformity with the needs of the working people.

It may be said that after 1902 the old educational policy of the Federation began to undergo a process of modification. Something had happened to shake the confidence of the rank and file in the sufficiency of the public school for labour. Persistent minorities were continually asserting that the organised worker needed more than the usual kind of education. Confronted with this state of mind among the rank and file, Mr. Gompers was compelled to adopt conciliatory measures. He raised the Standing Committee on Education to a position of importance by the appointment of John Mitchell as chairman. He recommended that local bodies establish trade union schools where at least the elementary principles of the trade union movement might be taught. He also reported that, as President of the Federation, he had already co-operated in a campaign for giving lectures in the evening schools, which he regarded as potential "working-men's universities."

This was a big step forward. By taking it, Mr. Gompers broke with the educational tradition of the Working Men's Party. But concession to the dissatisfied elements did not mean that the Federation had been finally converted to the necessity of Workers' Education in the strict sense of the term. The pressure which ultimately placed Workers' Education on the official programme of the American Federation of Labour came neither from England nor from the West. It came from two large groups within the organisation itself—the women workers and the Jews.

The fascinating story of the organisation of the women workers of America into trade unions and of their interest in education is too long to be included here, except in bare outline. Trade unionism among the earlier women operatives seemed to exist less to redress economic grievances than to raise an educational status that had always been low. The interest of the women workers in education is as old as the American woman worker herself. It dates from the entrance into cotton mills of the daughters of New England farmers and professional men. In 1825 women workers were of revolutionary stock. The tradition of resistance to oppression was fresh and inspiring. But this early phase was followed by a period of about half a century following the organisation of Reform Associations during which women responded feebly to the appeals of the movement. In 1886 a group of women, calling themselves the Working Women's Society, was founded in New York City for the purpose of inquiring into and finding remedies for poor working conditions. It was composed of operatives and women of independent means. Their intention was to gather together all those devoted to the cause of organising women, to collect and publish facts and to undertake a campaign of education among the more fortunate classes in the community. A similar attempt was made in Chicago in the 'nineties. But women's trade union membership did not become important till the beginning of the new century, though even in 1902 it was less than 16,000 and formed less than 5 per cent of the total number of trade union members and an even smaller proportion of the million women gainfully employed.

Although the International Ladies' Garment Workers' Union, the Tobacco Workers' International Union and other crafts in which women predominated carried on a vigorous policy of organisation the problem was not faced with any degree of determination until the establishment of the National Women's Trade Union League in Boston in 1903. The names of many remarkable women are associated with this league, including Mary Kenny O'Sullivan, a bindery woman, Jane Addams, the present Warden of Hull House, Chicago, Mary M'Dowell, Lillian Wald and Leonora O'Reilly. The first president in New York City was Mary Dreier. The League proposed to organise all female workers into unions, then to secure equal citizenship for women, an eight-hour day, equal pay for equal work and a living wage. Compared with the progress made by women workers before it entered the field, the League was very successful in its organisation work. By 1908 it had placed women organisers in four cities and with the support of sixty-one international unions it induced the Federation to appoint another.

But the League recognised the need, on which the Federation had insisted, for a better instructed body of organisers and rank and file membership. It therefore undertook a campaign of instruction which may be described as a form of Workers' Education. At the first biennial convention in 1907 a recommendation was made that each local league establish classes for the discussion of the struggle going on between workers and employers. In 1911 the New York League carried the matter a step further by proposing a series of pamphlets for class use on such subjects as *The Development of Society*, *The History of Industry*, *Land*, *Labour*, *Capital*, *Rent*, *Wages*, *Profits*, *The Structure of Trade Unions in America*, and *The History of the Labour Movement in England and America*. In the same year, after the great garment strike, the Chicago League offered instruction to foreign-born working women in which English and trade unionism were taught at the same time. In 1914 the League opened, in Chicago, a School for Organisers to train women for their trade union vocation. Classes were organised, with the assistance of neighbouring universities, to give them a systematic knowledge of the movement in which they were to work, and the American Federation of Labour assisted the School with a gift of money.

The history of Workers' Education among the Jews is similar to that among women. Its development in each case was due to a desire to secure emancipation from burdensome economic and social disabilities and to aid trade union organisation. As aliens, however, the Jews laboured under the additional difficulties of the foreign-born. As the most depressed and dependent nationality in Europe they brought with them from Russia and Poland a diminished sense of personality and the determination to find an outlet that usually goes with it. These factors together with racial homogeneity, industrial solidarity and an intellectual tradition tended ultimately to strengthen collective action. Educational undertakings were pursued with great vigour and the American Federation of Labour was finally forced to capitulate to the new movement.

Several experiments were made by Jewish workers in the first decade of the twentieth century. Among the first of these was the Workers' School established in 1899. Courses in economics, the sciences and socialism were given for several years, after which the school was reorganised into the Workers' Educational League. In 1901 John Deitsch organised the Jewish Workers' League for the purpose of studying industrial and economic problems from a non-partisan standpoint. In 1899 systematic instruction similar to that given later in labour colleges was begun by Thomas Davidson. Davidson was a Scotsman, born in Aberdeen and educated in the university of that city. Opportunities for university teaching came his way but he chose the life of an intellectual free-lance, earning his livelihood by lecturing, writing and teaching private classes but keeping time for leisurely study and long visits to Europe. He regarded University students, animated mainly by the desire to fit themselves for a congenial and comfortable berth in life, as unpromising material. Only during the last years of his life did he succeed in finding a class of students with whom he could work with entire satisfaction.

In the winter of 1900 Davidson was asked to give a lecture to an audience composed largely of working men and women. This New York East Side audience of Russian, Polish and Hungarian Jews were made up of Marxian socialists, anarchists, single-taxers and the like who showered questions upon the lecturer which were, however, in his words "good-natured, completely serious and deserving of utmost consideration." This lecture was succeeded by many others which formed the instruction offered by what came to be known as the Breadwinners' College.

After the death of Davidson the enthusiasm which had helped to make the Breadwinners' College so important a factor in the intellectual ferment in the East Side of New York was continued. Classes, lectures and educational committees were organised in local unions. When in 1914, the task of creating stable unions and a loyal rank and file was approaching a satisfactory conclusion, the International Ladies' Garment Workers' Union led the way in establishing the Workers' University and secured for the undertaking the blessing of the American Federation of Labour.

II. *The contemporary position in the United States*

In spite of the retarded development of working-class consciousness, the modifying influence of a middle-class educational tradition and the obstructive tactics of the American Federation of Labour, Workers' Education in the United States has become a fact. Twenty years after the foundation of the Breadwinners' College and the School for organisers, two hundred separate classes for the instruction of working men and women had opened their doors. In 1924 these agencies were scattered from coast to coast, in thirty-one States and about ninety cities. In New York City there were more than twenty; in Boston, five; in Chicago, five. Twenty-five thousand men and women are said to have been enrolled. Since then there has been considerable development.

With the exception of the schools organised by the women workers and the Jewish clothing unions, none of them, however, traced their lineage to earlier experiments in the United States. Nor were they begun early in the twentieth century. The educational ideals of Thomas Davidson fell for fifteen years on barren ground. The movement did not actually get under way until the outbreak of war in Europe. And for some time after the inspiration of leaders seems to have been drawn from British rather than American sources.

It is impossible in a short account of this kind to follow all the post-war developments in detail. No such attempt, therefore, will be made here. But this review cannot be brought to a close without something in the nature of a picture of the contemporary position of adult and workers' education. Accordingly, the author has hit upon the device of reproducing here, with the permission of the Editor, an article he wrote for *Cambria*, a journal of Adult Education and Social Service in Wales, immediately after his return from America. As will be seen it is an impressionistic sketch rather than a report based on a comprehensive investigation and obviously it is not up-to-date but it is hoped it may serve its present purpose.

"ADULT EDUCATION IN THE UNITED STATES"

"The United States is a country of extremes—extremes of climate, ranging from 40 below zero to 112 in the shade; extremes in the distribution of wealth, ranging from multi-millionaires like John D. Rockefeller, Henry Ford and Harkness, to miners in the Pennsylvania bituminous coalfield whose lot is more miserable than that of the South Wales miners even to-day; and extremes of thought, from the most advanced thinking about religion and social customs to the lowest level of superstitious ignorance. Similarly, the field of adult education ranges from a Department of Workers' Education in the University of California at Berkeley —I have yet to see University notepaper in this country adorned with the heading 'Department of Workers' Education'—to Adult Education Classes which are nothing more than classes designed for the instruction of immigrants in the elements of the English language and the requirements of American citizenship with a view to naturalisation.

"Adult Education in America is in a chaotic state. In this brief article I shall not attempt an adequate explanation—the main factor is that it is such a huge and comparatively new country —and can do no more than refer to the chief institutions and the most promising developments.

"There is nothing in America corresponding to the Workers' Educational Association. There is no network of classes covering the whole country, particularly the industrial districts, which is an outstanding and one of the finest features of the social life of Great Britain. There are universities everywhere. Every State has its university, endowed by the State and almost free to students resident in the State, and in addition there are universities ranging from the great privately endowed and expensive institutions like Harvard, Yale and Princeton for men, and Bryn Mawr, Vassar and Smith College for women, to hundreds of local, denominational colleges studded all over the States, distinct from a national denominational college like Swarthmore, Philadelphia (a Quaker institution), or Howard University, Washington, D.C., which is the national negro university. And the majority of these universities have extension and correspondence departments. Columbia, in New York City, for example, meets the needs of something like 20,000 extension students, and an even larger number of men and women who are taught by correspondence. At Fairmont, West Virginia, I met an old farmer and his wife, both obviously over sixty, who were taking correspondence lessons under Columbia University in English Literature. They had worked hard all their lives, he said, had saved enough to live on, and now wanted to enjoy life! The University of Wisconsin (at Madison, probably the best State University in America) also has a huge extension department. But I found that the great majority of the extension students were studying in order to improve their qualifications for jobs. When the economic motive was not predominant, the desire was for more or less aesthetic studies, such as the appreciation of music, painting, sculpture, literature, dramatic criticism, elocution. Only at Berkeley, California, did I find extra-mural students of a university who studied the social sciences because they were intelligently interested in the social and industrial organisation, and had no axe to grind. Nowhere else is there anything resembling the British Joint Committee system.

"The nearest approach to the W.E.A. in America is the Workers' Educational Bureau (W.E.B.), with Headquarters in New York. The Secretary, Mr. Spencer Miller, is an enthusiast in the cause of adult education, and would make an admirable Secretary of the English W.E.A., but he seems to occupy in the field of adult education much the same place as that held in the whole field of organised labour by the American Federation of Labour (A.F. of L.), which, judged by European standards, is a decidedly reactionary body. He gives one the impression of having a bigger conception of adult education than he is able to put into practice, bound as he is by the horizon of the A.F. of L. which finances the classes and publications of the W.E.B. This organisation sponsors a number of so-called Labour Colleges, which roughly correspond in point of organisation to the classes supported by the London Labour College in the industrial areas of Great Britain, but the resemblance ends there. As for the character of the teaching in the two types of classes, the American Labour Colleges are palest pink compared with the deepest red of the Central Labour College here. I attended a Labour College Class at Pittsburg. The lecturer possessed academic achievement, industrial experience and courage. (He resigned his instructorship later because the university authorities objected to his activities in connection with the killing of a Polish miner by 'coal and iron' police.) But though he was an excellent teacher, the content of his lecture was distinctly puerile, and the students were the most 'milk and watery' types I have seen anywhere. Not a coal-miner or steel-worker in the class, in Pittsburg!

"I came into contact with various groups of Communists, but so far as I could discover, there are no systematic classes for the study of Marxian Economics sponsored by any trade union. The Rand School of Socialism, in New York, conducts many day and evening classes, offers a great variety of courses, and runs an apparently prosperous publishing and bookselling business. As its name implies, all of its activities are avowedly propagandist. New York contains a number of interesting institutions and workers in one phase or another of adult education. The Labour Temple is smaller and less socialistic than the Rand School, but provides courses designed for the more popular type of student, specialising in debates conducted by well-known economists, psychologists, sociologists, educationists, etc. The New School of Social Research conducts courses given by distinguished scholars who for the most part are no longer attached to universities, e.g. Mr. H. W. L. Dana, formerly a professor at Columbia, and Dr. Harry Elmer Barnes, till recently a professor at Smith College—rebels against the university system. Cooper College is a remarkable institution and attracts a large number of working men and women of all kinds of occupations. Dr. Everett Dean Martin is head of a People's College, and writes and lectures on adult education all over the country. Dr. E. C. Lindeman, another authority, is a free-lance lecturer, and has done much by his writings to stimulate interest in this field. The New York School of Social Work has an excellent staff, including Dr. John Fitch and Mr. Walter Pettit, has done more than any other institution I know of in this country to give social workers a scientific training for their job, and turns out graduates of an excellent type, entirely different from the traditional, philanthropic type of 'social worker.' In New York, too, is the office of the Institute of Adult Education, which attempts to co-ordinate the various institutions working in the field of adult education, publishes a useful magazine, and serves as a kind of clearing-house. The extension work of Columbia University has already been referred to. The University of New York and the New York City College are also very active in extension work; a large proportion of the students of these Colleges are Jews (New York has a population of two million Jews) and 'foreigners' of all kinds, and very keen students they are. There are also the classes of the Greater New York Central Trades and Labour

Council, and of the Workers' University of the International Ladies' Garment Workers Union.

"I visited the Illinois, Pennsylvania (anthracite and bituminous), West Virginia, Alabama and Colorado coalfields, spending about a month in each, and while my research was specifically an economic and social study of the coal industry, I was greatly interested in the educational life of the coal-mining communities, and never missed an opportunity of visiting schools of different types and of investigating facilities in the way of classes for adults. In each coalfield there are classes where the men can study the different technical aspects of the industry—surveying, physics and chemistry of mining, mining engineering and the like, and also first-aid classes—usually meeting in the local high school in the evenings, or in remote isolated camps, as, for example, in West Virginia, in the local community centre, supported by the local operator. But in not a single coalfield to-day are there any classes in the social sciences. Some few years ago the United Mine Workers of America (Sub-District Five in Illinois) appointed a director of workers' education who conducted classes in Economics attended by coal-miners, but after a brief run of success, the classes more or less 'fizzled out,' and the teacher, Mr. Tom Tippett, an excellent man for the work, is now on the staff of Brookwood College as Director of Extension work.

"Brookwood is a co-educational residential workers' educational institution, situated in lovely country about forty miles from New York, near the small town of Katonah. It thinks of itself as part of the labour movement of America and of the world. It tries to assist its students to an understanding, by means of study, analysis and discussion, of the philosophy and policies of the American Federation of Labour and other organisations and groups in the labour movement of America and of the world, endeavouring primarily to teach students how to think, not to tell them what to think. The Chairman of the Staff, Mr. A. J. Muste, formerly a Nonconformist minister, is in a difficult position, for the A.F. of L. regards the College as being too 'red' and the Communist group accuses it of a partiality for 'pink.' As he put it to me, he is 'between the devil and the deep blue sea.' He has a few well-to-do supporters, but the present situation of Brookwood is precarious, and the only thing certain about its future is that it is decidedly uncertain.

"Another interesting residential college is Commonwealth College in the State of Arkansas, the main feature of which is that the students earn their education, so to speak, by working at the college in various occupations. I can do no more than refer to it here. Better known on this side is Antioch College, in Ohio, where an attempt is made to combine practical experience of manufacturing, engineering, agriculture, etc., with an academic training, the practical and theoretical courses covering alternate periods of six weeks. Dr. Meiklejohn's Experimental College (a school of the University of Wisconsin) is an intensely interesting place, but this perhaps would more fittingly be included in a survey of university education. Dr. Meiklejohn, himself, however, is keenly alive to the importance of all phases of adult education, and one of the most treasured memories of my sojourn in America is an afternoon spent at his home, where for three hours he and Dr. Joseph K. Hart (an authority on the Danish High Schools) and I discussed American and European experiments in adult, workers' and university education.

"One of the most promising developments in the States is the movement for the education of women industrial workers. For several years a highly successful Summer School for women has been held in the beautiful buildings and grounds of Bryn Mawr, one of the finest women's colleges in America. The students are drawn from a considerable variety of occupations and are of varying degrees of preliminary equipment, some of them incapable of composing a simple essay. The staff is recruited from different universities, the assumption being that the best is not too good for such students, though occasionally a professor new to this kind of enterprise fails to adapt himself to the requirements of the students. The story is told of one of the students at the Bryn Mawr Summer School, who, urged by some of her fellow students, ventured at length to blurt out to the lecturer, who was gaily sailing over their heads: 'Say, Mister, your language just skids off our domes!' The moving spirit behind these Summer Schools is Miss Hilda Smith, a graduate of Bryn Mawr, a charming woman who is devoting her life to the education of women engaged in industry. In recent years a Summer School was established at Madison to serve the North and within the last two years another has been started in the South. In connection with the Summer Schools, a residential college has been organised near Poughkeepsie where Vassar College (Women's) is situated; students and staff of Vassar give their services to the industrial women's college.

"An extremely interesting summer school is held at the University of California at Berkeley. This is attended by about 150 teachers and others interested in the cultural, sociological and administrative aspects of Adult Education.

"Reference may also be made to the Y.W.C.A. which does a considerable amount of educational work among women all over the States–far more and better work than that of the Y.M.C.A.; the Chatauqua, which specialises in summer camps where educational work of a popular and of a somewhat religious flavour is done, the enrolment (men and women) in some cases amounting to several hundreds; forums, which are conducted in all large centres of population, where various aspects of educational, political and social problems are discussed by the audience after a debate or address from the platform—quite a remarkable feature of American life; and lastly, the multitudinous men's and women's luncheon clubs which meet regularly throughout the winter months to hear lectures by experts on a wide variety of topics—a far more highly developed form of popular adult education (made appetising by an attractive meal) than we have over here, especially among women.

"Such is a rough picture of American adult education. It is certainly in a chaotic condition, but let us remember that the pioneers over there are faced with tremendous difficulties, and while one can sympathise with the almost pessimistic despair of pioneers in the American field, one cannot help feeling an immense admiration of their achievements. May they, and their sons and daughters, continue with the great work."

CHAPTER V

INFLUENCE OF THE PHYSICAL AND SOCIAL
ENVIRONMENT ON THE LIFE OF THE MINER

CHAPTER V

INFLUENCE OF THE PHYSICAL AND SOCIAL ENVIRONMENT ON THE LIFE OF THE MINER

THERE is no need at this time of day to devote much attention to the hereditary *versus* environment controversy, which raged so fiercely in the Victorian era. The author's own view will be stated quite briefly. It is that while heredity, which may itself be favourably affected by improved social conditions operating over long periods of time, sets the limits to original equipment, environment, including agencies of training, determines the limits of development. It follows that, where there is no variation of original stock, a bad environment will prevent full development and a healthy physical and social environment will promote development to the fullest capacity. In an earlier chapter an attempt was made to analyse the stock from which the American and British mining population has been drawn. We found that the American miners shew an extremely wide range of racial composition, including native-born, white and black, and a tremendous influx of varied European elements; and that, apart from a relatively insignificant influx of foreign workmen, the miners of Great Britain are all English, Scottish, Welsh or Irish—"all British," in fact, with the doubtful exception of the Pats and the Mikes!

It now remains to describe the physical and social environment of the two mining populations and to consider its influence upon them. We shall then be able to see what manner of man the British miner is and how, if at all, the American miner differs from him.

With regard to British conditions and type the author, instead of writing a long description himself, proposes to rely largely on the following extracts: they are taken from a batch of essays written at a Summer School in 1932 by his own students who for the most part are themselves miners in the South Wales coalfield. The subject of the essay was the same as the title of this chapter, but when it was set the students had no idea that use might be made of their work and the author had no intention at the time of exploiting it. It should be explained that the essays, several of them covering ten pages of foolscap, were written in the students' own time amid all the allurements of sea-bathing, warm evenings and a general holiday atmosphere and that no assistance whatever was given in the way of treatment, composition, etc. Not all of the students were miners: a few were teachers, clerks, iron and steel workers and fitters and one was a retired postman, sixty-two years of age. The three women teachers were daughters of miners and the other teacher was the son of a miner. It may be added that some of the essays have not been made use of at all, partly because other essays made the same points more effectively, partly because of a lack of originality. The initials and occupations of the students are given.

The extracts are grouped under four heads and are given just as they were written:

  I. Working and Living Conditions.
  II. Ameliorative influences.
  III. General Observations.
  IV. Characteristics of the Miner.

THE SOUTH WALES COALFIELD

I. Working and Living Conditions

T. J. M. (Miner, married, unemployed.)

"The existing conditions must have a terrible psychological effect and cause unnecessary suffering and life becomes a series of monotonous gasps. The working surroundings of the miner are obviously unnatural and are as hard and cruel as any nature ever designed, and it is imperative that his entire mental and physical faculties are expended to produce what is expected of him. To return home to squalid or over-crowded dwellings cannot appease the reaction of hard and almost savage labour. If the home is within the vicinity of the mines even the eye finds no rest. However crude the natural landscape might have been it is now obliterated with scabs of derelict works or debris. . . . So life is devoid of variety so necessary to make life a little more possible. It may of course speed the change of the present system. But the effects upon the children is certainly to be lamented, and the life of the women is unbelievably miserable. The children must worry her beyond reason when there is a lack of room,

SOCIAL SCIENCE CLASS, GLAMORGAN C.C. SUMMER SCHOOL, UNIVERSITY COLLEGE, SWANSEA, 1932
These are the students from whose essays extracts are given in Chapter V. The lady on the right of the author (centre) is his colleague, Dr. Ida Saxby.

Inset the author and his wife "on top" after a visit underground in a mine in Colorado.

while her home work appears uncompleted, tending to strain the domestic relations of man and wife."

B. D. (Miner.)

"Primarily his occupation is an arduous one that has little use for the weaklings, it demands good physique, and quite soon shows that the 'survival of the fittest' law is exemplified. His work is conducted amongst poisonous gases, and an impure atmosphere, bad lighting almost darkness, dirt and uncomfortable positions, a constant possibility of falls from the roof, continual minor injuries, repeated difficulties continually presenting themselves, and in some of the deeper mines and even in the return sections of the more shallow undertakings, he is fatigued by the rather warm and partially vitiated atmosphere. In different seams, different depths of mines, different qualities of the stratum the general conditions set out above are oft-times altered, but one factor may be generally considered as balancing another, so that it will be within the bounds of truthfulness to allow of these conditions being general of the miners' physical working hours environment."

R. M. (Costings clerk.)

"Everyone will agree that there is no other industry that presents such risks, and that has more hazardous working conditions, than that of coal mining. The burning of coal has become so commonplace to some people that the thought of the steps taken to procure it never enters their mind, and their only interest is directed towards their Coal Merchant, and the fear of being overcharged.

"If mining is really then so dangerous to the worker, how important must it be for his life above the surface to be one of contentment, and a life where he can forget all about 'conveyors' and 'main headings.' . . .

"Consider the district in which he lives, and in which the greater part of his life will be spent. A visit to the mining valleys of our districts tells its own story. Gaunt, black tips, rearing their heads to the sky, with the fields around in which the grass looks a dirty green. Terraces of houses perched precariously on the mountain sides, with the smoke hanging lazily over the valley, and add to this the scene in the valley below. Houses almost

BB

unfit for habitation, shops with the windows boarded in, a dirty, sluggish stream winding its way down to a still more dreary district, and even the chapels have such a drab outer appearance, surely a scene hardly fit for a man after having toiled below underground."

C. W. (Clerk, insurance agent, unemployed, student at residential college for working men, now doing valuable voluntary work at settlement centre for unemployed.)

"I have it is true spent some time among a community composed entirely of miners. A time composed of some of the most impressionable years of a man's life—the very early twenties—but so tremendous a subject and so great a cause as that of the miner requires a searching examination over a considerable period and it is regrettable that so little is known by many people and so little information is forthcoming of the actual social conditions of the British miner. Let us hope that in the near future both these omissions will be rectified and that the necessary steps will be taken to give the miners that very high standard of living, economically, socially and intellectually, which is his by virtue of the great sacrifice he has made for and the tremendous contribution he has made to the advance of civilisation. . . .

"Take a common scene. Long rows of houses situated along or up on the mountain side. Badly designed, badly constructed. Lavatories situated next to the larder and over both a bedroom the window of which cannot be opened otherwise the exhalations come in and with many other discomforts hinders the occupants sleep. In the streets the ceaseless noise of children playing in this case the disgraceful lack of playing fields force the children on to the streets while the older girls are treated likewise not from lack of employment but because they are not given a decent standard of living. . . . Bedrooms like mouse traps, kitchens like cells. The whole resembling more vaults that are hiding the dead than houses that are sheltering the living. Nearby the railway with its snorting and whistling engines its bumping and clanging trucks. The funnels of the engines competing with the stacks of the collieries in belching forth clouds of filthy and acrid smoke. This is not exaggerated description. It may be the worst aspect of the case. Let us hope it is. God forbid that there be worse than what I have seen and attempted to describe."

J. R. R. (Tailor in mining town, unemployed, son of a miner.)

"He exists, rather than lives in a home or more often a hovel, a four, five, or six roomed house with usually no bathroom (the percentage of bathrooms to the average collier's home is very small) and situated quite close to the colliery. He leaves his home about five o'clock in the morning, arrives at the Pit-head, a noisy, stuffy glade amid the towering buildings that house the various types of machinery; he walks heavy-footed from the lamp-room, with lamp slung from his braces or his pockets, to the cage and is presently descending into those black dusty depths. Arriving at the 'bottom' he walks perhaps two or three miles along the 'levels' dodging under low hanging roofs and timber and jumping abruptly into a 'man-hole' or gap left in the side when a 'journey of trams' approaches, for there is no room to spare in these narrow levels . . . and eventually reaches his 'stall' or working place. Removing his coat and vest, and as it often happens in collieries where the air supply is faulty, his shirt and trousers too, and working only in shorts, he proceeds to 'hew' or cut the coal away from the 'face' or wall of coal. In most collieries there is a superabundance of insect and rodent pests, and the miner has often to hang his superfluous clothes from a piece of rope with a wire hook at the bottom, to prevent the Blackbeetles and Cock-roaches from swarming over them. Also there are thousands of rats or mice to be found or rather obtruding themselves. In the course of a 'shift' or working day of eight hours, the collier may with the help of a 'boy' remove eight to ten tons of coal, a few tons of 'small' and a great deal of rubbish, and may also put up some timber, with which to 'hold the roof'; he is not paid for any small coal he may load into the trams, and for every ton of coal he raises a penny also goes to the Miners' Welfare Fund, an ingenious institution whereby the Coalowners assure that this money is not spent in any way detrimental to their interests. About two or three o'clock the miner leaves his stall for home and after negotiating the crowded levels is presently on his way up the street. During his day's work he has faced the many dangers of a collier's normal working day—falls of roof, runaway 'trams,' gas in 'pockets,' or a flood of water or as sometimes happens, gas, danger of an explosion and the many smaller but disagreeable incidents that crowd around the collier's working hours.

"He walks or, if the distance is too great, rides wearily homeward, past dusty, dirty heaps of rubbish, coal heaps, rusty piles of metal,—in short he passes through the colliery yard, reaches the first rows of cottages and if in a reflective mood, notes the general dirt, dustiness and air of moral degradation of the average collier's home. He reaches his own, and perhaps a little more cleanly and comfortable home (for he may be of a more thoughtful and careful type) steps through the doorway, carefully avoiding his wife's clean floor, removes his clothes and proceeds to bath himself in the familiar tub, which his thoughtful wife has all ready for him. Having finished this very necessary task, he seats himself for a very welcome meal. Often he falls asleep without having eaten, too tired for anything else."

T. B. (Miner, of considerable experience of miners' union organisation.)

"A chat with our fathers or other old miners on the conditions under which they worked and lived 40 and 60 years ago would enlighten us in our study. Indeed, it is very interesting when one reflects of the changes which have taken place in the short life of us the younger miners. Such improvements give us optimism and hope for bigger and more permanent improvements in a different system of society.

"Many an old miner living to-day can tell a pitiful tale of his boyhood days, and the conditions under which he and his lived.

"At nine or ten, and sometimes even younger than that, they were taken by their fathers to the pit, in most cases before they were given a day's schooling. Not to work seven or eight hours, but twelve and sometimes fourteen hours a day. For certain months in the year they saw daylight but once a week—that once being on a Sunday. The work they did was often more suitable for ponies than boys. For this they were paid a few pence a day, which they received at the end of the month or six weeks. We must remember that safety regulations at these times were very limited, and their methods of ventilating the mines were what we would call to-day primitive and antiquated.

"They returned home to hovels in most cases, and the instance in mind is a two-roomed house, occupied by his four brothers, four sisters, father and mother. To augment the family income two lodgers were boarded, both being pit workers. To complete the picture some of the girls also worked at the pit. Needless to say that at the end of the day it was a case of mixed bathing. This was not an exceptional case, but typical of the time. The lad referred to here when he was twelve years of age spent what leisure time and money he had in the public house. The environment was conducive to this kind of habit. Home comfort there was none, and the very bad working conditions demanded some relaxation. There were but scanty facilities for healthy recreation in the way of sports. The village boys would have an occasional game of 'bando': a game what our higher schools call 'hocky.' One village team would play against a neighbouring team. Educational facilities were even less. Newspapers were a luxury which the better type of family would indulge in once a week. Libraries and reading rooms were out of the question. Their lives under such conditions were distorted, and they had no vision. They had little conception of better housing and sanitary conditions, not to mention educational and recreational; their lives were narrow and their disposition selfish.

"Improvements have been brought about in the working and social conditions of the miners by Parliament from time to time. These may be crumbs from off the rich man's table, and times may have demanded them, nevertheless they have given the miner a fuller life and a better conception of what life should be. The goal has not been reached, but the small reforms that we have had have been beneficial inasmuch as they have made the miner think—and have broadened his outlook. He begins to realise that he is intended for more than to be a pawn in the game.

"Free education to children up to fourteen years of age and better facilities for a secondary education, evening classes for young workers is undoubtedly the greatest boon the workers of the nation have had. In the words of Trotsky 'The education of the young is for us a matter of life and death.' Here is the foundation stone.

"Improved safety regulations, better lighting; shortening of the working day; the minimum wage act; miners' welfare schemes; all have, it is true helped to improve and brighten the draby environment of the miners.

"The social environment, in spite of the present day trade depression, has been improved by building better houses under a better planning system. Pit head baths, which are unfortunately not yet compulsory go a very long way to make more happy the miner's family.

"A good deal can be said for our free libraries and reading rooms, cheaper literature and free lectures; cinemas and theatres; parks and playing fields.

"The injured and sick miner is somewhat better cared for than he was at the very early part of the century. The compensation acts and the national health insurance scheme—very imperfect admitted—yet a decided improvement.

"We have yet a long way to go. The path may not be strewn with roses; but it is for the miners and all other workers to take advantage educational and otherwise to bring about a system of society, which will give them a heritage which is theirs."

II. Ameliorative Influences

(NOTE.—Initials only are given where the student has already been described.)

R. M.

"As good a way as any to probe the subject of this essay would be to try and imagine two miners returning from work say before and after the war. Consider first the pre-war miner. He comes out at the Pithead and perhaps it is raining. Everything around is dull and gloomy. His journey home leads him through puddles and streams, perhaps an ugly tip on the right and rows of dilapidated houses on the left. By the time he reaches home—thoroughly wet through, with a temper none too good, he is certainly in no fit state to greet his wife. Perhaps he has to wait some time before he can bath, incidentally in the same room that he takes his food, and when he is washed and dressed where can he go? Education facilities (if he is that way inclined) may not be any too good in his district, and nearly always he is left with the alternative of having to spend the time at the Street Corners. Here with his fellow men he breeds discontent and a dislike against those who are better off than himself, so that when he does return to work, rather than feeling contented with his lot, he is more ready to take part in any movements of disturbance and unrest among the workmen.

"Now turn to the present day miner, living in a well developed social community. He laughs at the rain that greets him at the

top, because he knows as he walks to the Pithead Baths that there
a complete change of dry and well-aired clothes await him.
After having bathed and dressed in comfort he leaves the Baths,
after having made sure that his Pit clothes will be quite dry and
ready for him, when he returns to work. His way home may lead
him through new housing sites with garden plots and pleasant
surroundings. He, too, may possess one of these new houses,
with all modern conveniences, and when he arrives there (in a
happy frame of mind), partakes of his food with a wife who has
infinitely less work to do, than she did 20 years ago. He is happy
also in the thought of his child who is attending the Secondary
School, and of the Class also that he intends to attend at night.
Or if he wishes he can go down to the Bowling Greens, etc.,
that have taken the place of the years-old-tips. Everything around
him goes towards improving his environment, and although it
would not be well to paint too rosy a picture of it all, it would be
safe to say that he is a better workman and citizen for it all."

J. C. (Miner, unemployed.)

"Pithead Baths should be as necessary to a pit as the winding
gear."

A. D. (Miner who has worked underground in the United States
and in South Wales.)

"One of the bright spots in the communal life of the British
miner is the great strides made in Welfare work."

H. M. (Miner, unemployed.)

"The houses have been built by the . . . Rural District Council.
It is a little garden city of about 200 houses, all fitted with inside
lavatories, water supply, and bathrooms. They have also been
fitted with electrical equipment, in readiness for a scheme now
under construction by the council, for lighting the district.

"A large percentage of the people, who now occupy these
new houses, came from the basement hovels that surrounded the
old iron works. The authority having had State aid to build a
large number of these houses, to replace basements and condemned
houses were now obliged to give these people first choice. This
has given us an excellent opportunity of studying these people
in a changed environment.

"Some of these people were of a low type and their children were destined to follow in their trend, but a change of surroundings has saved the majority from that fate. Spacious rooms, water facilities, bathrooms, pretty outside greens, and sizable gardens have created a desire to furnish the inside of the house, so as to compare favourably with the outside. Some families have undergone a complete change, the children can be seen going to school early and clean, rather than dirty and late. Some of them have gained scholarships to the secondary school. This has in some cases I know, stimulated such an interest in the parents, that they have completely changed their habits, previously they were content on drink and gambling, now they have turned to evening classes, and the cheap recreational facilities given by the Miners' Welfare. There are, of course, exceptions but they are very few, only complete change in working and living conditions could alter these people."

H. J. O. (Miner, unemployed, married.)

"The only relaxation offered to the men in the older days was a visit to the Public House.

"If they refrained from drinking, then their only outlet was in the church or chapel.

"Small wonder is it then, that they were narrow-minded, dogmatic and intolerant.

"As the conditions of the houses and the towns grew better and the children having an elementary education, the miner became a better informed and better type of person. Improvement of the environment led to an improvement of the mind." . . .

"The advantages of houses with bathrooms, kitchen ranges, built in wardrobes and electric light, are realised, and they are becoming more and more realised.

"Beauty and convenience are combined, the love of beauty is stimulated, the good things of life are appreciated, because they (the miners) have seen the sordid and ugly things of life. Much of the beauty of life, whether in possessions, or persons, is hidden, but I believe that the miner, with his general alertness and his natural ability to adapt himself to changing conditions is quick to realise the beauty that surrounds him and the beauty that could be, if the people only willed.". . .

"*The musical associations* are many and varied, first we have

the choral Societies, second Symphony Orchestras, third Brass
Bands. These three form the main interest, although Dramatic
Societies have a strong footing in parts.

"At least 90 per cent of the members of the 'South Wales and
Monmouthshire Brass Band Association' are working miners.

"The development and continuation of these societies depend
solely on the economic prosperity of the coal industry. Though
even in difficult times, the men struggle to keep them going, as
proved by the number of competitors from practically derelict
areas in the last National Eisteddfod. The works of the Masters,
are the most enjoyed i.e. Beethoven, Handel, Wagner, Bach etc.
The urge to achieve something grand is predominant, and the
execution of the pieces compare favourably with any amateur
society in the country.

"*Workmen's Halls and Institutes.*—There has been a great
advance in the numbers erected during the last few years. The
need for a place to hold meetings that affect the life of the workers
have been fully realised.

"A typical institute comprises a reading room, library, lecture
room, band room and a billiard room. Above, is the cinema, or
large hall, where the mass meetings are held. The workmen pay
a weekly contribution towards the upkeep of such institutes.

"Among other organisations that the men maintain, are some
very interesting and useful schemes. First, a Benevolent Fund,
from which a member receives assistance if he has been ill, or
had an accident in work, after he has been home a certain length
of time. Second, Funeral and Coffin Fund. This provides a coffin,
hearse and coaches, at the death of a member or his wife, besides
a sum of money, usually £10. In this, you see a tendency to form
a community unto themselves, the end in view being, mutual
assistance in time of need. These funds were started originally
to prevent exploitation, which was rampant.

"*Trade Union Life.*—Practically all believe in and support the
trade union movement. They have a keen and militant organisation.
The miners have long realised that 'united we stand, divided we
fall.' Firm believers in the Trade Union Congress, by co-operation
all things are possible.

"It appears to me that the social life and environment of the
miner, has enabled him to see and recognise men for what they
really are. That sympathy without action is useless.

"The reason that better housing facilities have not been demanded in larger numbers is due to the depression in the industry, with its resultant effects on the men. Low wages, part-time employment and unemployment, have made it impossible for them to have made an *effective demand*. If, and when, prosperity returns to the South Wales coalfield, the development of the social life, and the social consciousness of the miners will be a tremendous surprise in its size and magnitude to all but the keenest observers."

T. J. M.

"Better housing would affect the psychology of the worker in an advantageous manner. His work with its economic difficulties would produce the essential stimulus towards changing the system, and the comforts of home life with the accompanying ease of domestic estrangement, would assist clearer thinking, and lay the foundation for a true and humane society.

"To meet housing difficulties many schemes have been devised. The two important are Company and municipal building schemes by direct or indirect labour. In some cases the Company schemes have proved up to a point a success, but from the workers' standpoint they can never satisfactorily meet the needs of workers, as the municipal endeavours in this direction could. There is always a danger of workers having to submit to unjust treatment to maintain his house if Company owned.

"One particular Company built a group of houses, made their own reservoir to supply water, undertook to carry out repairs on the road to save costs in rates. This went well for a time the tenants were expected to do repairs of roads etc., also a fund was created to pay for certain labour. After a time these houses were bought by instalment or other means by private individuals who either moved from the district or let them to others. The reservoir cracked and the water became contaminated. Sidewalks and roads became shapeless and the roads developed into cesspools, which was inevitably unpleasant. Funds could not be collected, tenants would not pay while owner tenants objected because the others would not pay. The local council could not take over the system until a sum per house was paid. Economic conditions made this difficult so they suffered under protest.

"Municipal building is by far preferable as it can be controlled by the worker, and the site planned for his benefit, while the question of repairs would be a general concern to maintain the value.

"With regard to recreation the welfare schemes appear to have functioned successfully and have, whatever may be one's opinions, supplied to a great extent what the workers have demanded in recreation. It is futile to argue that schemes of this kind obscure the intrinsic evils. The mass in all economic epochs demand reforms, and although students see a little beyond and realise that reforms would not be necessary were there not a cause, we must face the fact that the sooner reforms are tried and as we prognosticate will be found wanting the quicker will the mass appreciate the necessity for changing the system. Often the more the worker attains in the minor things of life the more he demands, and he becomes just as dissatisfied when he becomes accustomed to a reform as before he acquired it.

"To argue it is detrimental, or that it appeases the essence of change, is to imply that our forefathers should not have advocated for less hours, old age pensions, reliefs or education. We are no more satisfied than our predecessors. All reforms are educational and more is desired until the system fails to meet the demand upon it, then it will have to pay the penalty. If the system had no demands made upon it, it might live indefinitely and it is humanly impossible to visualise a scheme of things wherein the mass could remain docile asking for nothing until all attain the same mental outlook, then suddenly evolving from comparative cave dwellers to modern houses with hot and cold water and garage. Thinkers of economics may realise the ultimate of economic felicity, they must not ignore the conflicting psychology factors. We know too well the futility of charity, but the various emotions essential to communal life coerce us to help a fellow sufferer, does this act assist the system or do we revolt at the need for charity, as the receiver revolts at the need of applying for such. A great economist said the psychology reacts to economic circumstance. Therefore the demarcation line of economic pressure must be reached before the psychology diverts into broader channels.

"The instinct of self-preservation forces the mass to clamour for reform, while the parental instinct demands better education for the children, to avoid the privations the parents suffered.

"But innovation does not permanently satisfy but only whets the appetite for more."

C. W.

"Together with the conditions in the home and the conditions in work there is a third factor to be considered—educational and recreational facilities. Notwithstanding the provision that has already been made in the shape of welfare grounds and playing fields the actual enjoyment of such facilities is forbidden to the miner in a great number of cases, by the insuperable cash nexus between him and the controller of the facilities. Prohibitive charges are often made for the use of tennis courts and cricket fields, and the necessary equipment to play such games is so costly as to prevent the miner obtaining it. There is another important factor which must be considered here. While not wishing to underestimate the miner's ability to do either his work or play games . . . it is not surprising that after a long and arduous day's work in the stifling atmosphere of a modern coal mine the miner finds repose in his arm chair more attractive and even more essential than the further exertion required by the playing of games. There is also considerable feeling among miners to-day —especially the more intelligent—that the money used in the provision of recreational activities should be used in the provision of pensions. This is not to be wondered at when one thinks of the tremendous change in the attitude of the miner towards life in the later ages when the desert of old age has been transformed to the paradise of adequate pensions.

"The case against the educational facilities is somewhat similar. I do not wish to enter into a discussion of the ethics or economics of the various evening classes, extension courses or Summer Schools. These things certainly do cater for the felt need of education on the part of the miner. But education was never intended to benefit only one or a few individuals and unfortunately the tendency has been in the past to use the facilities provided to further the interests of the student or the coal owner. The existence of the Miners' Welfare Scholarships for study at Universities has certainly not eliminated this tendency. If anything it has accentuated it, as only a disappointingly small number of those awarded Scholarships return to work with and for their former fellow workers. R. H. Tawney in his recent work *Equality* says 'Surely the greatest use of a noble endowment is not merely to benefit the individual possessor—to allow him to escape from the whirlpool undeterred by the thoughts of his drowning companions.' Yet this is what is done."

B. L. (Teacher.)

"Being the daughter of a miner I know how difficult it is for a miner to take part in a game of tennis. The courts are usually used by women and men who are not miners, and who do not wish to play with an 'ordinary collier.' Imagine the feelings of a miner, who has worked hard all day and therefore deserves a little recreation, but when he joins the so-called aristocrats or 'snobs' in a healthy game of tennis is often ignored. This is truly the position of a . . . miner.

"Having made enquiries concerning the recreational facilities of the Rhondda Valley, for instance in . . . and . . . I have discovered that the miners make great use of the recreational grounds, especially when the work is irregular and they have leisure time. It is very pleasing to think that some miners can join in these pleasures, for they undoubtedly feel brighter after a good game of tennis or cricket.

"It is of vital importance that the miner should avail himself of these recreational facilities. Lack of finance makes it difficult to make these recreational grounds pay, and the result is that many miners' tennis courts have been transformed into putting grounds. It is the duty of the miner to spend his leisure time in these grounds; he is compelled to pay his weekly contribution towards them and any miner who refuses to make use of these facilities by joining in a game of tennis or cricket has himself to blame if the grounds are closed down.

"During the last twenty years considerable progress has been made in the way of educational facilities. Many new senior and central schools have been built of late years. There has been great need of a new school at . . . , and the Central School has come as a great boon to the district. Miners' children are able to enjoy the good education that other children enjoy.

"An important feature in educational equipment is the Miners' Welfare Scholarship. Each year eleven to fifteen scholarships are awarded for entrance to a University College to miners or miners' sons and daughters. It is encouraging to know that

during one year eleven completed this course satisfactorily, and
only five were unsuccessful, due to lack of secondary education.
It would be a valuable feature if more Miners' Welfare Scholarships
were awarded, for there are thousands of brilliant miners, who
through lack of finance are unable to continue with their studies."

NOTE.—It is somewhat surprising that none of the students has referred
to the influence of the cinema, broadcasting, political meetings, billiard
halls, dance halls, attendance at big football and cricket matches, dog
races and boxing fights. These institutions may all be regarded as being
either educational or recreational, although one might not regard them
all as ameliorative agencies! They certainly play a big part in the social
life of the coalfields.

III. General Observations

(NOTE.—As the essays were not arranged under the headings chosen,
some difficulty has been experienced in placing the extracts under their
appropriate heading. It is hoped that the reader will not be too critical
of the classification.)

C. W. (Woman teacher; same initials as unemployed clerk,
        student.)

"It is possible, even common, to under-rate the interacting
influences of industrial prosperity and social conditions. Without
the one the other is not possible. Before the miner may accomplish
anything, before he may even contemplate action, his position in
the mine must be secure and lasting. To-day, the reverse is the
case, and we find that the miner instead of moulding his environment, making of it a fairly habitable land, is weighed down by
it. Depression in trade is everywhere deplorable, but infinitely
more so when the daily outlook of the unemployed miner consists
of his neighbour's back yard, sundry coal and ash tips, the dusty
pit stacks and a dust-parched land. Much is being done nowadays
to alleviate the physical outlook, such as the efforts of the Miners'
Welfare Fund in making a thing of beauty out of the unseemly
places; but this does not attack the root of the evil. Until the man,
the boy, the youngster, obtains work of a lasting character, accompanied by a decent living wage, he will be discontented, unhappy,
a burden on his family and the community. Industrial prosperity
then is the first adjunct of a happy social environment."

J. C.

"Disillusionment and despair now flourish in the mining valleys. The reasons are short time, continued low wages, conditions of work, low roof, broken timber, neglected packing, all making for accidents and death. The industry is run with callous disregard for human values. Some of the officials speak with loathing of what they have to do in the mine. As one said to me, we are compelled to be nigger drivers. It has been the pent-up resentment of workers against nigger driving, the dangerous conditions, the low wages that has provided the stimulus for the stern struggle in the mining areas. . . .

"With all these new developments, housing conditions are still bad for the great majority. Bad housing is a tremendous evil, and has a very bad effect on a miner's life. (1) It has a depressing effect. (2) It breeds tremendous discontent. Not of a social type which would be valuable. But of a peculiar domestic type. Which is bad from a social and cultural outlook generally. It makes people restless and gives them a craving for places where they can get quiet, or change, from uncomfortable home conditions. It drives men to the public house, to the company of other women, anywhere where they can find some kind of quiet and comfort. There is no chance of quiet or cheer in their own home. No companionship even, with their own women. Women get harassed, beyond endurance, nerves frayed, life is hard and unbearable. They become a bundle of nerves and make life a misery for those around them.

"Day after day, they struggle on, lingering out a miserable existence. Without hope or colour. The woman sacrifices everything for her family. I know a large number who are unable to go down to the Welfare park because their clothes are so poor, to enjoy the sunshine and laughter of children, which they enjoy.

"One wonders why they stick out such an existence. My Mother died 56 years of age. I asked the Doctor 'Why? What was wrong?' I was told there was nothing wrong organically. She was simply worn out. Lack of convenience in the home makes a woman's life in the mining area mere slavery. No facilities for bath, constant hot water having to be prepared, pit clothes always drying in front of the fire, as soon as one lot of cleaning is done. Everything again gets covered by dirt and grime when the worker arrives home from work. Only those

who live in a mining valley can appreciate the work entailed for
the women. The constant repetition of work caused through
lack of facilities in the home make them almost beasts of burden.
To-day one can say there is not much interest taken in overcrowding or for better facilities in the home.

"Everything is subordinated by the hard struggle to exist.
The struggle to live is now of primary importance. Can any class
of worker get excited over better housing conditions, when
living conditions progressively worsen. Workers lose all their
independent outlook and spirit. Everything is in a state of flux.
No worker in any home can feel certain he will remain there.
The dread prospect of being sold up for debt hangs over every
miner's home. (Which happened to the writer, after ten years of
continuous bad times, drained of all resources.) To those who
don't get enough to eat, good housing or bad housing assume
small importance in the scheme of things. It is of primary
importance that all culture needs must, if they are to assume
anything, be built up on the foundation of the stomach needs first.

"The majority of mining towns are drab and dreary in nearly
every detail. It is boring to wander from one to the other. One
sees the same long straggling rows of houses, perched on the
hillsides and valleys. The same type of Pits. Same huge sidings,
black with coal, with coal dust flying everywhere. The same
hills, covered with great stacks of slag and rubbish. The same
standardised film advertisements. The same girls with painted
faces, to hide their pale pallor underneath. With their slang
phrases hot from the cinemas, Oh-yea, Baby, Its O.K. with me,
I'll be right there, etc. The same weary looking women, marked
by the hand of hard toil. The same long rows of men aimlessly
rotting their lives out, waiting. The same children looking ill
nourished, ill clad. The same pathetic little attempts of the welfare
schemes to brighten village life. The same petty housing schemes.

"Which only serves to accentuate the general ugliness of everything. One feels one would like to blot it all out and start afresh. . . .

"But apparently the destruction of wealth by the war, the
helpless position the workers find themselves in, through unemployment, etc., as both incited and encouraged the capitalistic
class of Britain and U.S.A. to drive back the mass of the population,
to transfer the huge burdens capitalism has accumulated, off their
shoulders on to the stomach of the working class, through attacking

social services and wages, etc. Not only have wages been attacked but hours of labour and drastic speeding up has developed.

"Also the proportion of the national income allocated to such vital services as health and education has been diminished in order to reduce the income tax. In every industrial town or district, the overcrowding of families, in insanitary and indecent conditions is becoming worse.

"There has also developed a more insidious attack, an attack on popular liberty of action. The practical withdrawal from the trade unions, of their right (Statutory) to determine by majorities their industrial and political activities. Activities of checkweighmen are limited. Such action is bound to develop revolutionary feeling on a large scale. Even the right to sympathetic action in support of others is denied. It is the terrible hard life of the working class, that I feel is responsible for this restless craving for excitement, for pleasures of any kind, a feeling of restless social instability that dominate the people to-day. It is a reaction from the hard realities of life. A craving for something that will help them to forget it, if only for a short period only.

"The Welsh miner is not a natural revolutionary. He is stubborn, when driven, but treated decently, he is much like any other class of worker.

"The revolutionary urges that are now developing is because workers are driven to feel there is no other way out. When milllions are being driven to below any reasonable level of existence, especially those who have enjoyed a better existence and have been educated up to something finer, then the stimuli must develop mass feeling, must bring resentment to boiling point. When that arrives, because everywhere workers are meeting the same difficulties, then it will spread like wild fire. As a student one cannot be afraid of mass movements. Crowds act, like those microbes which hasten the dissolution of enfeebled bodies. When the structure of a civilisation is rotten it is always the mass that bring about its downfall. It is at vital moments in history that their chief mission is visible, that for a little longer the philosophy of numbers seems the only philosophy of history."

V. B. T. (Miner, unemployed, secondary education.)

"The Great War, though it took its toll of the mining community in the way of using its young men as cannon fodder, also brought increased prosperity to the mine owners and incidentally the mine workers, who found their standard of life considerably improved with the increased purchasing power, but Nemesis soon overtook them in the shape of the post-war slump, due to the increased use of other sources of energy, such as oil, electricity, and so on, and the consequent over-production of that previously indispensable source of energy, coal.

"This had a natural repercussion in a lessening number of men being employed, but it is a true saying 'It's an ill wind that blows nobody good'—this enforced idleness was not altogether without its advantages. Men who previously were only cogs in the machine of Capitalism, with the hard work and wear borne by such a position, found themselves free, with time and enough to spare, and turned avidly towards the free libraries and reading rooms of the many workmen's institutes (provided in many cases by that much maligned body—the Committee of the Miners' Welfare Fund).

"Whilst it is true that in the sudden freedom, the bulk of the miners turned to recreation and yet more recreation, a small proportion in numbers, but a fairly high proportion, in terms of effects, took the opportunity of studying sociological and psychological works, with a consequent very useful diffusion of political knowledge being made amongst the mass.

"Despite the abortive attempts, by means of temporary schemes, by the now scared capitalist fraternity to allay the discontent of the more and more freed wage slaves, this is, in my opinion, above all, what is sounding in no uncertain fashion the death knell of Capitalism—Unemployment, and so paving the way to that long dreamed of social community termed 'Utopia.' "

H. M.

"To come to a higher stage of social influence on the life of miners, I believe the continual depression and unemployment of the post-war years is a classic example. It has created a revolution in the attitude of miners toward life and things in general. Though confusion reigned supreme, there is a decided tendency toward conscious and logical thinking. His attitude to religion, convention and morals are gradually changing, he is not content with the old ideas, and is not prepared to accept any new suggestion without careful examination. He seems to be awakening to a higher culture, and were it not for a contrary force, which continually holds him in check, he would go on triumphantly to emancipation. I am referring to the economic problem, for it creates a conflict, a doubt, and a spirit of hopelessness and insecurity in the minds of all.

"This, I believe, is due to the little attention paid to economic and social subjects in our educational schemes. These conflicting forces, trade depression and its consequences, and the all-round improvement in social conditions, have a very marked effect on marriage and family life in general. Small families are the order of the day, in contrast to the large families of a generation ago. Marriage too is postponed till later in life, some authority recently ventured to say, that in a few years, there would be three women to every man in Wales. This of course is due to emigration in quest of work, and to be single is a decided advantage in this matter. This is also applicable to women in a lesser degree, some of them have good posts, which make them think more than once before leaving their jobs to marry a man who is earning less.

"It is a very debatable question, whether we can by improved social conditions completely eliminate all our economic troubles. Be that what it may, we must admit that the social influences that have been at work during the last generation have decidedly produced a better type, than was the case in the previous generation."

S. N. (Rate Collector, formerly miner.)

"It is no happy situation for a boy of 14 to be called upon to follow the life of a miner. The very time when ample opportunity should be given for a free development of his physique the unnatural conditions of underground work is thrust upon him. When his impressionable mind should be allowed to develop in surroundings that are clean and among boys of his own age, he is thrown into the company of men often brutalised and vulgarised by inhuman working conditions. Under such unfortunate conditions 'Jack soon becomes as good as his master.' The boy being father to the man, what chance as the man got when springing from such beginnings?

"The boy when employed as a collier's help soon discovers that the job is no sinecure. He can be very useful particularly where seams are very narrow, in such cases a boy of 14 is much more agile than a fully grown man. So we find a little specialisation goes on in the coal face, the miner hews the coal, while his young helper carries the loose coal to the tub near by. The boy now starts his apprenticeship to the coal industry, and if he is of the average physique, he soon discovers that at the end of the shift he hasn't much surplus energy for sport and means for advancing his position in life. He accepts the life of the mine as his, having been trained for nothing else. . . . It must be borne in mind the task of finding alternative work to that of mining is very much limited. . . .

"This interest in the Community has showed itself in a high degree of political education. One of the striking things about Local Government in mining districts to-day is the number of Local Authorities manned by miners. One of the pleasing things about Authorities so manned is the very real interest taken by them in advancing the well-being of the district.

"The attempts of these Authorities to deal with overcrowding by the creation of houses is very praiseworthy. These attempts are far from being adequate, but most of them have reached the limits of their powers.

"These authorities have been in the forefront in the promotion of Municipal undertakings such as Gas, Electric, Bus and Tram services, which are but a few of their many activities. Mining Communities have sent their representatives, men who have worked in the coal face up to their entry into public life to represent them on such important bodies as County Councils, and practically every M.P. representing the South Wales Coalfield has in some way or other worked in or about the mines.

"Viewing the miner of to-day and comparing him with his forefather his position in society appears to be raised.

"To assess any economic advance is somewhat more difficult. He with other members of any other industrial community is reaping the advantage of certain scientific advancements. The provision for his leisure hours is more varied, the advent of the talkies, the improvement of gramophones, the improvement in communications, the institution of a Miners' Welfare Fund resulting in the institution of Rest Homes, Recreational Schemes, such as bowling greens, tennis courts. The serious attempt on the part of the Welfare Fund Committee to erect pit-head baths: the provision to assist miners who are educating themselves, and also the grants in aid given to educate the sons and daughters of miners, these are but a few of the activities of the Miners' Welfare.

"The growth of Social Services is another consideration in trying to arrive at an assessment. The Maternity and Child Welfare Centres that many authorities have developed to the limits of their powers. These and many other things have to be taken into consideration to judge the miners' present position.

"In unhappy contrast is the miners' weakened position in the colliery. The post-war trade depression has been fully felt in the coal industry. Unemployment has sapped the miners' interest in many of his former activities, trade unionism is at a low ebb, though his working conditions never demanded a keener interest.

"His fighting position being weakened he is often compelled to accept conditions his father would consider intolerable. The older miners remember when the hours of work were much longer than they are at present, but with a corresponding reduction in the hours of labour, there has been a speeding up in the pace of the work. The old working hours were allowed to pass fairly leisurely, the present shorter working day is crowded with bustle.

"Perhaps one of the worst characteristics of the present working conditions is that though dissatisfaction is deep, the fear of unemployment is also great."

C. B. (Fitter.)

"The work of getting coal is drab enough and in years gone by before the recreational side of a man's life was catered for he had to find an outlet somewhere from his environment, and it is possible that it was one of the reasons why so many public houses were built in the mining villages. Incidentally I might mention that in the early days the public houses were built and owned by the colliery owners, it is said to recover some of the wages which they had paid at the pits. The owners saw the demand and they catered for it. It naturally follows that recreation in the open air will fit a man for his work more than the atmosphere of a drinking den. Healthy recreation is not so expensive as the drinking habit. When it came to a dispute with the owners perhaps leading to a strike, the weakest link is always the strongest and those who had spent their wages as they received it were

soon in difficulties, thereby weakening the resistence to the
Employers. . . . The reader must excuse me taking the example
of the public house, being an advocate of temperance it has
always distressed me by the amount of intoxication that was
typical of the mining community and have always put it down
to their drab work and lack of other pursuits."

D. J. D. (Teacher, son of a miner.)

"In a coal producing area there are generally no other mass
workers of other vocations. Miners constitute the bulk of the
population. Two or three decades ago, the administration of the
district was entirely in the hands of the few, whose occupations
were any other than that employed in mining. They were to a
great extent property owning individuals whose claims to literacy
and social position were above that of the worker. They had the
reins of local government entirely in their hands and the worker
had to be contented to trust in the goodwill of such people for
any reforms that they thought necessary for their (miners')
welfare. . . .

"Yet while there is coal we shall still have miners. The world
should be grateful for this class of worker, indeed more than is
actually attributed to them. They are a class that is little understood and tolerated. Does not the Old Book say somewhere that
the hands of the dyer are imbued with his craft—*ipso facto*,
miners' social activities are black because coal is black. But do
they not produce the nation's greatest asset? England owes her
prosperity (or did?) to this type of worker but he is but little
appreciated for it. He grovels in the earth, let him grovel for his
existence above it. For such is the attitude of the many toward
him. . . . We read accounts of visits of certain highly placed
personages to mining districts. They compliment and praise the
housewife for tidiness and the cleanliness of the home. The home
may be tidy but their reports are exaggerated. I have yet to see
a miner's home such as described by them. How can it possibly
be spotlessly clean amidst the grime and dust of belching smoke
from surrounding stacks? I say this with no disrespect to the
housewife for she is undoubtedly a very courageous person.
Her time is chiefly used up in the preparation of her husband's
going and coming from work. His clothes are impregnated with

dust and grime. These have to be dried before the kitchen fire before he is able to don them again.

"I picture this as I personally experienced it in my own home in my boyhood days."

B. D.

"The U.S. miners have a quite different environment, due to the cheapness of motor cars in the U.S.A., a very large number of the workmen possess their own cars, as a result they travel much more and acquire a better knowledge of how their neighbour fares. They are also more inclined to go 'Whoopee!' as the expression has it, really meaning a lively sort of do."

H. J. O.

"In America the way the miners spend their leisure time is extremely different. This is due to the fact that the American miners are composed of so many different nationalities, who have gone there with the definite intention of making as much money as they can in the shortest possible time. They have no social life, nor do they desire it, purely individualistic.

"The life and environment of the miners of both countries, coupled with their ideals, excuse and reveal the great difference between the two types of men."

(NOTE.—Before a more adequate comparison of "the two types of men" is attempted the reader will be presented with a fuller description of the British miner. It is hoped that the following extracts, disjointed though they may be, will serve this purpose.)

IV. Characteristics of the British miner

E. J. (Miner, unemployed.)

"One of the chief influences on the life and also on the outlook of the miner is his method of obtaining a livelihood. The extremely dangerous character of his work makes him keen and alert, compelling him to think and plan out his day's work before he has actually started. Variations in the conditions of his working-place, which change almost hourly, owing to geological causes make him continually change his method of working. This develops in him a faculty for logical thinking, first analysing then generalising, finally deciding on the best method to adopt in order to cope with the ever changing conditions. . . .

"The unhealthy environment of mining generally, lack of sunshine, fresh air, the inhaling of coal dust, working in low and wet seams and the arduous nature of his work are all important factors in moulding the miner's character and outlook. . . .

"The ready consent of the owners to the scheme (Miners' Welfare) may be accounted by their desire to provide the miners with some means of occupying their leisure hours in a pleasant manner and so detract their attention from the sordid conditions that prevailed in the mining districts generally, making them more satisfied with their lot, and also to counteract the element of militancy which is more pronounced in the mining industry than any other.

"That they obtained their object is doubtful for the strikes of recent years particularly that of 1926 show that the militant element if not increasing is still strong in the miners and that the only thing lacking is a strong and capable leadership.

"The totality of these factors together with the advantage taken by the miners of every opportunity for education, evening classes, home study etc., accounts largely for the fact that they are the most intelligent and revolutionary band of workers in this country."

P. H.

"His daily work necessarily sets its mark on a man and helps to mould his character and general outlook on life, of course there are various types of miners, as regards their character and conduct.

"The roughest specimens are usually found in the new collieries where there has been a demand for miners, and all who come along are signed on.

"A much better class of miners prevail in the long settled communities, where these miners and their fathers have worked, these miners are of an advanced type."

B. D.

"The typical miner is not, to external appearance, a very prepossessing type of individual, rather is the reverse mostly the case, inasmuch that he is a dour, hard sort of type being no great respector of persons or positions, but he is typically constant, knowing what he wants to quite a large extent, and when he places his respect it remains there. If one is allowed glimpses of the character that is underneath the surface, he is a very pleasing and desirable sort of person.

"This external casing, as it were, is just a cloak that the physical conditions under which his work is accomplished, fits around him. A brief summary of his working environment soon convinces one, that there are certainly influences that tend towards causing him to be of the rugged type that I have stated him to be. . . .

"Too many, unfortunately, go through their lives, accepting, with a feeling of apathy, all things, just as they come, bringing to one's mind the thoughts of beasts of burden and their ploddings with the loads of others.

"He, the miner, is working hard, he is not living any too well, somebody is putting on him, he wishes he knew *exactly*."

H. J. O.

"His working conditions are therefore responsible for his being a vigorous combatant throughout life."

J. R. R.

"After dinner and a short sleep in a chair, he takes his wife to the pictures (if they can afford this comparative luxury) or more often take a short stroll up the hillside seeking the fresh air and green fields above. Much adverse comment has been made upon the manner in which the average miner spends his leisure time. A great deal of this is true but let it be remembered, that when a man or boy arises as early as 4.30–5.30 of a morning, rushes in a hurry to the pit-head and does not emerge, tired and grimy, till 2–3 o'clock in the afternoon, his reaction to the welcome sunlight and fresh air must necessarily be much like that of the average schoolboy, suddenly freed from a rather boring study.

"Also there is the less pleasant, alleged lewdness and general disgusting sexual behaviour of some miners. To understand, if not to criticise these tendencies one must enquire more closely into the Psychological side of the miners' life. The average miner, worn and stunted from his hazardous labour, coarse and often (and natnrally) childish in his habits and thought, must necessarily be neglected by the more attractive of the opposite sex. Indeed, though the standard of feminine beauty among the miners wives and daughters is as high as that of any other section of the working class, the coarse laborious life too often stamps its worst features upon the minds and bodies of both sexes. Thus it is that the miner occasionally or habitually neglects his toilworn and unattractive wife to seek such doubtful pleasures as the local pub, gambling in some secluded spot or worst, hangs about the hillside dodging after courting couples in search of whatever sexual exhibitions he may occasionally see. Besides these unpleasant deviations, the standard of marital faithfulness is probably as high among the mining classes as that of other sections of the workers and probably much higher than that of his 'betters'! Another regretful feature of the miners life is his carelessness regarding the spending of his earnings; again there is a wise thrifty section and a loose living disreputable minority; but take for example, the war era, when the miners suddenly found themselves in the rare position of being able to dictate to their employers. Unused as they undoubtedly were to a really decent standard of living, it was only natural that they should squander away their earnings in a very reckless manner. In any case no one has ever yet succeeded in establishing thrift as one of the essential moral virtues. A very high percentage of the miners devote their spare time to various kinds of hobbies, many of which are decidedly instructive and all of a harmless nature. Indeed some of them have devoted their spare time to the arts and sciences, and it can be said, quite confidently, that when a miner devotes himself to an art or science his devotion, if not his products, rank with the best."

V. J. T.

"Coming from a mining community, from a family of men who have wrested their living from Nature in the bowels of the earth, and being myself at one time a miner, I may have a strong bias in favour of my own kin, but still I will say unreservedly at the outset that, having regard to the hideous unnatural conditions under which they have to work, and taking into consideration the dismal, gloomy and often unhealthy surroundings in which they live, or more correctly spend the time not occupied in work, it would be extremely hard to find a finer, more intelligent and deeper thinking worker than the British miner.

"This would seem, on the surface, to be a contradiction—intelligent, thinking workers evolved under conditions where these qualities are least necessary, but I believe, on second thoughts, that I do the miner an injustice; surely, wrestling with Nature at her cruellest, and although she might gain sporadic victories in the form of death dealing explosions and mighty falls of earth, consistently maintaining a superior position requires a fairly high degree of intelligence. Except in exceptional cases, however, the arduous nature of their calling so saps their energy and vitality that there is very little left to fire them to seek knowledge and experience of the higher arts, the great majority only having the desire for easy and necessarily cheap entertainment, which found outlet in such sports as whippet racing, rabbit-coursing, quoit throwing, and so on, and of course, the minor sports provided by the village 'pub'—darts, dominoes, card games and such like.

"And this is the environment in which the budding miner is brought up—dismal, smoky villages or towns, small overcrowded houses where toilet and other health facilities are few and limited, where opportunities for recreation and health giving exercise are correspondingly limited, where it is true, facilities for education are at least the equal of other corresponding working class areas, but what a picture! What an indictment of this so-called Christian, civilised country of ours! And from this morass of humanity, this murk of monotone, this canvas in mid-greys, have arisen men of unquestionable ability and even genius in the higher arts! Who knows what a galaxy of wasted talent may be laid at the foot of the juggernaut—the capitalist system?"

B. L.

"The miner's living standard have improved and we hope will continue to improve, for his physical and social environment have caused him to become more self-respecting and more prone to be assertive of his rights."

E. C. (Teacher, daughter of miner.)

"Since that time, world factors such as rationalisation, the inability of the capitalist to adjust production to consumption and the economy campaign expressed in the Means Test, etc., to which the masses have been subjected have all resulted in a state of change. The unsheltered trades particularly that of coalmining have suffered most up to now—which makes it impossible to separate the miner from his local and world environment.

"A rapidly changing environment results in a rapidly changing human being and what is true of our grandfathers is not true of our fathers and what is true of our fathers is not true of our brothers though they may all be colliers. Again thousands of men of other trades sent their sons to work underground, possibly it was the only work available at the time and with them they brought characteristics which even environment cannot completely eradicate.

"The old miner was responsible for his place on the coal and it depended mostly on his skill as to his achievement underground. This gave him a certain pride in his work and an amount of satisfaction in this expression of himself. He often negotiated on his own for prices, etc., which developed in him a strong strain of individuality and independence.

"To-day the young colliers turned twenty are still 'boys' in the old sense of the word which gives them a feeling of inferiority and injustice. Those who are 'men' work to a large extent on conveyors and so have no occasion to outstrip their fellows in skill and achievement. The work is more monotonous and is consequently more wearing. There is scarcely any pleasure derived from achievement—you fill so many trams because the company expect it—and when it comes to bargaining each miner gets the same wage whatever his ability to fill may be. This is good in that it helps the weaker—yet it causes dissatisfaction among the younger men when the disparity is too great. Neither do the young men get the experience of standing on their own feet but they do develop the power of collective bargaining and the realisation of their dependence one on the other. In no section of the community is this feeling of smallness and ineffectiveness unless all the units unite, felt so strongly as in the mining community.

"But to come to more concrete characteristics. The collier especially one born of collier stock is usually small and stunted, the result of arduous work in dark and airless tunnels underground.

How few colliers reach the age of fifty without suffering from disablement, chest trouble, asthma, silicosis and anthracosis, and what collier does not realise that all this could be modified were he not a money making tool for the employing class? Is there any race of men who value life as lightly or who realise more than they, the insignificance and yet power of each unit in the universe? When money interests are put first and human life and suffering are merely the means to that end can it be wondered that a type is produced that acts regardless of consequences? This dangerous calling makes men speak out, they detest servility and it is only now since unemployment is so bad and victimization the result that a few are beginning to count ten before they speak.

"In spite of his outspokenness so dangerous is the work that the miner must be cautious too—the unwary get killed and yet because he must risk his life in his effort for bread we find him reckless too.

"The monotony, unhealthy conditions and strain of work brings him home fatigued and too worn out to bath before he eats, yet he always has his joke ready to make his wife and children laugh. Once the grime is washed off and he has rested a little, he finds he must take interest in pleasant pursuits—something to erase the underground atmosphere and so we find in the mining valleys more so than anywhere else groups gathering to discuss art, education, politics, to debate on topical events and to study the drama, all of which tend to make the miner the class conscious individual he is.

"Although the miner was inclined always to live fully as he went along he had a certain amount of self respect which urged him to save, to own his own house and the like. He usually paid into a sick society because accidents and illness were so frequent, but by to-day we find that every third miner is on the Unemployment Insurance once his standard Benefit runs out and if he is on Transitional Benefit he loses part of his Unemployment Benefit should he happen to own a house. The man who is ill and may receive money from a Sick Society gets that amount deducted from his public assistance allowance and so we see the tendency in those who have touched rock bottom to neglect the future. Foresight in the past has not put you in any better position than the one who didn't bother and while conditions are worsening this idea is gaining ground amongst the younger and weaker section of the community. The Standard of Life is so low that Insurance and the like have to be dropped after tremendous effort to keep them going, and so many of the younger generation are beginning to regard themselves as the State's responsibility.

"The risks and hard work of underground have in the past been counteracted to a large degree by a high standard of living particularly of food. This has meant a more vigorous outlook. Long periods of unemployment reduce the physical strength and vitality of the miner. The miners have been the most militant section of the community from a political and industrial point of view. Even when times are good the miner has to be on the alert. The management are always trying to cheat individual colliers of their due by a confused method of working out their dockets always are they endeavouring to cheat them of the compensation due to them because of accident until we find a defensive attitude taken up urging him at all costs to keep up the Standard of Life and whatever happens not to be 'done' if he can help it. Fighting in this way becomes second nature to him and it is only when the standard of life goes down to below subsistence level that he is inclined to lose his militancy.

"This militancy is a feature in the expression of his political and industrial life. It is displayed by the fact that in our valleys nearly all the representation on local councils are working men out to get through social means the rights denied them in their private lives. And so we find more health and maternity clinics in a mining area than almost anywhere else. Militancy is again expressed during strikes and lock-outs. If militant action is necessary the better type of collier is prepared to lose all in order to ensure a better standard of life for the future. So forceful is he that where there is a large group of people the ones who might feel inclined to sneak and blackleg are kept steady by the fear of the scorn and social ostracism of the remainder of the community.

"In this the miner as a type is intolerant. Once a miner black-legs he has lost prestige which can never be recaptured even amongst men who blacklegged themselves. This atmosphere binds the men together as one and it is only in localities where people of other occupations are strongly represented, introducing a snobbish element, that there is any tendency to break away.

"A characteristic of the collier too is his youthful outlook, his love of fun and a good time after the extreme confinement of the colliery. This love of fun and freedom has been termed hooliganism but it is no different in essence and certainly more harmless than our university rags. It is only expressed this way once or twice a year. For the rest his youthfulness is expressed in advanced thinking particularly in politics. New problems continually arising out of their economic life keep their minds active and always anxious to seek a solution from their own point of view. Strongly critical of each other, the mine, with its bad conditions, its dangers, its disasters, is a common enemy before which they must all unite. . . .

"One cannot write of the miner himself without including the effect of environment on wife and children. A characteristic of the wives of colliers is their kindness to their men folk. I have lived with families whose occupations were either farming, railway or road work, but rarely have I seen the wives so considerate and thoughtful of the men as I have seen it in colliery homes. The wife thinks her husband has to do the worst kind of work a man can do and there is always the fear that he may come home injured or never at all, and so she is usually a self-sacrificing type, oftentimes more so than is good for her own personality.

"On the other hand it is the woman who has to bear the brunt of a strike or of victimisation—the result of her husband's activity —so that the women are inclined to view progress more from the point of view of the family than that of the community.

"The children of the miners are on the whole quick-witted and intelligent—perhaps because most of them come from big families where they have to be fit to survive. With a minimum of good conditions the children have the ability to enter all of the professions as illustrated by the number of applications for Scholarships under the Welfare Scheme."

G. G. (Miner, unemployed.)

"If an inquiry was made as to the number of miners who had had training in working out figures, the number would be small, yet it is surprising the great number who can work out the total of their pay at the end of the week. As in arithmetic, so in the other branches of general education there are only a small number who are prepared to devote the necessary time to learning, yet despite the lack of any special study, the miner is well informed on all the leading questions of the day. He gets most of his information from the daily papers, which he reads very carefully, especially for news of the activities of the federation, and also for the winner of the three o'clock race. Through this medium of education, he keeps in touch with all the events that occur. Through the press he also reads of the activities of the local authorities, and if he does not agree with the actions of his representatives, he is not long before he tells him. . . .

"The home life of the miner must also have improved much during the last few years. The building of better types of houses, for years they had to put up with low and small roomed houses. But the building of new houses including baths has made him look at things from a higher standard, it as awakened a desire for a more beautiful surrounding, that can be seen by the way he cultivates his garden and flower beds.

"Therefore it can be seen that with an improvement in his conditions, the miners' outlook on life improves, and that for the better. He has had a taste of the nice things and he is thirsty for more."

C. W. (Teacher.)

"The miner of to-day has much to contend with, apart from trade depression. Overcrowding in towns and villages, lack of repairs to substantially built houses, and a comparatively low standard of living help to make the miner's life very undesirable. The miner is not, of course, unique in this respect, but it is true that one usually finds the worst conditions in coal mining areas. It is impossible even to guess the physical, psychological and spiritual effect on a working man, of being a member of a large family living in one, perhaps two, rooms of a house. Physically it makes him little better than the beast, for he finds sanitary equipment insufficient, toilet facilities an indulgence and independence of thought and action, so vital to self-development, an impossibility. Home life is unendurable, and one could paint lurid pictures of the pastimes many such are driven to.

"Again, insufficient money tends to make the miner and his family, not more frugal, but more improvident, more fatalistic, less inclined to fight his troubles, since, in fact, they are not to be beaten, and in fact, slackens his whole moral fibre. The social conditions then, following trade depression, have a tremendous moral effect on the miner."

D. J. D.

"Thirty years ago, clothes, conduct and other class distinctions were so marked that when Rhondda miners came to Cardiff for a week-end jaunt, they could easily be distinguished. Their solid clothes, swaggering carriage and a predilection for the more gaudy and bright entertainment and attractions, always betrayed them. To-day this has changed. Miners mingle with town and country people unobserved in the main, except on occasion when some atavistic strain evidences itself.

"Briefly the change is due mainly to the Advancement in Education, which has reduced illiteracy to a minimum. The publication of newspapers of a national character, national movements, political and economic, and not forgetting religion, all have sought and valued miners' adherence. Mass distribution of clothes, shoes, food, ideas, interests, recreations, all of standard-ised mass production, have helped to level out the difference in their past and present social order.

"The advancement in Education as already indicated has undoubtedly created the greatest change in the life of the miner in recent years. The greed for learning hitherto unattainable they ravenously sought in order to free themselves from the shackles that held them to their dire and grim existence. . . .

"What are the physical effects upon the miner? He works in cramped positions, in low seams. This gives rise to a tendency of low backs, to shorter legs. The Rhondda Battalion in the late war was recruited from Miners and was generally known as the 'Bantams.' And it is a qualifying fact that the Welsh men and women are shorter than the average British group, not because of mining but racial inheritance—the more Welsh they are, the shorter they come.

"Owing to the exhaustive nature of his work, he readily accepts any kind of ideal doctrines, which hold promise of a solution or even abolition of danger, dirt and distress. Where mining villages were closely integrated—Rhondda and Aberdare valleys—the job of the propagandist was always easier because ideas and doctrines were more easily placed before large groups with a

proportionately higher emotional content. By far the steadiest
elements among the membership of the South Wales Miners'
Federation were the detached isolated groups of men in smaller
collieries. These were very much less erratic in their behaviour
and adherence to the principles of the Trade Union than the
larger groups in the concentrated mining areas.

"Finally a word on the recreation of the miner. The Welfare
Movement, in bringing parks with provision for Tennis, Bowls,
etc., is removing the sports blight. Twenty years ago even
colliers who played tennis or golf in the Rhondda would have
been accused with aping a class beyond their rights or status.
This development is making a better man of the miner than he
hitherto was, both educationally and socially. If you like to say
so he is now associating himself with such a class, but the latter
now are very reluctant to acknowledge their superiority over their
unfortunate brothers in games of contest. Jack has become as
good as his master.

"Of course we have the fellow, and who blames him, whose
sole recreation and literature is the *Mid-Day Echo*. A tanner
flutter each way keeps things going. As a Cinema fan, no one
equals him. He knows the stars and amongst themselves discuss
the superiority of one over the other. In short the Cinema has
ousted the pub.—This evidences itself in less family and domestic
quarrels and deprivations.

"The Miner has made tremendous strides in the past, more
than any other class in so short a period."

R. W. (Miner.)

"We have the unintelligent type of miner and there are many
of these, they seem to be well satisfied with their conditions, they
work hard and live in circumstances that are not conducive to
raising the standard of intelligence, and appear to be settled in
a certain groove, and however much you try to induce them to
their emancipation, it is of no avail, you are replied with such
remarks as these 'What's the use of the Federation?' 'Blow the
Labour Party.' If their manager says 'Good day, John' they feel
themselves in an exalted position, this leads on to their subservi-
ency to their master, this has an unwholesome outlet in the fact
that they sneak, and carry tales to the higher officials. It is a
known fact that the management of a colliery knows what is

being carried on at every lodge meeting. The proof of this statement is evident in the . . . Area.

"Then we have the average minded, the type of person who after being crouched up in the mine in various positions according to the nature of their seam, feel that they should exercise their limbs in various sports, but the tendency is after playing these games for a while, they develop a certain amount of high mindedness (*note*: snobbishness) and they are prone to be indifferent to the well-being of the community at large. At the local libraries, what do we find when enquiring of the Librarian as to an illustration of what type of literature is being read, we find the great majority are light fiction:—Love stories, Dare devil stories and all that type of trash that leads nowhere.

"There are however another type who read what must be admitted to be high class literature in Economics, Philosophy, etc. This leads us on to the individual who in this time of speed and bustle, stands one side and looks on at life as it appears in his community. He is conscious of stark poverty and misery, bad housing which results in consumption and other diseases, children whose growths are stunted, old men having worked themselves to the marrow, facing the Workhouse, others crippled with Rheumatic through working in which they get soaking through every day by droppers and water in the bottom, they are told there is no compensation for Rheumatic, he feels there is something wrong in a social order that will allow these injustices to prevail. People in want, while nature provides in plenty, he then sets himself in earnest to understand the whole economic structure, he decides where the evil lies and sets about to organise, his industrial organ is the 'Miners Federation of Great Britain.' Politically, he has a strong movement called the Labour Party, but in recent years we have the advance of a new party namely the Communist Party. This party is thoroughly class conscious but personally I feel that their emotions overpower their common sense. . . .

"There are other various activities in the life of the miner such as Operatic Societies, Dramatic and Choral, but these must be laid aside, in order to discuss what I consider an important phase in the life of the miner, 'his religion.' There are many who state quite definitely that Religious Institutions are merely dope institutions where the working class are implored upon to accept their circumstances and to be thankful and satisfied on them, but this is entirely wrong, as the church stands to-day its mission is 'Be satisfied *in* the circumstances but not *on* the circumstances,' two very small words but very important indeed.

"One is tempted to use four lines of poetry of which I am very fond:—

> These things shall be,
> A nobler race than ere before shall rise,
> With flame of freedom in their souls,
> And light of knowledge in their eyes.

We deride the churches in which the miner has had and does have a certain spiritual betterment. We say we are sure of the realisation of a Socialistic State, but are we sure that this kind of state is possible without some spiritual progress from where we are to-day."

The foregoing extracts relate almost exclusively to the South Wales coalfield. It is not easy to state precisely the degree to which the field is typical of British coalfields. Working and living conditions are perhaps unusually difficult, owing mainly to the steepness of the hills and the narrowness of the valleys. Ameliorative influences, particularly institutes, libraries, educational classes (especially in Economics), lectures, musical and dramatic societies have operated on a larger scale proportionately here than in the other coalfields. And it is probably true that the South Wales miners are better educated and more militant than any other body of miners in Great Britain. There are differences of language and institutions. Welsh is still commonly spoken in the coalfield, especially in the anthracite section, and no other coalfield has anything quite like the Welsh National Eisteddfod. But apart from these differences the physical and social environment of the South Wales coalfield may be regarded, especially by American readers, as being fairly representative of British coalfields generally.

It now remains to describe the corresponding environment of the American coalfields. Not being fortunate enough to make use of essays written by American students living and studying in a coalfield, the author must rely on his own experience and observation. In any event, no coalfield in America can be taken as typical, so that the method of painting a national picture with colours drawn from one field would be misleading.

Working and Social Conditions

It is hoped that the following excerpts from the author's diary may give a general composite picture of working conditions underground in American coal-mines with occasional flashlights on social conditions aboveground. They relate to visits made in the following fields:—Illinois, West Virginia, Pennsylvania (West-bituminous), Pennsylvania (East-anthracite), and Colorado. Each of these fields is typical of a larger main area, and a point was made of exploring different kinds of mines—shaft, slope, strip, drift and anthracite—so as to get an insight into the varied conditions of American mining. Conditions in the Alabama field are described in Chapter IV (f) in the section headed "Difficulties in Alabama."

"*Belleville, Illinois, Friday, November* 30, 1928.—Visited No. 7 mine of the Southern Coal and Coke Mining Co., by courtesy of Mr. Kavanaugh, President. (*Note:* the visit was arranged by Mr. Edward Wieck, the best-educated and most widely-read miner the author met in America. His wife, formerly a teacher, had contributed excellent articles on coal problems to the American *Nation.* During his stay in Belleville, the author lived for some time with this remarkable couple, who assisted him in many valuable ways in his investigations.) First went to the office in Belleville where Mr. Kavanaugh introduced me to the Superintendent, Mr. Frank Davies, the engineer, Mr. Brandenberger, and the sales official, Mr. Webb. After a general talk on the coal situation in America and abroad, including discussion of 'dole' system and relations between employers and men in England, I was taken in Webb's car with Brandenberger to the mine, five or six miles out, Davies going in his own car. I donned the clothes lent me by Wieck and was provided with a cap (lamp attached—naked acetylene flame) and hand torch. Only a slight drop in the cage to the bottom. General first impressions—lighter, cleaner, more headroom than in English or Welsh mines, could stand upright most of the way and I must have walked about five miles in all. Not so much timbering as at home, a good deal of the roof being rock. Steel pillars used in some places to hold up roof. Chief feature of the mine was the use of mechanical loaders and shearers. The shearer bores into the coal vertically preparatory to 'shooting,' which loosens large quantities of coal. The loader scoops up the coal, even very large blocks, which travels up the machine to be tipped into trucks (drams) which are drawn by mules to the main track, along which they are drawn by an electric locomotive (about 24 trucks to the load) to the cage, up which they are drawn and tipped into wagons, ready in the pit-head railway sidings, different grades of coal being tipped into different wagons. Mules are used because they are more 'flexible' and more economical than locomotives for conveyance from the 'rooms' (places) to the main road. (*Note:* Mules, not ponies, are the usual 'live stock' used in American mines.) Mr. Davies told me that since 1925, 6,000 feet of coal had been cleared as the result of the use of mechanical loaders—an average of 700 feet a year, allowing for a six months' stoppage. The men operating the loader are paid more than $10 a day (£2 +) and the wages ranged from this figure to $5 +. I talked with several of the men, including one from Talywain, Monmouthshire, and another from Wigan, who had visited England last year. The relations between Davies and Brandenberger (representing the management) and the miners seemed to be remarkably friendly, and the general impression was one of harmonious working. About 130 men employed, including a number of Germans who I was told are good workmen. The stables for the mules were very well kept. The coal is 'shipped' to St. Louis, mainly 'steaming' coal for domestic and industrial (boiler) use. No need for a bath as I was not in the least dirty."

(NOTE.—In every mining town he investigated the author inquired into the educational facilities provided, and in particular the proportion of miners' sons and daughters attending the schools. The following diary entries are included here, although they have nothing to do with the working conditions: they may be of interest to educationalists.)

"*Belleville, Tuesday, December* 14.—Had valuable talk in morning with Mr. Calhoun, Superintendent of Schools. The most interesting points—percentage of children of miners 22 per cent—(*Note:* this figure was specially prepared—Belleville has several other industries), 'opportunity school' (where backward pupils are given special opportunities to improve in their weak subjects), and the system of classifying pupils and arranging sizes of classes according to Intelligence Quotient and Mental Age, the best pupils being organised in largest classes. Average size of classes about 30 in primary schools. Went over Junior High School in afternoon. Addressed a group of teachers (about 30–40, mostly women) on English educational system for three-quarters of an hour—questions for about half an hour. In the evening Calhoun drove me to the High School. Had an interesting talk with Mr. Schmidt, Headmaster—excellent type of man—first on Psychology and then on organisation of night classes. Made a tour of all the classrooms. Special features—machine shops, music appreciation and art rooms. Usual commercial subjects but no class in Economics. Finely equipped building. Saw basket-ball match between Belleville High School Boys and Lebanon High School Boys. Girls acting as 'cheer leaders.' Introduced to Headmaster of Lebanon High School, Welsh on his mother's side—name Griffith Mayes."

"*Friday, December 7th.*—Spent day with Butts, Head of Junior High School. Had lunch at the School Cafeteria, and after visiting all the classes Butt took me out in his car to the High School. Biology compulsory subject. Agriculture given unusual attention. Interesting class in Journalism—teacher bright and keen, daughter of President McKendrick (denominational) College. Class in Economics—teacher—Trabue. Doing banking at the time."

"*Benton, Illinois (southern). Wednesday, December 12th.*—Saw Mr. H. A. McCreery (friend of Butts of Belleville) who phoned to Mr. John Foster (manager of New Orient, No. 2 Mine) who replied that we could go down at one o'clock. Meantime saw Mr. A. C. Lewis, Chief Counsel of U.M.W., whom I had met with Wieck at St. Louis, for a few minutes. McCreery called and ran me out to the Orient Mine, owned by Chicago, Wilmington and Franklin Co. The manager (John Foster) seemed a very good type of mining engineer. Escorted below ground by Mr. Wentworth, who proved an excellent guide. The tipple (pit-head) extraordinarily clean and spacious. Parking of hundreds of automobiles a remarkable feature. Drop in cage of about 500 feet Ample head room. Clean roads. Extraordinarily fine engine room —one of three. No mules used—all cars electrically propelled. Struck by size of cars—five or six tons load. Walked $2\frac{1}{2}$ miles to see the McKinley machine, 'entry driver,' which cuts out the coal in circles—about 30 feet a day, at night—scoops it up into cars which are propelled to bottom of cage where they are emptied, two at a time, into a large curved iron receiver which slips the coal into basins which are electrically hoisted up to the top and emptied into railroad cars. Ascended the cage the same time with the men coming off the shift. About 1,200 men employed. Average wage now (rough estimate) 38–40 dollars a week. Not very dirty, and after a wash finished with an interesting talk with Foster and McCreery, who ran me back to Benton. This mine, commonly spoken of as the biggest in the world, meaning the mine having the largest output, averages now 12,000 tons a day, though it has reached 15,900 tons—a world record."

"*Thursday, December* 13*th.*—Left Benton and arrived in West Frankfort . . . called on Superintendent of Schools (Waller) who shewed me round some of the classes and gave me some interesting information. About 90 per cent of the children tested in 3 classes the sons and daughters of miners. Visited Public Library —miserably poor institution."

"*Belleville, Thursday, December* 20*th.*—Spent day in visit to R. C. Moore, Secretary, Illinois State Teachers' Association, at Carlinville—70 miles distant. (*Note :* the author had been specially advised to see Mr. Moore as a man of wide experience of the education of immigrant children of a number of different nationalities and as one who was interested in the sociological aspects of education.) Went on Illinois Traction System from St. Louis—electric tramway through the mining towns Edwardsville, Staunton, Beneld and Gillespie. Had long and very fruitful talk with Moore on environment (educational) and its effects on Russians, Italians, Germans, British, Roumanian, Lithuanians, Poles, Hungarians, etc. He gave striking instances of influences of change of environment, economic and educational, on European races coming from inferior circumstances and educational facilities to better. Described aims of Illinois State Federation of Teachers. Emphasised the importance of equalisation of opportunities in State of Illinois and the problem of inequalities of taxable resources of different districts (approximately 12,000) in the State, e.g. Winnetka, rich, West Frankfort, poor. Effects on children of type of school, teacher, facilities, etc. Formerly Principal of a School and County Superintendent of Schools in mining area. Very thoughtful and progressive educationist."

"*Charleston, West Virginia. Thursday, March* 5, 1929—

MINERS' HOUSES MADE OVER FROM FREIGHT CARS, ILLINOIS

Taken by car by Mr. James Martin, General Superintendent of mines of Wyatt Coal Co., up Cabin Creek. Crossed river in car on a ferry. First stopping place Sharon, where we entered the Company Store, machine shops, etc., and the Grades School, where at the request of Mr. Thomas, Headmaster, a pleasant, very shy young fellow, I spoke to his class of about thirty boys and girls of about thirteen years of age. Drove on to Wake Forest, where we visited the Store, machine shops, etc. Then on a short distance to Laing, so called after the President of the Company. Here we ascended at an angle of about 60° on an open hoist to a height of 1,500 feet to the drift mine. Equipped with lamps we entered the mine and walked 1½ miles, most of the way with body bent, Martin being a very quick walker and used to walking bent. At face came upon half a dozen men, including one Scotsman, with whom we had a short talk. After a rapid walk back I felt pretty tired and very hot, but soon got cool on emerging into a heavy snowstorm. Descended on the open sled, sitting on the snow, accompanied by eight coloured men coming off the shift. In spite of the snow, the view of the surrounding hills on the descent was magnificent. The coal is sent down on separate rails in trucks called monitors and at the bottom is separated into three sizes by an automatic machine called a shaking screen. Output between 2,000 and 3,000 tons a day. This mine working full time but we saw a number of abandoned mines and camps, Martin saying that one-third of the smaller and less efficient mines had closed down—the old story of unnecessary production owing to competition. 150 million tons of coal produced in West Virginia annually. Eight-hour shift. Martin took me into two miners' houses (company) at Wake Forest—quite nicely finished off inside—4 rooms, rent 2 dollars per room per month. Unable to return to Charleston owing to floods, we stopped the night at home of Manager of Company Store. Following morning Martin took me in his car as far as Cabin Creek, beyond which car could not go on account of flood, but he accompanied me over the hillside to the Interurban R.R. station where I took the trolley to Charleston. The whole creek extremely interesting industrially, rich in coal, natural gas and oil. Passed remarkable oil field at Giles—my first sight of oil derricks. In the Kanawha valley the Du Pont Company is erecting enormous chemical and by-product plant.''

"*Pittsburg, Thursday, March 21st.*—Set off by train to Logans Ferry. Visited West Pennsylvania Power Co.'s mine at Springdale. Superintendent and General Manager out, so I visited the scene of the explosion at the Kinloch mine (Valley Camp Mining Co.) which occurred early this morning—I had read about it in the train. There was a big crowd round the tipple, which was badly blown up. I got a pass from the Superintendent (Morgan), but when they were about to bring bodies up all who were not directly concerned were ordered off by the police, much to the annoyance of the cinema-operators and photographers. I had seen one man, a negro, carried out, earlier, alive but 'petered out.' I met Burke, a journalist I had known in Pittsburg, who told me that 180 of the 280 had been saved but that there was too much gas (98 per cent) for rescue operations. I saw men with all kinds of recue and testing apparatus going down the slope. It is a slope mine but worked by a shaft, 300 feet. Morgan said it was a dust explosion, caused by the breaking of a conveyor. Red Cross and rescue parties were apparently more than adequate. There were also several clergymen and I noticed a number of women in tears. The Bureau of Mines of Pennsylvania was much in evidence, and it looked as if McGregor, the Chief Inspector, was directing rescue operations. The two features that struck me most were the tremendous number of cars and the great variety of languages spoken by men and women in the crowd. Butler asked one man, a Pole, who was shivering after having been in the water waist-high for hours, how he spelled his name, but he couldn't say and the journalist had to get the spelling from someone else."

"*Pittsburg, Friday, March 29th.*—(*Note:* made a tour of Tarentum, 22 miles distant, Curtisville, mining camp of Ford Collieries Co., and drove on to Russelton, where we called at the office of the Republic Iron and Steel Co. mine.) The Superintendent (McVicker) arranged for us to go down the shaft, drop of 230 feet. Chief feature the remarkably fine rock roof. Six foot seam. No 'live stock.' This is a 'captive' mine. Caught train back to Pittsburg. Chief impressions—'deadness' of unionism of any sort among the men, but operators maintaining certain Union features, e.g. eight-hour shift, payment for dead work. Housing conditions much better than in most of West Virginia I had seen, though not so good as in Glen White or Holden. These mining camps not so isolated as those of West Virginia and not so entirely under the control of the companies, due partly to geographical conditions, partly to influence of recent unionisation."

"*Lansford, Pennsylvania (east), Friday, May 10th.*—In morning called on Mr. J. B. Warriner, General Manager, Lehigh Coal and Navigation Co., to whom I had a letter of introduction from Mr. Edward W. Parker, Secretary of the Anthracite Bureau of Information, Philadelphia, and on Mr. H. S. Gilbertson, Director of Personnel. Both men received me very kindly though I hadn't rung up beforehand. Had half an hour's talk with Mr. Warriner, who called in the Chief Engineer, Mr. Rausch, and asked him to arrange visits to the Lansford breaker and a strip mine to-day and to go underground in one of the mines to-morrow morning. In the afternoon Mr. Whildin (of Welsh descent) took me over the breaker and was a most helpful guide as well as being a pleasant companion. The Breaker is a building 200 feet high where the coal (anthracite run of mine) is cleaned, sorted and prepared for shipment. First the refuse (usually 50 per cent) is separated from the coal. The coal is then automatically propelled along running tables according to size of lumps, men sitting at the sides to throw out rock or slate. Special automatic machinery for treating each size of coal, from large lumps down to No. 5 Buckwheat, about the size of small peas. The smallest sizes (4 and 5 Buckwheat) are combined with bituminous coal in the manufacture of briquettes. The next smallest (Buckwheat 1, 2 and 3—'rice' and 'barley') are used for steam coal in small factories, laundries, etc. The 'chestnut' size is popular for domestic fuel. A motor for each size, all the motors being worked by one man in the engine room. Each size automatically tipped into wagons on railroad sidings right in the building. Inspectors employed by the Company to inspect the final results, which, if condemned, are returned to the breaker for further treatment. Even so, complaints are received, as consumers are very critical— 'they almost want the coal wrapped in tissue paper!' 5,000 tons of steel in the breaker. Not many men employed as so much automatic machinery used. Only one shift—8 hours. The 'dumping' of the refuse quite a problem—huge hills of it outside. . . .

"Later taken by Mr. Samuel E. Thorne (of English descent), Superintendent of Strip mines, to see two strip mines at Summit Hill, two or three miles out. This, I was told, is where coal was first mined in America, also the scene (Panther Valley) of Conan Doyle's novel about the Molly Maguires—*The Valley of Fear*. The strip mines reminded me of the Rucksack Lignite mine, eight miles from Cologne (Rhine Valley). At Summit Hill electric 'shovels' (162 tons) automatically load 50–60 fifty-ton wagons a shift (eight hours). No coal being loaded just then, rock and soil having to be excavated first. The 'shovel' like a large 'tank.' I went inside one of them and was fascinated by the machinery. The coal not deep enough to be mined 'inside' and another reason for stripping operations was the presence of fire in the hillside (Summit Hill mine fire) which has been burning since 1858. . . .

"In the evening Mr. Gilbertson showed me a four-part film in his office illustrating the history and practice of anthracite coal-mining—a most interesting film lasting about two hours. Suitable for an audience of anything up to 500. Advertising film of the Lehigh Coal and Navigation Co., but would have a general interest. I also had a long, useful conversation with Gilbertson. He was a student at University of California and at Columbia University. Excellent man for his job. Gave me a copy of his booklet *Mine Management Policies*. He has done investigation work for the Coal Commission. Interested in the human, social aspects of coalmining."

"*Saturday, May 11th.*—Mr. Le Vann (of French descent, Alsace Lorraine), Assistant Mining Engineer to the Company, called for me in his car about eight o'clock. We went out to No. 3 shaft at Nesquehoning (Indian for Narrow Valley). Equipped with rubber Wellington boots (necessary because of water, often six inches deep), overalls, cap and Edison lamp (battery), we descended 450 feet. First impressed by tremendous amount of water and dirty appearance generally compared with bituminous mines I had seen in Illinois, West Virginia and West Pennsylvania. Mr. Sterner (engineer of the mine, of German descent) and Mr. Ronemus (foreman of the mine, also of German descent, wife named Watkins, of Welsh family) explained that the water was due to the fact of different levels and we were on the bottom (third) level, the water finding its way to the lower levels. After walking a few hundred feet we came to a pitched seam, with a slope of forty degrees. Two manways on either side of the breast (i.e. the mass of coal itself), one for ascending and descending, the other for ventilation. I found mounting the slope, notwith-

standing the wooden props spaced about a yard apart all the
way up, hard 'sledding,' and was glad of the rest at the top on
the breast, where we talked for a few minutes with the man
(a Slav) who was drilling. Part of the breast had recently been
shot and the man was waiting till all trace of gas had disappeared.
We then descended the manway in a sitting position on the
small coal. This was much easier than ascending, though one was
apt to slide down too quickly on the zinc bottom where there
was not a thick covering of coal. Once I slipped, but Ronemus
was prepared and put out his foot to serve as a brake. Both men
looked after me very carefully and considerately. They next took
me to see a 'straight' (vertical, 90°) pitch, and I was content
merely to see it! The coal from the breast is guided through a
battery (opening) into cars, which are conveyed direct to the
breaker. The men getting the coal at the breast work on contract
(piecework) and earn anything from $5 to $7.50 a day. Not much
machinery in use in this mine and Sterner told me that he did
not think mines in which there were pitched seams were at all
likely to be mechanised to any great extent, though he had been
told some development in this direction had been made in
Belgium. On reaching the office we discussed many technical
points as the result of studying his plans of the mine, etc. Mr.
Le Vann returned from the main office to take me back to
Lansford."

"*Hazelton, Monday, May 13th.*—. . . Opposite the Overall
Factory is a Mining and Mechanical Institute. I called on the
Principal, a man named Bray, of Cornish descent—quite a good
type. The Institute was established and endowed by an operator
and his wife (Mr. and Mrs. Coxe) for the purpose of training
executives in the mines. Endowment of $200,000. Excellently
equipped but apparently the classes were neither numerous nor
large. Bray seemed to think the prospect of a Class in Economics
a remote dream! He talked interestingly about the changes in
ethnic composition of the Classes from British and German to
Eastern European ('many of whom could hardly speak English')
and more recently to Spanish and Portuguese ('who have no
ambition') because conditions in this coalfield were so much
better than anything they had known in their own countries."

"*Wyoming, near Wilkes-Barre, Pa., Thursday, May 23rd.*—
Visited mine of Harris, Denley Coal Co. 'Billy' Harris a quaint

'self-made' little fellow whose people lived at Neath, Glamorgan-shire. His speech was the weirdest and most amusing mixture of Neath (Welsh) accent and American slang. A kindly little man, somewhat seared by his occupational experience (started work in a mine at the age of nine), he did all he could to make my visit fruitful. The mine itself a very small affair but it was interesting as being the first slope mine I had explored. I was conducted over the mine by the foreman Robert Donald, of Scottish descent. After coming up I had a remarkable talk with Harris, who shewed me in his books the wages which his men earned in 1924–5, in many cases reaching more than 200 dollars a fortnight (£20 weekly). He also told me of the way certain operators used to instruct their clerks to 'cook' their figures in such a way as to deprive the miners of part of their earnings. He worked himself into a state of indignant excitement as he described the 'cheating' methods of some of the operators. A remarkably interesting case of an operator (one of three owning this mine) who spoke freely of the exploitation of the men.''

"*Friday, May 24th.*—Visited the No. 4 mine of the Kingston Coal Co. (*Note :* a few miles from Wilkes-Barre.) Mr. T. H. Williams, Vice-President of the Company, a native of Cwmtwrch, near Swansea, who also started working in a mine at the age of nine. Before going down the mine I had a very informative talk with Mr. Williams and one of the officials who once lived and worked at Gwauncaegurwen and knew J. H. Davies (*Note :* one of my colleagues, a specialist in Geology), who, it seems, had visited this same mine, on his visit to America last year. The most interesting thing they told me was that they had recently introduced the system of paying wages by cheque. I examined some of the cheques with interest (average wages for the fortnight about $65—about £6 10s. weekly). Williams said the system fostered thrift and an interest in banking and that another reason for adopting it was that there had been numerous cases of way-laying clerks carrying large sums of money, and of miners on paydays. This company was the pioneer in methods of 'silting,' i.e. conveying by pipes the refuse aboveground into the mine where it was used as support under rocks which had been 'under-cut.' The Company had presented six equipped playgrounds to the town of Kingston, planted trees in many of the streets, built and furnished a library (1,800 books), looked after 'hard cases' among the employees' families, supplying sons and daughters of widows with clothes, boots, etc., and even 'bobbing' the hair of the girls till they were able to earn. The Company also conducted technical classes in mining. Each man gives one shift's pay annually for Community Welfare. The mine itself was extremely well engineered, the engine-room being especially well equipped, the roads were spacious, exceptionally free from water and well lighted. I walked erect everywhere. Seams mostly flat, though there were some of 30°–40°. The best mine I had seen since I visited the No. 2 Orient mine, West Frankfort, Illinois. Nine hundred men employed in this mine, 3,000 altogether by the Company. The 900 comprised various nationalities—Lithuanian, Polish, Russian (I saw churches of these three from the mine), Slavonians, Italians, Germans, Welsh, Irish, Scots, Negroes (I saw some underground), Serbians, Austrians, Dutch and native-born Americans (by far the largest percentage)."

"*Monday, May 27th.*—Visited, with Mr. Brislin, of the International Board of the U.M.W.A. as guide, the Hanover Memorial High School (*Note :* in the neighbourhood of Wilkes-Barre). Had a good talk with the Principal (Finnegan) and addressed two of the Classes in Economics. Intelligent and well-trained boys and girls of 16–17 years of age, a dozen or so being of exceptional calibre. Questions were asked on Causes of the Industrial Depression in England, Disarmament, Kellogg Pact, Growth of Socialism in England, The World Court and the 'dole' system. The teacher, Charles J. Morris (Course in 'Problems of American Democracy,' text-book by Williamson, of Smith College), a very good type of fellow, who had been a member of the Pennsylvania Legislature as a Democrat-Labour but relinquished political life because of 'graft,' of which he gave me some astounding instances. The pupils, of whom a considerable percentage were sons and daughters of miners, were of various nationalities, including a goodly proportion of Welsh."

"*Monday, June 3rd.*—Spent day at Scranton, which I had previously visited to arrange for the inspection of one of the mines. In morning visited the offices of the U.M.W. and talked with Mr. Enoch Williams (native of Aberdare, Glamorganshire). In the afternoon taken by Mr. Daggar and Mr. Martin Williams (both Welsh, Daggar being a cousin of George Daggar, M.P. for Abertillery, Monmouthshire) in Daggar's car to Storrs Mine,

about six miles out, the property of the Glen Alden Co. Remarkably fine approach (grass lawns, etc.) to the mine—the finest
thing of its kind I have seen. Went down the mine with the mine
foreman, Mr. James Jones, native of Clydach Vale, Rhondda—
a charming old fellow with a Rhondda accent despite his thirty
years in America. Conditions underground excellent. Next drove
past several breakers to Pyne, small mining 'patch' where we
entered two miners' houses (company)—quite good houses,
though without bath and inside toilet but unusually good gardens.
Rent 9 and 11 dollars a month. Small Grades School in the
village. High School 2½ miles away at Taylor. Pupils conveyed
by 'jitney' by municipality. Drove past Taylor High School and
on to Grades School at Hyde Park (one of the wards of Scranton).
Entered the school and went through various classes. Children
of several nationalities, Welsh the highest percentage. Williams'
own boy in one of the classes, another being now at Dartmouth
College. Both Williams (specialist in 'cave-ins' for the company)
and Daggar (Office Engineer) the sons of mine foremen. Mine
foremen's houses very good, having bathrooms, etc."

"*Tuesday, June 4th.*—Had interview with Mr. Zeiser, Superintendent of Schools of Wilkes-Barre. 53½ per cent of elementary
pupils proceed to High Schools. 16 per cent of high school pupils
proceed to Universities, Technical Institutes, etc. Very mixed
ethnic composition of population, British stock predominating
—Welsh, Irish, Scottish—but strong representation of Slavs
(Poles), Italians, and, in recent years, of Germans. About 30 per
cent of the children sons and daughters of miners. Discussed
Adult Education. Good man for his post, able and unassuming,
though evidently hadn't given much attention to these points
before, the data having to be specially prepared."

The scene shifts to the Colorada coalfield. Unfortunately, the
author did not keep a detailed diary of his investigation in this
field and the brief entries he made at the time are hardly worth
reproducing here. His main interest was the Colorado Plan for
Industrial Relations and the Rocky Mountain Fuel Company's
scheme, of which he has given a close examination in Chapter IV,
Section F. He found time, however, to visit several mines, both
in the Denver district and in the southern field, and investigated
conditions underground in one mine of the Rocky Mountain
Fuel Co., near Denver, and one mine of the Colorado Fuel and

STREET SCENE SHOWING TYPES OF HOUSES, PENNSYLVANIA

Iron Co., at Trinidad in the south, each of which may be regarded as typical of its section. Here, as almost everywhere in the States, he was impressed by the high standard of engineering—roof work, ventilation, roadways, lighting, etc. He also visited schools, colleges, housing settlements and investigated recreational and social conditions generally. The impression that has remained is that the social conditions were far in advance of those of the Alabama Coalfield and compared very favourably with those prevailing in the eastern coalfields. Indeed it was somewhat astonishing to find such a high level of civilisation in a coalfield so far West, but perhaps in retrospect one is inclined to exaggerate, or maybe one's mind dwells less on the conditions underground or on the surface than on the glorious sun-capped, snow-peaked mountains of beautiful Colorado!

Housing conditions and welfare schemes have been compared in Chapter IV, Section G and facilities for education in Section H. We are now more adequately equipped for a comparative study of the American and British types of miner.

THE BRITISH AND AMERICAN COAL-MINER COMPARED

Stress has already been laid on the racial contrast. The American mining population has been recruited from many sources. The older types are still pronouncedly national—British, German, Swedish, Hungarian, Italian, Russian, Lithuanian, Roumanian, Polish, etc. The process of Americanisation has been carried on so long and so successfully that the younger men may be regarded as an American type, though compounded of so many elements. In Great Britain, while there are differences between the older and younger miners they are all racially essentially British. That is one outstanding differential feature.

To what extent this difference influences the two types it is difficult to say because of other factors that have to be taken into account. To take one instance. It may be said that the American miner is more excitable, less stable, than his British counterpart. How far is this due to genetic considerations? How far is it to be explained by differences in the industrial and social conditions in the two countries? Is the excitability induced by working in a relatively new country to which immigrants have come in their millions in the expectation of high wages, "good and plenty"?

Miners as a type everywhere are probably quicker and more emotional than other types of workers, and in an analysis of the American miner due weight must be given to the economic factors but the racial factor cannot be ignored. Leaving out of account on the American side the miners who emigrated from England, Scotland and Germany, who may be described as somewhat phlegmatic, and on the British side the Welsh and Irish miners who are "temperamental," we are left with a large proportion of American miners drawn, comparatively recently, from southern, eastern and south-eastern European countries, and the negro element, all of whom may be described as more lively, noisy and excitable than the English type, which is essentially stolid and equable. In his tour of the American coalfields the author mixed with all sorts of miners and everywhere he met this happy-go-lucky, boisterous, rollicking, dare-devil type. This characteristic may possibly prove to have some economic and political importance in the future. There are quite responsible people in America who think that a "revolution" is more likely to occur in that country than in Great Britain, and one of the reasons they give is that when the workers of America feel the full effects of the continued Great Depression they will not pause to consider ways and means of handling them but that, like an excitable, spoilt child baulked of its desire, they will "break out" and "upset the whole apple cart."

Physically, the American miner shews to advantage. He is taller, more shapely, better set up, has more regular features, his face is unspotted by "coal marks" and he has fine teeth. His superior bodily frame is probably due to hereditary influences though better working conditions underground are a factor— he is not obliged to bend his body as much as the British miner. Generally, he is not so greatly affected by the coal environment underground. His fine teeth may be due partly to heredity but the careful dental treatment from childhood throughout life, which is a feature of American life, is certainly an important factor.

There can be little doubt that the working conditions of the miner exercise a considerable influence on his character and outlook. They tend to make him at once reckless and cautious, quick to think and act, combative and independent. To the extent that American conditions differ from those in British mines— and that they are generally easier has been proved in Chapter

IV (B)—there is a difference in the two types of miner. The American miner has all the characteristics indicated above but not to such a marked extent as the British miner.

The range of comfort, as expressed in housing conditions, is very great in American coalfields. In the Pennsylvania anthracite field the miner's family live in a well-built, roomy house, containing several electrical devices which alleviate household drudgery, with a fair-sized garden—in short, something in the nature of a decent home to which the miner and his sons can return after a day's work at the mine. At the other extreme the Alabama miner has nothing better to look forward to at the end of his shift than a flimsy shack where he exists in a miserable frame of mind till it is time to go to work again. If his skin is permanently black his living conditions are even "blacker." The higher standard of comfort is reflected in a brighter, more alert, happier, more spirited type of miner—he and his family have "something to live for." The miners of Alabama are nothing more than hewers of coal and drawers of water for their own domestic purposes. In Great Britain there are not the same extremes of living conditions. And in the author's experience nowhere in the British coalfields are there such cheerful types as the mining men, with their wives, daughters and sisters, of Scranton, Wilkes-Barre and Hazelton, in Pennsylvania, or such abject types as are to be seen in Alabama.

It may be stated generally that the social environment of the British miner is superior to that of the American miner. In the matter of welfare schemes, particularly those catering for the recreational, health and educational needs of the miners, Great Britain is far ahead, while the difference in origin and control of such schemes in the two countries, which have a bearing on the self-respect and independence of outlook of the miner, has already been emphasised (see Chapter IV, G). Such schemes have done far more to mitigate some of the more ugly features of the colliery districts and to brighten the lives of the miners of Great Britain than has been effected by schemes, largely personal and voluntary in character, for the improvement of American mining communities.

Apart from the nature of the environment, the British miner seems to function more fully and more variously as an individual within the environment. There are more miners proportionately in Great Britain who play football (Association and Rugby, "Soccer" and "Rugger"), cricket, tennis and bowls than there are American miners who play baseball and football. Curiously enough, the large crowds who watch football matches in America are mainly college crowds, present and past students, women forming half the crowd, everybody seated in comfort, fur coats predominating, large numbers with rugs for the legs and foot-warmers for the feet. Baseball crowds are more "democratic." In an American coalfield there is nothing to compare with the large crowds, composed of miners and other industrial workers, to be seen on a Saturday afternoon from October to April in any of the British coalfields—crowds who certainly do get a "kick" out of the games they follow so eagerly and so critically. And even the relatively smaller crowds who attend the leisurely cricket matches in Northumberland and Durham, Lancashire, Yorkshire and South Wales contain a large number of miners who are able to appreciate every fine point in the game. There are those who regard big watching crowds as a sign of decadence and others who regard them as dupes of "capitalist dope,"designed to keep the workers contented. Certainly it would be much better if all those who flock to look on at these big games were able to play themselves but at least they bring a little healthy excite-ment and much-needed colour into the drab life of mining districts. And there is more of this element of change in the British than in the American coalfields.

The average British miner is better educated and more cultured than the average American miner. An attempt has been made to shew that this is due to the much better provision, quantitatively and qualitatively, of facilities for the education of the adult worker in Great Britain. Even though a larger proportion of American miners have had a secondary school education this by no means compensates for the loss, from which the overwhelming majority of American miners suffer, of a kind of revival of learning which affects such large numbers of British miners. Apart from the fact that the British miner is better educated and far more interested in economic and political questions, he is altogether a more cultured person. Large numbers of miners are active members of choral societies, orchestras, brass bands, literary, debating, religious and dramatic societies. A great many of them are remarkably well-read and well-informed on a great variety of subjects. They read the classics and the latest novel with equally avid interest. The works of writers like Shaw, Wells, Bertrand Russell, Tawney and Laski are devoured by them. Einstein's Theory aroused far greater interest among them than among American miners.

It may be that the author is a little biassed in admiration of the South Wales miner with whom he has been in close contact for a quarter of a century, but if the reader, especially the American reader, will allow for this he may regard the following testimony as being fairly applicable to the British miner generally. It is given by Mr. H. V. Morton in his recent book *In Search of Wales*, pp. 247–249. Mr. Morton is a writer of established reputation as a descriptive, investigative critic and is the author of *In Search of England, In Search of Scotland, In Search of Ireland, The Call of England, The Heart of London* and other similar studies.

"The Welsh miner is a proud, sensitive—I use the word with deliberation and in its true sense—gentleman. I have met him in crowds: I have met him individually. I have seen him at work; I have sat at his fireside and talked to him for hours. I would like to think, if I had entered a pit at the age of fourteen and had grown to manhood in it, that I would retain the outlook and the intellectual curiosity of the average Welsh miner.

"His intellectual interests are remarkable. At a street corner in Tonypandy I heard two young miners discussing Einstein's Theory of Relativity. I know this was exceptional, but it is significant; and it is true.

"It will not seem out of the way to anyone who knows South Wales. It will be believed by the manager of Smith's bookshop in Cardiff, who recently delivered Murray's *Oxford English Dictionary*, which cost £45, to the Workmen's Institute at Ton-yr-efail. This £45 was saved by miners in twopences! And they followed it up by saving £39 for the *Encyclopædia Britannica*!

"I have met miners whose culture and gift of self-expression seem to me nothing short of miraculous. These men know how to think. They have a mental curiosity which leads them into all kinds of queer paths. Music is one of their passions." (*Note:* The author is reminded of one of his students, a miner's daughter, who once said to him "Economics is my passion!"

The young woman attended the author's weekly class in Economics
for seven winters in succession and was never absent, though her
attendance meant a walk of nearly three miles over a mountain
in all sorts of weather. She won a scholarship to Ruskin College
and later married a student she met there.) "It does not consist
of putting a record on a gramophone. In one miner's home there
are four framed objects on the wall, and three of them are
L.R.A.M. certificates.

"I was introduced to a miner who had taught himself to play
music by studying the Welsh Hymn Book. This has the tonic
sol-fa on one page and opposite is the ordinary notation. He
translated them painfully and became proficient.

"How can you withhold admiration from a community in
which this is not an exceptional achievement? It is going on
every day.

" 'Hugh So-and-So,' said an ex-miner, 'was so mad on music
that he could hear it in the rhythm of the wheels of the journey.'

"(The 'journey' is the line of loaded coal 'trams' which
travels, often for miles, from the coal seam to the pit bottom.)

" 'The wheels make different sounds on the gradients. Hugh
heard music in this, and he used to keep a bit of chalk in his
pocket and write melodies on the ventilating doors. They made
wonderful blackboards.'

"Imagine that! Think of a man hearing music in the darkness
of a pit and writing melodies by the light of a safety lamp!

" 'Where is Hugh now?' I asked.

" 'Teaching music in America.'

"I asked this man to explain to me the exceptional interests
of the miner.

" 'Every miner has a hobby,' he said. 'Some are useful; some
are not. Some miners take up hobbies as amateurs; some study
to escape from the pit. I did. Even now I sometimes marvel that
it is possible to earn money except with my hands. Why do we
do so many things? It's difficult to say. It may be a reaction
from the physical strain. The miner works in a dark and strange
world. He comes up into the light. It is a new world. It is stimulating. He wants to do something. It may be, in good times,
pigeon racing, fretwork, whippet racing, carpentry, music,
choral singing or reading. Think what reading means to an active
mind that is locked away in the dark for hours every day! Why,

in mid-Rhondda there are 40,000 books a month in circulation from four libraries. . . !' "

The Welsh miners are certainly keen readers. The author has been asked by hundreds of his miner students for lists of books on Economics, Economic History, Philosophy, Psychology, Sociology, etc., for submission to the local Workmen's Institute or Public Library and has even been called to book by certain librarians for encouraging a demand which increases the local rates! As a rule, librarians do all they can to cater for the needs of such readers but the depressed areas are hard hit financially and find it almost impossible to supply the demand. There was a time when a miner would think nothing of spending ten shillings on a book but to-day he has to rely on boxes of books supplied to classes or on the local library.

Let it not be thought that there are no well educated and cultured American miners. In every coalfield in America are to be found groups of miners who are remarkably well read, internationally minded, able thinkers and men of varied accomplishments, including music. Reference has already been made to the miner with whom the author lived for a time in the Illinois coalfield, Edward Wieck. And the best of British miners would have nothing but admiration for that fine young American miner, Powers Hapgood, a Harvard graduate who has worked underground in Wales, Germany, France, Belgium and Russia and in a number of American coalfields. American miners also make use of libraries, some of which in the mining towns are very well equipped. The author has listened to excellent glee parties, composed mainly of American miners. Literary and dramatic societies are not unknown. But the plain fact remains that the average is not high. So far as education in Economics is concerned it would not be making too strong a statement to say that the mass of American miners are illiterate. Even to-day, when there are between 10 and 12 million unemployed in America, the average American miner could probably tell you more about the latest models of automobiles than about the causes of unemployment.

Trade union and political activities play a big part in the lives of British miners. A considerable proportion of them devote a good deal of their leisure time to lodge meetings and to other forms of activity in connection with their union, the best speakers being frequently elected as delegates to conferences and chosen to assist in the work of propaganda. Quite a number serve as members of various local authorities in the coalfields and it is a common thing to find a miner as Chairman of an Urban District or County Council or Mayor of a Borough. The majority of British miners take an active and intelligent interest in politics and not only during general elections: they are all-the-year-round politicians, regular attenders of political meetings, keen, critical questioners (woe betide the speaker who cannot "stand up" to hecklers!) and voracious readers of newspapers and political periodicals. Their knowledge of international politics is amazing, particularly of developments in America, Russia, Germany, India, China and Japan and especially of the economic significance of such developments. Of the unionised American miners a certain proportion attend their lodge meetings but their activities are relatively limited. The standard of speaking among them is poor and the points which the author heard discussed were mainly of a purely "craft" character. It is an exception to find a miner taking an active part in local government. If there are any miner members of Congress—the author has not heard of one—they cannot number many, whereas it is exceptional to find members of the British Parliament representing mining constituencies who are not miners. Political meetings are not a feature of life in American coalfields. During a presidential election a certain amount of enthusiasm is aroused but when this dies down there is very little interest shewn in political questions. The traditional attitude has been to "leave politics to the grafters." The recent tremendous increase in unemployment, which was predicted by the author in a talk he gave at the Harvard Liberal Club (see *The Harvard Crimson*, December 11, 1929, "Watkins Predicts Fall in American Wealth"), has greatly stimulated an interest in economic and political issues on the part of the American workers. One has only to contrast the main issues in the Presidential election of 1932 with those of 1928 to realise that, and the probability is that henceforth this interest will grow and become better informed and more critical.

Finally it is to be remembered throughout that the miners in each country are influenced by the prevailing national industrial and social "atmosphere." In America up till recently there has been a kind of "get-rich-quick" atmosphere. In Great Britain this stage has long since passed and for some time now the challenge to the supremacy of *laisse-fairer* has taken the form of increasing legislative regulation and a growing demand even for a change of controlling ownership. The difference is reflected in the general attitude of the miners in each country.

It is hoped that the student and the general reader are now in a position to know and understand the differences between the two types of miner. The author's aim has been to describe them as faithfully as he could: if it would appear that the British miner is the superior type let it not be counted against him as a matter of national pride. Scientific truth is indifferent to praise and to blame, to national pride and to national shame. The author is as sympathetic with the American miner as with the British miner: he has unbounded admiration for both. But they are different in many respects and an attempt has been made to shew how the two types have been evolved. Broadly speaking, one may say that each is the product of hereditary equipment or original endowment and all the forces and institutions that go to make up the physical and social environment.

On a beautiful, sunshiny day about four years ago the author stood in a little Polish graveyard on the brow of a hill overlooking the peaceful mining village of Lattimer, Pennsylvania. His eyes were glued upon a row of seven small tombstones bearing the inscription of the names of seven simple Polish miners, the date and the eloquent word "Shot"—shot for the heinous offence of trying to persuade some of their mates on their way home from the local colliery to join the Union! In the Catholic cemetery across the road were seven other similar graves. He entered the car to view the scene of the shootings with leaden feet and a heavy heart but with feelings of reverential gratitude and a renewed consecration to the cause of the miners' freedom.

For what do the miners want? Assuredly they want a better living as miners but they also want a more dignified status as men. And the more intelligent, finely integrated and more courageous of them have their feet set on the road leading to emancipation and a higher level of civilisation. It is a steep and stony road but when the story of the long ascent comes to be written the miners of Great Britain and of the United States of America will be found to have an honourable place in it.

BIBLIOGRAPHY

REFERENCES FOR SUPPLEMENTARY READING

ABERCONWAY, LORD: The Basic Industries of Great Britain. Benn & Co., Ltd., 1927.

ABERCROMBIE, P., AND OTHERS: The Coal Crisis and the Future. Williams & Norgate, 1926.

ARBER, E. A. N.: The Natural History of Coal. Cambridge University Press, 1912.

ARCHBALD, HUGH: The Four-Hour Day in Coal. The H. W. Wilson Co., New York, 1922.

ASHTON, T. S., and SYKES, J.: The Coal Industry of the Eighteenth Century. Publications of the University of Manchester, 1929.

BELLERBY, J. R.: Coal Mining: A European Remedy. Macmillan, 1928.

BLANKENHORN, HEBER: The Strike for Union, a Study of the Somerset Strike, 1922–23. The H. W. Wilson Co., for Bureau of Industrial Research, New York, 1924.

BOYD, NELSON: Coal Pits and Pitmen. London, 1895.

BRAMWELL, HUGH: The Economics of the South Wales Coal-Field. Cardiff, 1920.

BULMAN, H. F.: Coal Mining and the Coal Miner. Methuen & Co., 1920.

BURT, THOMAS: An Autobiography. T. Fisher Unwin, Ltd.

COLE, G. D. H.: Labour in the Coal Mining Industry. Oxford University Press, 1923.

COMMONS, JOHN R., AND OTHERS: History of Labor in the United States. Macmillan, 1918.

DAVIDSON, THOMAS: The Education of Wage-Earners: A Contribution Toward the Solution of the Educational Problems of Democracy. Boston: Ginn, 1904.

DAVIES, D. CHAS.: Organisation and Scientific Management as Applied to the Coal Industry, 1926. Published by the author, Port Talbot, South Wales.

DAVIES, DANIEL: Safety in Mines. Published by the author, Aberdare, South Wales.

DEMANT, V. A., AND OTHERS: Coal: A Challenge to the National Conscience. Hogarth Press, 1927.

DOBBS, A. E.: Education and Social Movements, 1700–1850. Longmans, Green & Co., 1920.

DRON, R. W.: The Economics of Coal Mining. Ed. Arnold & Co., 1928.

EDINGTON: Essay on the Coal Trade, 1803.

EDWARDS, NESS: The History of the South Wales Miners. Labour Publishing Co., 1926.

EVANS, CHRIS: History of the United Mine Workers of America from 1860 to 1900. U.M.W.A., Indianapolis, 1920.

FRANKFURTER, FELIX, and GREENE, NATHAN: The Labor Injunction. The Macmillan Co., New York.

GALLOWAY, ROBERT L.: A History of Coal Mining in Great Britain. London, 1882.

GEORGE, GLEN: The Future of the Coal Trade and the Alternatives to Nationalisation, 1925. Published by the author, Aberdare, South Wales.

GILLMAN, F. J.: The Workers and Education: A Record of Some Present-Day Experiments. Allen & Unwin, 1916.

GLÜCK, ELSIE: John Mitchell, Miner: Labor's Bargain with the Gilded Age. John Day Co., 1929.

GOODRICH, CARTER: The Miner's Freedom. Marhall Jones Co., Boston, 1925.

GREENWOOD, ARTHUR: "Labour and Education" in Cambridge Essays on Adult Education. Cambridge University Press, 1920.
    The Relation of the Board of Education, the Universities and the Local Authorities to Adult Education. National Labour Press, London, 1919.

HAMILTON, WALTON H., and WRIGHT, HELEN R.: The Case of Bituminous Coal. Institute of Economics, Washington, D.C., 1925.
    A Way of Order for Bituminous Coal. Institute of Economics, Washington, D.C., 1927. The Macmillan Co., New York.

HAPGOOD, POWERS: In Non-Union Mines. Bureau of Industrial Research, New York, 1922.

HAY, W. F.: Education and the Working Class. District Council for Independent Working Class Education, Liverpool, 1920.

HINRICHS, A. F.: The United Mine Workers of America and the Non-Union Coal Fields. Longmans, Green & Co. for Columbia University Studies in History, Economics and Public Law, 1923.

HODGEN, MARGARET T.: Workers' Education in England and the United States. Kegan Paul & Co., Ltd., 1925.

HODGES, FRANK: Nationalisation of the Mines. Allen & Unwin, Ltd., 1920.

HOLE, JAMES: An Essay on the History and Management of Literary, Scientific and Mechanics' Institutions. Longmans, Green & Co., 1851.

HORNER, ARTHUR, and HUTT, G. A.: Communism and Coal. Communist Party of Great Britain, London, 1928.

HORRABIN, J. F., and WINIFRED: Working-Class Education. Labour Publishing Co., 1924.

HUDSON J. W.: The History of Adult Education. Longmans, Green & Co., 1851.

HUGHES, E.: Socialism and the Mining Industry.

HULL, EDWARD: The Coalfields of Great Britain. Hugh Rees, Ltd., London, 1905.

HUNT, TRYON, and WILLITTS: What the Coal Commission Found Williams and Wilkins Co., Baltimore, 1925.

JEFFREY: Coal and Civilization. Harvard University.

JEVONS, H. STANLEY: The British Coal Trade. Kegan Paul & Co., Ltd., 1915.

JEVONS, W. STANLEY: The Coal Question. Macmillan, 1865

LANE, WINTHROP D.: Civil War in West Virginia. B. W. Huebsch, Inc., 1921.

LAUCK, W. JETT: Combination in the Anthracite Industry, Report presented by U.M.W.A. to United States Anthracite Coal Commission, 1920.

LAWSON, JOHN: My Life. Hodder & Stoughton, 1932.

LOWE, DAVID: From Pit to Parliament: The Story of the Life of Keir Hardie. Labour Publishing Co., 1923.

LUBIN, ISADOR: Miners' Wages and the Cost of Coal (Bituminous). Institute of Economics, Washington, D.C., 1924. The Mac-. millan Co.

LUBIN, ISADOR, AND EVERETT, HELEN: The British Coal Dilemma. Institute of Economics, Washington, D.C., 1927. The Macmillan Co.

MANSBRIDGE, ALBERT: An Adventure in Working-Class Education: Being the Story of the W.E.A. Longmans, Green & Co., 1920.
The Workers' Educational Association. International Labour Review, September, 1922.
University Tutorial Classes. Longmans, Green & Co., 1918.

MERRETT, H. H.: I Fight for Coal. Printed for the author by Spottiswoode, Ballantyne & Co., Ltd., 1933.

NEF, J. U.: The Rise of the British Coal Industry. Routledge, 1932.

NICHOLLS, W. J.: The Story of American Coals.

NORTH, F. J.: Coal, and the Coalfields in Wales. Cardiff, 1926.

PARRY, R. St. J.: Cambridge Essays on Adult Education. Cambridge University Press, 1920.

PARRY-JONES, T. J.: The Other Story of Coal. Allen & Unwin, 1926.

PICHT, W. R. V.: Toynbee Hall and the English Settlement Movement. Bell, 1914.

RAUSHENBUSH, H. S.: The Anthracite Question. The H. W. Wilson Co. for Bureau of Industrial Research, New York, 1924.

RAYNES, J. R.: Coal and Its Conflicts: A Brief Record of the Disputes Between Capital and Labour in the Coal Mining Industry of Great Britain. E. Benn, Ltd., 1928.

REDMAYNE, SIR RICHARD: The British Coal-Mining Industry During the War. Oxford, 1923. Economic and Social History of the World War, British Series.

Modern Practice in Mining, Vol. 5. Longmans, Green & Co., 1932.

ROCHESTER, ANNA: Labor and Coal. Modern Books, Ltd., 1932.

ROCKEFELLER, J. D., JR.: Brotherhood of Men and Nations.

The Personal Relation in Industry.

ROBERTS, PETER: The Anthracite Coal Industry (American). 1904.

ROWE, J. W. F.: Wages in the Coal Industry. P. S. King & Son, 1923.

ROY, ANDREW: History of the Coal Miners of the United States. Columbus, 1907.

SARGENT, A. J.: Coal in International Trade. P. S. King & Son, 1922.

SELEKMAN, BEN, and VAN KLUCK, MARY: Employees' Representation in Coal Mines: A Study of Industrial Representation Plan of Colorado Fuel and Iron Co. Russell Sage Foundation, 1924.

SHURICK, A. T.: The Coat Industry (American). George G. Harrap & Co., Ltd., 1924.

SMART, R. C.: The Economics of the Coal Industry. P. S. King & Son. 1930.

SUFFERN, ARTHUR E.: Conciliation and Arbitration in the Coal Industry. Houghton Mifflin, Boston, 1915.

The Coal Miners' Struggle for Industrial Status. Institute of Economics, Washington, D.C., 1924. The Macmillan Co.

TOYNBEE, ARNOLD: Education Through Settlements. Allen & Unwin. 1917

TRYON, F. G., and SCHOENFELD, M. H.: Comparison of Physical Conditions in British and American Coal Mines. Reprint from Coal and Coal Trade Journal, 1926.

WEBB, SIDNEY: Story of the Durham Miners, 1662–1921. Labour Publishing Co., 1921.

WHIPPLE, LEON: The Story of Civil Liberty in the United States. Vanguard Press, New York, 1927.

WILKINS, CHARLES: The South Wales Coal Trade. D. Owen & Co., Cardiff, 1888.

WILLIAMS, D. G.: Capitalist Combination in the Coal Industry. Labour Publishing Co., 1924.

WILLIAMS, MORGAN D.: Practical Machine Mining. Published by Oxford University Press, 1928.

PUBLIC DOCUMENTS AND PERIODICAL OR PAMPHLET MATERIAL

Adult Education in the United States. London A.E.C., 1919, pp. 359, 364.

Adult Working-Class Education in the United States. *Monthly Labour Review*, July, 1919, pp. 1301–1309.

BROPHY, JOHN: Miners' Problems and Workers' Education. First National Conference on Workers' Education, America, pp. 65–67.

CHAFER, ZECHARIAH, JR., AND OTHERS: Manuscript Report on *Civil Liberties in the Coal Fields*, filed with the United States Commission. Copy is in files of American Civil Liberties Union. A summary by Winthrop D. Lane was published in 1924 by Doran (in the *Christianity and Industry* Series) under the title *The Denial of Civil Liberties in the Coal Fields*.

Christian Social Council: Research Committee. The Miners' Distress and the Coal Problem: An Outline for Christian Thought and Action. Report prepared by V. A. Demant, 1929.

Coal and Power: the Report of an Enquiry presided over by D. Lloyd George, 1924.

Coal Mines Reorganisation Commission Report, 1933.

Coal Mining Industry: What Mr. Lloyd George was Not Told. A Reply to *Coal and Power*. Mining Association of Great Britain.

COHN, FANNIA M.: What Workers' Education Really Is. *Life and Labour*, October, 1921, p. 230.

COLE, G. D. H.: Workers' Education in America, and Its Lessons for Us. *Highway*, March, 1923, p. 83.

DANA, H. W. L.: Teachers' and Workers' Education. First Annual Conference on Workers' Education, America, pp. 98–99.

DE LEON, SOLON: Workers' Education in the United States. A Review. *Advance*, November 18, 1921, p. 5.

EVANS, ERNESTINE: Workers' Education in the United States. *Labour Monthly*, January, 1922, pp. 1307–1309.

GIBSON, FINLAY A.: The Coal Mining Industry of the United Kingdom, the Various Coalfields thereof, and the Principal Foreign Countries of the World: Supplement with Statistics for the Completion of the Yearly Tables to December 31, 1930, and for the Monthly Tables to September 30, 1931. Cardiff, 1931. Typed Script.

GLEASON, ARTHUR: Workers' Education. American Experiments (with a Few Foreign Examples). New York Bureau of Industrial Research, 1921.

HANDY, FRANCES: The Life of a Miner's Wife. *Labour Magazine*, April, 1924.

Independent Working-Class Education? What is. London: Plebs League, 1920.

International Labour Office: Wages and Hours of Work in the Coal-Mining Industry. Geneva, 1928. Studies and Reports, Series D, No. 18.

JOHNSEN, JULIA E.: Selected Articles on Government Ownership of Coal Mines. Compiled by J. E. Johnsen, New York, 1923.

League of Nations, Economic and Financial Section: International Economic Conference, Memorandum on Coal (C.E.I. 18), Geneva, 1927.

League of Nations: Economic Committee. The Problem of the Coal Industry: Interim Report of Its International Aspects. Geneva, 1929. Series of League of Nations Publications, II. Economic and Financial, 1929, II, 19.

MACTAVISH, J. M.: Education in Its Relation to Labour and Industry. Oxford, 1919.

MILLER, SPENCER, JR.: Workers' Education: Its Achievements and Its Future. *American Federation*, December, 1922, pp. 881–7.

Mines Department (British Government Department): Publications of, particularly Annual Reports, Reports of Inspectors of Mines, Description of the Miners' Welfare Fund by the Chairman (1927) and Annual Reports of the Miners' Welfare Committee. All published by H.M. Stationery Office, London.

Price of Coal, The: Annals of the American Academy of Political and Social Science, January, 1924.

Report by the Board of Trade under Section 7 of the Act on the Working of Schemes under Part I of the Coal Mines Act, 1930, during the Year 1933.

Report of Court of Inquiry Concerning the Coal Mining Industry Dispute, 1925. The Macmillan Report.

Report of Royal Commission on the Coal Industry, 1919.

Report of Royal Commission on the Coal Industry, 1925.

Report of United States Coal Commission, 1925.

Report on the Trial of Pitmen for the Riot at Walbridge Colliery, Newcastle local pamphlets.

STITES, SARA: The Teaching of Economics. Second National Conference on Workers' Education, pp. 170–173.

SWEENEY, C. P.: Adult Working-Class Education in Great Britain and the United States. Washington, Government Printing Office, 1920.

United States Bureau of Labor Statistics. Hours and Earnings in Anthracite and Bituminous Coal Mining: Bulletins 279 (1921); 316 (1922); 416 (1926). Hours and Earnings in Bituminous Coal Mining: Bulletins 454 (1927); 516 (1930).

United States Bureau of Mines: Mineral Resources of the United States. (Until 1923 this annual volume was published by the United States Geological Survey). The Coal Section is also published separately.

United States Children's Bureau: The Welfare of Children in Bituminous Coal Mining Communities in West Virginia, 1923. Child Labor and the Welfare of Children in an Anthracite Coal-Mining District, 1922.

United States Senate, 70th Congress, 1st Session, Interstate Commerce Committee, Hearings under S. Res. 105: Conditions in the Coal Fields of Pennsylvania, West Virginia and Ohio, March–April, 1928. Second session, same committee, Hearings on S. 4490 (Watson Bill), December, 1928, and January, 1929.

World Association for Adult Education, The Inauguration of the: London: The World Association for Adult Education, Bulletin I, July, 1919.

World Power Conference: London, 1928. Transactions of the Fuel Conference: World Power Conference, London, September 24–October 6, 1928, with a Foreword by C. H. Lauder. 4 Vols. Vol. I—The Coal Industry; the Oil Industry.

PERIODICALS

AMERICAN

The American Miner—Weekly. Formerly *The Illinois Miner*.

The Anthracite Miner: Hazleton, Pennsylvania. Weekly.

The Coal Age: New York. Monthly.

Federated Press: New York and Chicago. Mimeographed releases.

United Mine Workers' Journal: Indianapolis. Fortnightly.

United Mine Workers of America, *Proceedings* of Annual and Biennial Conventions.

BRITISH

Coal Merchant and Shipper. Weekly.

Coal Seller. Bi-Monthly.

Colliery Engineering. Monthly.

Fuel. Monthly. British and American.

Iron and Coal Trades Review. Weekly.

The Colliery Guardian. Weekly.

The Miner: London Weekly. Commenced publication June 4, 1926. Ceased publication October 29, 1930.

The Mining Journal. Weekly.

NOVELS, PLAYS, ETC., HAVING A BRITISH OR AMERICAN "COAL" INTEREST

NOVELS, ETC.

BODEN, F. C.: The Miner.

DATALLER, ROGER: From a Pitman's Notebook.

DAVIES, RHYS: Count Your Blessings.
    Rings on Her Fingers.
    Red Hills.

DOYLE, A. CONAN: The Valley of Fear. (Descriptive of activities of the Molly MacGuires in the Pennsylvania anthracite field.)

FLETCHER, JOSEPH S.: Heronshawe Main: the story of a Yorkshire Colliery.

GRANT, J. C.: Back-to-Backs.

HERBERT, EVELYN: Anna Priestly.

IRWIN, WILL: Youth Rides West: a Story of the Seventies. Adventures in the Rockies of Colorado and among miners.

KEATING, Joseph: Son of Judith: a Tale of the Welsh Mining Valleys, 1901.

LAWRENCE, D. H.: Sons and Lovers.

MURRAY, D. CHRISTIE: Old Blazer's Hero.

NEVINSON, H. W.: The Valley of Tophet.

OPPENHEIM, E. PHILLIPS: The World's Great Snare. A romance of adventure and love in an American camp and in England.

SINCLAIR, UPTON: King Coal.

WELSH, JAMES: The Underworld.
    The Morlocks.

YOUNG, E. BRETT: The Black Diamond.

PLAYS

BRIGHOUSE, HAROLD: The Price of Coal.

FRANCIS, J. O.: Change.

GALSWORTHY, JOHN: Strife.

HUGHES, RICHARD: Danger.

INDEX

GEORGE ALLEN & UNWIN LTD
LONDON: 40 MUSEUM STREET, W.C.1
LEIPZIG: (F. VOLCKMAR) HOSPITALSTR. 10
CAPE TOWN: 73 ST. GEORGE'S STREET
TORONTO: 91 WELLINGTON STREET, WEST
BOMBAY: 15 GRAHAM ROAD, BALLARD ESTATE
WELLINGTON, N.Z.: 8 KINGS CRESCENT, LOWER HUTT
SYDNEY, N.S.W.: AUSTRALIA HOUSE, WYNYARD SQUARE

The Industrial Development of Birmingham
and the Black Country, 1860–1927

by C. G. ALLEN

With an Introduction by PROFESSOR J. F. REES. 8 Illustrations and 2 Maps

Demy 8vo. 28s.

"No more valuable addition to the knowledge of our own industrial development has been recently made than this volume. . . . Here we have a book of genuine, first-hand, historical and descriptive economics, worth ten of most essays in abstract economic theory."—*Spectator*

"It is a model of its kind . . . his book raises a number of questions of profound importance to the historian, and is full, both of introduction and of sober encouragement."—*Times Literary Supplement*

The History of Trade Union Organization
in the North Staffordshire Potteries

by W. H. WARBURTON

Introduction by R. H. TAWNEY

La. Cr. 8vo. 10s. 6d.

"Unusually interesting . . . a valuable addition to our knowledge of industrial development."—*Northern Echo*

"Lucid and well written."—*New Statesman*

"The whole of this study is full of interest."—*Church Times*

Work and Wealth

Demy 8vo. by J. A. HOBSON 7s. 6d.

"It offers an acute and penetrating analysis of the psychological and ethical aspects of both production and consumption. . . . It is a book that demands close and concentrated attention, but the labour is amply repaid."—*Journal of Education*

The Other Story of Coal

by T. J. PARRY JONES

Cr. 8vo. Cloth, 3s. 6d. Limp Cloth, 2s. 6d.

"A very interesting study by a working Welsh miner of the miner's point of view in the coal controversy."—*The Times*

Work and Wealth in a Modern Port

AN ECONOMIC SURVEY OF SOUTHAMPTON

Demy 8vo.   *by* P. FORD   10s. 6d.

"In this volume Southampton, the newest and in many respects the most interesting of our great seaports, is laid bare in all its statistical complications. . . . If it does not become the handbook of social reformers . . . he will have received less recognition than his painstaking work merits. . . . A book that everyone might read with profit."—*Observer*

"A really important contribution to the modern study of economics."—*Hampshire Advertiser and Independent*

"A thoroughly comprehensive survey."—*Liverpool Post and Mercury*

The Industrial Crisis

ITS CAUSES AND ITS LESSONS

by LIEUT.-COL. K. E. EDGEWORTH, D.S.O., M.C., A.M.I.E.E.

Cr. 8vo.   5s.

"An unusually clear statement of the causes that led up to the crisis, and the lessons to be drawn therefrom."—*New Britain*

"Should be of value to the layman, for the ground is well covered. The importance of industrial, as opposed to monetary, reorganization is clearly set forth."—*The Times*

The Conditions of Industrial Peace

by JOHN A. HOBSON

Cr. 8vo.   4s. 6d.

"The most independent and the most consistent of our thinkers on economics."—*Manchester Guardian*

"It is refreshing to read Mr. Hobson's lucid analysis of the problem . . . his proposals are as stimulating as they are logical."—*Times Literary Supplement*

"Like everything that Mr. Hobson writes, it is full of a wise insight into economic conditions."—*Observer*

The Prospects of Industrial Civilization

by BERTRAND RUSSELL and DORA RUSSELL

Cr. 8vo.   *Cheaper Edition. Third Impression*   *Cloth*, 5s. *Paper*, 3s. 6d.

"It has undoubtedly contributed very greatly to the knowledge of our own stage of civilization, and this addition is in itself of great value."—*The Times*

"Highly stimulating and suggestive."—*Westminster Gazette*

The Coal-Tar Tree Chart

Illustrating the various chemical products derived from Coal and Coal-Tar, designed in the form of a Genealogical Tree

by WALLACE C. NICKELS, F.C.S.

Revised Edition   *Coloured*, 7s. 6d. *Mounted on Rollers*, 10s. 6d.

Democracy in Crisis

by H. J. LASKI

La. Cr. 8vo.   *Second Impression*   7s. 6d.

"Professor Laski faces fearlessly the implications of a situation new in its conscious pressures, and definitely revolutionary in its possibilities."—*Manchester Guardian*

"A highly disturbing book; immensely able, lucid, profound."—*Listener*

"Reveals its distinguished author at his best."—*English Review*

Unemployment Relief : the Basic Problem

by E. F. STEVENSON

Cr. 8vo.   6s.

"His presentation of the question, particularly in the stress it lays on the possibilities of economic organization, may prove helpful."—*The Scotsman*

"The general reader . . . will find here a clear and readable account of the problem and its implications."—*Aberdeen Press and Journal*

Rationalisation and Unemployment

by JOHN A. HOBSON

Cr. 8vo.   *Enlarged Second Edition. Third Impression*   3s. 6d.

"Deserves to be carefully read at the present time for the light which its wise remarks on high wages, industrial reorganization, and the evils of economic nationalism throw on our immediate economic difficulties."—*Nation and Athenaeum*

"One is considerably stimulated and unusually interested in Mr. Hobson's thesis."—*Manchester Guardian*

"He deserves endless credit for focussing attention on the problem of 'under-consumption.' "—*New Statesman*

Education Through Settlements

by ARNOLD FREEMAN

Demy 8vo.   *Paper, 1s. 6d.*

"The reader must be impressed by the fine enthusiasm of the author, and no one can doubt that much good would result if something could be done to carry out his proposals."—*The Times*

Industry and Civilization

by C. DELISLE BURNS

Demy 8vo.   10s. 6d.

"In this illuminating analysis Mr. Burns brings his readers from the dangerous realm of phrase into the dispassionate world of realities. . . . After reading it, those whose concern is to understand the world in which they live will certainly be wiser."—*Times Literary Supplement*

All prices are net

LONDON: GEORGE ALLEN & UNWIN LTD